T5-AFC-739
Mass. 02668

THE RESIDENTIAL REAL ESTATE APPRAISER'S PORTABLE HANDBOOK

Leland R. Hill
Phyllis M. Hill

PRENTICE HALL
Englewood Cliffs, New Jersey 07632

Prentice-Hall International, (UK) Limited, *London*
Prentice-Hall of Australia Pty. Limited, *Sydney*
Prentice-Hall Canada, Inc., *Toronto*
Prentice-Hall Hispanoamericana, S.A., *Mexico*
Prentice-Hall of India Private Limited, *New Delhi*
Prentice-Hall of Japan, Inc., *Tokyo*
Simon & Schuster Asia Pte. Ltd., *Singapore*
Editora Prentice-Hall do Brasil, Ltda., *Rio de Janeiro*

10 9 8 7 6 5 4 3 2 1

Library of Congress Cataloging-in-Publication Data

Hill, Leland R.
The residential real estate appraiser's handbook / Leland R. Hill, Phyllis M. Hill.
p. cm.
ISBN 0-13-775321-7
1. Real property—Valuation. 2. Dwellings—Valuation. I. Hill, Phyllis M. II. Title.
HD1387.H516 1990
333.33'823—dc20 90-34068
CIP

ISBN 0-13-775321-7

PRENTICE HALL
BUSINESS & PROFESSIONAL DIVISION
A division of Simon & Schuster
Englewood Cliffs, New Jersey 07632

Printed in the United States of America

WHAT THIS BOOK WILL DO FOR YOU

Real estate appraisal . . . What is it? How is it done?

Although many books provide expansive discussions of theoretical principles and traditional standards, little has been done to put the sometimes confusing maze of principles, regulations, and standards into proper perspective, in nontechnical terms, in a single reference guide that will help the appraiser produce the highest-quality appraisal in the shortest amount of time: a book filled with practical information that can be used on a daily basis. This book is designed to fill that need; it takes you beyond theory to the real "nuts and bolts" of appraising residential real estate.

This book is a comprehensive, thoroughly practical working guide for present and potential appraisers, tax assessors, real estate brokers, loan agents, owners and investors in real property, and mortgage lenders; both commercial and savings and loan institutions.

The foundation of a well-written appraisal report is adequate documentation. Adequate documentation, or a fully justified final estimate of value, describes all the steps taken so completely that the reader, whether or not he or she is familiar with the appraisal process, could duplicate the exercise and concur with the appraiser's conclusions.

This comprehensive guide is packed with real insider secrets for structuring your investigation and analysis to help you achieve that goal, including proven, well-accepted techniques for

- defining the appraisal assignment.
- timesaving methods for researching and analyzing market data.
- what to do when you can't find pertinent data.
- defining the neighborhood.
- efficient methods for conducting accurate fieldwork.
- recognizing economic forces that influence value.
- logical, step-by-step instructions for the development of the appraisal with suggested commentary.
- completing the cost approach.
- making value adjustments.

This book covers virtually every practical aspect of appraising residential real estate. We have studied many of the major problems you are likely to encounter and we tell you how to deal with each of them, in the quickest and most effortless ways possible. The entries are complete without being exhaustive.

The comprehensive table of contents, detailed index, arrangement of the entries, and examples provide easy access to practical solutions for dealing with a wide variety of appraisal problems, such as functional and external obsolescence, non-conforming zoning, illegal additions, overimprovements, property in poor condition, cash equivalency, and depreciation.

- This book offers step-by-step blueprints to follow for appraising single-family residences, planned unit developments, condominiums, and cooperative units.
- The market approach is generally given the greatest emphasis in arriving at a final estimate of value; therefore, we have devoted an entire chapter to selecting and analyzing comparable market data effectively.
- Chapter Five shows you how to appraise different classes of property including new construction, entire subdivisions, custom-built homes, manufactured housing, and mobile homes.
- Chapter Fifteen shows you how to proceed in the orderly development of a concise and effective presentation of an appraisal review.
- An example narrative-style appraisal report is presented to demonstrate possible ways to organize written reports and to illustrate the application of established principles and professional standards for report writing.
- Checklists can be critical if they catch even a single error. To reduce your margin of error, we have included checklists and illustrations derived from a collection of common errors and all-important facts that are often overlooked.

We have designed this book so you can read it straight through or can skip around to find the chapter or entries that suit your particular needs. The entries are arranged in the sequence that proper appraisal procedure normally prescribes and in the general order that the topics appear in residential appraisal reports. You will find, however, that there are some cumulative benefits from reading it in sequence.

This handbook of practical, down-to-earth advice is based on many years of research and the authors' personal depth of experience in the real estate industry, including appraising all types of real property, reviewing thousands of appraisals, negotiating listings and sales, investing in real estate, underwriting mortgage loans, and serving as members of loan committees. We believe that our extensive and diversified experience in this fascinating and rewarding field gives us the leading edge to help you to make informed, productive real estate decisions.

Grateful acknowledgment is made for the assistance, encouragement, and support of our friends, family, and colleagues.

Leland R. Hill
Phyllis M. Hill
ASSOCIATE APPRAISERS OF AMERICA, INC.

CONTENTS

WHAT THIS BOOK WILL DO FOR YOU iii

CHAPTER ONE PROBLEMS AND PITFALLS IN APPRAISING 1

Increased Regulation: Financial Institutions Reform, Recovery, and Enforcement Act of 1989 2
Greater Burdens of Responsibility 2
Undue Influence: Cause and Effect 3
Problems Caused by Omissions 4
Consequences of Errors and Omissions 5
Achieving Maximum Results 5

CHAPTER TWO MARKET VALUE AND FACTORS INFLUENCING VALUE 7

Market Approach to Value 7
Market Value, Defined 8
Cost and Price Versus Value 10

Finding Sales That Represent Market Value 10
Economic and Environmental Forces Influencing Value 11
Recertification of Market Value 14

CHAPTER THREE ORGANIZING APPRAISAL DATA 17

Defining the Scope of Your Investigation 18
Identification of the Property—Checklist 19
How to Quote Fees for Appraisals 20
Valid Reasons for Rejecting Appraisal Assignments 21
How to Deal with Owner's Illusory Values 21
Qualifying Appraisals Limited in Scope 22
Organizing Your Time Strategically 23
Advantages of Preliminary Access Arrangements 24
Cancellations and Postponements of Assignments 25
Using the Plat Map 26
Using Microfiche Data 27
Why Assessor's Descriptions Could Vary from Appraiser's Descriptions 28
How You Will Benefit by Enlisting the Agent's Help 29
Disclosure Statements and Sales Contracts 30
The Critical Importance of Timeliness 30
- Restrictive Deadlines 31
- Interest Rates and Loan Terms 31
- Appraiser's Time Schedule 32

Expiration Date of Appraisal 32

CHAPTER FOUR HOW TO USE COMPARABLE SALES IN APPRAISALS 35

Obtaining Comparable Sales 35
How to Determine Sales Prices by Using Tax Stamps 37
Using the Most Effective Order of Importance When Selecting Market Data 38
Dealing with Subjective Adjustments 38

When to Bracket Comparable Sales 39
Across-the-Board Adjustments—Examples 39
Bracketed Adjustments—Examples 39
What Is a Neighborhood? 40
Defining Neighborhood Amenities 40
Using Common Interests and Characteristics to Define Neighborhoods 41
Natural and Man-made Boundaries 41
Locational, External, and Environmental Factors 42
Civic Amenities, Conformity, and Property Rights 43
Using Market Data from Alternate Cities 44
How to Use Builder Sales 45
Suggestions for Documenting Your Conclusions 46
Avoiding Comparable Sales Mistakes 47
Using the Cost Approach to Estimate Values 48
Determining the Price per Square Foot of Gross Living Area 50
Handling the "Tricky" Problem of Choosing from a Wide Range of Sales 50
Eliminate Inconsistent Comparable Sales 51
How to Overcome the Insufficient Recent Market Data Problem 52
Don't Forget Listings and Sales in Escrow 54
Defining the Upper Limits of Value 54
Why Consideration of Sales Terms and Concessions Is so Important to the Appraiser 55
Establishing the Date of Sale 55
How to Use Multiple-Listing Books 57
Summary 58
The Right Way and the Wrong Way to Analyze Market Data 59

CHAPTER FIVE HOW TO APPRAISE DIFFERENT CLASSES OF PROPERTY 63

Appraising Custom-Built Homes 63
Effective Ways to Learn Building Costs 64

Acknowledging Discrepancies in Building Costs 65
Supporting Values of Higher-Priced Homes 65
Identifying and Accurately Appraising Nontypical Property 66
How to Find Market Data for Unusual Property 67
How to Analyze New Residential Tracts 68
Finding Competing Developments 69
How to Appraise Entire Subdivisions 69
Using Builder's Plans to Define Dimensions 69
How to Establish Lot Sizes 70
How to Handle Upgrades 70
Key Information Needed for Tract Appraisals 70
Cautions When Appraising Model Homes 71
Why You Should Create Sample Appraisals 72
Checklist for Appraising New Subdivisions 72
How to Analyze Older Homes Located in Areas with New Construction 73
The Significance of Past Evidence of Value 74
How to Deal with Overimprovements and Underimprovements 74
The Buyer's Options 76
Price and Value Considerations 76
Development of Neighborhood Age/Life Cycles 77
The Best Way to Document Your Conclusions 78
How to Classify Modernization in Older Homes 78
Advantages of a Range of Sales 79
Dealing with Economic Characteristics 79
How to Handle the Compatibility Factor 80
Primary Neighborhood Considerations 80
Traditional Improvements in Higher-Priced Neighborhoods 81
How to Differentiate Between Over- and Underimprovements 81
Judgment Decisions: An Alternative 82
Comparability of Number of Bedrooms 82
Market Adjustments for Amenities 83
How to Appraise Manufactured Houses 83
How to Classify Manufactured Housing 84
How to Appraise Mobile Homes 85

Summary 86

CHAPTER SIX PHYSICAL INSPECTION OF THE PROPERTY, NEIGHBORHOOD, AND COMPARABLE SALES 87
Scheduling Appointments 88
What Equipment You'll Need 88
Using an Architect's Scale 90
Taking Photographs That Provide More Effective Appraisals 90
How to Plan for Property Inspections 91
Making the Neighborhood Inspection the Framework of Your Appraisal 93
The Importance of Thorough Inspections 94
Physical Inspection of the Neighborhood 95
How Buffers Diminish Negative Influences 96
Traffic Patterns, Maintenance, and Civic Amenities 96
Neighborhood: Static or Changing? 97
Analysis of the Site and Location 98
Identifying Incompatible Uses 99
Rating Lot Utility 100
Identifying Favorable Site Factors 101
What to Look for in Judging Design and Appeal 101
Nonconformity and Misplaced Improvements 102
Rating Architectural Styles in Older Neighborhoods 104
How to Judge Quality of Construction 105
Quality Is Revealed by the Shape of the House 106
Significant Exterior Characteristics of Quality 106
Quality and Types of Roofing Materials 107
Rating Interior Characteristics 108
Characteristics of Very-Good-Quality Homes 110
Achieving Proficiency in Judging Quality 110
How to Write a Description of the Property 112
Confirming the Year Built 112
Common House Styles 113

Common Window Styles 113
Types of Flooring 114
How to Inspect and Classify Insulation 114
Wall Finishes, Roofs, and Foundations 116
Illegal Outside Entrances 117
Parking Facilities 117
How to Document Deferred Maintenance 117
Procedures for Dealing with Personal Property 118
Appearances Can Be Deceptive 119
How to Make a Physical Inspection of the Property 120
How to Differentiate Physical Depreciation from Deferred Maintenance 120
When to Recommend Professional Inspections 121
Distinguishing Characteristics of Yard Improvements 121
Drainage and Slippage Problems 121
Ways to Spot a Worn-Out Roof 122
Inspection of Foundations and Exterior Walls 123
Ways to Unearth Dry Rot and Termite Damage 124
How to Recognize Additions 124
Modernization, Refurbishing, and Remodeling 125
Inspection of the Garage 126
How to Handle Nonconforming Uses 126
What to Look for When You Inspect Basements 126
Factors to Consider When You Inspect Attics 127
How to Conduct Interior Inspections 128
Room Layout and Functional Utility 128
Classifying Conformity and Condition 129
Kinds of Energy-Efficient Items 131
How to Reduce Your Errors 131
Reconciling All the Facts 133
How to Measure Property Accurately the First Time 133
Increase Your Efficiency by Estimating Dimensions 134
How to Conduct Visual Inspection of the Comparable Sales 139
The Importance of the Date of Sale 139
Factors Adding to Relative Value 139
Summary 142

CHAPTER SEVEN EFFECTIVE COMMUNICATION AND REPORTING REQUIREMENTS 143
How to Evade Touchy Situations 143
Avoiding Last-Minute Crises 145
Disclosing the Final Estimate of Value 146
Appropriate Uses of the FNMA Form 1004 146
  Single-Family Residential Property 146
  Two-Family Properties 147
  Guest Houses 147
The Written Report—Compliance with
  Reporting Requirements 148
  Avoiding Needless Explanations 149
  Using Abbreviations 149
  Documenting Discrepancies in Public Records 150
Exhibits and Addenda to FNMA Form 1004—
    Checklist 150
  FHLMC Form 442, Satisfactory Completion
  Certificate 153
  Recertification of Value 153
  Building Diagram—Example 155

CHAPTER EIGHT DESCRIPTION AND ANALYSIS OF THE PROPERTY AND NEIGHBORHOOD 157
How to List Property Addresses 158
The Right Way to Show the City 158
How to Present Legal Descriptions 158
Owner's, Occupant's, and Borrower's Names 159
Census Tract Numbers 160
Sales Price and Date of Sale 160
  Sales History 160
Loan Charges and Concessions 161
  Acknowledging Sales Concessions 162
Real Estate Taxes and Tax Year 162
  Effective Tax Rate 162

Special Assessments 163
Identifying Lenders and Clients 163
How to Identify Property Rights 164
Leasehold Land 164
Planned Unit Developments 165
Homeowner's Association Dues 167
General Description of the Neighborhood 168
Percentages of Built up Areas 168
How to Show Growth Rates 168
Property Value, Demand, Supply, and Marketing Time 169
How to Recognize Declining Market Trends 170
Present Land Use Percentages 171
How Land Use Changes Affect Property Value 172
Establishing Predominant Occupancy 172
Neighborhood Vacancy Ratio 173
Single-Family Housing Price and Age Ranges 174
Age Range and Predominant Age 174
How Price and Age Ranges Affect Marketability 175
Establishing Predominant Price 175
Dealing with Values Exceeding Predominant Price 176
How to Handle Overimprovements 177
Neighborhood Analysis Ratings 177
Stability of Employment 179
Convenience to Employment 179
Convenience to Shopping 180
Convenience to Schools 180
Adequacy of Public Transportation 181
Recreational Facilities 181
Adequacy of Utilities 181
Property Compatibility Rating 182
Protection from Detrimental Conditions 183
Police and Fire Protection 183
General Appearance of Properties 183
Appeal to Market 184
Practical Suggestions for Writing Neighborhood Comments 184

Socioeconomic Characteristics 185
Adverse External Influences and Mixed Uses 186
Other Factors to Consider 187
Rating Stability of Value 189
Neighborhood Comments—Examples 190

CHAPTER NINE GENERAL DESCRIPTION AND ANALYSIS OF THE SITE AND LOCATION 193

How to List Dimensions and Site Area 194
Zoning Classification 194
How to Classify Mixed Uses 195
How to Handle Legal but Nonconforming Uses 196
What Is a Grandfather Clause? 196
Variances in Zoning Regulations 196
Identifying Legal But Nonconforming Uses 197
Highest and Best Use 197
Determining Uses: Factors to Consider 198
Development of the Site to Full Zoning Potential 200
Multiresidential Zoning 200
Public and Private Utilities 201
Description of the Site Improvements 201
Streets 202
Curbs and Gutters 202
Sidewalks 203
Street Lights 203
Alley 203
Topography, Size, and Shape of the Lot 204
Drainage 205
View Amenities 206
Landscaping and Driveway 206
Apparent Easements and Detrimental Conditions 207
Easement 207
Encroachment 207
Restrictions 207
FEMA Flood Hazard Areas 208
Site Comments and Review of Value Factors 209
Reporting Geological Hazards 209

Special Assessments 210
Flood Control Channels 210
How to Classify Air Traffic 210
How to Classify Railroad Traffic 211
Summary 212

CHAPTER TEN GENERAL DESCRIPTION AND ANALYSIS OF THE IMPROVEMENTS 213

Number of Units on the Site 213
Number of Stories 214
Type of Residential Unit 214
Design and Style of the Improvements 215
Existing Improvements 215
How to Handle Proposed Units and Units Under Construction 215
Building Plans 216
Photos of Uncompleted Construction 216
Actual Age of the Structures 216
Effective Age of the Structures 217
How Architectural Obsolescence Affects Effective Age 217
Cosmetic Improvements and Value 218
Neighborhood Relationship to Effective Age 218
Exterior Description of the Improvements 219
Exterior Walls 219
Roof Surface 220
Gutters and Downspouts 220
Window Types 220
Foundation 221
Basement 221
Insulation 222
Reporting Unhealthy Insulation 222
Rating Adequacy of Insulation 222
When to Use the Energy Addendum Residential Appraisal Report 223
How to Classify Energy Ratings 223
Room List—FNMA Form 1004 224

Why You Should Use the Same Levels of Adjustment 224
How to List the Number of Rooms 225
Descriptions of Interior Finishes 226
Wall Finishes 227
Adequacy of Trim and Finishes 227
Bath Floors and Wainscot 228
Interior Doors 228
Rating Quality of Interior Surfaces 228
Number and Kinds of Fireplaces 229
Heating Equipment 229
Cooling Equipment 230
Kitchen Equipment 230
Assigning Value to Attics 230
Autos and Parking Requirements 231
Classifying Interior Garage Finishes 231
Outside Entries into the House or Basement 231
Analysis of the Improvements 232
Explanations Required by Lenders 232
How Improvement Ratings Are Affected by the Neighborhood 233
Requirements for Reporting Detrimental Conditions 233
Quality of Construction 234
Condition of Improvements 234
Room Sizes and Layout 234
Closets and Storage 236
Energy Efficiency 236
Adequacy and Condition of Plumbing 236
Adequacy and Condition of Electrical Equipment 237
Adequacy and Condition of Kitchen Cabinets 237
Compatibility to Neighborhood 237
Appeal and Marketability 237
Estimated Remaining Economic Life 238
Estimated Physical Life 238
Additional Features, Modernization, and Rehabilitation 238
Reconciling Your Descriptions 241
How to Classify Personal Property 241
Assigning Value to Insignificant Improvements 241
Preferred Methods for Dealing with Additions 242

Garage Conversions 243
Kitchen Facilities: Zoning Compliance 243
Building Regulations and Permits 244
How Code Violations Are Discovered 244
Problems Created by Discrepancies in Public Records 245
Does Everything Need a Permit? 246
How to Handle Nonpermitted Additions 247
How to Handle Permitted Additions 247
Depreciation Factors 247
The Importance of Rating Consistency 248
Repairs and Overall Value 249
How to Deal with Minor Repairs 250
Appraised Value: As is or Subject to 250
Considerations of Health, Safety, and Security of the Occupants 250
General Market Conditions and Sales Concessions 251
Financing Statements—Examples 252
Descriptions of the Property—Examples 252
Summary 253
Illustrations: Poor Utility and Functional Obsolescence 254

CHAPTER ELEVEN THE COST APPROACH TO VALUE 259
Advantages of the Cost Approach 260
Using the Cost Approach to Eliminate Errors 262
Obtaining Cost Estimates 262
How to Calculate Building Sizes 263
Why Consistency is Important 263
Considerations Given to Hillside Property 264
How to Present Building Calculations 264
How to Estimate Building Costs 265
Estimating Building Costs for Unique Property 267
Why Cost Estimates Should be Rounded 268
Additional Considerations: Extras 268
Special Energy-Efficient Items 269
Porches and Patios 269
Garages and Carports 269

New or Proposed Construction 270
Adjusting Base Costs 270
When and How to Include Cost Sources and Land Sales 271
Total Estimated Cost New 271
Procedures for Estimating Depreciation 272
Physical Depreciation 272
Curable and Incurable Physical Depreciation 272
How to Estimate Physical Depreciation Based on Economic Life 273
Why You Should Refine Estimates of Depreciation 273
How to Extract Percentage Rates of Depreciation from the Market 274
Using Cost Handbooks to Estimate Depreciation 274
Defining Functional Obsolescence 275
Estimating the Dollar Amount of External Obsolescence 276
Reconciliation of Depreciation 277
Site Improvements "As is" 277
Overimprovements and Repairs 278
Site Improvements: Planned Unit Developments 278
How to Estimate Site Value 279
Land Estimate Using an Abstraction Technique—Example 279
Documenting Speculative Land Values 280
How to Present Land Sales 281
Indicated Value by the Cost Approach 281

CHAPTER TWELVE PRESENTATION AND ANALYSIS OF THE COMPARABLE SALES 283

The Right Number of Sales to Use 283
Why You Should Eliminate Redundant Sales 284
Using Additional Market Data 285
How to Use Listings in the Market Analysis 286
How to Make Value Adjustments 287
Requirements for Comparability 287
Using Rules of Thumb 288

Determining the Relevancy of Market Adjustments 289
When to Bracket Sales 290
Basing Market Adjustments on Cost 291
How to Round Market Adjustments 291
Upgrades in New Tract Homes 291
Rounding Gross Living Area Adjustments 292
Using the Same Levels of Adjustment 292
How to Make Market Adjustments 293
Explanations Required by Lenders 293
How to Handle Financing Concessions 294
FHA/VA Transactions 295
Rating Builder's Incentives 295
Unfavorable Financing 296
Adjusting Sales for Cash Equivalency 296
Reasons for Seller Financing 297
Cash Equivalency and Mathematical Calculations 299
Using Market Data for Cash Equivalency Adjustments 300
Using Loan Payments for Cash Equivalency Adjustments 301
How to Present Your Market Analysis 303
Listing the Proximity to Subject 303
Price per Square Foot of Gross Living Area 304
Data Sources 304
Reporting Requirements for Date of Sale 305
How You Will Benefit by Using Current Sales 306
How to Confirm Market Trends 306
How to Make Time Adjustments 307
When and How to Make Location Adjustments 307
Site and View Adjustments 310
Adjustments for Design and Appeal 312
Adjustments for Quality of Construction 313
Actual and Effective Ages 314
How to Document Adjustments for Condition 316
Above-Grade Room Count 318
Gross Living Area Adjustments 322
Basement and Finished Rooms Below Grade 323
How and When to Adjust for Functional Utility 324
Heating and Cooling 328
Garages and Carports 329

Patios and Porches 330
Yard Improvements 330
Special Energy-Efficient Items 331
Adjustments for Fireplaces 332
Other, Kitchen Equipment, and Remodeling 332

CHAPTER THIRTEEN RECONCILIATION AND FINAL ESTIMATE OF VALUE 335

How to Define the Estimate of Market Value 335
Reconciling Net Adjustments 336
Analysis and Reconciliation of the Comparable Sales 336
Indicated Value by the Sales Comparison Approach 338
Comments on Sales Comparisons 340
Sales Comparison Comments—Examples 341
Indicated Value by the Income Approach 342
Value As is, Value Subject to 344
Comments and Conditions of Appraisal 346
Final Reconciliation of Value Estimates 346
Final Reconciliation Comments—Examples 347
Final Estimate of Market Value 348
Certification and Statement of Limiting Conditions 349
Effective Date of Value Estimate 350
Appraiser's Signature 350
Additional Requirements for Appraisals 351
Summary 352
Uniform Residential Appraisal Report—Example 354

CHAPTER FOURTEEN CONDOMINIUMS, COOPERATIVE UNITS, AND PLANNED UNIT DEVELOPMENTS 357

How to Differentiate a Condominium from a Town House 358
Declaration of Ownership 360
Public Subdivision Report 360
How to Appraise Condominiums and PUD Units 360

Present Land Uses 361
Predominant Price and Age Ranges 361
Potential for Additional Condominium and PUD Units 362
Neighborhood Ratings 362
Distance to Civic Amenities 362
Defining the Site, Lot Dimensions, and Location 363
Listing Zoning Classifications 363
Off-Site Improvements 363
Project Ingress/Egress, Topography, Size/Shape, and View 364
Drainage and Flood Conditions 364
Site and Location Comments 364
Descriptions of the Project Improvements 365
Original Use of the Unit 365
Condominium Conversions 365
Proposed Units and Units Under Construction 366
Differentiating Row Houses from Town Houses 366
Primary Residence, Second Home, or Recreational Use 367
How to List the Number of Units 367
Project Classification 369
Security Features 369
Elevators 369
Vertical Soundproofing 369
Horizontal Soundproofing 370
Parking Facilities 370
Common Elements and Recreational Facilities 371
Leased Common Elements and Recreational Facilities 371
How to Rate the Project 372
Location of the Project 372
General Appearance, Amenities, and Density 372
Classifying the Unit Mix 372
Condition of the Improvements 373
Appeal to Market 373
Inclusionary Zoning Restrictions 373
Description of the Individual Unit 374
Unit Livable Area 374
How to Measure Condominiums 374

Parking for Unit 375
Unit Rating 375
Estimated Effective Age and Remaining Economic Life 375
Analysis of the Budget—Page Two of FHLMC Form 465 375
Unit Charges 376
Utilities 376
Fees Other than Condominium and PUD Charges 376
Identification of the Management Group 377
Condominium and PUD Documents 377
Insurance Requirements 377
Key Elements of the Cost Approach 377
Depreciation 378
Land Value 378
Value of Amenities 378
Market Data Analysis 378
Price per Gross Living Area 379
Location: The Prime Factor for Variances in Prices 380
Garages and Carports 382
Common Elements 383
Monthly Assessments 383
Income Approach to Value 383
Reconciling the Data 384
Additional Requirements for Planned Unit Developments and Condominiums 384
Exhibits and Addenda to FHLMC Form 465 385
How to Appraise Cooperative Units 388
Requirements for Addendum A and Addendum B 391
Project Analysis—Page One, Addendum A 392
Section I—Project Analysis 392
Project Analysis—Page Two, Addendum A 394
Section II—Project Analysis 399
Analysis of Annual Income and Expenses, Addendum B 400
CHAPTER FIFTEEN HOW TO CONDUCT EFFECTIVE APPRAISAL REVIEWS 403
Review Procedure—Checklist 404

Uniform Standards of Professional Appraisal Practice 410
How to Summarize Review Appraisals 412
Review Summary—Example 412
Advantages of Proper Communication 413

CHAPTER SIXTEEN NARRATIVE APPRAISAL REPORT 415

Requirements for Narrative Appraisal Reports 416
Letters of Acceptance 422
Acceptance Letter—Example 423
Narrative Appraisal Report—Example 424

APPENDICES 443

- A:Example: Cost Calculations 443
- B: Example: Land Comparable 445
- C: Example: Area Computations 446
- D: Principal Information Sources 448
- E: Abbreviations 450
- F: Checklist—Subject and Comparable Sales 454
- G: Checklist—Subject and Comparable Sales: Site Improvements and Amenities 456
- H: Checklist—Neighborhood Description: External Obsolescence, Environmental Deficiencies 458
- I: Glossary 460

INDEX 469

CHAPTER 1

PROBLEMS AND PITFALLS IN APPRAISING

In former times, investing in real estate, listing and selling property, and appraising were not complex, difficult, and time-consuming enterprises. There were relatively few transactions, and prices increased at such a snail's pace that we could use comparable sales that were more than a year old and we could go all over the place to find them. We seldom had to bother with verifying permits and other records because zoning and building departments were virtually nonexistent. Lenders accepted the appraiser's conclusions at face value, and few, if any, explanations were required or provided.

Lenders didn't have to be overly concerned because there were few variables that required subjective adjustments which could distort the value. Moreover, we really couldn't stray too far off the mark since most houses were conforming, small bungalows with minimal variances in design and quality.

Today, however, this dynamic, rapidly changing profession is characterized by in-depth regulations and standards, new lending policies, and voluminous reporting requirements. Professional societies, state and federal government agencies, financial institutions, and other concerned parties are continuously seeking greater control and demanding an increased level of performance from appraisers and people in related professions.

INCREASED REGULATION: FINANCIAL INSTITUTIONS REFORM, RECOVERY, AND ENFORCEMENT ACT OF 1989

The trend toward increased regulation and competent, well-supported valuations was partially brought about by the many troubled or failed institutions wherein questionable real estate values were involved. The federal government's answer to this problem was the "Financial Institutions Reform, Recovery, and Enforcement Act of 1989." This federal law requires certification and licensing of appraisers.

All federally related transactions involving commercial and residential property with a value over $1,000,000. must be completed by a state-certified appraiser. All federally related transactions that do not require a state-certified appraiser must be performed by either a state-certified or a state-licensed appraiser.

Certified appraisers must meet the requirements for certification established by the Appraisal Foundation, which include a passing grade on a uniform examination as well as experience requirements. Licensed appraisers must meet state or territory requirements for licensing.

GREATER BURDENS OF RESPONSIBILITY

Along with greater burdens of responsibility brought about by intensified regulation, real estate professionals are now exposed to greater risks than ever before because of the short supply of land created by high demand. Residential property is being constructed over old oil wells, adjacent to and over toxic landfills, next to freeways, on unstable land, in flood plains, and every other place developers can find a square inch of land to build on. Considering today's powerful technology, skills, and regulations, new construction shouldn't create new hazards, but it does.

Essentially, then, appraisers are expected to be soils, structural, and environmental engineers, geologists, and health inspectors because they are required to inform consumers of both man-made and natural forces that could have an adverse impact on the value of the property or the health and safety of the occupants.

UNDUE INFLUENCE: CAUSE AND EFFECT

The assignment seemed simple enough: refinance of an older, two-story home in an established neighborhood with no outward signs of any problems.

The interior of the dwelling, however, was in fair condition. The appraiser disclosed required repairs of more than $20,000. in his report, including major plumbing and electrical problems.

The client's conversation with the appraiser, after the appraisal was received, went something like this: "I didn't mention this in the beginning, but the borrower is getting the loan specifically to make the repairs, and we need a higher value to make sure that there is enough money to complete the work. I really need to make this loan, so how about giving me a break, just this once? Rewrite the appraisal, but show the house in good condition and don't mention any repairs. I'm sure we can do a lot more business in the future if you take care of this favor for me."

The borrower ran off with the money and the property

went into foreclosure. Because the selling price was reduced to make allowances for the substantial amount of necessary repairs, the proceeds from the foreclosure sale were not sufficient to cover the loan. It was subsequently determined that the property was in fair condition when the loan was funded and the appraiser failed to disclose this information in his report.

The appraiser was found negligent; the judgment against the appraiser was for the entire amount of the loan. This appraiser not only lost his credibility, he also lost his business and his home due to the substantial dollar amount of the settlement.

PROBLEMS CAUSED BY OMISSIONS

The owners of property A sold their home without the benefit of a real estate agent. They bought property B, which was listed and sold by real estate agents. The owners of B bought property C.

When property B was appraised, the appraiser noticed some cracks in the exterior stucco. The appraiser dismissed the damage as typical signs of settlement; therefore, the damage was not mentioned in the appraisal report.

When the transaction was due to close, the selling agents scheduled a final walk-through of the property. Upon close inspection, the buyer noticed the cracks in the stucco. The buyer then asked an associate, a licensed contractor, to take a look. The contractor, in turn, recommended an inspection by a licensed structural engineer who found strong evidence of severe structural damage. Further investigation revealed extensive structural damage in a number of other homes in this development, which was built on unstable land.

The potential buyers canceled the sale of their house (property A), as well as their purchase of property B. The owners of property B joined with other owners to sue the developer. Because they had to resell their existing home, the owners of property C lost the opportunity to purchase their new home.

The listing agent, selling agent, and the appraiser were held equally liable for damages for failure to disclose the evidence of possible structural damage, which should have been obvious to all of them.

CONSEQUENCES OF ERRORS AND OMISSIONS

As demonstrated, errors and omissions can reach far beyond the appraiser's relationship with his or her client. An error in the appraiser's judgment or negligence can affect several transactions, each one dependent on the other, resulting in great emotional and financial harm to any number of people.

Even when a case based on possible errors and omissions goes to court and, ultimately, it is shown that the appraiser did not make any errors in judgment, the thorn in your side caused by countless wasted hours defending the issue, substantial costs for legal defense, and the irreparable damage to your reputation are not commensurate with the extra time it takes to document appraisals to the greatest extent feasibly possible.

ACHIEVING MAXIMUM RESULTS

The best defense always has been a good offense: meet the challenge of greater responsibility and higher standards by relinquishing old concepts and creating new, streamlined methods for discovering and presenting factual information. Positive effects can be also be achieved by eliminating preoccupation with the vast array of guidelines and getting on with the essential activities of collecting and processing data for the appraisal.

Make every effort to verify your facts and document your findings to the fullest extent possible so the reader will not be misled, which in turn, will establish credibility and trust in your judgment.

We will show you what to watch out for and how to proceed in the orderly development of a concise, yet complete and effective, presentation with due consideration given to all factors that might influence value. Most problems you will encounter along the way have been addressed in this book. It would be impossible, of course, to identify all the potential hazards lurking in some dark corner waiting for an unsuspecting appraiser, but we do hope to reduce your errors, omissions, and unsupported judgment decisions to a minimum.

CHAPTER 2

MARKET VALUE AND FACTORS INFLUENCING MARKET VALUE

While it is not your job to predict what will happen in the future, to minimize appraisal problems you must convince your readers that you have considered stability of value and future marketability of the property. The best way to do this is to obtain information from a variety of sources so you don't overlook any factors adding to or detracting from market value. You can also avoid problems by keeping the definition of market value in mind throughout the appraisal process.

MARKET APPROACH TO VALUE

The market approach, as used to estimate the value of real estate, is based on the theory that an informed and prudent buyer would not pay more for a property than the cost of acquiring another property of equal desirability and similar utility. It is, therefore, based upon the "principle of substitution." This approach is based upon an active market and the availability of other properties from which a person can make his or her choice.

The application of this approach produces an estimate of value of the subject property by comparing it with similar or comparable properties that have sold recently. The comparison approach used in determining the degree of comparability between two properties involves judgment as to their similarity with respect to many elements of value, such as location, size, quality of construction, age, condition, and amenities.

Adjustments to the selling price of the sold property are made, if required, that will reflect the inferior or superior qualities of the subject property as compared to the sold property. The adjusted sales price of the properties deemed most comparable tend to set the range in which the value of the subject property will fall. Thus, application of the units of comparison to the subject property will indicate to the appraiser a figure that represents the value of the subject property, that is, the probable price at which it could be sold by a willing seller to a willing buyer as of the date of the appraisal.

MARKET VALUE, DEFINED

Of the several possible definitions of market value, following is the definition of market value to be used for residential appraisals prepared in conformance with Federal National Mortgage Association (Fannie Mae) and Federal Home Loan Mortgage Corporation (Freddie Mac) lending guidelines:

> The most probable price which a property should bring in a competitive and open market under all conditions requisite to a fair sale, the buyer and seller, each acting prudently, knowledgeably and assuming the price is not affected by undue stimulus.

Implicit in this definition is the consummation of a sale as of a specified date and the passing of title from seller to buyer under conditions whereby:

1. buyer and seller are typically motivated;
2. both parties are well informed or well advised, and each acting in what he considers his own best interest;
3. a reasonable time is allowed for exposure in the open market;
4. payment is made in terms of cash in U.S. dollars or in terms of financial arrangements comparable thereto; and
5. the price represents the normal consideration for the property sold unaffected by special or creative financing or sales concessions[1] granted by anyone associated with the sale.

---

[1]Adjustments to the comparables must be made for special or creative financing or sales concessions. No adjustments are necessary for those costs which are normally paid by sellers as a result of tradition or law in a market area; these costs are readily identifiable since the seller pays these costs in virtually all sales transactions. Special or creative financing adjustments can be made to the comparable property by comparisons to financing terms offered by a third-party institutional lender that is not already involved in the property or transaction. Any adjustment should not be calculated on a mechanical dollar-for-dollar cost of the financing or concession but the dollar amount of any adjustment should approximate the market's reaction to the financing or concessions based on the appraiser's judgment.

COST AND PRICE VERSUS VALUE

These words, although they are closely related, have different meanings, and you should not use these terms interchangeably as though they were synonymous.

Cost: The total dollar amount of an expenditure of money; the price paid to acquire or create a thing.

Price: The amount of money asked for something to be sold; the amount of money the seller agrees to accept for something to be sold; the amount of money the purchaser agrees to pay.

Value: The worth of a thing as measured by the amount of other things for which it can be exchanged, or as estimated in terms of a medium of exchange; equivalent worth or adequate return.

An appraisal is not an *estimate of price;* it is an *opinion of value* and sales prices are not to be interpreted as market value.

FINDING SALES THAT REPRESENT MARKET VALUE

How can you find out whether the sales price is the probable price which a property should bring in a competitive and open market under all conditions requisite to a fair sale? How can you determine whether the buyers and sellers were typically motivated, well informed, and well advised? How can you find out whether a reasonable time was allowed for exposure in the open market? Even if you had time, it would be an impossible task to examine every sales transaction to determine these factors.

You can narrow the scope of your investigation by studying the pattern of recent sales in the subject neighborhood. As you analyze market data, typically, a definite range of sales prices will emerge. Disregard the unreasonably high and low sales that are outside of the range because these sales are usually the result of extraordinary buyer or seller motivation. When sellers are typically motivated, informed, and well advised, they do not sell their property for less than it is worth, and prudent buyers do not pay more for a property than it is worth.

WATCH OUT FOR THIS

The preceding rule of thumb works well in a stable market, but it could cause problems in a changing market. Always study recent market trends before you automatically eliminate sales. If you don't review sales in escrow, pending sales, and listings, you could overlook the very real possibility that prices are increasing or declining.

ECONOMIC AND ENVIRONMENTAL FORCES INFLUENCING VALUE

Well-prepared appraisal reports give readers some indication that the appraiser has studied all the factors that govern value and has also given some thought to stability of value. Therefore, it is important always to monitor change, supply and demand, competition, and other economic factors that control market value, as well as environmental forces that may have some impact on value and marketability.

Ongoing studies of market trends will save you countless hours of research during your assignment because you will be able to identify quickly relevant facts that are directly related to the appraisal problem. By staying in tune with the market, you will know what type of research is necessary for your assignment and where to find the data you need. When market trends indicate an increase in prices, you will be prepared to use the most recent sales, listings, and sales in escrow to support price increases or time adjustments. You will also have ready access to regional descriptions, neighborhood descriptions, commercial and industrial activity, quality of educational facilities, and other pertinent information. Most important, by becoming more involved, you can at least show your readers that current happenings did have some impact on your thinking.

Consistently consult with real estate agents, bankers, investment counselors, builders, loan agents, and other people who are knowledgeable in the field of construction and financing. Know whether interest rates are increasing or declining, whether funds are available for financing residential property, the dollar amount of current loan points, financing costs, building costs, the stability and types of employment in the area, the demand for residential property, and the supply of housing in the area.

You can obtain a wealth of information about the latest developments and trends from local newspapers, libraries, planning departments, community development agencies, and chambers of commerce, including

- The wave of the future: attached homes emerging during the 1990s as the dominant new-home product.
- The newest concept in planned and existing projects: offices, retail stores, child care centers, recreation centers, shopping facilities, and other uses on the same site.
- Home price indexes illustrating price increases in various cities in the United States. For example, in Orange County, California, the average price of homes increased from $34,000. to $233,000. within 15 years.

- The average number of days a resale home or condominium sat on the market, average sales prices, financing concessions being offered by builders, and the impact of new construction in the area.
- The availability and prices of vacant land.
- Population statistics, income levels, number of vacancies, rental rates, and tax rates.
- Construction and development costs.
- Locations of planned transportation arteries.

Include news articles as addenda to the report to add further support to your conclusions and to show that you have considered economic factors that could affect stability of value. For example, include economic studies to support time adjustments, marketing time, price increases, demand for housing in the area, and types of employment opportunities. When the building cost of the appraised property is $90,000. and the land value is $300,000., it helps to include published data that validate the high cost of land.

Many appraisers have discovered that news articles help them identify defects in property caused by man-made and natural forces that are sometimes difficult to detect upon visual inspection. For example, our files now include

- The location of a tract of homes plagued for years with toxic oil waste. This tract was built on a site that had been used as a dumping ground for toxic wastes about 20 to 30 years before the houses were built.
- The location of a tract of homes built on unstable land. Within a year after people moved in, as they added yard improvements and watered their lawns, cracks formed along interior walls, concrete patios cracked, covered patios pulled away from the houses, pools began slowly

to sink, and the excessive settlement caused roofs to buckle and block wall fences to fall over.

- The locations of other new tracts of homes of substandard construction showing evidence of extensive structural damage within the first few months.

Many examples of shoddy workmanship, which could seriously affect stability of value, have been found in new attached and detached housing projects throughout the United States, such as water leaks from substandard pipe, sagging second story floors, bathtubs and sinks that did not drain properly, open gaps between walls and floorboards, and other structural defects. In some areas, the problems are so severe that many units must be reframed and whole walls must be ripped out and rebuilt.

RECERTIFICATION OF MARKET VALUE

New housing developments are typically appraised from blueprints before or during construction. When the loan is ready for funding, the appraiser reinspects the property and recertifies the value. The FLHMC Form 442, "Satisfactory Completion Certificate," to be signed by the appraiser, reads as follows:

"I certify that I have reinspected the subject property, the requirements or conditions set forth in the appraisal report have been met, and any required repairs or completion items have been done in a workmanlike manner."

Rather than waiting until the loan is ready to fund, look for evidence of poor workmanship, structural defects, and drainage problems during construction of the dwelling unit. If you notice any problems, inform your client at once.

When the dwelling is complete, don't forget to inspect

the interior of the dwelling. If you find any major defects in the property, list the defects on the satisfactory completion certificate and state whether the defects adversely affect any property ratings in the appraisal or the final estimate of market value. If you suspect problems, but you are not certain, recommend an inspection by a licensed geologist, structural engineer, or soils engineer.

CHAPTER 3

ORGANIZING APPRAISAL DATA

A well-written appraisal report reveals the appraiser's uncompromising regard for details and accuracy. The barriers to a well-written appraisal lie in the way that the appraisal is organized. The right way to organize appraisals is to always work with a definite plan and do everything the same way each time. By following a structured procedure, you will be less likely to make errors or miss a step, which is easy to do when you have a magnitude of data to contend with and interruptions plague you at the same time.

Appraisers sometimes expend so much time and energy compiling market data and doing research that by the time they get around actually to writing the appraisal and finalizing the value, they no longer have the energy and interest needed to do a thorough analysis of the property. It is virtually impossible to gather all the data needed for the appraisal assignment and then make a final decision. Starting with the initial order, you should be making notes and decisions as you proceed through the various steps of appraising a property. In this manner, a pattern should emerge that will lead you to a logical value conclusion; hence, it will then be quite easy to write the appraisal report.

DEFINING THE SCOPE OF YOUR INVESTIGATION

To make a preliminary estimate of the time, labor, and expense involved in the assignment, the first step is to establish the scope of your investigation by clearly defining the appraisal assignment. To ensure that no important aspect is overlooked, obtain a detailed description of the property to be appraised.

The importance of obtaining a detailed description of the property to be appraised cannot be overemphasized. Details are critical because every erroneous detail results in great losses in time and income for everyone concerned. For example, a "minor" error in the address, such as avenue instead of street or north rather than south, could have a major effect by directing the appraiser to the wrong property at the opposite end of the city.

Or suppose the appraiser quoted a fee and completion date for an appraisal assignment, and, because the property description was wrong, it was later discovered that the assignment would involve much more research and time than the appraiser had anticipated. The appraiser would be hard pressed to extend the time limit or increase the fee accordingly because most people would assume that the appraiser has the experience to quote a commensurate fee and they will expect to receive the appraisal within the proposed time frame.

An accurate and detailed description of the property to be appraised not only eliminates errors and speeds the appraisal process, but it is also vitally important in order to quote an appropriate fee and completion date. Make certain that all names of streets, cities, and especially owner's names are spelled correctly as this will facilitate verification of the information.

IDENTIFICATION OF THE PROPERTY—CHECKLIST

It may not be possible to obtain all the information that you need during your initial conversation with your client; therefore, to avoid overlooking valuable information, highlight the missing items so you will remember to obtain the data from another source. This list can also be used as a guide when you write cover letters and proposals.

1. Complete address of the property to be appraised including north, south, east, or west; unit numbers; and street, avenue, lane, or boulevard.
2. Full name and telephone number of the person requesting the appraisal and, if applicable, the company he or she represents.
3. Full name and title of the person to whom the appraisal will be directed, telephone number, and mailing address.
4. Find out whether the fee will be paid in advance, collected at the site, or paid upon presentation of the completed appraisal.
5. Date your client needs the appraisal and delivery instructions.
6. Full name of the borrowers.
7. Name of the person to get in touch with for access; business and residence telephone numbers (including

area code); and the interest they have in the property to be appraised, for example, broker, loan agent, seller, owner, or borrower.

8. Description of the property, including
   a. type of property, for example, single-family residence, residential income property, industrial, commercial, vacant land, planned unit development, or condominium.
   b. number of units on the site.
   c. locational influences, such as water or view orientation, equestrian zoning, golf course, or private security-gated community.
   d. age, size of buildings, and lot size.
9. Sales price or owner's estimate of value, loan amount requested, and separate amounts of all the existing mortgages on the property.

10. Date of valuation for special-purpose appraisals, such as divorce or estate settlements, tax appeals, or insurance claims, a valuation date as of some date in the past may be specified.

11. Define the purpose of the appraisal, for example, to establish market value for a sale, refinance, line of credit, second trust deed, foreclosure, construction loan, or employee transfer.

HOW TO QUOTE FEES FOR APPRAISALS

When your client requests a preliminary fee quote, subject to modification, make sure you have all the information needed to define the scope of the assignment properly.

Never quote a *firm* fee and delivery date until the property description has been verified. The fee should be agreed upon before the appraiser accepts the assignment. Written confirmation of the assignment and the amount of the fee can be presented in the form of an acceptance letter. A copy of the letter, signed by the client, should be kept with the file.

VALID REASONS FOR REJECTING APPRAISAL ASSIGNMENTS

Appraisers cannot allow themselves to be influenced; they must, at all times, maintain an objective and impartial perspective. Therefore, appraisal assignments should be declined when

1. the appraiser has an undisclosed financial interest.
2. clients suggest that a certain value is needed.
3. clients exert pressure on the appraiser to meet deadlines that do not allow sufficient time for a thorough investigation.
4. clients request an appraisal that is beyond the appraiser's ability or the appraiser cannot complete the assignment within a reasonable time or the time requested.

HOW TO DEAL WITH OWNER'S ILLUSORY VALUES

After making a preliminary analysis of market data, the appraiser could determine that the sales price of the property or the owner's projected estimate of value is very unrealistic. In this event, rather than risking endless conflicts with respect to value, it may be in everyone's best interest to decline the assignment because "sufficient market data are not available to support the value." If your client wants an appraisal with a solid value, however, you will probably be directed to proceed with the assignment.

It is important always to maintain communication with your clients as the appraisal progresses because people do not like to wait until the last minute, when the loan is ready to fund, to find out that the appraised value is much lower than they anticipated.

WARNING

Sometimes the person who originates the appraisal will assure you that the appraisal will only be used for a specific objective. Never assume that the objective will not be changed or that the appraisal will be used for the purpose stated. Always presume that your appraisal will be submitted to, and reviewed by, any number of lenders.

There may be times when you will be asked to overlook certain items or to write an appraisal that is not fully up to standards because "it won't be used for lending purposes." You will more than likely discover, however, that the appraisal is being shopped all over town in an attempt to obtain a loan on the property. When your client is applying undue pressure on you to overlook certain elements or expects you to provide a specific value, it is better to lose the client because the net result could be irreparable damage to your reputation and a lawsuit could evolve if a loan was made based on an appraisal that was not up to standards.

QUALIFYING APPRAISALS LIMITED IN SCOPE

When your client requests an appraisal that will be limited in scope or content, advise the client, prior to beginning the assignment, that the appraisal will be less than, or will be different from, appraisals that strictly adhere to specific appraisal guidelines. To make certain that your client understands this, include a qualification in your acceptance letter that reflects the limited extent of the appraisal. Your client should sign and return a copy of the acceptance letter. A copy of the signed acceptance letter should be included with the appraisal.

Even though an appraisal that is limited in scope or content is acceptable to your client, the appraisal should still reflect professional appraisal standards, and it should not be so limited in scope that your client is misled or is uncertain as to the context of the appraisal. Keep the appraisal simple and easy to understand. Do not include a lot of meaningless demographics, regional descriptions, definitions, statistics describing real estate cycles, or explanations that could be misunderstood or misinterpreted.

When the scope of your investigation is limited, to avoid any misunderstandings

- Include a statement to the effect that the scope of your investigation and the availability of data were restricted by your client's choice.
- Describe the limits or scope of your investigation.
- Reference the sources of your data.
- A precise value should not be provided. Instead, show a range of values. Include a statement that the range given is a preliminary estimate only and further investigation of the property could produce a value that is outside of your range.

ORGANIZING YOUR TIME STRATEGICALLY

People have been known to give the appraiser a mailing address rather than the property address, wrong or incomplete addresses and telephone numbers, inadequate loan information, and inadequate descriptions of the property. Therefore, whenever anyone (other than the property owner) requests an appraisal, the first thing that you should do is to call the owner or the participating real estate agent and verify all of the information. The time to rectify errors is *before* you assemble comparable sales data or go into the field to inspect the property.

Clarifying the description of the property always results in much greater efficiency because you will not waste any time selecting comparable sales that are unrelated to the subject property. For example, a more appropriate selection of comparable sales can be assembled if, at this time, it can be determined whether there are any special features that should receive specific consideration, such as swimming pools, views, extensive upgrading, or room additions.

If the property to be appraised is an older residence, find out whether the home has been remodeled or modernized. If so, use comparable sales that are in the "effective age" range of the property to be appraised. For example, if the home has been completely remodeled and modernized, the age of the home could be "effectively new," in which case, the comparable properties should be similarly remodeled or modernized. If there are no current sales in comparable condition, use sales of new homes to ten-year-old homes in your sales analysis.

If you uncover any relevant diversities from the information originally given to you that could create a problem, inform you client at once. This way, your client can help you reconcile the differences or solve the problems before you continue with the assignment.

ADVANTAGES OF PRELIMINARY ACCESS ARRANGEMENTS

Making a preliminary call for access expedites your fact-finding because it gives you the opportunity to activate the assemblage of documents (tax bills, building permits, legal description, or receipts for improvements to the property) that you will need to complete your assignment. A preliminary call also apprises interested parties that you are initiating your investigation of the property, thereby allowing them sufficient time to coordinate their time schedule with your schedule.

When you make preliminary access arrangements, explain that it will take a day or so to complete your initial research and that you will call back for an actual appointment at a later time (because, more often than not, they will want to know why the property will not be appraised right now). Depending on your schedule, you may be in a position to make an actual appointment at this time; however, do allow yourself ample time to compile comparable sales and, if needed, time to obtain additional appraisal requests in the same area, or on your route, which is more time effective than having to return to the same area several times.

CANCELLATIONS AND POSTPONEMENTS OF ASSIGNMENTS

If you select your comparable sales before you have made a preliminary call for access, you may find that you have wasted your time because the person who requested the appraisal may not be aware of circumstances that could result in a cancellation or postponement of the appraisal assignment. Thus, the comparable sales may not be needed or they could be outdated by the time the owner or agent is ready to proceed. Some of the circumstances that you could encounter are

1. The property description is wrong, and the fee that was quoted may have to be revised, which may or may not be acceptable.

2. The borrower or owner has not been informed of the amount of the fee, disputes the amount, refuses to pay, and cancels the appraisal.
3. The appraisal cannot be initiated until the appraisal fee has been paid.
4. The owner, borrower, or agent does not wish to have that particular appraiser assigned to appraise the property.
5. The sale may have been canceled without notification to the lender.
6. The sales price or terms are being renegotiated.
7. Unexpected absence or illness of any of the principals involved.
8. Postponements by owners to provide time to complete additions, repairs, or property maintenance.
9. Inability to schedule appointments because of the lack of cooperation on the part of an owner, borrower, or agent.

Always alert your client immediately if there are any circumstances that affect the timely completion of your assignment.

USING THE PLAT MAP

A clearly legible copy of the plat map must be included with every appraisal. If you do not have a service that provides plat maps on microfilm, a copy of the plat map can usually be obtained from a title company, or you may be able to obtain a plat map from the participating lender if they have the preliminary title report for the property.

If a plat map is not available, the appraiser must show all

the required information on the building diagram, that is, distance to the nearest cross street in feet or number of intervening buildings, names of the subject street and cross streets, dimensions of the subject lot, and a north arrow. Plat maps must also clearly show the preceding data.

Appraisals of condominiums and planned unit developments should include plat maps with all the same information. The location of the condominium project or planned unit development is usually not acceptable; hence, identify the subject unit by showing the distance in feet or number of intervening units or buildings to the nearest cross street on the building diagram or plat map. Two plat maps should be combined, when necessary, to present an overall picture of the subject property and surrounding area.

The appraiser must indicate, on the plat map, the type of property that the subject backs and sides to when the plat map does provide a clear indication of the type of adjacent properties.

USING MICROFICHE DATA

If you have microfiche data, start with the "address register," which shows the owner's name, street address, legal description, year built, building size, and lot size. Check the ownership of the adjacent lots. If the adjacent lots are owned by the subject property owner, find out if they are supposed to be included in the appraisal report

Next, examine the "parcel list," which shows the type of improvements, and the plat maps. Note the type of improvements (residential, apartments, commercial, or industrial) on the adjacent and surrounding lots because this will help you describe the neighborhood. This will also help you assemble better selections of comparable sales because you may have to survey a wider than typical area for market data if there are mixed uses, such as apartments, condominiums, or commercial or industrial properties in the immediate area. Comparables must have similar amenities and locational influences; therefore, note nearby traffic streets, flood control channels, other external influences, and typical building and lot sizes of surrounding properties.

WHY ASSESSOR'S DESCRIPTIONS COULD VARY FROM APPRAISER'S DESCRIPTIONS

If you are using microfilm, or other data sources, that provide building sizes based on assessor's records, the total square footage of the livable area indicated by the data source could vary from the appraiser's physical measurements of actual livable area for one or more of the following reasons:

1. Real estate appraisers tape property to the nearest half foot while some county assessors tape property to the nearest foot.
2. Sometimes in homes located on hillsides, with one or more areas below street level, only the areas at or above street level are identified as "total livable area" while the balance of the structure is identified as "basement area." Hence, the total livable area indicated by assessor's records is sometimes misleading because the "basement area" may, in fact, consist of actual living area on a *first* level, such as a kitchen, living room, dining room, or other living areas that cost the same price per square foot to build as the rest of the structure.
3. Bonus rooms or recreation rooms are sometimes referred to as "attic" area by assessors; therefore, the rooms are

not included in the total livable area, as they should be, if the rooms are, in fact, finished living area.

4. Additions without permits might not be included in the total livable area shown.
5. Incorrect information provided by the source.
6. Incorrect information input on the microfilm.
7. In some instances, lot sizes shown on microfilm for newer subdivisions are not actual lot sizes; they are typical lot sizes for the subdivision. When all of the lot sizes in a particular tract are listed as, say, 6,000 sq. ft.; it is reasonable to assume the 6,000- sq. ft. figure is an average or typical lot size rather than the actual lot size. To find out if this is the case, check the size of a cul-de-sac lot, corner lot, or irregular-shaped lot to see if they are listed as 6,000 sq. ft. as well. If they are, then most of the lot sizes will be incorrect. It is the appraiser's responsibility to *verify* all the data contained in the appraisal report; never assume that any information is correct

HOW YOU WILL BENEFIT BY ENLISTING THE AGENT'S HELP

Whenever real estate agents have some association with your appraisal assignment, even though you may already have all the market data you need, always ask the agents for comparable sales. If no attempt is made to collaborate with participating agents, and the appraisal falls short of either description or value, you can be absolutely certain that your client will immediately be informed of your lack of cooperation.

Your expertise, most definitely, will be open to question if your client already has possession of your completed appraisal and a real estate agent (or owner) subsequently provides comparable sales or other information that alters your final estimate of value.

DISCLOSURE STATEMENTS AND SALES CONTRACTS

In some states it is mandatory that sellers provide disclosure statements detailing known deficiencies in the property and the status of permits for additions, remodeling, and so forth. Ask the seller or real estate agent for a copy of the disclosure statement so you can be assured that all the points are covered in your appraisal.

Because you have to provide the date of the sale and define sales concessions in the appraisal report, if you have not received a copy of the complete, ratified sales contract from the lender for the property that is to be appraised, obtain a copy from the listing or selling agent. Always find out if there are any amendments to the original contract of sale because, quite often, the terms of the sale are subsequently modified

THE CRITICAL IMPORTANCE OF TIMELINESS

Appraisers lose more clients because of time than for any other reason. Lenders often dispense with an appraiser's services because they do not appreciate complaints from owners and agents who were inconvenienced because the appraiser was either late for an appointment or didn't even show up. Appraisers lose clients, however, mainly because the appraisal was not completed on time. Because it is in everyone's best interest, we feel that it is important to point out some of the reasons why appraisers should provide timely, well-prepared documents.

Restrictive Deadlines

Many people are dependent on appraisers to sustain their responsibility to conclude assignments in a timely manner. Typically, real estate agents, loan agents, escrow officers, and lenders are very restricted with deadlines that cannot be altered. Delays on the part of the appraiser can result in cancellations of transactions, frustration, wasted time, lost income, and additional expense for redrawing loan documents and other paperwork.

Homes are usually sold with stipulations that the sale must record within a certain number of days, and, more often than not, the sale of one home is dependent on the sale of another home or even several other homes. Thus, rigid schedules have to be maintained by real estate agents in order to correlate recording dates that are suitable to all parties concerned. When the real estate transaction cannot be concluded because the appraiser failed to complete his or her assignment on time, everyone associated with the transaction will suffer great losses in time and money.

Interest Rates and Loan Terms

Daily changes in the market can affect the dollar amount of real estate loans, types of loans, interest rates, and availability of funds for loans. If the changes are not suited to the borrower's needs, the loan might be canceled. For this reason, it is imperative to fund loans before any changes in the market can alter the terms of the loans.

Appraiser's Time Schedule

Some lenders wait until a borrower's credit is approved, which can take several weeks, before they order an appraisal in order to avoid unnecessary expenses for the borrower in case the loan is rejected for credit reasons. Unfortunately, this leaves little time for appraisers to complete their assignment because the appraisal still has to pass through several stages of review, after the lender receives it, before the loan can finally be funded. Therefore, every effort should be made to produce a reliable product because errors and omissions delay the process even more.

When something or someone is hindering completion of the appraisal, your client should be advised immediately so that alternate solutions can be considered and expedient results can be obtained. All requirements, letters, additional forms, or addenda that are requested by the lender, after the appraisal has been completed, should be presented to the client *immediately upon request* to ensure a timely funding of the loan.

EXPIRATION DATE OF APPRAISAL

The appraisal is normally considered current for a period of 120 calendar days from the date of valuation. If, prior to closing, 120 days have elapsed, the original appraiser may be required to certify whether the property value has or has not changed. Appraisal reports on new construction may be up to 180 days old if the construction of the mortgaged premises is completed after the mortgage application.

In the event the property value has declined, the appraiser will be required to document the conditions that have affected the market value of the property. Additional comparable sales may be required if the loan is not funded within the required time period. If the loan is not funded within 120 days (or 180 days for new construction), a new appraisal may be required.

CHAPTER 4

HOW TO USE COMPARABLE SALES IN APPRAISALS

The process of arriving at a final estimate of value begins with a search for comparable sales. The importance of a thorough search for comparable sales cannot be overemphasized —for several very important reasons. Time is the most important reason: if you select appropriate market data to begin with, you will save countless hours down the road when you are writing the report, analyzing the market data, and finalizing the value.

In this chapter we will show you how to save time, how to identify a neighborhood, how to avoid comparable sales mistakes, how to document your conclusions, and how to analyze market data, correctly and incorrectly.

OBTAINING COMPARABLE SALES

Comparable sales can be obtained from market data books that are published by data research centers primarily for appraisal use, multiple-listing services, real estate agents, sellers, buyers, title companies, on-line computer services, certificates of value, market data services that provide recorded sales on microfilm, and the appraiser's files. Properties that have been appraised for sale purposes are acceptable comparables if the sales have been recorded.

Sales prices and descriptions of the comparables must be verified, and two legitimate data sources should be shown in the appraisal report. Personal inspection is not a legitimate data source. When you obtain comparable sales from listing agents, selling agents, or anyone else having a financial interest in the sale, always verify the details of the transaction with a disinterested third party.

Include multiple-listing numbers when market data are obtained from a multiple-listing service to enable reviewers to verify the information readily. When information is obtained from a published source (market data books), the month and year of the publication should be shown in the report. Include names and telephone numbers when the referenced data sources are agents, owners, or buyers. Because reviewers often refer to the same data sources that you have used to assemble your market data, always describe any discrepancies that you find in published data in an addendum to the appraisal so you will avoid having to provide explanations at a later date.

Select a range of sales, rather than just three or four sales, so the most suitable sales can be singled out after the subject property has been inspected. Make sure the sales prices of the comparables are not more than they were listed for—which is a sure sign that sales concessions may have influenced the sales price; hence, the sale may not be appropriate. Do not use sales of homes that are in very bad condition because these homes usually sell far below market prices.

The neighborhood price range, age range, the predominant price, and predominant age should be established while you are selecting your comparable sales and then refined after a field inspection of the subject property.

HOW TO DETERMINE SALES PRICES BY USING TAX STAMPS

In many localities, transfer taxes must be paid when an interest in real estate is sold and conveyed by deed. Payment of the tax is usually made by purchasing stamps from a state or local official, affixing them to the deed, and having them canceled. To determine the sales price of a property, divide the dollar amount of the stamps by the tax rate. For example, the dollar amount of the stamps is $341.00 and the tax rate is $1.10/1,000.

$341. ÷ 1.1 = $310,000. sales price

If the mortgage has been assumed, add the amount of the assumed mortgage to the actual cash amount paid (represented by the amount of the tax stamps) to find the approximate sales price.

$69. ÷ 1.1 = $62,727., rounded $63,000.
$63,000. + $357,000. = $420,000. sales price

In the example, the dollar amount of the tax stamps was $69. The amount of the assumed loan was $357,000.

The amount of the transfer stamps give an indication of the sales price, however, tax stamps are generally not considered to be a reliable source of exact selling prices because the tax rate might be based only on the actual cash amount paid at the closing of the sale, thereby excluding assumed mortgages, or too many or too few stamps are sometimes put on the deed deliberately to mislead anyone trying to find the selling price of the property.

USING THE MOST EFFECTIVE ORDER OF IMPORTANCE WHEN SELECTING MARKET DATA

Select market data in this order of importance: neighborhood, zoning, location, date of sale, terms of sale, age (comparable sales should be similar in effective age), size of dwelling, lot size, room count, quality, condition, amenities, and price.

Every effort should be made to select comparables that are as similar as possible in date of sale, neighborhood appeal, locational appeal, physical characteristics, and terms in order to make the least adjustments possible and, especially, to avoid making "subjective adjustments."

DEALING WITH SUBJECTIVE ADJUSTMENTS

Subjective adjustments are those adjustments that cannot be supported by factual justification at this time; hence, the adjustments are based on the appraiser's experience and judgment. Subjective adjustments should always be avoided. The best way to do this is by using at least two like properties in the appraisal report to provide a basis for market adjustments.

Typically, adjustments for variances in neighborhood appeal are highly subjective; therefore, it is extremely important to use comparable sales that are located in the same neighborhood. When market data are selected from an alternate neighborhood, provide good reasons for extending your search for comparable sales and explain the relationship of the alternate neighborhoods to the subject neighborhood.

Every effort should be made to document subjective adjustments to the fullest extent possible because the dollar amount of any adjustments for controversial items is always open to question by reviewers, clients, owners, and lenders.

Appraisers should always be fully prepared to provide answers to inquiries regarding their investigation, opinions, and value conclusions. Therefore, if necessary, in addition to current sales from the subject neighborhood, include dated sales, sales in escrow, listings, or sales from other neighborhoods to provide a basis for your adjustments and conclusions.

WHEN TO BRACKET COMPARABLE SALES

When market data are limited, bracket the sales to demonstrate a basis for adjustments; for example,

1. Use one or more sales in your market analysis that are greater in size than the subject dwelling, one or more sales that are equal in size, and one or more sales that are smaller in square footage.
2. Use one or more sales that have an inferior view, one or more sales that have an equal view, and one or more sales that have a superior view.

Bracketed Adjustments—Examples

Subject	Sale No. 1	Sale No. 2	Sale No. 3
Good View	Superior −5,000	Comp View 0	Inferior +5,000
2,280 sq. ft.	2,500 −8,000	2,100 +6,000	2,300 0

The subject is the standard against which the comparable sales are evalu ated and adjusted. Comparable sales are adjusted to the subject property. When an item in the comparable property is superior to the subject a minus adjustment is made. When an item in the comparable property is inferior to the subject, a plus adjustment is made to bring that item equal to the suibject. In the example, minus and plus adjustments were made to bring the items equal to the subject.

Always bracket sales comparables when the adjustments cannot be supported by two like properties, when the adjustments are substantial, when the adjustments are subjective, and when you are appraising higher-priced properties because across-the-board, unsupported adjustments should always be avoided.

Across-the-Board Adjustments—Examples

Subject	Sale No. 1	Sale No. 2	Sale No. 3
Good View	Inferior +8,000	Inferior +3,000	Inferior+ 5,000
2,280 sq. ft.	2,500 −8,000	2,400 −4,000	2,600 −11,000

In the example, because all of the comparables have a plus adjustment for inferior views, and a minus adjustment for size, a basis for the adjustments cannot be defined.

WHAT IS A NEIGHBORHOOD?

Many people are under the impression that a neighborhood consists of a $\frac{1}{4}$, $\frac{1}{2}$, or 1-mile radius in a Thomas Bros Map or street directory. This simply is not true.

A neighborhood consists of an area where housing characteristics (houses are similar in age, quality, size, and value range), concerns of the inhabitants (comparable earning power, educational levels, similar cultural interests, and social backgrounds), land uses, and amenities are similar. Neighborhoods are smaller in geographic area than are locations or areas; thus, typically, several neighborhoods can be found within a particular location.

Defining Neighbornood Amenities

Amenities are the advantages, appeal, pleasing features, or circumstances that one particular location has over another, such as climate, recreational facilities, views, water orientation, or hillside locations. Civic amenities can include desirable political or governmental influences, a highly desirable school system, and close proximity to shopping centers, employment centers, banks, restaurants, libraries, cultural centers, churches, and parks.

Several neighborhoods, located in close proximity to each other, can enjoy the same or similar amenities; nevertheless, the housing characteristics, value range, land uses, and concerns of the inhabitants may differ substantially. Therefore, a neighborhood should not be defined only on the basis of common amenities.

USING COMMON INTERESTS AND CHARACTERISTICS TO DEFINE NEIGHBORHOODS

When you are defining neighborhoods, selecting comparable sales from within the neighborhood, and especially having to obtain comparable sales from outside of the immediate neighborhood, always look for common interests and characteristics (which should be described in the neighborhood section and the sales comparison comments section of the appraisal report), such as the following:

Natural and Man-made Boundaries

1. Neighborhoods are often defined by natural or man-made physical barriers or boundaries, such as rivers, ravines, flood control channels, topography, elevation, climate, city boundaries, traffic arteries, railroad tracks, commercial or industrial centers, proximity to other land uses, and percentage of built-up area.

2. Neighborhoods are sometimes defined by street patterns, such as a grid pattern as opposed to a pattern that inhibits the free flow of traffic through the neighborhood by incorporating dead-end streets, cul-de-sac streets, or curving roadways in the layout of the neighborhood.

3. Neighborhoods are sometimes divided into two or more segments by natural or man-made physical barriers. Since your readers recognize natural or man-made physical barriers or boundaries as typical neighborhood perimeters, they will surely question the appraiser's selection of comparable sales when the sales are not located within the neighborhood boundaries as typically defined. When you select comparable sales from both sides of a divided neighborhood, describe the actual neighborhood boundaries, in detail, addressing similarities in land uses, housing characteristics, appeal, and amenities. Also, clearly define the boundaries of the neighborhood on a location (area) map and include the map with the appraisal.

Locational, External, and Environmental Factors

1. Waterfront property must be compared to like property. When sales prices are based on a price per front foot on the water, appraisers must use comparable sales that have sold on the same basis.

2. When property owners have to drive through an undesirable area to enter the housing development, always obtain comparable sales from within the development. Sales history should also be studied to determine long term stability of property values; that is, are property values likely to remain stable, increase, or decline?

3. Homes located on flat or level terrain should not be compared to homes that are located on elevated or rolling terrain.

4. The neighborhood, subject property, and comparable sales should have similar proximity to airports, vehicular traffic influences, and other hazardous or undesirable influences.

Civic Amenities, Conformity, and Property Rights

1. Buyers are usually willing to pay more for a home when their children can attend a school located within the neighborhood or within walking distance or when the school district is proclaimed to be highly desirable.

2. Generally, houses are worth more when they back and side to conforming (like) properties; therefore, comparable sales should have similar influences.

3. Do not compare property situated on fee simple land to property that is situated on leasehold land, or vice versa, unless you can clearly demonstrate the basis for market adjustments. Property on leasehold land should only be compared to leasehold property with similar land lease terms.

A leasehold status can usually be established by perusing a property profile of owner's names. When homes are situated on leasehold land, the lessor will be shown as the owner of all or almost all of the properties. The borrower's (lessee's) name will not be shown because the land is owned by the lessor. The borrower will not be listed as an "owner" until the land has been paid for in full. Property transfers usually will not be shown as recorded sales because the land has not changed hands.

4. Neighborhood maintenance levels must be comparable. Homes that are located in neighborhoods exhibiting only average maintenance levels should not be compared to homes in neighborhoods that reflect superior maintenance levels.

5. Age, size, architectural styles, and quality of the homes must be similar and should be conforming with respect to neighborhood appeal.

6. Proximity to employment centers, shopping centers, recreational facilities, and other public amenities should be similar.

7. Neighborhoods with common areas or association-owned recreational facilities and security-gated communities must be compared to like property. Equestrian and view-oriented neighborhoods and neighborhoods featuring estate size lots must be compared to like property. Homes located in neighborhoods consisting of mixed uses, such as income, commercial, or industrial property (other than small neighborhood convenience stores) interspersed with single-family residential property, should not be compared to homes located in a neighborhood with more conforming uses.

8. Comparable sales must have the same zoning as the subject property.

9. When you appraise a home in a neighborhood that consists of only one-story homes, the homes should not be compared to homes located in another neighborhood that consists of both one- and two-story homes. Apply the "Principles of Progression and Regression." A one-story home surrounded by larger homes will be worth more (progresses in value) than is the same home located in a neighborhood that consists of only one-story homes. A large home surrounded by smaller homes is worth less (regresses in value) than is the same home located in a comparable neighborhood.

USING MARKET DATA FROM ALTERNATE CITIES

Can you use comparable sales that are located in cities other than the subject city? Even though the comparable property is located within a block or two, or a few blocks, and the alternate city or neighborhood gives the impression of being similar, very careful consideration must be given to the definition of a neighborhood.

School systems, city government, and public facilities may be more or less desirable, the city tax base could be higher or lower, and special assessments could influence property value.

You might wonder how buyers know when the tax rate varies from one city to another, or how they know that there is a special assessment that has to be paid, because potential buyers wouldn't call city officials or the tax assessor for information every time they look at a different house. Typically, the first thing a potential buyer wants to know is, "How much is the payment?" By making a comparison of estimated payments projected by real estate agents, buyers can easily identify higher taxes and special assessments in different cities. If you could buy a similar home in a comparable neighborhood with a lower tax base, which one would you choose? If a lower tax base resulted in reduced payments, would you be willing to pay more for the property?

ALWAYS CHECK MAILING ADDRESSES

Always check the mailing address of the subject and the comparable sales because a mailing address that differs from the actual property address sometimes has a tremendous effect on property value. For example, the property may be located in an unincorporated county area, with a given community name, but the city listed as the mailing address might be more (or less) desirable. Most buyers are willing to pay more for a prestigious mailing address.

HOW TO USE BUILDER SALES

When market data are very limited, can you use sales of homes constructed by the same builder that are located in alternate neighborhoods? Sometimes; however, neighborhood appeal affects market value to such a great extent that you should not automatically assume that values are the same in different neighborhoods even though the houses were constructed by the same builder. When maintenance levels, locational influences, or economic factors vary substantially, sales prices also vary substantially. One neighborhood might have a very high turnover rate or an excessive number of rental properties resulting in inferior maintenance levels than an identical tract of homes that exhibits high pride of ownership because the homes have been occupied by the same owners for many years.

Two tracts, constructed by the same builder, are identical in quality, design, and maintenance levels. One of the tracts, however, has a beautifully landscaped park and an elementary school in the center of the tract. Would the two tracts be comparable in appeal? Would the homes sell at comparable prices? A study of market history in both tracts would probably reveal a distinct difference in sales prices attributed to the close proximity of the park and school.

The economy, demand, and the purchasing power of the buyers prompt builders to modify their specifications when they build in different neighborhoods. Builders also have been known to modify quality and amenities in different phases of the same project. The floor plans and exterior designs, however, could remain unchanged.

Suggestions for Documenting Your Conclusions

When you use builders' sales from alternate neighborhoods, use older sales, sales in escrow, and listings from the subject neighborhood to show that there is little variance in sales prices between the neighborhoods. Also, address similarities in housing characteristics, economic factors, maintenance levels, land uses, locational influences, and amenities. Consider the following illustration:

The subject property is a trilevel home of very good quality lath-and-plaster construction, containing 2,400 sq. ft. of livable area. Comparable 1 is the only recent, closed sale of a similar home in the immediate neighborhood. Comparables 2 and 3 are located in a tract, 3 miles north, that was constructed by the same builder.

This tract is identical in quality, design, amenities, and maintenance levels to the subject tract. The immediate and surrounding land uses; proximity to schools, shopping, and recreational facilities; and convenience to employment centers are equivalent to the subject development.

Comparables 4 and 5 are located in the immediate neighborhood. They are in escrow at this time and were included to lend additional support to the concluded value.

AVOIDING COMPARABLE SALES MISTAKES

We have reviewed a number of appraisals where values were overstated or understated because appraisers did not recognize differences in neighborhood appeal when they used data from outside of the subject neighborhood. This situation usually occurs when market data are limited and the appraiser assumes that the sales prices for the one or two sales that he or she does find in the subject neighborhood are typical. Hence, those sales prices are used to find sales in alternate neighborhoods.

Selecting comparable sales from alternate neighborhoods by price similarity alone, without a thorough analysis of every factor that contributes to market value, can lead to very distorted values:

Example 1: Comparables 1, 2, and 3 sold for about $180,000. The homes are similar in age, size, and location to the subject. Comparable 1 is located in the subject neighborhood, and comparables 2 and 3 are located in a nearby neighborhood. The appraised value of the property is $180,000. (which was easy to achieve because the appraiser selected comparables by price).

Comparable 1 had a recent, large addition that was not disclosed in public records. Comparables 2 and 3 are superior in quality, design, and appeal to the subject property. These value factors were overlooked, however, because the appraiser did not conduct a thorough market analysis. Consequently, the property was overvalued by more than $20,000.

Example 2: The subject property, which was highly upgraded, sold for $200,000. There were no homes that sold for about $200,000. in the subject neighborhood. To support the sales price, the appraiser selected sales from a nearby tract of homes, similar in quality and design, but superior in locational appeal. The locational appeal is superior because the homes are located in a highly desirable school district. Because the appraiser did not do a thorough analysis, adjustments for locational appeal as well as the subject's overimprovement were overlooked. Hence, the property was grossly overvalued.

When sales prices exceed the predominant price in the neighborhood, always find out why and never assume that houses or neighborhoods are similar simply because they have the same outward appearance. The only way to avoid making comparable sales mistakes is to verify the data and analyze all the factors that contribute to value, particularly, locational factors.

USING THE COST APPROACH TO ESTIMATE VALUES

After you have appraised a number of properties in various areas, and you have become familiar with land values, you can then use the cost approach to define a starting point for assembling market data.

For example, the property to be appraised is a 25 year-old, 2,500 sq. ft., average-quality home in Huntington Beach with air conditioning and a swimming pool. The home is situated on a typical 6,000-sq. ft. lot. The effective age is estimated at ten years because the home has been modernized and well maintained.

The typical replacement cost for an average-quality home in this city is $55/sq. ft. The base cost is increased by $1/sq. ft. because the home is air conditioned. Land values in this city typically represent 60 percent of the total value. Estimate an approximate value as follows:

Dwelling:	2,500 sq. ft. @ $56./sq. ft.	=	$140,000.
Garage:	320 sq. ft. @ $18./sq. ft.	=	5,760.
Total cost:			$145,760.

The house represents 40 percent of the total value; therefore, divide $145,760 by 40 percent or .4 to find the total value, before adjustments, which is $364,400. Next, subtract the total cost new from the total value to find the land value:

$364,400 less $145,760 = $218,640 land value.

Then, deduct 10 percent for depreciation (based on effective age of ten years) from the total cost new of $145,760. Add the average cost of yard improvements (6,000 sq. ft. x $1.25/sq. ft.), the market value of the swimming pool, and the estimated land value:

Total cost new:	$145,760.
Less: 10 percent depreciation:	14,576.
Plus: Yard improvements:	7,500.
Plus: Swimming pool:	10,000.
Add: Land value:	218,640.
Estimated value:	$367,324., rounded $370,000.

After you have established an estimated value, select comparable sales in this value range.

This is a good method to use to avoid being out in left field when you are selecting comparable sales. By working with an approximate value, you can select comparable sales before you go into the field to make your property inspections, which will eliminate return trips to the area.

DETERMINING THE PRICE PER SQUARE FOOT OF GROSS LIVING AREA

Determine the price per square foot of gross living area for each sale when you are assembling your market data. When the price per square foot of one comparable sale varies considerably from the other sales, the variance can usually be attributed to one or more missing pieces of information, such as locational influences, lot size, swimming pool, remodeling, additions, guest house, basement, financing, or some other value factor.

If you analyze the price per square foot range for all of the sales before you go into the field to inspect property, you will be prepared to find reasons for any variances. When the price per square foot is way out of line compared to the other sales or the subject's estimated value, the sale would not be appropriate because the end result would be excessive adjustments and sales with excessive adjustments should not be used in your analysis.

HANDLING THE "TRICKY" PROBLEM OF CHOOSING FROM A WIDE RANGE OF SALES

Older developments often exhibit a wide variety of sales prices because many of the homes have been extensively remodeled or upgraded and additions of living areas, swimming pools, and other improvements have also taken place. If you have a list of 20, 30, or more sales with a wide variety of sales prices, do you have to analyze the details of each sale to decide which sales to use?

Eliminate Inconsistent Comparable Sales

Because public records are not always accurate or up-to-date and full descriptions are not always provided, it could be difficult to select meaningful sales from a wide range of sales prices. Suppose, among others, the following sales prices for 1,800-sq. ft. homes are shown in public records:

$387,000., $400,000., and $420,000.

Would you look for comparable sales in the $390,000. range or $420,000. range? Use the cost approach to quickly narrow down the number of sales to analyze.

First, estimate a value for the subject in the same manner as previously illustrated. Next, divide the estimated value by the size of the structure to find the price per square foot of gross living area. Then, divide the sales prices of the comparables by the size of the homes to find the price per square foot for each sale (this only takes a few minutes). At this point you can concentrate on the sales that are closest to the subject in price per square foot as those sales will probably have similar characteristics.

In the following example, the subject 1,800-sq. ft. home is situated on an 8,000-sq. ft. lot. There are a spa, swimming pool, and covered patio. We have estimated a value of $400,000. or $222./sq. ft. The following meaningless comparables, which are out of line with the $222./sq. ft. range estimated for the property, can be eliminated:

$387,000. or $214./sq. ft. (no pool or spa)
$400,000. or $267./sq. ft. (addition not included in size shown in public records)
$420,000. or $210./sq. ft. (addition not included in size shown in public records)
$415,000. or $230./sq. ft. (completely remodeled home)

An alternative, but less reliable, way to narrow down the

number of sales to investigate is to study the subject's physical characteristics. When the property has not been upgraded or modernized and there are no amenities, the value will be toward the lower end of a range of sales prices. When there is a swimming pool, view, larger than typical lot, remodeling, or modernization, the value will probably fall in the higher end of the range. Check out a few sales from the price range that best reflects the subject's characteristics to find out whether the sales are relative. If so, a lot of time has been saved.

HOW TO OVERCOME THE INSUFFICIENT RECENT MARKET DATA PROBLEM

When market data are limited or nonexistent in the subject neighborhood, before you try to find sales in alternate neighborhoods, make a study of sales history in the subject neighborhood. Select several older sales in the subject neighborhood that are similar to the property being appraised. Then, apply an appropriate percentage rate of appreciation to the older sales, which will give you an approximate value to use as a starting point to begin searching for comparable sales in alternate neighborhoods.

Rates of appreciation and other statistics can usually be obtained from real estate agents because almost all realty boards continually evaluate rates of appreciation in specific areas as well as monitoring average marketing times and median prices. Rates of appreciation, median sales prices, unemployment rates, locations of local employment centers, and other market statistics can also be obtained from local newspapers, regional economic publications, and the local Chamber of Commerce.

It is always faster and easier to select suitable comparable sales from public records, multiple-listing books, and other data sources when you have an estimated value, or value range, to work with. Further, if appropriate, you could include the following statement in the appraisal report:

"The appraiser's selection of market data from outside of the subject neighborhood was based on the historical pattern of sales from within the subject neighborhood. We have applied an appreciation rate of 8 percent to the older sales, comparables 4 and 5, in the subject neighborhood. The rate of appreciation was established by market surveys as well as the appraiser's experience and knowledge of market appreciation in the subject and neighboring communities."

Use the cost approach as a double-check to find out whether the sales that you select from alternate neighborhoods are in line with your estimated value of the subject property. If the sales prices of the comparables do not relate to your estimated value of the subject property, reconsider the characteristics of the homes and the neighborhood—are they really comparable or did you overlook something? Do the sales prices in the alternate neighborhood relate to listing prices, pending sales, and sales history in the subject neighborhood?

Would a typical and informed buyer have looked at the comparable property if it had been for sale at the time? Buyers usually do not confine themselves to a single neighborhood when they are contemplating a purchase. They look for a specific type of home in neighborhoods with similar appeal; comparable school district; similar tax base; and comparable proximity to employment centers, recreational facilities, and shopping centers.

A comparable sale, selected from outside of the subject neighborhood, is acceptable only when the appraiser demonstrates that the alternate neighborhood has comparable appeal. The appraiser must also explain why it was necessary to extend his or her search for comparable sales. An analysis of sales history, sales in escrow, or listings from the subject neighborhood should be included in the appraisal report to lend further support to the appraiser's conclusions.

When market data are limited or nonexistent in the subject neighborhood, always discuss the subject's property value and the relationship of alternate neighborhoods to the subject neighborhood with real estate agents. Enlist the help of real estate agents when you are having trouble finding the right sales.

DON'T FORGET LISTINGS AND SALES IN ESCROW

Listings and sales in escrow should be reviewed because they reflect current market trends. If you evaluate only recorded transactions, your final value could reflect *past* evidence of value rather than present value because recorded sales are dated; the actual transactions may have taken place months or more previous to the date they were recorded.

Survey "for sale" signs in the subject neighborhood for listings, sold property, property in escrow, and names as well as telephone numbers of agents to get in touch with for assistance with the neighborhood description, comparable sales, and verification of comparable sales. This survey is also necessary in order to perform a proper neighborhood analysis with respect to demand, supply, and marketing time. The number and duration of "for sale" signs will give you an indication of current market trends.

Defining the Upper Limits of Value

Include two or more listings in your report, if appropriate, to define the upper limits of value. More than one listing should be referenced to show clearly that you are representing the "norm" and to indicate that you have considered more than just one higher or lower than typical listing in the neighborhood. This is particularly important when the appraised value differs from the sales price or the owner's estimate of value. When someone insists that their property is worth more than the appraised value, by including listings in the appraisal, you can show that their property cannot be worth more than comparable homes that are listed for less than they claim their property is worth.

WHY CONSIDERATION OF SALES TERMS AND CONCESSIONS IS SO IMPORTANT TO THE APPRAISER

Always carefully consider sales terms and concessions because the final estimate of market value must represent "cash or cash equivalency." When you appraise property in a neighborhood where few, or none, of the sales transactions are conventionally financed, study sales history to find out whether there is some relationship between past sales and current sales. A rapid increase in sales prices is sometimes caused by special or creative financing. Also, discuss current values with several local real estate agents, who are familiar with the subject neighborhood, to find out whether special or creative financing has resulted in inflated property values.

Eliminate market data that are not typical due to the circumstances of the sale. Do not use sales with unusual financing or sales concessions, foreclosure sales, forced sales, sales of underpriced or overpriced property, or sales that are not arm's-length transactions.

ESTABLISHING THE DATE OF SALE

Generally, the appraiser should use comparable sales that have been settled or closed within the last 12 months. However, the appraiser may use older comparable sales as additional supporting data if he or she believes that it is appropriate. The appraiser must comment on the reasons for using any comparable sales that are more than 6 months old. In addition, the appraiser may use the subject property as a fourth comparable sale or as supporting data if the property previously was sold (and closed or settled). If the appraiser believes that it is appropriate, he or she also may use contract offerings and listings as supporting data.

According to Fannie Mae guidelines, appraisers can use sales up to a year old; however, most lenders will not accept comparable sales that are over 6 months old. In most cases, the 6-month limit refers to the date the loan is funded, not the date of the appraisal. When sales are incorporated in the appraisal that are 5 or 6 months old, by the time the loan is ready to fund, the sales will probably be too old, and they may have to be supplemented or replaced.

In the event that lenders request additional sales, you might find it difficult, if not impossible, to locate additional supportive market data. Most certainly, it would be a great adversity to everyone concerned if additional data were required and sales prices, at this time, would not support the value represented in the appraisal report. For this reason, and because market value must reflect current market value, always use market data that are as recent as feasibly possible. This also illustrates another reason why it is important to review listings and sales in escrow—not only will supplementary sales be readily available if needed, you will not have a problem reaffirming your value.

CHECK THE ACTUAL DATE OF SALE

It is very important to note the actual date of the sale (rather than the recorded date) and the description of the property *at the time of the sale.* If you do not, as you are visually inspecting the comparable sales, you might overlook improvements to the sold property that took place *after* the sale. If any improvements have taken place after the sale, clearly describe the condition of the property at the time of the sale and list the improvements that took place after the sale. When the photo of the comparable depicts the property to be in a condition other than what is shown in the report, an explanation will be required.

HOW TO USE MULTIPLE-LISTING BOOKS

Become familiar with the format of multiple-listing books in different areas where you appraise property because this will enable you to find the information you need quite rapidly. Whenever you are appraising in different areas, ask real estate agents for a copy of an outdated multiple-listing book so you can study the format at your leisure. Or ask for their assistance so you can readily find of the data that you need.

This information is included in this book because many appraisers do not avail themselves of the opportunity to verify market data or to obtain listings and sales comparables from multiple-listing books because they feel it is too time consuming. Also, on a number of occasions, we have noted that appraisers have overlooked many very good comparables because they did not know how to use the books properly. Multiple-listing services typically publish sales information in weekly books for a specific period of time (usually three months). The information is then transferred to "comparable books." When appraisers do not check the comparable books, as well as the weekly books, they overlook all but the most recent sales.

Any number of good comparable sales can also be overlooked when the appraiser simply looks for actual sales without analyzing pending sales. Many agents do not report sales prices until the transactions have actually been recorded; therefore, the sales are shown as "pending." Appraisers should also should call on listings to find out whether the property may have sold because sales are not always reported to the realty board for publication as they should be.

Always verify sales prices and descriptions contained in multiple-listing books with the listing or selling agent, or the realty board, because the information may not be correct. Sales prices, particularly, should be verified because sales prices are sometimes changed and the agent may not have reported the new sales price to the board. Reported sales, sometimes, "fall out of escrow," that is, the transaction was not completed; hence, the property may have resold at a different price. Or the reported sales price may have changed because the property did not appraise at the right price; therefore, the buyer and seller agreed on a new price, which was not reported.

SUMMARY

The comparable sales used in the appraisal report must be the best comparables available; if not, an explanation will be required. The appraiser will have to explain why he or she didn't use the best comparables available or why certain comparables were ignored. This question usually presents itself when review appraisers survey the subject neighborhood and they find comparable sales that the appraiser apparently overlooked.

A satisfactory number of sales must be contained in the appraisal report to support the concluded value and to provide a basis for the adjustments, which could be three, four, five, or more, depending on the particular appraisal problem. More than three sales should always be provided when you are appraising higher-priced property, when the sales have other than conventional financing, when property values are increasing or decreasing, when the appraised value differs from the sales price, or when the market data are so dissimilar that numerous or large adjustments are applied.

Appraisers should analyze as many properties as necessary in an effort to isolate each significant factor that requires an adjustment in the sales comparison analysis. The greater number of properties that are reviewed, the better the statistics and the greater likelihood of an accurate estimate of value. If you are thorough when you are selecting market data, you will eliminate the need to follow up the report with a lot of explanations or additional supportive data, and you will spend less time finishing the appraisal report. When the sales are very complementary to the subject, it is easier to define a basis for the adjustments because the differences will be readily apparent.

Although you made every effort to select meaningful comparable sales and analyze the property appropriately, and have arrived at a concluded value based on substantial and verifiable evidence, when your client, the borrower, or the lender offers additional supportive data, you must make a conscientious effort to review all the information offered and report all your findings to your client in a matter-of-fact, professional manner. When additional information affects your concluded value, the value must be adjusted to reflect your current findings.

THE RIGHT WAY AND THE WRONG WAY TO ANALYZE MARKET DATA

The following examples of a market data analysis illustrate the importance of a thorough investigation. Example 1 was written by a trainee appraiser. Example 2 was written by the review appraiser.

The appraisal problem was a 554-sq. ft. addition to an

existing residence. The property was one of the largest homes in the neighborhood before the addition. After the addition, the home was a gross overimprovement for the neighborhood.

In the market analysis, comparable 1 was used because it was the largest home in the subject development that sold within the previous six months. Comparables 2 and 3 were used because they were the only sales of large homes in the area that were similar in quality, condition, and locational appeal.

Example 1: Because the appraiser did not know how to deal with functional obsolescence, many errors were made in the market analysis.

1. Notice the range of the indicated value to the subject: $490,500 to $511,000. This wide range was the first tip-off that something was wrong with the analysis.

2. Comparable 3: Perhaps, because the appraiser wanted to bring the indicated value closer to the other sales, an inappropriate $15,000 adjustment was made for design and appeal and an inappropriate $10,000 adjustment was made for a superior location.

3. The dimensions were not calculated correctly. The gross living area should be 3,296 sq. ft. instead of 3,206 sq. ft. Consequently, the adjustments for size were off by $3,500.

4. The major factor that was overlooked, which caused the other problems, was functional obsolescence.

Example 2: Now take a close look at the market adjustments in this example. The adjustments for location and appeal were eliminated and the other adjustments were fine-tuned. Notice the major difference: an adjustment of $15,000 was made for functional obsolescence. The correct indicated value of the subject is

Comp. 1: $500,500. Comp. 2: $499,500. Comp. 3: $505,500.

A very close range! And, most important, the adjustments were based on market history, discussions with local real estate agents familiar with the subject property and the comparables, and the appraiser's files. There were no "fudge factors" used to distort the value.

THE RIGHT WAY AND THE WRONG WAY TO ANALYZE MARKET DATA, Example Number One

SALES COMPARISON ANALYSIS

ITEM	SUBJECT	COMPARABLE NO. 1		COMPARABLE NO. 2		COMPARABLE NO. 3	
Address	2312 Lemon Street	2412 West Street		2428 South Street		1824 Bolton Circle	
Proximity to Subject		2 blocks south		3 blocks south		1 3/4 mile southeast	
Sales Price	$ 500,000		$ 469,000		$ 465,000		$ 508,000
Price/Gross Liv. Area	$ 155.96 ¢	$ 179.35 ¢		$ 177.96 ¢		$ 161.63 ¢	
Data Source	Personal Insp	Title rec./MLS/CMDC		Title rec./MLS		Title records/owner	
VALUE ADJUSTMENTS	DESCRIPTION	DESCRIPTION	+(-) $ Adjustment	DESCRIPTION	+(-) $ Adjustment	DESCRIPTION	+(-) $ Adjustment
Sales or Financing Concessions		Cash		Cash		Conventional $406,400 1st	
Date of Sale/Time	3/89	2/17/89		12/2/88		10/13/88	
Location	Good	Good		Superior	-3,000	Superior	-10,000
Site/View	6000	6000		7931/Sup. Ut.	-4,000	7700/Sup. Ut.	-3,500
Design and Appeal	Good	Good		Good		Sl. Superior	-15,000
Quality of Construction	Good	Good		Good		Good	
Age	1980	1980		1975		1978	
Condition	Good	Good		Good		Good	
Above Grade Room Count (Total / Bdrms / Bath)	10 / 4 / 3	8 / 4 / 3		8 / 3 / 2.5	+2,000	9 / 5 / 3	
Gross Living Area	3,206 Sq. Ft.	2,615 Sq. Ft.	+25,000	2,613 Sq. Ft.	+25,000	3,143 Sq. Ft.	+2,500
Basement & Finished Rooms Below Grade	None Doc. #'s	None 89-86739		None 88-629310		None 88-523562	
Functional Utility	Good	Good		Good		Good	
Heating/Cooling	FAU/None	FAU/None		FAU/CA	-2,000	FAU/None	
Garage/Carport	3 Car Garage	3 Car Garage		2 Car Garage	+3,000	3 Car Garage	
Porches, Patio Pools, etc.	Pool & spa Patio & deck	None Patio & deck	+15,000	None Cov. patio/Eq	+15,000	None Solarium	+15,000 -2,500
Special Energy Efficient Items	Typical Gd.Lndscaping	Typical Inferior	+2,000	Typical Gd.Lndscaping		Typical Gd.Lndscaping	
Fireplace(s)	3 masonry	3 masonry		1 masonry	+2,000	2 masonry	+1,000
Other (e.g. kitchen equip., remodeling)	Built-ins Upgrades	Built-ins Upgrades		Built-ins Upgrades		Built-ins Sup.Upgrades	-5,000
Net Adj. (total)		[X] + [ ] - $	42,000	[X] + [ ] - $	38,000	[ ] + [X] - $	17,500
Indicated Value of Subject			$ 511,000		$ 503,000		$ 490,500

THE RIGHT WAY AND THE WRONG WAY TO ANALYZE MARKET DATA,
Example Number Two

SALES COMPARISON ANALYSIS

ITEM	SUBJECT	COMPARABLE NO. 1		COMPARABLE NO. 2		COMPARABLE NO. 3	
Address	2312 Lemon Street	2412 West Street		2428 South Street		1824 Bolton Circle	
Proximity to Subject		2 blocks south		3 blocks south		1 3/4 mile southeast	
Sales Price	$ 500,000	$ 469,000		$ 465,000		$ 508,000	
Price/Gross Liv. Area	$ 151.70 ¢	$ 179.35 ¢		$ 177.96 ¢		$ 161.63 ¢	
Data Source	Personal Insp	Title rec./MLS/CMDC		Title rec./MLS		Title records/owner	
VALUE ADJUSTMENTS	DESCRIPTION	DESCRIPTION	+(-) $ Adjustment	DESCRIPTION	+(-) $ Adjustment	DESCRIPTION	+(-) $ Adjustment
Sales or Financing Concessions		Cash		Cash		Conventional $406,400 1st	
Date of Sale/Time	3/89	2/17/89		12/2/88		10/13/88	
Location	Good	Good		Good		Good	
Site/View	6000	6000		7931/Sup. Ut.	-4,000	7700/Sup. Ut.	-3,500
Design and Appeal	Good	Good		Good		Good	
Quality of Construction	Good	Good		Good		Good	
Age	1980	1980		1975		1978	
Condition	Good	Good		Good		Good	
Above Grade Room Count (Total / Bdrms / Bath)	10 / 4 / 3	8 / 4 / 3		8 / 3 / 2.5	+3,000	9 / 5 / 3	
Gross Living Area	3,296 Sq. Ft.	2,615 Sq. Ft.	+28,500	2,613 Sq. Ft.	+28,500	3,143 Sq. Ft.	+6,500
Basement & Finished Rooms Below Grade	None Doc. #'s	None 89-86739		None 88-629310		None 88-523562	
Functional Utility	Average	Superior	-15,000	Superior	-15,000	Superior	-15,000
Heating/Cooling	FAU/None	FAU/None		FAU/CA	-1,000	FAU/None	
Garage/Carport	3 Car Garage	3 Car Garage		2 Car Garage	+5,000	3 Car Garage	
Porches, Patio Pools, etc.	Pool & spa Patio & deck	None Patio & deck	+15,000	None Cov. patio/Eq	+15,000	None Solarium	+15,000 -2,000
Special Energy Efficient Items	Typical Gd.Lndscaping	Typical Inferior	+3,000	Typical Gd.Lndscaping		Typical Gd.Lndscaping	
Fireplace(s)	3 masonry	3 masonry		1 masonry	+3,000	2 masonry	+1,500
Other (e.g. kitchen equip., remodeling)	Built-ins Upgrades	Built-ins Upgrades		Built-ins Upgrades		Built-ins Sup.Upgrades	-5,000
Net Adj. (total)		[X] + [ ] - $	31,500	[X] + [ ] - $	34,500	[ ] + [X] - $	2,500
Indicated Value of Subject			$ 500,500		$ 499,500		$ 505,500

CHAPTER 5

HOW TO APPRAISE DIFFERENT CLASSES OF PROPERTY

It would be impossible, of course, to provide information in this book about appraising every unique property in existence, but we will show you how to handle many unique properties including custom-built homes, overimprovements, and misplaced improvements.

Because we have appraised a countless number of entire subdivisions, we have been able to develop time saving, accurate methods for putting together all the necessary documentation that you will need to appraise an entire tract of homes. Use the checklist for appraising new subdivisions to eliminate errors, omissions, and problems.

APPRAISING CUSTOM-BUILT HOMES

When you appraise custom-built homes, always obtain an itemized list of the construction costs from the owner, seller, builder, or authorized agent. Find out when the land was purchased, the purchase price, and the terms of the transaction. This information, along with the builder's estimate of construction costs, must be included in the appraisal report when you appraise

1. proposed residential construction.
2. dwelling units under construction.
3. homes that have recently been completed.
4. homes that are being extensively remodeled.

Keep this information in your files and use it to learn construction costs, typical amount of contractor's profit and overhead, and land costs. Use the subject land sale for subsequent appraisals in the area.

Calculate and verify building sizes, lot sizes, and garage sizes taken from building plans because sizes have been known to be wrong even though the plans were drawn by a professional architect. Don't forget to rate functional utility, cross ventilation, orientation of the structure on the lot, lot utility, economic factors, zoning and use restrictions, and other value factors.

CAUTION

Unfortunately, builders and owners occasionally attempt to mislead appraisers by misrepresenting their costs to obtain a high value for the property, which should never happen if the appraiser conscientiously distinguishes price, or cost, from value. To avoid misrepresenting values, appraisers must be able to recognize projected building costs that deviate from the norm.

Effective Ways to Learn Building Costs

Look for homes under construction when you are appraising in different areas. Whenever you have the opportunity, ask contractors working on the project for typical building costs.

Always ask owners and builders for installation costs of swimming pools, room additions, remodeling, enclosed patios, concrete driveways, block wall fences, and any other items that will help you to learn costs. When you are completely familiar with these costs, you can easily verify costs and refine costs found in cost handbooks, and you will find that you can finish the cost approach in a matter of minutes.

Acknowledging Discrepancies in Building Costs

Building costs always have to be verified. When there is a wide discrepancy between your estimated costs and the builder's costs, or a disputed amount, obtain copies of paid receipts or other forms of verification and, if appropriate, include the data with the appraisal to validate your conclusions.

SUPPORTING VALUES OF HIGHER-PRICED HOMES

Lenders usually require at least five comparable sales to substantiate the value of custom-built homes and higher- priced homes because, typically, there are many variances that will require adjustments. You must include a sufficient number of sales to provide a sound basis for any adjustments and your concluded value; therefore, you may have to include more than five sales.

You may find that it is necessary to survey a much wider than typical area for comparable sales when you appraise custom-built homes and you may have to select comparable sales from alternate cities, which should be acceptable as long as you provide detailed rationale for transcending the usual requirements regarding the location of comparable sales.

Use the guidelines for defining a neighborhood that are presented in this book to determine whether alternate locations have comparable appeal. You should also consider construction costs and land costs in the alternate neighborhoods; for example, the alternate neighborhood is probably not comparable if construction costs or land costs in the alternate neighborhood vary significantly from costs in the subject neighborhood.

IDENTIFYING AND ACCURATELY APPRAISING NONTYPICAL PROPERTY

The preceding illustrations regarding comparable sales for custom-built homes also applies to appraising other nontypical properties. Some examples of nontypical properties are homes that are not suitable to their environment, newer homes located in older neighborhoods, very old Victorian-style homes surrounded by newer or different styles of homes, homes featuring nontypical or unusual designs, larger or smaller than typical homes for the neighborhood, and homes that are situated on much larger or smaller than typical lots for the neighborhood.

A structure could be well designed and architecturally very attractive; however, if the age, size, style, or design does not conform to other houses in the neighborhood; the house should be classified as a "misplaced improvement." For misplaced improvements or highly unique properties, comparable sales from similar neighborhoods, outside of the subject neighborhood boundaries, or dated sales of similar houses, are preferred to more recent sales in closer proximity that require very large or subjective adjustments.

How to Find Market Data for Unusual Property

A survey of neighboring or distant neighborhoods, or even other cities or communities, to locate comparable sales is usually not an easy or rapidly accomplished task. If you don't have an on-line computer service, the most expedient method to find comparable sales is to peruse the listings of sold properties in market data books provided as a service to real estate appraisers.

To avoid making subjective adjustments, look for the most important factor of consideration first. Next, look for the second most important factor, and so forth. For example, if you are appraising a new home, look for any sales of new homes. Then, select the sales that are most similar in size, location, quality, and so forth. If you are appraising a home situated on a 20,000-sq. ft. lot, look for sales of homes on similar size lots.

Begin by searching for comparable sales in the immediate area and keep expanding your search to other areas until you find similar properties. Also, whenever possible, estimate the subject's value, using the cost approach, to define a beginning point for your data research.

SPECIAL PROBLEMS

When the characteristics of the property are so significant or unique that you are unable to find evidence of market acceptance, or you are unable to establish a reliable estimate of market value, get in touch with your client immediately for further instructions because the property may not be eligible for maximum financing.

HOW TO ANALYZE NEW RESIDENTIAL TRACTS

For properties in new subdivisions or for units in new (or recently converted) condominium or PUD (planned unit development) projects, the appraiser must compare the subject property to other properties in its general market area as well as to properties within the subject subdivision or project. This comparison should help demonstrate market acceptance of new developments and the properties within them.

Generally, the appraiser should select one comparable sale from the subject subdivision or project, one comparable sale from outside the subject subdivision or project, and one comparable sale, which can be from inside or outside of the subject subdivision or project as long as the appraiser considers it to be a good indicator of value for the subject property. In selecting the comparables, the appraiser should keep in mind that sales or resales from within the subject subdivision or project are preferable to sales from outside the subdivision or project as long as the developer or builder of the subject property is not involved in the transactions.

The major concern with new construction has to do with builders setting their own market. For this reason, if the project is less than 25 percent developed, Fannie Mae will accept only one sale by the subject builder. The other sales must be from competing builders or resales in the subject area. When appraising new construction, it is imperative that the appraiser provide the names of the builders of the comparable sales. Similarities in locational appeal should be aptly described when outside sales are used.

Finding Competing Developments

To find competing developments, survey publications describing new housing in the area and advertisements in local newspapers. Discuss competing developments with sales representatives or the developer of the subject project. Developers usually monitor all their competition in the area on a regular basis in order to stay competitive in the market, and, almost all the time, they will disclose the results of their surveys.

HOW TO APPRAISE ENTIRE SUBDIVISIONS

When you appraise an entire subdivision (residential housing tract), obtain at least two or three comparables from the sales agents for each plan in the subject tract. Obtain two or three sales for each plan in competing developments as well, so you will not have to keep going back to various sales offices each time that you have a new request for an appraisal.

Double-check the appraisal form while you are at the property and the sales office to make sure you have all of the information necessary to complete the appraisal.

Using Builder's Plans to Define Dimensions

Do a "takeoff" (list all the building dimensions) from the blueprints for each different building plan while you are at the sales office. Make certain all of the houses "square-off" (check to see whether the net dimensions on opposite sides of the house are equal) and all open areas, stairways, garage dimensions, setbacks, and lot sizes are included in your notes.

Calculate the building sizes while you are at the site. When your building calculations differ from the gross livable area represented by the builder find out why, because the total livable area represented by the builder and the appraiser should be fairly close.

How to Establish Lot Sizes

To find the lot sizes for all the homes in the tract, ask the sales representative, or the developer, for a plot plan that shows the dimensions of all the lots in the tract. If you are appraising an entire tract, most builders will give you an extra set of blueprints and plot plans. When a plot plan is not available, the lots may have to be physically measured.

DON'T FORGET ABOUT THIS

Be sure to note all the setbacks, as well as level pad areas, upslopes, downslopes, and any other pertinent information, such as views, flag lots, cul-de-sac streets, corner locations, the shape of the lot, and possible drainage or slippage problems.

How to Handle Upgrades

List all the upgraded items (carpet, flooring, extra fireplaces, air conditioning, etc.) that are included in the sales price and itemize the costs. All the upgrades, along with specific costs, should be described in the appraisal report.

Buyers sometimes pay cash for added upgraded items; therefore, the cost of the upgrades might not be reflected in the sales price. In this instance, do not include the upgraded items in the appraisal report.

Key Information Needed for Tract Appraisals

Discuss location and view premiums, types of financing programs offered, sales inducements, and absorption rates with sales representatives. This information should also be obtained from competing developments.

The absorption period for the subject development as well as competing developments, should be considered and addressed in the appraisal report. For example, the following statement might be included in the appraisal:

"The subject project, consisting of a total of eighty- seven units, was released for sale on July 16, 1988. Forty-two units have sold to date for an absorption rate of 4.6 units per month, which is on the same level as competing developments."

To find the absorption rate, divide the number of units sold by the number of months the units have been available for sale. If the subject units are selling slowly as compared to competing projects, this should be so noted in the appraisal report.

Cautions When Appraising Model Homes

Do not include personal property when you are appraising a model home. Sometimes model homes are sold as a package deal that includes all the furnishings as well as the yard improvements. Furniture and other items of personal property included in the sales price should be identified as sales concessions and appropriate deductions from the sales price and the value of the property must be made.

Include at least two other model homes in your market analysis when you are appraising a model home. When there are no sales available of a comparable size model home—bracket the sales; that is, include sales of model homes that require upward adjustments and sales of model homes that require downward adjustments (larger and smaller homes) to define the subject's value, which should lie approximately midpoint between the higher and lower indicated values depending on the subject's amenities.

Why You Should Create Sample Appraisals

Work up a sample appraisal for each plan in the subject development and reconcile them so that appraisals of one plan make sense with relationship to the other plans. When you are completing the cost approach, the smallest plan should have the highest-base building cost per square foot and the largest plan should have the lowest-base building cost per square foot.

WATCH FOR CONSISTENCY

Land values should be consistent with varied lot sizes and locations. Price-per-gross living area adjustments should be consistent. Adjustments for location, views, garages, fireplaces, and all other elements of value should be also be consistent.

CHECKLIST FOR APPRAISING NEW SUBDIVISIONS

1. Obtain a complete description of development, including number of units, date construction began, anticipated date of completion, association dues, and special assessments.
2. List cost and type of upgrades.
3. Discuss sales concessions, location premiums, and absorption rate with sales representative.
4. Obtain at least two inside sales and two outside sales for each plan.
5. Take off dimensions from building plans and square- off the building.
6. Note dimensions for open areas and stairs.

7. Calculate size and compare with builder's size.
8. Obtain lot sizes and setbacks.
9. Check location: orientation of house on the lot, shape of the lot, and positive and negative influences.
10. Double-check the form for omissions.
11. For condominium and PUD developments, double-check Addendum A and Addendum B forms for omissions.

HOW TO ANALYZE OLDER HOMES LOCATED IN AREAS WITH NEW CONSTRUCTION

Appraisers should keep track of new and proposed single-family residential developments in areas where they appraise because the marketability and sales prices of older homes will be limited by the availability and prices of new homes with comparable locational appeal.

The offering prices of new homes might be higher than offering prices of resales in the area; however, buyers are usually attracted to new homes because they are new. Also, buyers are more prone to select a new home, rather than a resale, because builder financing programs are typically more favorable than are those offered in the open market. Lower interest rates, minimal down payments, and affordable monthly payments are persuasive reasons for buying a new home, especially for first-time buyers.

When you appraise an older home, the sales prices of new homes in the area should be considered because the price of new homes in the marketing area tends to establish the upper limits of value in the same manner as listings in the subject neighborhood tend to set the upper limits of value.

The Significance of Past Evidence of Value

When you appraise a home in an older neighborhood with strong competition from newer developments, the sales price or estimated value of the subject property might be supported if the value were based on recorded sales (past evidence of value); however, a review of listings and sales in escrow could provide an indication that values in the neighborhood are stabilizing or declining due to competition from new housing developments in the area.

Market value must reflect *current* market value; therefore, appraisers must use current market data as well as consider future value and marketability because lenders must consider the security of the property throughout the life of the loan. Refer to the neighborhood section of FNMA Form 1004 and consider the following items: percentage built-up, growth rate, property values, demand, supply, land use, and change.

HOW TO DEAL WITH OVERIMPROVEMENTS AND UNDERIMPROVEMENTS

Although statistics show that people do move quite frequently, the majority of people, when they purchase a home, usually intend to take up residence there for a long period of time, especially in inflationary times—who can afford to move? Consequently, owners (particularly first-time buyers and owners whose children have left the nest) have a tendency to make grand improvements to the property, and it never occurs to them that, someday, they might want to retrieve all their expenditures.

Then, the owners decide to buy a new house, the owner is transferred to another area, the older couple decides to move to a retirement area, or a divorce occurs. Consequently, the house must be sold. At this time, the owners decide that they should recapture all the money they spent for improvements, dollar for dollar, and then some, because the property is so highly upgraded. Few people realize, however, that extensive upgrading or remodeling usually results in an overimprovement for the neighborhood, and their expenditures will only be returned as the market dictates.

Suppose the buyer was willing to pay the asking price, which includes all the money spent for upgrades? Many people think that a sales *price* is the same as *value*. That is, if someone purchased an overimproved property for a certain price, the property must be worth the price paid even though other homes in the neighborhood sold substantially below this price. When price is confused with value, the net result is always inappropriate sales comparables in the market analysis accompanied by subjective market adjustments.

Just because one particular buyer (emotional or uninformed?) liked the property well enough to pay too much for it does not mean that the home could be resold for the same price. Market value, as defined, refers to a typical, informed buyer. Overimprovements usually have very limited market appeal because typical, informed buyers will tend to look for similar homes in more conforming neighborhoods.

Suppose, for example, the property in question is a 25-year-old, 1,500-sq. ft., medium-quality home. The owners spent

$15,000	to modernize the kitchen (new cabinets, floors, appliances)
8,000	on new carpet, window coverings, wallpaper, and paint
5,000	to modernize two bathrooms, add tile, install new flooring and new fixtures
15,000	to add a family room
1,000	on miscellaneous items
$44,000	Total cost

The owner now wants to sell the home for $274,000., which is $44,000. more than the typical selling price for the neighborhood.

First, the appropriate reproduction cost to use in the cost approach is $55.00/sq. ft.. The total cost of the improvements, less the family room, is $29,000. or $19.33/sq. ft. Could you, realistically, add $19.33/sq. ft. to the appropriate cost of $55.00/sq. ft. and use $74.33/sq. ft. in the cost approach? A sharp-eyed reviewer would spot this discrepancy immediately.

Second, This house, although partially modernized and upgraded, is still a 25-year-old house in a 25-year-old neighborhood. And, among other items, the roof and heating equipment should be replaced.

The Buyer's Options

1. Would you buy a different home in this housing tract for $230,000., or perhaps less, and spend $44,000. to remodel, upgrade, and modernize the house to your own liking?
2. Would you (a typical and informed buyer) pay $274,000. for this 25-year-old house in a 25-year-old neighborhood? Or would you pay $274,000. for a better quality, perhaps newer, house in a different neighborhood?

Price and Value Considerations

It is more expensive to modernize, add rooms, and remodel than it was to incorporate many of these features in a house when it was originally constructed. Therefore, you could buy a better quality home, or a newer home, with the same features for the same price.

Occasionally, as we have pointed out, overimprovements can be overvalued when the appraiser is more concerned with price than value. When overimprovements are not appraised properly, the net result could be great financial losses to lenders if the property is taken back through foreclosure proceedings, especially if the lender has been forced to discount the value substantially in order to market the home within a reasonable period of time.

Know what an overimprovement consists of and how to deal with the situation effectively and dispassionately. Would the property actually sell at the estimated value and within the specified marketing time indicated in the appraisal report? Considering the overimprovements, is there really a wide market for this home? How many buyers will this home appeal to? How much would the price have to be discounted to sell the property within the *normal* marketing period for the area?

THE IMPORTANCE OF OBJECTIVITY

While it is sometimes difficult to appraise property when you know that the owners will only retrieve a portion of their expenditures; your job is only to report the facts as you see them and as they are supported by market data. Appraisers should not discuss overimprovements with the owners or anyone else associated with the property. Complete the appraisal, which must be an objective, and impartial report of market facts and let the client, lender, or real estate agent explain overimprovements to the owners because it is their job to counsel their clients.

Development of Neighborhood Age/Life Cycles

Consider the age/life cycle of the neighborhood. As families increase in number and the need for additional space (extra bedrooms, baths, recreation rooms) increase, and the income levels of the occupants increase, many additions will take place in the neighborhood. This is an expected happening, and, generally, improvements of this type are not overimprovements if they are consistent throughout the neighborhood.

The Best Way to Document Your Conclusions

A sufficient number of sales comparables from the subject neighborhood, with like improvements, should be included in the appraisal report to provide a basis for your assumptions and an explanation must be included referencing reasons for your conclusions. Sales comparables could be obtained from similar, outside neighborhoods when sufficient supportive data are unavailable in the subject neighborhood. When you use outside sales, include dated sales, listings, sales in escrow, or other supportive data from the subject neighborhood as well.

How to Classify Modernization in Older Homes

When you appraise homes in older neighborhoods, modernized kitchens or bathrooms, replacement of older equipment (furnaces, hot water heaters, plumbing, wiring), and refurbishing, such as new paint, wall coverings, floor coverings, fencing, roof, driveway, or landscaping are usually not classified as overimprovements unless the quality, materials, and the extent of the refurbishing, remodeling, or updating exceeds the standards of the neighborhood, in which case, the cost of the improvements should be discounted accordingly.

If almost all the homes in the neighborhood have been well maintained, modernized, refurbished, or upgraded, dwellings that have not received similar care and improvements are *underimprovements* for the neighborhood. To market the underimproved property within a reasonable period, the price may have to be discounted substantially to allow a buyer to bring the home up to the standards maintained throughout the neighborhood.

Advantages of a Range of Sales

To avoid returning to the area a second time to inspect the sales visually when you appraise an older home that has been remodeled or refurbished, before you go into the field to appraise the property, select a range of sales so you will be prepared to select the comparables that are most befitting the subject property. Select a few sales that are similar in age that may have been similarly remodeled or refurbished and a few sales in the "effective age" range of the subject.

Dealing with Economic Characteristics

Consider the economic characteristics of the area and the neighborhood, that is, the stability of employment, proximity to employment centers, types of employment, governmental influences (tax base and maintenance of publicly owned property), and convenience to schools, shopping, and other public amenities. A small number of properties that are well-maintained cannot change a neighborhood that is declining due to economic factors. When the area is declining economically, major improvements to a property would not be worthwhile. Therefore, any major improvements should be classified as overimprovements related to economic factors. Discuss economic factors, maintenance levels, and other factors relative to long-term stability of value in the appraisal report.

How to Handle the Compatibility Factor

All property improvements must be considered with respect to neighborhood compatibility. Evaluate the income levels of typical occupants in the neighborhood when you are considering adjustments for improvements. When the owners cannot afford the extra tax burden and maintenance, added improvements, such as a swimming pool, may contribute little, or no value, to the property and, in some instances, a negative adjustment for the cost of removing a misplaced improvement might be appropriate.

Primary Neighborhood Considerations

Lower-income neighborhoods can attain a complete about-face when income levels increase or buyers with higher-income levels move into the neighborhood. When prices escalate in neighboring communities, lower-income neighborhoods are sometimes taken over by buyers who can no long afford the higher-priced homes. Standards, maintenance levels, and prices will increase as new owners renovate the homes and add improvements.

Standards and maintenance levels can also change, often quite rapidly, when owners become cognizant of increasing prices in the area. Neighborhoods with a high ratio of tenant-occupied properties often experience rapid changes. As the tenant-occupied properties are sold, and the occupancy changes from tenant to owner, maintenance levels typically increase, which usually results in higher sales prices and greater return on investments for improvements.

We are familiar with several neighborhoods where prices increased as much as $50,000. to $60,000. in one year because the predominant occupancy in the neighborhoods changed from tenants to owners and the new owners painted the homes; added new landscaping, new roofs, concrete driveways; and so forth. The return on their investment was far more than they had anticipated.

The preceding representations were presented to emphasize the importance of evaluating the entire neighborhood (rather than just a few homes or a block or two) to find out whether the neighborhood is in a stage of transition before you automatically assign ratings for overimprovements. Consider whether neighborhood maintenance levels are likely to decline, remain static, or improve.

Consider the number of owner occupants versus nonowner occupants because neighborhoods that exhibit an oversupply of nonowner occupied property typically reflect less than average maintenance. Get in touch with local real estate agents, who consistently list homes in the neighborhood, to find out the status of owner- and nonowner-occupied property.

Traditional Improvements in Higher-Priced Neighborhoods

Swimming pools, spas, patios, patio covers, extensive landscaping, and extensive upgrading are expected items in higher-priced neighborhoods; therefore, properties without these items are usually rated as underimprovements for the neighborhood. Typically, homes that are underimproved for the neighborhood take longer to sell, and, in some cases, prices have to be discounted considerably to market the home.

How to Differentiate Between Over- and Underimprovements

Each home that is appraised must be considered on a case basis because every situation is unique. Depending on the factors previously mentioned, elements labeled as overimprovements in one neighborhood might be considered as conforming and expected items in other neighborhoods. To determine whether an element is, in fact, an overimprovement or an underimprovement, always evaluate the economic and social characteristics of the neighborhood along with making a thorough study of all available market data. A sufficient number of sales should be included in the appraisal to support your conclusions.

JUDGMENT DECISIONS: AN ALTERNATIVE

When there are no sales available to provide a basis for the adjustments, or lack of adjustments, the appraiser can make a judgment decision; however, the amount of deduction, or lack of a deduction, based on the appraiser's experience and judgment, must be realistic, and an explanatory statement must be included in the appraisal report.

COMPARABILITY OF NUMBER OF BEDROOMS

When you appraise a three-bedroom home and there are no sales of three-bedroom homes, use sales of four-bedroom homes that are similar in size (or vice versa for four-bedroom homes) because they will probably have similar utility. Four-bedroom homes do not always sell for more than three-bedroom homes. When the bedrooms are larger or utility is superior, three-bedroom homes often sell for more than four bedroom homes that are similar in size.

DO NOT COMPARE APPLES TO ORANGES

Do not compare one- or two-bedroom homes with any other types of property unless sales of like properties are nonexistent because there is usually as much as $10,000. to $15,000. variance in value between one-, two-, and three-bedroom dwellings. Normally, it is difficult, if not impossible, to support the dollar amount of adjustments for the number of bedrooms.

MARKET ADJUSTMENTS FOR AMENITIES

How would you determine the difference in value between homes located near the end of a channel where boats are anchored as compared to homes that are located in an area where boats pass freely by?

How would you find out whether sales prices are based on front footage on the water, which golf course location commands the highest premium, which locations command view premiums and the dollar amount of the premium? How would you assign a market adjustment for favorable or unfavorable proximity to community recreational facilities?

Adjustments of this type cannot be defined by simply looking at listings or gathering sales prices. When you appraise higher-priced property, or when subjective adjustments might affect the value of the property, always consult with real estate agents specializing in the area to ascertain their opinions of market value, typical location premiums, and view premiums.

HOW TO APPRAISE MANUFACTURED HOUSES

Modular houses, or prefabricated houses, are basically appraised in the same manner as a single-family residence. The comparables should have the same or similar characteristics.

When comparable sales of similar properties are not available, site-built housing can be used for comparable sales; however, the appraiser must provide satisfactory explanations for using site-built comparables. Appropriate adjustments should be made to reflect any market preferences for site-built housing.

How to Classify Manufactured Housing

A manufactured housing unit must

1. be legally classified as real property.
2. be permanently affixed to a foundation.
3. assume the characteristics of site-built housing.

Foundation:

The perimeter or pier foundations must have footings that are located below the frost line. The foundation system must have been designed by an engineer to meet the soil conditions of the site.

Other Requirements:

The manufactured unit must also have been built under the Federal Home Construction and Safety Standards that were established by HUD in June 1976. Other factory-built housing, such as prefabricated, panelized, or sectional housing, must assume the characteristics of site-built housing and must meet local building codes.

The appraiser must address the marketability and value of manufactured housing units in the subject market area in comparison to the marketability of site-built housing in the area. The materials and construction of the improvements must be acceptable in the subject market area.

HOW TO APPRAISE MOBILE HOMES

The Fannie Mae Form 1004 can also be used for mobile homes. Mobile homes are appraised in the same manner as single-family residences and manufactured houses; however, the appraiser must also evaluate and incorporate the following data into the appraisal report:

The mobile home must be legally classified as real property and must be permanently affixed to a foundation. The wheels, axles, and trailer hitches must be removed when the unit is placed on its permanent site. Anchors must be provided if state law requires them. Identify the make, model, year, and serial number.

If the land is leased, provide a meaningful description of the principal terms of the lease as well as rent, options, and negotiation provisions. When the space is rented, specify the amount of the space rent and state whether the rent includes gas, electric, trash, or sewer.

Describe the project including the number of mobile homes in the project, density per acre, amenities, recreational facilities, number of units for sale, and number of units rented. Rate the project to competing projects considering location, condition, general appearance, amenities, and recreational facilities.

The materials and construction of the mobile home must be acceptable in the subject market area. Discuss excessive rents or unusual restrictions and regulations that could affect marketability and address the likelihood of rezoning. The appraiser should compare single-width units to single-width units and multiwidth units to multiwidth units.

SUMMARY

Explain the similarity of the comparables to the subject, in the appraisal report, addressing similarities in design and appeal, housing characteristics, concerns of the inhabitants, land uses, and amenities. Include past sales (sales history), sales in escrow, or listings from the subject neighborhood to further substantiate your concluded value.

DON'T FORGET TO RATE MARKETING TIME

The more unique a property is—the fewer buyers it will appeal to; thus, an extended marketing time may be indicated. Carefully consider the marketing time for custom-built homes; homes with substantial remodeling, misplaced improvements, under- and overimprovements; and higher-priced properties. Document your findings in the appraisal report.

CHAPTER 6

PHYSICAL INSPECTION OF THE PROPERTY, NEIGHBORHOOD, AND COMPARABLE SALES

Does it seem like it sometimes takes forever to inspect the property, neighborhood, and comparable sales? Is there a way to eliminate unnecessary steps, so you can get the job done more efficiently and in less time? By using the proper equipment, scheduling your time effectively, and following the recommended procedures for property inspections, you will find that you can get the job done quickly without sacrificing quality.

Probably the greatest way to waste time is by retracing your steps because you missed something during your initial inspection. This is very easy to do when you are distracted by other people during your inspection or when the day is getting long and your concentration is waning. To make sure that you don't overlook important value factors, we designed a checklist for property inspections (included in this chapter) as well as checklists for describing the property, comparable sales, site improvements, amenities, and neighborhood, which are included in the appendices to this book. The list of abbreviations, in Appendix E, can also be used as a checklist for property descriptions.

SCHEDULING APPOINTMENTS

Poorly prepared appraisals can be blamed, in part, on unrealistic schedules that cause the appraiser to rush from one appointment to another leaving an insufficient amount of time to complete the neighborhood and sales analyses. Rather than returning to the property to finish a thorough survey, the appraisal is written up based on the information at hand. Inadequacies in the report, noted by reviewers, normally impel the appraiser to return to the property to assemble more data anyway; therefore, why circumvent the inevitable? Distance and time are important elements to consider; to avoid having to return to the area, always schedule an ample amount of time to complete your assignment.

Along with delays caused by traffic, schedules can be interrupted by real estate agents or owners who do not meet with you on schedule and unforeseen circumstances encountered during property inspections generating a much more time-consuming analysis than anticipated. To allow yourself some flexibility, explain the possibility of a delay so the person who is meeting you at the property won't wonder why you are late. Also, schedule appointments between a certain period of time rather than at a specific time because a relaxed schedule is more compatible for everyone.

WHAT EQUIPMENT YOU'LL NEED

Never cut costs when you are purchasing equipment for appraising real estate because it typically costs much more in the long run (in wasted time) to use poor equipment. For example, a poor camera could result in a return trip to retake photos and an inadequate tape measure will slow you down considerably.

One requirement is a good 35mm camera with a wide-angle lens. Some cameras have built-in exposure compensation features that allow you to take good photos when the sunlight is behind the subject. Taking photos without this feature usually results in poorly exposed pictures or pictures that clearly show the effect of the sunlight while you can barely make out the outlines of the structure. A camera that indicates proper film loading is also a very wise investment.

You will need a good 100-foot-long measuring tape. Make sure that it winds easily and rapidly and that it fits well in your hand, that is, that it is not too cumbersome. It is also a very good idea to have an extra tape with you in case one breaks.

A very helpful "second pair of hands," which will make it easier to tape property, can be fashioned from a clothes hanger. Bend the clothes hanger into the shape of a question mark and attach it to the end of your tape (like the accompanying figure). Flatten the top end of the hook with a hammer so it will have a better gripping surface. The straight, or bottom, end of the hook can be inserted into the ground if the hook cannot be attached to the structure or any other object.

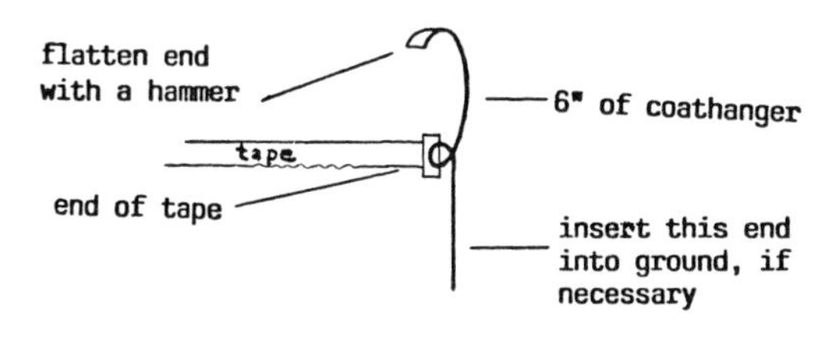

Other items that you will need are a map book for each county in your territory, cost handbook, legal-size clipboard, plenty of plain paper for sketches and notes, appraisal forms, a flashlight, a screwdriver or pocket knife, and an Architect's

Scale. Always keep one map book in your office and one in your car.

Using an Architect's Scale

An Architect's Scale will come in handy when you are doing a takeoff from builder's plans because all the dimensions might not be shown on the plans.

An Architect's Scale may be flat or three-sided. A three-sided scale is preferable. The three-sided scale has one edge marked in inches, as does the common 12-inch ruler. The other edges contain ten scales. These are the $\frac{1}{8}$- and $\frac{1}{4}$-, the 1- and $\frac{1}{2}$-, the $\frac{3}{4}$- and $\frac{3}{8}$, the $\frac{3}{16}$- and $\frac{3}{32}$-, and the $1\frac{1}{2}$- and 3-inch scale.

Practice with an Architect's Scale as you will find that it is a useful tool. To interpret the scale (using the $\frac{1}{4}$- inch scale as an example), note the edge marked "$\frac{1}{4}$." This edge is read from right to left. It is divided into spaces that are each $\frac{1}{4}$-inch apart. Each of the $\frac{1}{4}$-inch spaces represents 12 inches or 1 foot. At one end, one of the $\frac{1}{4}$ inch spaces has been divided into halves, quarters, and twelfths. One of the halves, in the space divided into 12 equal parts, represents 6 inches, one of the quarters represents 3 inches, and so forth. What you are doing is simply substituting quarter inches for feet. The other scales function in the same manner as the $\frac{1}{4}$-inch scale.

TAKING PHOTOGRAPHS THAT PROVIDE MORE EFFECTIVE APPRAISALS

Find out whether your client requires one, two, or three sets of photos. Almost all lenders require three sets of photos of the subject street, the front of the subject dwelling, and the rear of the subject dwelling as well as three sets of photos of each of the comparable sales used in the appraisal report.

In addition to street, front, and rear photos of the subject, always include photos of all of the positive and negative influences that substantially affect the value. For example, major causes of external or functional obsolescence; swimming pools; tennis courts; extensive yard improvements; extensive interior upgrading, refurbishing, or remodeling; and views. When any of the structures, swimming pools, or decks are supported by pilings or caissons, as is sometimes the case when a property is located on a hillside, show the supports in the photos.

The photo of the front of the dwelling should be taken at an angle that fully illustrates the architectural design of the home. In other words, do not take the photo straight on; take it so the front and a portion of the side of the house are detailed in the picture. Stand back far enough to show the house and the yard improvements, but not so far back that viewers cannot make out details of the property. The location of the subject property should be discernable in the photo of the street scene.

Make notes when you are taking photos, especially photos of comparables, so you can identify them later on. Explanations are always required when appraisers do not provide the required photos.

For properties valued at $500,000. or more, additional photographs of the interior and exterior are required. Include photos of the kitchen, living room, master bedroom, and other areas of the home that are extensively upgraded.

HOW TO PLAN FOR PROPERTY INSPECTIONS

Always follow a definite plan and *do everything the same way each time,* and you will be less likely to miss a step if you are interrupted. Inspect the neighborhood, property, and comparables in the following sequence:

1. As you are entering the neighborhood, make notes describing the neighborhood and the surrounding area.
2. Note any positive or negative external influences that may influence the value of the property. Take photos, if applicable.
3. Take photos of the street and the front of the subject dwelling.
4. Enter pertinent data in the site section of the appraisal form.
5. Enter pertinent data in the improvement section of appraisal form.
6. Tape and inspect the front of the property.
7. Tape and inspect the interior of the garage.
8. Tape and inspect the basement.
9. Tape the interior of the dwelling, as needed.
10. Tape and inspect the attic area, if applicable.
11. Inspect the interior of the dwelling.
12. Take photos of the back of the house, amenities, and any other positive or negative factors that may influence the value of the property.
13. Tape the back and sides of the dwelling, setbacks, swimming pool, patios, and any other buildings or elements that will be assigned value.
14. Complete the subject's description on the form including all the yard improvements.
15. Square-off the building and any other structures.

16. Verify the lot size with public records or check the size shown on the plat map.
17. Verify data with owner or agent.
18. Double-check the form for missing data.
19. Reinspect the neighborhood.
20. Visually inspect the comparable sales.

The checklists in the appendices do not list all the data needed for completing an appraisal; the lists contain only those items that could easily be overlooked by appraisers. When you have completed your inspections of the subject and the comparables, use the appropriate checklist to make certain that you have not overlooked any relevant information.

MAKING THE NEIGHBORHOOD INSPECTION THE FRAMEWORK OF YOUR APPRAISAL

A proper neighborhood analysis is the framework for your appraisal. It is important to make a very thorough study of all of the elements that contribute to value, for example, location, economic factors, social factors, governmental influences, demand, supply, marketing time, land uses, and growth rate in order to make appropriate adjustments and define a proper conclusion of value. Every single item listed in the neighborhood section of the single-family residential appraisal report form has either a positive or negative influence on value. Therefore, as you drive through the neighborhood, think about every element listed and evaluate the long term effect of the elements on the subject's value and marketability. The entire surrounding area must be considered as well because a neighborhood cannot sustain its value when the surrounding area is declining.

The Importance of Thorough Inspections

You will not be wasting your time by devoting an extra hour or two, or however long it takes, to acquire knowledge of many different areas and neighborhoods because eventually, in one way or another, it all comes back to you. There are many reasons why appraisers should be completely familiar with different neighborhoods. Some of the reasons are as follows:

1. When you have future assignments in the area, if you have a good mental picture of the neighborhood, market data can be selected quite readily because you will know which characteristics to consider when you are selecting comparable sales.
2. Rather than requesting a physical inspection, suppose your client wants your opinion of the feasibility of making a loan in a certain area or an approximate value of a property, based on your experience, knowledge, and good judgment. Could you answer questions regarding neighborhood appeal, land use, and stability of value in the neighborhood? Could you provide an estimated opinion of value without making a physical inspection of the site and neighborhood? It is in your own best interest always to be prepared to provide answers to these and other questions because your clients will remain very loyal when they can always rely on your good judgment and reliable opinions of value.
3. Suppose your client requests a desk review of an appraisal. Could you properly evaluate the appraisal and

the appraiser's performance when you are not familiar with the neighborhood? It is not very likely.

When you are performing a desk review of an appraisal, if you find deficiencies in the neighborhood description, you must be prepared to explain why you disagree with the description in addition to providing an accurate description of the neighborhood. Errors and omissions in appraisal reports can easily be detected when you are cognizant of all the elements that contribute to value in different neighborhoods and you are familiar with property values in different areas. When you are not familiar with property values in the neighborhood, in all fairness to the client as well as to the appraiser who wrote the appraisal, a field inspection should be made or the assignment should be declined.

Physical Inspection of the Neighborhood

To get a better picture of the neighborhood and surrounding areas, enter the neighborhood from one direction and leave the area from another direction. Make notes describing the neighborhood and the surrounding areas as you are entering and exiting the area.

Examine land uses, conformity, appeal, maintenance levels, and traffic patterns in the neighborhood. Look for adverse external influences, such as sources of air pollution, toxic waste sites or dumps, freeways, flood control channels, high-tension power lines, railroads, or airports. When mixed uses (commercial or industrial properties, apartments, condominiums, or planned unit developments) are evident in the neighborhood, or are making their way into the neighborhood, remember to study market history to determine whether property values appear to be declining, remaining static, or improving and the length of time it takes to market property in the neighborhood.

Look for other environmental deficiencies, such as overcrowding; improper location of structures on the land; excessive dwelling unit density; conversion of buildings to incompatible uses; obsolete buildings; unsafe, congested, poorly designed, or otherwise deficient streets; inadequate utilities; and inadequate community facilities.

How Buffers Diminish Negative Influences

If there are any adverse external influences present, are buffers provided that will effectively reduce or eliminate the effects of the adverse influences? Landscaping, trees, block wall fencing, concrete sound walls, upsloping or downsloping hillsides, and earth berms can effectively reduce sound levels and disguise the presence of adverse influences. The negative effect of high-tension power lines, in some instances, has been partially overcome by the installation of landscaped parks or commercial nurseries beneath the high- tension power lines. Are the adverse influences noticeable throughout the entire neighborhood? Is residual traffic noise audible in the interior of the dwelling? Is it likely that the adverse influence will worsen and property values will decline?

Traffic Patterns, Maintenance, and Civic Amenities

Consider traffic patterns and parking congestion in the neighborhood. The entire neighborhood could decline in value if it is hazardous or very inconvenient to enter or exit from the area or when the area is heavily congested with parked cars. Heavy traffic or fast traffic throughout a neighborhood is noisy, hazardous, inconvenient, and detrimental to property value. Is it likely that the traffic or parking congestion will continue, lessen, or become worse?

Are the parkways and streets well maintained throughout the neighborhood? Is there an overabundance of unsightly power lines or power poles, unkempt alleys, overgrown parkway trees, or broken sidewalks? Even little things like curbs and gutters are an important consideration to the long-term sustainment of property values. Neighborhoods that do not have curbs and gutters (where lawns run out into the street) will often deteriorate faster than will neighborhoods that are similar and do have curbs and gutters; therefore, curbs and gutters are considered to be desirable, long-range amenities.

Are there an unusual number of "for sale" signs displayed in the neighborhood? If so, why? Are there an unusual number of tenant-occupied properties? Are the homes well maintained? If vacant land is located nearby, will the zoning and potential development influence property values in the neighborhood?

Check the proximity and convenience to neighborhood convenience stores, schools, parks, recreation facilities, shopping centers, public transportation, and local employment centers. Is there any evidence indicating a change in land uses or maintenance levels that could result in increasing or decreasing property values?

Neighborhood: Static or Changing?

Consider the type of neighborhood and the life cycle of the neighborhood because neighborhoods can change. For instance, a neighborhood could exhibit a lot of traffic and congestion because every teenager in the neighborhood owns a car; however, in a few years, the situation will change as teenagers move to other areas, empty-nesters sell their homes and move to a retirement area, young couples buy the homes, and the cycle begins again. Always consider change and keep long-term stability of value in mind when you are evaluating a neighborhood. Think about it—what is changing and what are the changes leading to? Are property values likely to decline, remain stable, or improve?

Check the appraisal form before you leave the area to make sure you have not overlooked anything. Refer to the checklist "Neighborhood Description: External Obsolescence and Environmental Deficiencies" in Appendix H to this book.

ANALYSIS OF THE SITE AND LOCATION

The dimensions of a lot can be obtained from the owner's legal documents, title companies, city public works departments, city engineering department, or from the county surveyor's office.

It is the appraiser's obligation to tape the subject property physically. When the appraiser's physical measurements are not the same as the dimensions shown on the plat map, the appraiser should provide apparent reasons for the difference. Plat maps available on microfilm are typically dated; therefore, care should be taken to ascertain the validity of the information. When a plat map has been obtained from a title company, the lot size must still be verified because recent changes, such as divisions of larger lots into smaller lots or encroachments may have altered property lines.

The total area of the site should be calculated and compared with the size indicated on the plat map before you leave the property. If the size differs, recheck the dwelling size and retape the front, rear, and side yard setbacks. If there is still a discrepancy, look for possible reasons for the difference, such as loss of a portion of the site due to road widening or easements, a portion of the lot could have been sold, a portion or some of the adjacent lots could have been purchased by the subject owner, there may be an encroachment of the subject property onto a neighboring property, or a neighboring property could be encroaching onto the subject property.

Always investigate the possibility that adjoining properties could be owned by the subject property owner. If this is the case, find out which properties are going to be included as security for the loan applied for by the borrower.

Accurate measurements of the subject property are essential. If the boundary lines are not readily apparent, the topography is unusual, encroachments are apparent, or there are any other factors present that affect the size of the site or prohibit you from verifying the size of the site; recommend a site survey and notify your client, as soon as possible, to provide them with an opportunity to attend to the situation in a timely manner.

Identifying Incompatible Uses

Check the subject and neighboring properties for any incompatible or nonconforming uses, such as proximity to apartments, condominiums, commercial or industrial property, neglected vacant land or vacant land that could be put to an incompatible use; nonconforming residences that could affect the value of the subject property; and adverse influences from aircraft, traffic, trains, high-tension power lines, or flood control channels. If there are any adverse influences present, are buffers (the depth of the lot, fencing, double- paned windows, landscaping, shrubs, or trees) provided to insulate the subject from the effect of the adverse influences?

Consider the maintenance of the subject street, location of stop signs or bus stops close to the property, parking congestion, traffic patterns on the subject street, and hazardous ingress or egress. Steep slopes, near to or a part of the subject property, can affect drainage, cause soil problems and erosion, make it difficult to maintain lawns, and prohibit safe and easy access to the property.

When the subject is located in an older neighborhood, and the property fronts on a heavy-traffic street, or one that is likely to become heavily traveled, consider the possibility that the street could be widened to permit additional traffic or a better flow of traffic. If this situation is suspect, check with the city planning department to ascertain the likelihood of street widening in the near future because a portion of the lots could be lost to the street widening. A decline in property values could result from the loss of site utility and heavier traffic. When the plat map shows that a portion of the front of the lot is already dedicated to street widening, do not include this portion of the lot in the overall size and provide an explanation in the appraisal report.

Rating Lot Utility

Lot utility is a very important factor to consider. The main consideration is conformity to the neighborhood. Lots should be typical in size and utility to appeal to a wide number of typical buyers. When lot utility has been reduced by the addition of a room or a swimming pool that consumes almost all the yard area, the appeal to a wide number of typical purchasers would be limited. The appeal would be limited to buyers that prefer little or no yard area or buyers that desire a swimming pool. Properties with little usable yard area typically take much longer to sell. Actual lot sizes of different properties in the same neighborhood can sometimes vary a great deal; however, if the level, usable pad area of the different properties can be put to the same or similar uses, site utility should be considered as comparable. Hence, adjustments for variances in actual lot sizes would not be warranted.

Identifying Favorable Site Factors

Look for positive influences that can affect value and marketability, such as desirable locations within the neighborhood; views; superiority in shape, size, frontage, or depth; water orientation; or wooded areas. The positive and negative effects that a certain site or location has on value and marketability must be related to the neighborhood and typical buyer's attitudes in that particular neighborhood.

Take photos of all the positive and negative influences that have a major effect on the subject's value and marketability. Check the form to make certain nothing has been omitted.

All the preceding criteria also apply to the lot sizes and locations of all the comparable sales used in the appraisal report.

WHAT TO LOOK FOR IN JUDGING DESIGN AND APPEAL

Carefully consider the design and appeal of each property that you appraise as well as the design and appeal of the comparable sales because these factors have a tremendous influence on marketability and value. A buyer's first impression of a property is visual appeal. If the house is poorly oriented on the site, doesn't "fit in" (is nonconforming) with the neighborhood or its surroundings, has little of the architectural details or refinements that give homes their unique character, or is poorly landscaped, or the property is poorly maintained, a prospective buyer might not even consider looking at the interior of the property. The design and appeal of a home must attract an ample number of typical buyers to generate a sale within a reasonable period of time to sustain value.

Weigh the difference in appeal between a home with bay windows and attractive brick ornamentation on the front elevation versus another home, comparable in architectural design, with wood siding and planter boxes used as ornamental trim. You might prefer one style over the other, thus giving it a rating of superior appeal. Ornamentation, however, is simply a matter of buyer preference; it does not warrant an adjustment for design and appeal. Always look at a property as it would appeal to a typical buyer and do not let your personal preferences influence your judgment when you are rating overall appeal.

Study the appeal of the home with respect to the *overall* attractiveness of architectural design and style. Is the design well proportioned and well balanced? Does any single element detract from the others? Consider the attractiveness of the interior design and special features in addition to exterior design and appeal.

Nonconformity and Misplaced Improvements

Homes that have been designed, or remodeled, to suit one person's individual tastes, incorporating many mixed features throughout the home (entrances, type of roof, windows, trim or ornamentation, or type and quality of building materials) that do not relate to the overall design, age, and style of the home, or the neighborhood, will not appeal to very many buyers.

Color has a great deal to do with appeal. The color of the exterior should blend in with surrounding homes. A red, blue, black, or green roof might be nonconforming and have little appeal. Mixed, bright, or loud colors on the interior and bold or mixed wall coverings will deter marketability in certain neighborhoods. The effect on marketability must be related to the neighborhood; in some neighborhoods, color may have little or no influence on marketability and value. Typically, the more affluence a neighborhood exhibits; the greater marketability will be affected.

THE KEY WORD IS CONSISTENCY

The use of fair-quality materials in an average-quality home will detract from the value. Good-quality items in an average-quality home will not be consistent; therefore, the good-quality items should be considered as overimprovements. A Mission Tile roof in an area that displays inexpensive asphalt shingle roofs is a misplaced improvement (an overimprovement for the neighborhood). A highly upgraded home in a lower-priced neighborhood will also fall under this classification. The design, style, quality, types, and kinds of materials used must conform to neighborhood standards and to the original structure. The key word is *consistency.*

A second-story addition in a neighborhood of one-story homes would be a misplaced improvement even if the addition were very consistent with the original structure. There are times when the pioneers of a neighborhood pay the price for nonconforming additions by not realizing full return for their investment because the addition was an overimprovement for the neighborhood at the time. As time passes, many second-story additions might take place in the neighborhood, in which case, if the additions are conforming to the original structure and the architectural design is pleasing, the additions would not be classified as an overimprovement for the neighborhood due to consistency with the neighborhood trend. Thus, the owners would be more likely to receive a return of almost all or all their investment.

Additions to the front of a property, unless they are professionally designed and well planned, usually alter the overall design of a home to a point where the home no longer appeals to a typical buyer. On the other hand, many well-planned, attractive additions as well as customizing and upgrading, can transform a neighborhood from the appearance of tract or stock-built homes to the look of a custom-built neighborhood, thereby enhancing the value of all the homes.

Consider the type and style of the property with relationship to the size and location of the site in addition to the placement of the home on the site. Is the structure well placed with respect to lot size, shape of the lot, views, topography, exposure to the elements, and other amenities? Does the home blend in well with other homes in the neighborhood and its surroundings? A modern-style home might look out of place in a wooded area, a newer home located in an older neighborhood would probably be an overimprovement, a ranch-style home would not fit in with more conventionally styled homes or smaller bungalows, much larger or smaller homes than typical for the neighborhood would be nonconforming, and so forth. The more unique the property is and the less it conforms to the neighborhood and its surroundings; the fewer buyers it will appeal to.

Rating Architectural Styles in Older Neighborhoods

Homes located in older neighborhoods often exhibit a variety of ages, sizes, and architectural styles. Consider the overall concept of the neighborhood. Are the designs and architectural styles consistent with the neighborhood? Are almost all the homes fairly similar in age, quality, size, and value range? If so, they would be comparable in appeal. Compare an older home with wood siding to an older home with a stucco exterior. The architectural styles and exterior finishes differ, but the quality of the basic building materials is the same. Would you make an adjustment for a difference in appeal because of the differences in exterior finishes and architectural style? If so, what would you use as a basis for your adjustment?

Select a sufficient number of comparable sales that represent both types of property. Make all the other adjustments that are appropriate and then correlate the sales prices between the different types of homes to find out whether there is a difference in sales prices that can be attributed to a difference in appeal. By comparing properties in this manner, a definite pattern will appear which will provide a basis for making adjustments, or not making adjustments, when you appraise properties in older, mixed improved neighborhoods.

You should also consider the possibility that a property that is superior in appeal to another may sell faster, but not necessarily for more money, because buyers are usually inclined to believe that they could upgrade a similar home, in the same manner, or perhaps in a better fashion, for less money. Hence, adjustments for design and appeal must be related to buyer attitudes, or preferences, in the subject neighborhood.

HOW TO JUDGE QUALITY OF CONSTRUCTION

Appraisers must have the ability to rate quality of construction effectively to select the proper dollar amount to apply to the various component parts of the subject improvements when they are defining the "Estimated Reproduction Cost New of the Improvements." Additionally, appraisers must be able to recognize differences in quality readily when they are rating the subject property as well as when they are comparing one property to another. Almost all the time, overvalued and undervalued properties are the result of comparing the subject property to homes of superior or inferior quality with no consideration given to variances in quality.

Do not confuse design and appeal with quality of construction, for example, one home could be more pleasing in design and appeal because it has more "gingerbread" (ornamentation) or a somewhat more elaborate design; however, the *quality* of construction could be identical. To make a clear distinction between the factors, determine the quality of construction first and then rate the design and appeal. Carefully consider the cost and quality of the materials used in the basic construction of the home. Rate the quality of the exterior and interior finishes and the quality of workmanship throughout. One or two components of a different quality is normal and should be generally disregarded as influencing the classification for general quality.

Quality Is Revealed by the Shape of the House

Study the shape of the house. A low-quality dwelling is usually a square or oblong box that is basically a shelter and nothing more. Low- or fair-quality homes seldom have recessed or covered entries and entry is directly into living areas. Low- or fair-quality homes typically have no covered parking, a one-car garage, or a carport.

As quality increases, the shape of a home gets farther and farther away from a square or oblong appearance. An average-quality home may still have somewhat of a square or oblong appearance, but added trim and detail tend to diminish the plain appearance recognizable in lower-quality homes. Recessed entries found in average-quality homes are smaller, and covered entrances are typically not as wide as those featured in better-quality residences. The architectural design of a good-quality home is generally attractive, resulting in a more custom-built appearance as opposed to average tract or stock-built homes. Average-quality dwellings usually have a two-car garage, whereas good-quality dwellings feature two- and three-car garages.

Significant Exterior Characteristics of Quality

Consider the amount of trim and finishes, the detailing and width of the trim, the slope of the roof, and the depth of the roof overhang. Low-quality homes have little or no trim and little or no roof slope or roof overhang. Better-quality homes have more trim or ornamentation and the trim is more detailed. Wider and heavier wood trim and wider and heavier shutters are used as quality increases. The slope of the roof and the depth of the roof overhang also increases as quality increases. A good-quality home will feature common brick or stone exterior finishes, whereas a medium-quality home usually has brick veneer finishes.

Examine the windows and doors. Cheaply constructed homes often have small windows and poor window placement or, sometimes, unsuitably large windows designed to cut construction costs rather than being functional and appealing. Less expensive homes have little or no window trim, and the window casings are usually narrow and ill- fitting. Stock windows, standard casings, and trim are characteristic of average-quality homes, while good-quality homes feature different styles of well-placed windows with attractive ornamental finishes. Doors range from laminated-wood hollow-core doors in minimal-quality dwellings to good- quality laminated or solid wood, more decorative, single- or double-entry doors in better-quality homes.

Quality and Types of Roofing Materials

Notice the type and style of roofing in addition to the quality of roofing materials. A very thin coating of ceramic granules on a very thin asphalt shingle is not going to last very long as the weather takes its toll. A medium-grade (or medium-heavy) asphalt shingle roof will last approximately 15 to 25 years depending on the orientation of the home on the lot and the area the house is located in. A good grade of heavier asphalt shingle will last 25 to 35 years, or longer. Typically, as the quality of the roof increases, it will have more of a textured appearance. Some roofs have a "drip edge," which is a metal lip that extends a few inches beyond the actual edge of the roof sheathing. It is an added measure of protection against water coming in under the edge of the roofing. When a roof has a drip edge, consider it a sign of quality.

Low-quality homes:

Asphalt rolled roof, lightweight shingles (very thin with minimal ceramic granule coating), or built-up tar and gravel roofing.

Fair-quality homes:

Lightweight asphalt shingle or built-up roofing with gravel or small rocks.

Average-quality homes:

Medium-weight asphalt shingles, wood shingles (medium quality–medium density), lightweight shakes, built-up tar and gravel roofing, or built-up roofing with a rock surface.

Good-quality homes:

Concrete or clay tile, Mission Tile, slate, heavy wood shingles or shakes, built-up rock roofs with larger rocks, or good-quality asphalt shingles.

Rating Interior Characteristics

Lower-quality homes ordinarily have masonite or laminated-wood hollow-core doors along with a minimum of cupboards, closets, and storage space; small pullmans; laminated plastic countertops and bath wainscots; minimal-quality appliances and plumbing fixtures; inexpensive vinyl or asphalt floor coverings; and minimal-quality carpeting. Note: Laminated wood is formed by rolling or compressing wood particles or other types of materials, which are usually bonded together by glue, while veneer is a thin piece of wood.

The typical characteristics of an average-quality home are medium-grade laminated-wood hollow-core doors and cabinetry with average-grade hardware; narrow baseboards; vinyl or asbestos tile flooring; average-grade carpeting; laminated plastic or ceramic tile countertops; laminated plastic, ceramic tile, or one-piece fiberglass tubs and showers; small pullmans; adequate wardrobe closets; and some storage space.

Notice the quality of materials in an average-quality home as opposed to the quality of materials incorporated into a good-quality home. Ceramic tile has more density and more of a custom appearance and window sills, door frames, and baseboards are wider, more tightly mitered, and have more of a custom appearance as quality increases. Good-quality homes feature ample kitchen cabinets, linen closets, and storage areas; walk-in wardrobe closets; large double-pullmans; ceramic tile or simulated marble countertops, splash, and wainscots; better-quality appliances and plumbing fixtures; sheet vinyl, vinyl tile, wood, or linoleum flooring; better-quality carpeting; veneered hollow-core doors; and wider, more attractive entry foyers. Fireplaces found in good-quality homes typically have a hearth and mantle, and they will consist of better-quality materials, for example, used brick, marble, or stone.

Lower-quality homes typically have only a kitchen with an eating area, living room, bedrooms, and bathrooms. Average-quality homes may feature small dens, family rooms, and dining areas in addition to basic living areas. Good- quality dwellings usually feature formal dining rooms, large family rooms, and separate laundry rooms in addition to basic living areas.

Characteristics of Very-Good-Quality Homes

Very-good-quality homes will be located in the better residential districts of a community and are usually custom designed and custom built. High-quality materials and workmanship will be found throughout, and the homes will feature many interior refinements and detail. Well-finished woods are used for cabinetry, paneling, moldings, and other ornamentation. Other characteristics of a very-good-quality home include hardwood veneer or solid wood doors; good-quality hardware, appliances, and plumbing fixtures; sheet vinyl, wood, ceramic tile, or linoleum flooring; good-quality carpeting; cooking islands; ample cabinetry and closets; built-in bars, wetbars, desks, and bookshelves; high-quality ceramic tile or marble countertops and bath finishes; spacious wardrobes with built-in features; dressing areas; and fully shelved, large linen and storage closets.

The exteriors of very-good-quality homes are attractive with good fenestration and custom ornamental features; well-designed, ornamental windows; heavy wood shake or tile roofs; good roof slope; large eaves; and gracious entrances.

The esthetic appeal, quality, refinements, and finishes of mansion- or luxury-type homes will exceed those found in a very-good-quality home. The homes will be professionally decorated and customized throughout including lavish professional landscaping as well as other customized yard improvements.

Achieving Proficiency in Judging Quality

Take the time to visit several new housing developments and note the variances in quality. Look closely at the interior trim and finishes, appliances, room layout, and quality of the materials used throughout. Particularly note the exterior building materials and types of roofing, windows, exterior trim, and garages because you will be judging the quality, design, and appeal of your comparable sales based only on an exterior inspection.

Whenever possible, go to home shows that feature the latest materials being used to upgrade and remodel homes so you can learn more about costs and quality. Also, visit local building centers, remodeling centers, and gardening centers. Study advertisements in newspapers and magazines. Compare the differences in quality of various materials and note the prices of all the different building materials, including the prices, types, and descriptions of materials of patio covers, spas, swimming pools, fencing, and even plants, shrubs, and trees as there is a large variance in costs between small 1-gallon plants and larger, mature plants or trees. When homeowners have invested a substantial sum to landscape their property with fully grown (mature) or nearly fully grown plantings, you should be prepared to estimate the cost of the yard improvements accurately.

Take advantage of every opportunity to learn more about construction materials so you can readily recognize differences in quality, which is prerequisite to assigning appropriate costs. A comprehensive knowledge of quality and costs will enable you to complete the cost approach rapidly and effectively, itemize costs of repairs, itemize costs of items to be completed when owners are in the process of remodeling or refurbishing, validate owner's costs, and to validate contractor's construction costs efficiently when you appraise proposed or new construction.

PRICE AND QUALITY

You can't equate price and quality. Many homes that sell in the upper price ranges ($400,000. to $700,000.) are basically average quality homes. It is the cost of the land that drives the prices up; not the quality of the residence.

HOW TO WRITE A DESCRIPTION OF THE PROPERTY

To describe property appropriately in the appraisal report, to complete the cost approach effectively, and to make appropriate adjustments, you should note the size, age, condition, and type of construction materials of all the elements that are assigned value, including patios, patio covers, decks, landscaping, fencing, driveways, sidewalks, swimming pools, perimeter pool decking, spas, sheds, storage buildings, barns, corrals, and any other elements of value.

The size, age, condition, and building materials must be considered when you are assigning costs and depreciation as well as when you are making your adjustments. Almost all buyers will pay more for a home when it has a swimming pool, block wall fencing, feature fireplace, or other amenities that are newer, are in good condition, and are constructed with good-quality materials; therefore, appraisers should also consider these items when they are making their adjustments.

If the typical adjustment for swimming pools is $10,000., this adjustment must be modified to reflect the age, quality of construction materials, condition, and size of the subject pool and the pools the subject is being compared to. A statement should be included to identify adjustments that differ from the norm. For example, "The adjustment for swimming pools is less than typical because the subject swimming pool is older and is in inferior condition to the comparable pools." All the elements assigned value should be considered in this same manner. The adjustments must also be refined to reflect over-improvements for the neighborhood.

Confirming the Year Built

Because data sources cannot be guaranteed to be 100 percent reliable, the age of the subject property and comparable sales must be confirmed. Study the pictures in cost handbooks to determine the ages of older homes. For other homes, using the known ages of different properties as a guideline, learn to estimate ages of homes by becoming familiar with the dates when architectural styles changed and the dates when different components of construction were introduced, for example, types of roofing, slab floors, aluminum sliding windows, sliding glass doors, attached garages, aluminum siding, drywall, built-in appliances, fiberglass stall showers, forced-air furnaces, or wall furnaces. For example, drywall replaced lath-and-plaster in the 1940s to 1950s, and steel swing-out windows were introduced around 1959 to 1960. It is also important to know when the different components of construction were introduced to provide a means of identifying additions and modernization and the approximate time the changes took place.

Common House Styles

Common house styles are modern or contemporary, ranch style, bungalow (one-story, small, or compact home), "conventional" (typical tract or stock-built home), Victorian, Spanish style or Spanish villa, French Normandy, French provincial, English Tudor, English regency, colonial American, A-frame, saltbox, Mediterranean, Georgian, Williamsburg, farmhouse, adobe, and Swiss chalet.

Common Window Styles

Common window styles are fixed, sliding aluminum, single or double hung (moves up and down), casement (swings open like a door), awning (basement window that opens up and out), hopper (like an awning window, only swings inward), transom (basement windows that open at the top), center pivot, jalousie (looks like a venetian blind), clerestory (window usually placed high in the wall and does not open), and bay windows.

Types of Flooring

"Resilient" floor coverings are available in either sheet or tile form. Common types of resilient flooring are vinyl composition tile (VAT), asphalt tile, vinyl tile, linoleum, vinyl, or rubber sheet. Other types of flooring are ceramic tile, terrazzo, different types of hardwood flooring, and carpet.

How to Inspect and Classify Insulation

The appraiser is not expected to inspect the interior of the walls or inspect the attic area to find out whether there is insulation. However, since many people are becoming more cognizant of the value of energy-efficient items, every effort should be made to determine the presence and type (including the "R" value) of insulation because of the possible effects on marketability.

There are many different types of insulation. Batts or blankets, loose fill, and rigid board are common types of insulation. Loose fill can be rock wool, fiberglass, vermiculite, or cellulose. Rigid board may consist of polystyrene, urethane, fiberglass, or other materials.

Defining R-Values:

The following table lists typical thicknesses required for specific R-Values:

Harmful Insulation—Reporting Requirements:

Two types of insulation that may be harmful are urea-formaldehyde and asbestos. Asbestos was widely used in

	BLANKETS/BATTS		LOOSE FILL (BLOWN)		
R-Value	Fiber-glass	Rock Wool	Fiber-glass	Rock Wool	Cellu-lose
R-11	3 1/2"	3"	5"	3 3/4"	3"
R-19	6"	5 1/4"	8 3/4"	6 1/2"	5"
R-22	6 1/2"	6"	10"	7 1/2"	6"
R-30	9 1/2"	9"	13 3/4"	10 1/4"	8"
R-38	12"	10 1/2"	17 1/2"	13"	10 1/2"

homes and businesses from the 1940s to the 1970s; however, it is no longer used because of the danger of inhaling the asbestos fibers from deteriorating insulation. Urea-formaldehyde foam, like loose fill, can be pumped into the attic and walls of a house. If urea-formaldehyde is improperly installed, at an incorrect temperature, it might not solidify, thereby producing noxious odors and toxic fumes.

If you have reason to believe that the insulation is of a type that is related to possible health hazards, request an inspection by a knowledgeable person for affirmation. The possibility of the presence of hazardous insulation should be reported to the lender immediately because marketability of the property could be seriously affected. If you are not certain whether there is insulation, what type of insulation is present, or the R-Value don't guess; only *factual* information should be provided in an appraisal report.

Ask the property owner for a description of the insulation. Or check attic areas for insulation, remove the cover from an electrical receptacle on an outside wall to see if there is insulation in the space between the electrical box and the wall, or check the outside walls in a room. If they feel cold, there probably isn't any insulation in the walls.

Wall Finishes, Roofs, and Foundations

To detect plaster walls as opposed to drywall, knock sharply on the wall. If it hurts your knuckles, the walls are probably plaster. Plaster finishes are heavier and not as smooth as drywall. Look for seam lines that identify drywall and look for nails. Nails are usually detectable close to the ceiling because they have a tendency to pull out a little as the house settles.

The foundation of a house is the substructure on which the superstructure rests. The term "foundation" includes the footings, foundation walls, slab, columns, pilasters, and all other parts that provide support for the house. Common types of foundations are cinder or concrete block, cut stone, brick, field stone, treated wood, wood blocks or sills, poured concrete (concrete slab), and piers or posts on concrete footings.

The three basic types of foundations are poured concrete, basements, and pier and beam. In a pier-and-beam foundation, the foundation slab rests on a series of posts, or piers, that extend above ground level and rest on footings. The piers support the sill which is attached to the pier by an anchor bolt. The floor joists that provide the major support for the flooring are placed on top of the sills. The floor joists, which run parallel from wall to wall, support the boards of a floor. The space between the ground and the floor is called the "crawl space." Crawl spaces can by identified by air vents along the bottom portion of the structure. Slab (poured concrete) foundations do not have air vents.

Aluminum "shingle-shakes" are preformed, embossed panels whose irregularly grooved or textured surfaces have been molded to simulate the coarse surface of hand-split wood shakes. The shingle-shake panels have their edges formed so that during application a four-way interlock of shingle to adjacent shingle is provided, making them impossible for the wind to lift. Distinguishing wood shingle roofs from wood shake roofs, shakes are split from the tree while wood shingles are sawed. The shakes are usually thicker and they have a more textured look as well as a longer life expectancy.

Illegal Outside Entrances

If you notice outside entrances to room additions, bonus rooms, or recreation rooms, find out if the room is being used as a rental unit. If so, it should conform to zoning and use regulations. The most important criterion of a nonconforming use is rooms or structures with separate entrances that have a kitchen, or cooking facilities, and bathrooms. When this is suspect, verify permits for the room, or structure as well as the cooking facilities and baths. If the unit is not legal, inform your client immediately and let them know you will probably have to make a deduction from the value for the cost to convert the structure to its legal use; that is, deduct the cost to remove the kitchen or bath facilities.

Parking Facilities

Detached garages are free-standing buildings with independent structural systems; that is, foundation, roof, and walls. Attached garages share a common wall with the house. Built-in garages have living area both adjacent to and above the garage.

How to Document Deferred Maintenance

When the property reflects excessive deferred maintenance, list the items needing repair on a separate addendum and include a total estimated cost to complete the repairs. The following format is suggested for an addendum detailing needed repairs:

ADDENDUM
14897 Ash Street
Orange, California

The following repairs are needed to raise the subject property to a good marketable condition:

1. Install new concrete driveway.
2. Remove weeds, trim shrubs and trees, clean up and re-seed front and rear yards.
3. Sandblast and paint exterior stucco, eaves, and all the wood trim.
4. Install new screens where needed.
5. Repair (3) broken windows.
6. Install new carpet throughout.
7. Install new tile flooring in kitchen and both bathrooms.
8. Remove wallpaper in (2) bedrooms, patch and paint the walls in both bedrooms.
9. Clean the entire interior of the dwelling.
10. Service and repair all electrical, heating, and plumbing fixtures and equipment.
11. Install new window coverings throughout.

TOTAL ESTIMATED COST TO COMPLETE ALL
THE RECOMMENDED REPAIRS IS: $6,500.00
DATE: ______
SIGNATURE: ______

Procedures for Dealing with Personal Property

Never include personal property in the appraised value. Describe the items in the report and show "personal property, no value assigned." If the item is included in the sales price, consider the item as a sales concession and make appropriate deductions in the market analysis. Above-ground spas and pools should be considered personal property. Ranges, ovens, refrigerators, and air-conditioning units that are not built in should be considered personal property.

Anything that is attached to a building with the intent that it be made a permanent part of the building is generally considered to be "real property" and automatically goes with the structure for the purchase price of the property.

California courts have employed several general tests to determine whether an item of personal property has become a "fixture." Fixtures are items of personal property attached to or incorporated into the land or building in such a manner that they become real property. The fixtures are then considered to be part of the land or building. Two of the most critical tests are (1) the intent of the person attaching or incorporating the personal property into the land or building and, (2) the particular method by which the property is actually incorporated or attached and the degree of damage that might result to the property if the item was removed.

Appearances Can Be Deceptive

Never allow the ambience of the property to influence your opinion of value; picture the home without the furniture, wall hangings, and other decorations—as if it were vacant. Window coverings, chandeliers, mirrors, shelves, and other items have been known to be removed or replaced when a home is sold. Occasionally, owners will retain items that they value personally, or they might substitute items they wish to keep for a corresponding item that may vary in value. Get in touch with the listing or selling brokers to find out if the home is being sold "as is." The listing and sales agreements should include detailed descriptions and acceptance by the buyer referencing all substitutions and items that are not included in the purchase price of the home.

HOW TO MAKE A PHYSICAL INSPECTION OF THE PROPERTY

Before you begin inspecting or taping the property, complete as much of the site and improvement sections of the appraisal report as practicable to avoid omissions.

Following the suggested sequence for inspecting property, make notes describing the property and condition as you are taping the property. If you use the same abbreviations to describe the property and follow the same pattern each time that you appraise a property, you will find that it is much easier to decipher your notes and you can proceed much more efficiently. Refer to "Abbreviations" in Appendix E.

Because standards vary from one market segment to another, rate the property in terms of the standards established by the market. In other words, "typical purchasers for this particular type of property in this particular neighborhood."

How to Differentiate Physical Depreciation from Deferred Maintenance

"Physical depreciation" reflects the wearing out or deterioration in the structure or impairment of condition as a result of wear and tear or disintegration. It may be curable or incurable. If the cost to repair or cure the condition is not economically feasible or profitable, as of the date of valuation, the depreciation should be identified as "incurable." "Deferred maintenance" consists of items in need of immediate repair, such as replacement of broken items or replacement of worn-out items. Deferred maintenance is the basis for "curable" physical depreciation. If applicable, costs to correct defects should be included in the appraisal report.

When to Recommend Professional Inspections

The appraiser is responsible for recognizing and acknowledging *hidden as well as obvious defects* in the property. Therefore, if you have reason to believe there might be some kind of defect in the property, but you are uncertain—always recommend an inspection by a professional person who can confirm or deny your suspicions, for example, a geologist, soils engineer, structural engineer, termite inspector, or electrical, plumbing, or roofing inspectors.

Distinguishing Characteristics of Yard Improvements

Describe the yard improvements and landscaping. Note the age, size, condition, quality, and construction materials of the driveway, fencing, planters, automatic sprinklers, walkways (flagstone, brick, concrete, wood), lawn, retaining walls, patios, patio covers, swimming pools (gunite, vinyl lined, fiberglass), spas, gazebos, barbecues, decks, and any other elements that will be assigned value. Items that have little or no value should be described in the appraisal report with an indication that "no value was assigned" to avoid any controversy or questions regarding omissions.

Drainage and Slippage Problems

Check for proper lot drainage. Particularly look for standing water near the dwelling; drainage must be away from the improvements to avoid the collection of water in or around the dwelling unit or other improvements. Also, investigate the possibility that water from adjoining property to the sides and rear of the subject could run off onto the subject site. When a house is built on a hillside, always examine the subject property as well as surrounding properties for signs of drainage and slippage problems. When there is evidence of drainage, slippage, or soils problems, these conditions must be addressed in the appraisal report and an inspection by a professional soils engineer, geologist, or termite inspector should be recommended. Note: Termite inspectors usually look for dry rot and water damage in addition to checking for termites.

Gutters and Downspouts:

Note the type of material, location (front or rear), and the condition of the gutters and downspouts. There should be adequate drainage away from the downspout. An inspection should be recommended when gutters are filled with debris because standing water and rotting debris in the gutters could result in rotted fascia boards. When there are no gutters, note the depth of the roof overhang.

Ways to Spot a Worn-Out Roof

Note the type of roof and the age. Inspect the condition of the roof, particularly the portion of the roof receiving the brunt of the sun and wind. Signs of deferred maintenance are curled, broken, cracked, or missing shingles; roof sagging and decay; a lot of debris on the roof; tree branches rubbing against the roof; heavy growth of vines or ivy on the roof; and water stains on interior ceilings caused by roof leaks. Very old roofs that need replacing can result in additional expense due to rotted sheathing boards underneath the shingles.

There are times when, rather than repairing or replacing a worn out rock roof, the owner simply has new rocks added to give the appearance of a new roof. Therefore, when a rock roof appears to be new, review paid receipts to find out if the roof actually was replaced, obtain the roofer's name for further verification, or recommend an inspection.

When there is evidence that a roof was recently replaced, always verify the status of permits with local governing agencies. A case in point: A local roofing inspector for the city, on his way to inspect a newly installed roof, noticed a new roof on another house down the street. He checked the records and discovered that the owner did not obtain permits. Consequently, the city forced the owner to remove the new roof and replace it according to code.

INSPECTION OF FOUNDATIONS AND EXTERIOR WALLS

Inspect the condition of the paint, wood or aluminum siding, and other exterior finishes. Look for disintegrating or loose stucco, decaying wood siding, rusted sheet metal, broken or rusted screens, and broken windows as well as damage caused by trees, ivy, vines, and plants that are growing too close to the structure.

Sticking or scraping doors and windows, ill-fitting joints, and ill-fitting door frames can be a sign of uneven settlement. Look for other evidence of uneven settlement, such as cracks in the foundation, walls, or chimneys. Eroding mortar in brick or stone walls or other types of foundations can cause the walls to settle unevenly. Small cracks are generally present and may be indicative of some settlement of the structure, earth movement, or may even indicate the presence of an addition.

It is not necessary to mention normal evidence of settlement, small cracks, or minor deferred maintenance that can easily and inexpensively be repaired or inconsequential items that will not affect the sustainment of value over the life of the loan. Major repairs and indications of possible major structural damage must be addressed in the appraisal report. Photos should accompany the report clearly showing evidence of structural defects. When there is evidence of major structural damage, an inspection by a licensed structural engineer and/or a geologist should always be *required,* and your client should be notified as soon as possible.

Ways to Unearth Dry Rot and Termite Damage

Check the house, garage, all the other structures on the property, patio covers, decks, wood fencing, and wood piles for evidence of dry rot or damage caused by termites and other wood-boring insects. Especially, pay close attention to the eaves, the garage door frame, and areas where wood comes in contact with the soil. Tree stumps that have been left to rot are also a good place to find infestation.

Termites can hollow out wood and cause extensive damage to the structure without damaging exterior surfaces; hence, termite damage to wood is usually not noticeable on the surface. To find out whether wood-boring insects are present, or were present, probe the wood lightly with a screwdriver; when it penetrates the wood easily and the wood appears hollow, you can assume that termites or other wood-boring insects have been at work. Termites can also be evidenced by a black pepper like residue which will be found in the hollowed-out wood or where pieces of wood are joined together.

Dry rot is a decay of seasoned wood caused by a fungus. It can usually be detected by actual evidence of decay. Examine the wood closely; wood affected by dry rot will feel soft or spongy, and it will easily disintegrate.

HOW TO RECOGNIZE ADDITIONS

Additions may be recognized by noting one or more of the following diversities from the original structure:

1. Design not conforming to the neighborhood
2. Different or newer roofing on one part of the structure;

the roof line of the addition doesn't correspond to the original structure

3. Small cracks in interior or exterior walls where the addition is joined to the original structure (caused by different rates of settlement)

4. Floors on different levels (step-up, step-down, or uneven)

5. Mixed colors, quality, or grades of carpet, flooring, or finishes

6. Different sizes and styles of windows, window frames, or doors

7. Newer or dissimilar quality and styles of plumbing fixtures

8. Variations in finishes, door frames, molding, and hardware (which can seldom be matched exactly to the original finishes)

Modernization, Refurbishing, and Remodeling

Many of the items described under additions can also be attributed to modernization, refurbishing, or remodeling. Look for additional evidence of modernization, such as updated appliances, countertops, plumbing, heating, electrical wiring, bath fixtures, bath wainscot, flooring, doors, and windows. It is important to note all the features of modernization, refurbishing, and remodeling to make an appropriate estimate of value of the property, define the effective age of the property, complete the cost approach, and assign appropriate adjustments. Note the date the improvements were installed and the condition, quality, and type of materials.

INSPECTION OF THE GARAGE

Test automatic garage door openers to make sure they are in good working condition. Laundry facilities should be shown on the building diagram. Storage areas, built-in cabinets, and workshops should also be indicated on the building diagram, and the condition, size, quality, age, and types of materials should be considered when you are assigning costs, depreciation, and adjustments. Make allowances for other elements of value, such as oversized garages, insulation, or finished walls. Look for water damage from leaky laundry facilities, plumbing, hot water heaters, and leaky roofs.

How to Handle Nonconforming Uses

When the garage is being used for anything other than a garage, find out whether the garage doors are in place and operable. Describe the status of the doors in the appraisal report. No consideration can be given to any use other than a garage unless the changes or conversions have been properly permitted. Assign garage value only less the cost to convert the structure to its original and intended use. Corresponding adjustments for the cost of the conversion should be considered in the sales comparison analysis.

When it is apparent that the garage was installed at some time after the house was built, verify the status of permits with local governing officials because the garage may have to be removed, or moved, if it was not built to code or the placement of the garage on the lot is not legal.

WHAT TO LOOK FOR WHEN YOU INSPECT BASEMENTS

Look for evidence of seepage, flooding, or settlement, such as cracks, water marks, scaling or flaking paint, white areas of discoloration or mineral deposits on masonry, wet wood, rotting wood, or musty odors. Completely dry basements under all conditions, however, are rarities because seepage of a small amount of water after heavy rains or a spring thaw is inevitable. Also, condensation often occurs on hot, humid days in the summer and this should not be a cause for concern.

When there is a sump pump in the basement, give the basement a second look for signs of leaks, water seepage, and flooding. Not all basements need sump pumps; therefore, its presence should alert you to potential problems. However, the sump pump may be there only as a precautionary measure in case of extensive rainfall or because laundry facilities, stall showers, or other plumbing fixtures located in basement might break or overflow. Take the cover off the top of the sump pump, if possible. If there is standing water in it, it is likely that it was recently in use. Discuss any potential problems with the owner of the property.

Look for evidence of faulty or unprofessionally installed electrical wiring, especially in finished basement rooms. Finished basement rooms should have enough light and ventilation to provide good healthy living space if they are to be considered generally acceptable to a broad market. Note the type of finishes and include photos with the report when you assign value to finished basement rooms.

FACTORS TO CONSIDER WHEN YOU INSPECT ATTICS

Include dimensions, full descriptions, and photos of finished attic areas that are assigned value. Finished attic rooms should have sufficient light and ventilation to provide good healthy living space if they are to be considered generally acceptable to a broad market. Electrical wiring should be adequate and professionally installed. Verify the status of permits with local governing officials.

HOW TO CONDUCT INTERIOR INSPECTIONS

Appraisers should always inspect the entire interior of the residence being appraised; however, when the home has been well maintained and you are unable to enter a room or two because of a sleeping child or there is someone in the room who is ill, you do not have to inspect every single room. When the property is in need of repairs, however, every attempt should be made to inspect the entire residence.

When you are identifying the room count, define a living area as a room only when the area actually is or could be a room with full utility. For example, a "dining area" is a part of another room. A "dining room" is a separate room or an area large enough to be effectively divided into a separate room.

Before commencing with the interior inspection, make sure that you have taped

1. all of the two-story open areas.
2. the area of the garage that extends into the livable area of the house.
3. other levels of a trilevel dwelling.
4. second story, basement, attic, and stairs.

If applicable, the area of the garage that extends into the livable area of the house should be deducted from the total area of the dwelling and added to the total area of the garage.

Consider the amount of natural light and cross ventilation with respect to overall livability and appeal. Dwelling units without good cross ventilation and good, natural light are usually considered to be undesirable.

Room Layout and Functional Utility

Go through each room of the subject property noting, on the building diagram, the location of the laundry room, kitchen, living room, bedrooms, bathrooms, other rooms, hallways, and stairways. Note the floor and wall finishes, kitchen equipment, number of bathroom fixtures, bath finishes, type of doors, and heating and cooling equipment.

Next, always recount the rooms and compare your room count with public records to make certain your room list is accurate. Continue your inspection by noting the functional layout of the dwelling. The room sizes must be acceptable based on market standards. Doors, stairs, and hallways must be wide enough to be functional (stairs and halls are generally 3 feet wide). Does the floor plan permit free traffic flow or is there too much walk-through traffic that diminishes the intended use of the room? Is there sufficient wall space to permit suitable furniture groupings? Is there ample room for furniture to be arranged so it is not too close to sources of heat? Have changes been made that alter room sizes so they are too small for good utility? If changes or remodeling have taken place within the structure, has the location of the main bearing wall been altered? If so, has proper compensation been made for this factor, for example, installation of new load-bearing beams that will adequately support the structure? If you are not certain, always recommend an inspection by a professional structural engineer.

Classifying Conformity and Condition

Consider the conformity of the decor throughout the home. Are the wall finishes, carpeting, flooring, built-in shelves, cabinets, and lighting fixtures compatible throughout? Will the improvements appeal to a typical buyer of a home of this type and quality? Rate the consistency of quality throughout the home.

Check the adequacy, quality, and condition of the kitchen equipment, hot water heaters, heating equipment, plumbing, and electrical wiring. Most older homes have 100-

amp service, which is adequate, generally, for a six-room dwelling of approximately 1,600 square feet. Older homes that only have 60-amp service do not have the capacity to utilize all of today's appliances and electrical conveniences. Newer houses typically have 200-amp service. An inadequate number of electrical outlets usually results in the use of too many extension cords, which can be extremely hazardous. Inspections should be *required* when there is evidence of inadequate or improper wiring or inadequate or unvented heating equipment.

Inspect exposed pipes under the kitchen sink noting condition and signs of corrosion or leaks. Check bath pullmans, bathtubs, showers, and toilets for evidence of major plumbing problems, leakage, and water damage. Closely examine marlite or plastic panels (bath wainscoting) to find out whether the panels are buckling, cracked, or pulling away from the wall, which is an indication that water is getting behind the wainscoting. If so, when this situation is not promptly attended to, the end result can be extremely expensive repairs.

Excessive moisture and water damage can be evidenced by ill-fitting or loose tiles on bathroom floors. If the bathroom flooring is carpet, always lift the carpet (if it is loose) to find out whether there is water damage to the flooring underneath because, sometimes, carpet is installed to conceal water damage.

Plumbing, or pipes, may be installed beneath the structure, in the attic, or between floors. Check ceilings for water stains, which can indicate major plumbing problems or leaky pipes. Water stains on the ceiling can also be caused by a leaky roof.

Check the materials and condition of the walls and flooring. Badly stained or warped hardwood floors are usually very expensive to refinish or replace. Walls covered with multiple layers of wallpaper and paint can also be expensive to restore to good condition. Moisture in the slab or subfloor can be a result of water seeping in from underneath caused by improper drainage or from broken pipes beneath the foundation. Excessive moisture can be evidenced by cracks in tile flooring, lifted tiles or sheet vinyl, bubbles in sheet vinyl or linoleum, warped wood flooring, carpet pulling away from the walls, carpet that crunches when it is walked on, mildew, or discoloration.

Uneven floors and walls or sagging beams could be the result of major settlement and structural damage. A sagging or soft feeling when you walk across a floor could be caused by plumbing leaks or other water damage, causing the floor to rot. Look for evidence of excessive moisture near the baseboard on outside walls. Recommend inspections when they are warranted.

Kinds of Energy-Efficient Items

Itemize all the energy-efficient items, noting the date of installation and the condition. Energy-efficient items include solar water heating systems, insulation, weatherstriping, insulated ducts, automatic-setback thermostats, electronic ignitions, insulated hot water heaters, and double-paned windows.

HOW TO REDUCE YOUR ERRORS

Take the time to verify everything, including the total number of rooms, bedrooms, and bathrooms, with the owner or agent, before you leave the property. By reviewing all the data at this time, you will never have to rewrite an appraisal because you failed to include a room or incorporate some element of value into the appraisal report.

Although you may have identified all the improvements

that have been made to the property and you are completely familiar with the corresponding costs, always obtain costs and detailed descriptions of additions, modernization, upgrading, and refurbishing from the owner or agent. Typically, when the value of the property does not fulfill the expectations of the parties involved, the first response your client will receive from the owner or agent will be "The reason the value is so low is because the appraiser did not take the time to notice all of the recent improvements that have been made to the property, the appraiser didn't even bother to ask what type of improvements had been made, and the appraiser did not discuss the cost of the improvements."

Therefore, to avoid any controversy, describe all the pertinent items in the appraisal report or include an addendum with detailed descriptions. Reference the owner's costs, if relevant, to demonstrate to your client that you were thorough in your investigation. This method is far more efficient than being compelled to follow up the appraisal with additional data or letters of explanation at a later date. Additionally, actual costs provided by owners can be an invaluable aid to keeping abreast with current costs in various areas as costs do vary per city as well as locations within a city. Reviewing owner's paid receipts can also help you to validate costs in cost handbooks.

ALWAYS AVOID PROBLEMS

Discuss only the information required to complete your report with owners, borrowers, or agents. Never discuss your opinion of value or any other subject that could affect your image of professionalism. All that is necessary is a simple statement; "I cannot formulate an opinion of value until I have analyzed all the facts and comparable sales." If you do discuss value, even a range of value, you will find that it is very difficult to defend yourself if your final analysis results in a different figure. Never disclose the value of the property to anyone other than the person that requested the appraisal.

Reconciling All the Facts

Complete all the relative items on the form before you leave the site. Make sure all your notes are legible and are labeled with the subject property address. No matter how good your memory is, by the time you have inspected the comparable sales, other properties, returned to the office, and have set the appraisal aside for a period of time, you may forget some important details if you do not do this at once.

A checklist of details usually overlooked can be helpful. Have you inspected the interior of the garage for finishes, built-in cabinets, work areas, or possible living area? Have you squared off all the structures and noted all the setbacks? Do your descriptions and calculations of the lot size and total size of all the structures coincide with the descriptions found in public records? Have you taken all the required photos? Collected the fee?

Make certain that you have not overlooked any positive or negative external influences. Check your map book to see if there are any possible adverse influences, such as airports, freeways, or traffic streets. Note the effect of the noise levels, on the interior and exterior of the property, if applicable. Is the entire neighborhood affected by the external influences or are they limited to the subject property?

HOW TO MEASURE PROPERTY ACCURATELY THE FIRST TIME

Before you begin taping the property, complete as much of the site and improvement sections of the form as practicable to avoid omissions. Survey the immediate area, noting any adverse conditions, such as high-tension power lines, traffic influences, nearby stop signs or bus stops, and hazardous ingress and egress. Take the front and street photos before you tape the property. Take the rear photos after you have completed the interior inspection and before you begin taping the rear and sides of the property.

When you are appraising a property that could be very time consuming to measure, visit the building or planning department in the city where the property is located because most building or planning departments retain copies of approved plans on microfilm. If the building plans are available, you can quickly define the dimensions of the property.

Increase Your Efficiency by Estimating Dimensions

Before you begin to tape the property, and while you are taping the property, estimate the overall size of the garage, the house, setbacks, overhangs, patios, and swimming pool. Step-off (estimate the size by the number of steps you take per yard or per foot) different areas of the improvements and the site and verify your accuracy in both instances. With enough practice, you will become quite proficient when you are estimating dimensions and overall building sizes. The ability to estimate dimensions and overall sizes accurately is very important because obstructions can sometimes prohibit the taping of certain areas. Also, proficiency in estimating dimensions (especially the depth of the overhang) will enable you to measure the second story at the same time as you tape the first story of the structure.

It is inefficient to measure swimming pools, spas, or tennis courts. You should be able step-off the areas to determine the size or estimate the dimensions accurately. When you are visually inspecting the comparable sales, because public records are not always accurate, you must have the ability to recognize any deviations from the size the homes are purported to be. When you appraise property for foreclosure sales, divorce settlements, or other reasons, and you are denied access to measure the structure, you must verify the size by making an accurate estimation.

Can you accurately estimate the number of feet to the corner, the height of the hillside behind the property, the distance to power lines, or the height of a concrete sound wall?

When you appraise income, industrial, or commercial property, you must be able to render accurate estimations of size because rents are usually analyzed on a price-per-square-foot basis for apartments, stores, and offices. It would not be practical or possible to measure every office, store, or apartment that you survey for rents; therefore, an accurate estimation of size is extremely significant.

The easiest way to learn how to estimate sizes is by retaining an image in your mind of a 2-ft. overhang, a 3-ft. overhang, a 15-ft. pool, the average depth of a house, typical garage sizes, and so forth. Practice the following method for estimating overall square footage: A typical garage is 20 ft. wide and the house appears to be one-and-one-half times the size of the garage or 30 ft. in width. The depth of the house appears to be 25 ft. Hence, 20 ft. (garage) + 30 ft. (front of the house) x 25 ft. depth = an approximate dwelling size of 1,250 sq. ft.

By using the following procedures, you should be able to measure a typical property accurately within 10 to 20 minutes.

1. Do not keep rewinding the tape because you can effectively drape long loops of tape and hold the loops in one hand when you are writing down information.

2. Measure to the nearest half-foot rather than to the nearest inch.

3. Never tape one small area at a time. Learn to run the tape

the entire width or length of the property. At the same time note the setbacks, garage size, recessed or protruding areas, patios, pools, and the dimensions of the second story of the dwelling. For example,

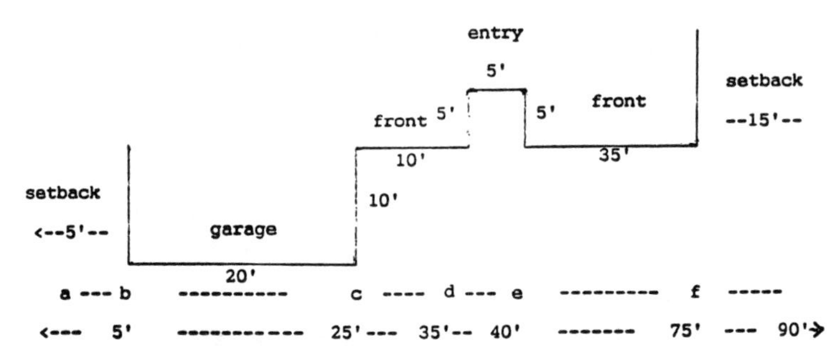

By picking up the dimensions from point a to b (5 ft. setback), b to c (25 ft. less 5 ft. = 20 ft. garage), c to d (35 ft. less 25 ft. = 10 ft. front of dwelling), and so on, when you run the tape from one end of the property to the other, you can measure the entire front width of the property without measuring one small section at a time. Now, pick up the dimensions that you missed: front setback, depth of entry, and so on.

4. Do not tape up to a fireplace or other obstruction, then tape the obstruction, then tape the balance of the wall. Rather, tape from one end of the house to the other ignoring the obstruction. Usually one side of a house will be free of obstacles; therefore, adjust the dimensions of the side with obstructions to the side without the obstructions. In this manner, you will learn how many feet to deduct from the dimensions when you tape around a fireplace or other obstacles. Until you are certain of your accuracy, tape all the individual areas separately as well.

5. The second story can almost always be taped right along with the first level if you notice where the second story

begins and ends and you can accurately estimate the depth of the second story overhang. If you measure the size of the second story from the interior; don't forget to add 6 inches (or whatever figure is applicable) to each side of the house to compensate for the width between the inside and outside walls because the total livable area of a single-family residence should be based on exterior dimensions.

Include only livable area in your dimensions, that is, make sure that you do not include open areas, such as two-story entries or open areas over the living room or other rooms in the total square footage of the dwelling. When storage areas or closets are located below the stairs, the stairs should be considered as livable area. When the area below the stairs is open and unusable as livable area, measure the stairs and deduct the area from the total dwelling size. When there are two sets of stairs, only one flight of stairs should be deducted from the total area of the house. Landings are considered to be livable area. If you have taped the second story at the same time as you taped the first level, do not forget to deduct the area of the stairways and the open areas when you define the dimensions of the second story.

Begin by taping the front "setbacks." Setbacks are the distance between the house (or garage) and the property lines. The front property line is typically located at the edge (the side of the sidewalk that meets the subject's front yard) of a public sidewalk or where a public sidewalk might be installed. When there is no sidewalk, the property line could be located at the curb or street. If this is the case, show "to curb" or "to street" on the building diagram. Verify the lot size with the city or county planning department if you are not certain where the property line is.

Next, tape the side yard setbacks, the garage (if built-in or attached to the dwelling), and the exterior of the front of the house to define the shape of the structure. Following this step, inspect the interior of the garage, basement, the residence, and the attic, as applicable. (If necessary, to avoid bringing mud or dirt into the house, inspect the interior before you measure the exterior.) Next, tape the rear setbacks picking up dimensions of patios, decks, pools, and other yard improvements as you proceed from the house to the rear property line. Then, tape the rear and sides of the dwelling, again noting setbacks and second story lines, if applicable.

When the lot is irregular in shape, side yard setbacks at both the front and the rear sides of the dwelling should be indicated on the building diagram. When an alley is located to the rear of the property, the property line typically ends in the middle of the alley. Verify the property line with city or county records.

Tape livable area *only*. Small storage cabinets, hot water heater cabinets, or chimneys that are attached to the house should not be considered as livable area; therefore, the dimensions of these items should not be included in the total gross livable area of the structure.

All the elements on the property that are assigned value must be accurately measured and described. Items of value include open, covered, and enclosed patios; decks; swimming pool; spa; tennis court; guest quarters; barns; free-standing recreation rooms; and free-standing garages. Descriptions should include the age, size, condition, quality, and type of construction materials.

DON'T FORGET TO SQUARE-OFF THE STRUCTURES

Never leave the property without rechecking to see that all of the structures or elements of value have been measured. Make sure building sizes correspond to those depicted in public records. And always square-off the structures, that is, the net dimensions on opposite sides of the structure should be equal.

HOW TO CONDUCT VISUAL INSPECTION OF THE COMPARABLE SALES

To avoid omitting an item of comparison, which might force you to return to the area to survey additional comparable sales, make preliminary adjustments on the form as you inspect each comparable sale. By attaining an approximate adjusted value for each comparable in this manner, the need for replacing sales that are not actually comparable or the necessity to obtain additional information should be illuminated; hence, the information or additional sales can be procured at this time. Additionally, you will be less likely to overlook adjustments.

The Importance of the Date of Sale

Pay close attention to the date of the sale as you are inspecting each comparable property to determine whether there has been an adequate amount of time between the actual date of the sale and your inspection to allow sufficient time for the buyer to repair or upgrade the property. If you have reason to believe that the property was improved after the buyer took possession of the property; always verify the condition of the property, at the time of the sale, with the buyer or participating real estate agents. Look for "for sale" signs in the neighborhood, ask property owners, or check multiple-listing books to find the name of the agents that listed and sold the property or the names of agents who consistently farm the neighborhood because they are usually familiar with the condition of all the homes in the neighborhood.

Factors Adding to Relative Value

While you should be concerned about overvaluing property, do not become overly conservative when you select comparable sales, apply adjustments, or define a final estimate of value. When homes have been updated, refurbished, or remodeled, these factors not only add value to the property; they also reduce the effective age of the property. When the effective age of the property has been properly estimated, the amount of depreciation will be correspondingly reduced.

It would not be possible to correlate the estimated market value of the property and the indicated value by the cost approach if proper adjustments are not made in the sales comparison analysis to reflect the upgraded condition of the homes. To reduce the likelihood of defining an inappropriate final estimate of value, make sure you have a complete description of the subject and comparables so appropriate costs and depreciation can be assigned in the cost approach and appropriate market adjustments can be made.

Adjustments are sometimes overlooked or they are not attended to in a proper manner; for example, adjustments for asphalt driveways versus concrete driveways; block wall fencing compared to wood fencing; variances in type, age, and condition of roofs; modernized kitchens and bathrooms; upgrading; or type and condition of heating and cooling systems. Errors are also made when appraisers assume that public records are correct; consequently, additions are overlooked because they are not included in the square footage shown in public records.

A lack of thoroughness on the part of the appraiser can be readily evidenced by studying the photos that accompany the appraisal report. For example, the photos show that the subject has a newer roof, extensive yard improvements, concrete driveway, and block wall fencing and photos of one or more of the comparable properties disclose several dissimilarities, that is, older roofs, asphalt driveways, wood fencing, or items in obvious need of repair. Yet, none of these factors has been addressed in the appraisal report, no adjustments have been made, and no explanations have been provided. The reader is left to wonder why none of these elements adds to, or detracts from, the value of the properties. Additionally, if such obvious items have not been mentioned, one can certainly assume that the condition of the interiors of the comparable sales has not been investigated in the manner they should be.

Sometimes, in appraisals of older properties, the condition of the subject and comparables is rated "good"; however, the appraisal does not contain any descriptions of modernization, refurbishing, or upgrading that would place these properties in good marketable condition. It doesn't make sense to make a thorough investigation of the subject property and comparable sales if you fail to provide details of your investigation and analysis in the appraisal report.

Suppose you were appraising your own property; wouldn't you make every effort to examine each comparable sale carefully for differences in age, quality, condition, design, appeal, site size, locational influences, and every other element that adds to the value of the property and describe those factors in the report? Appraisers should not overvalue property, but, at the same time, due consideration must be given to every element that contributes to value.

Investigate the sales vigilantly; walk around and check out the view and amenities. Look for positive and negative influences. If necessary, ask the owner or neighbors for a description of the property. Note the condition, age, quality, materials of construction, design, and appeal as well as the age, type, and condition of the roof, driveway, fencing, yard improvements, and upgrading. Don't forget to drive around the block to see what type of property the comparable sale backs to.

A full description (age, size, condition, and amenities) of comparable sales cannot be determined by an exterior inspection; therefore, it is the appraiser's responsibility to obtain full descriptions by reviewing published data sources and by consulting with owners, buyers, or real estate agents.

SUMMARY

Make certain that the value assigned to the subject property is realistic and fair by making sure every item of value has been given proper consideration. If you want your opinions and appraisals to be readily acceptable to clients and reviewers, be precise in your presentation of data to substantiate your adjustments, lack of adjustments, explanations, conclusions, and the final estimate of value. Don't forget to document large or unusual adjustments with photos.

Refer to the checklists contained in appendices to this book: Appendix F, "Checklist—Subject and Comparable Sales," and Appendix G, "Check List—Subject and Comparable Sales: Site Improvements and Amenities." To describe the property effectively and to complete the cost approach effectively, the items on the checklists should be considered.

CHAPTER 7

EFFECTIVE COMMUNICATION AND REPORTING REQUIREMENTS

Appraisers must conduct a thorough investigation of the property and are responsible for presenting all the facts in a professional manner. Appraisers must also exercise considerable discretion when they are interviewing people and should make every effort to help their clients complete the transaction in a manner that benefits everyone.

In this chapter, we have provided a few tips for handling delicate situations. Also, we have included the what, why, and when you should point out problems to your clients before problems become major tragedies. Guidelines for using the FNMA Form 1004 and a checklist of lending requirements are presented to help you avoid errors and omissions.

HOW TO EVADE TOUCHY SITUATIONS

Property owners will ask a variety of questions, such as, Do you think the property is priced right? Should the property be taken off the market until the market reflects more profit? Where do you think real estate prices are headed? Should something should be done to improve the property? No matter how you say it or what you meant to imply, people usually manage to turn words around, and your client will hear a version different from yours. Therefore, do not offer your personal opinions or discuss any subject that could affect your image of professionalism. Refer any questions from property owners to the participating real estate agent, loan agent, or lender, as applicable, because it is their responsibility to counsel their clients.

Consider the following true account:

While the appraiser was making an inspection, the owner asked the appraiser whether he knew how much the house on the corner sold for. The appraiser replied, "I think it sold for about $380,000." The final estimate of value of the appraised property was $365,000. The enraged owner called the vice-president of the lending institution and demanded to know why the appraiser told him that his property was worth $380,000., yet it was appraised for only $365,000. The appraiser spent many hours going back and forth between the vice-president and the owner trying, unsuccessfully, to explain that he told the owner the house on the corner sold for $380,000. and that he did not tell the owner his property was worth $380,000. Needless to say, lending officers do not like to be caught in the middle of situations like this.

When people ask questions about how you arrive at your final estimate of value, explain the basic procedures avoiding any controversial items. If they want to know what the value of the property is, simply state, "I cannot formulate an opinion of value until I have analyzed all the facts and comparable market data." If you do discuss value, even a range of value, you may find that it is very difficult to defend yourself if your final analysis results in a different figure.

AVOIDING LAST-MINUTE CRISES

If you observe any deficiencies in the property that could affect the outcome of the loan transaction, prior to the time that your appraisal report and value are finalized, ask your client whether the appraisal should be suspended until the deficiencies have been corrected, whether the property should be appraised "as is" or whether the appraisal should be made "subject to" the deficiencies being corrected.

Deficiencies that could have a serious impact on the eligibility of the property for a loan include poor condition, nonconforming property, additions without finalized permits, declining neighborhood, environmental hazards, and nonconformity to zoning and use restrictions. By getting in touch with your client before the appraisal is completed, your client is given an opportunity to rectify the problem or cancel the appraisal, if necessary, before a great deal of time and money is expended on a loan that might not be feasible.

When your preliminary investigation indicates a value that is much lower than what your client anticipated, don't wait until loan documents are drawn up and the loan is ready to fund to discuss your tentative value with your client. Give them time to modify the loan terms or work out some other solution to the problem.

Cooperate with clients insisting that they, and they alone, are informed of the value estimate and any special conditions relating to the property. This gives them the opportunity to present alternative solutions to their customers. Additionally, a straightforward approach will usually relieve undue pressure on the appraiser to appraise the property at a certain value or to overlook certain items.

Appraisals should not be delivered to the client without prior notification of circumstances that could affect the conclusion of the transaction in a satisfactory manner for everyone concerned; however, always remember that it is not your job to underwrite the loan—your job is only to state the facts as you see them. Report any deficiencies to your client and let them make the decision whether to proceed and how to proceed.

DISCLOSING THE FINAL ESTIMATE OF VALUE

Never disclose the final estimate of value until all the arithmetic has been checked and the accuracy of the appraisal report has been confirmed. When a verbal value is given to a client, make certain that they are also informed of any adverse conditions; requirements for permits, inspections, or needed repairs; nonconformity; and any other conditions that affect marketability and value.

APPROPRIATE USES OF THE FNMA FORM 1004

The FNMA Form 1004/FHLMC Form 70 (Uniform Residential Appraisal Report Form or "Universal Form") should be used for

1. single-family residential property.
2. planned unit developments.
3. properties that have a "true" guest house.

Single-Family Residential Property

The universal form can be used for detached single-family residences, duplex and fourplex-style single-family residences, patio homes, cluster homes, planned unit developments, prefabricated homes, and mobile homes.

Two-Family Properties

Fannie Mae Form 1004 may also be used for two-family properties if the value of the second unit is relatively insignificant in relation to the total value of the property. For example, if a two-family property consists of a legal basement rental unit and an owner-occupied main unit—and the property is located in a neighborhood in which rental basement units are commonly found—use of the Form 1004 is appropriate when the value of the basement unit is relatively insignificant. This is because the appraiser generally places more emphasis on the sales comparison approach to value rather than on the income approach to value that typically is used for most rental properties.

Guest Houses

The Fannie Mae Form 1004 can be used for single-family residential property with a "true" guest house. A true guest house, maid's quarters, or mother-in-law quarters is typically a "self-contained unit." A self-contained unit is a freestanding unit, or a separate area of a dwelling unit, that contains cooking facilities and a bathroom; thus, the unit or room is readily rentable.

To include a second unit, such as a guest house, maid's quarters, or mother-in-law quarters on the FNMA Form 1004, zoning and use regulations must allow the second unit on the site, and the value of the second unit must be relatively insignificant in relation to the total value of the property.

When the zoning is anything other than single-family residential zoning, use the form designated for two- to four-unit properties.

If the unit is situated on a lot zoned for single-family residential use and zoning regulations do not permit a second unit on the site, the kitchen, cooking facilities, or bathroom may have to be removed. The appraisal should then be made subject to the removal of any illegal elements found in the property or an appropriate amount should be deducted from the value to cover the cost of removing the items.

When the second unit does conform to zoning regulations, and the value is relatively insignificant in relation to the total value of the property, the second unit should be fully described, and comparable sales should be used that have a similar unit.

Include a statement, such as, "The appraiser has verified the status of the maid's quarters with Dave Smith, City of Stevensville planning department, telephone (213) 345-9867. Mr. Smith stated that the maid's quarters is a legal conforming use (or, if appropriate, show legal but nonconforming use) and the structure can be rebuilt to its present state if destroyed by natural causes."

THE WRITTEN REPORT—COMPLIANCE WITH REPORTING REQUIREMENTS

The written appraisal should be presented in such a manner that all readers of the report can easily identify the significance of all the data presented in the report. Descriptions and explanations should be comprehensive, but brief.

The appraiser's personal prejudices and personal opinions should never appear in an appraisal report and should never be discussed with his or her client or anyone else affiliated with the property or transaction. All explanations, analyses, and value conclusions must be based only on the appraiser's professional judgment.

Avoiding Needless Explanations

The use of "unknown" anywhere on the form is not acceptable and will always require an explanation. It is the appraiser's responsibility to make every effort to obtain the required information. In the event that the information cannot be obtained from any source, show "not available" on the form and state the reasons why the data could not be provided.

When the appraisal is intended for conventional lending purposes, all of the sections and spaces on the report must be filled in with the exception of the "Lender Discretionary Use" section, "Estimated Remaining Physical Life" (which is a HUD requirement), and the section (on page two) "Not required by Freddie Mac and Fannie Mae." Although it is not a Fannie Mae requirement, many lenders require an estimated physical life; therefore, to avoid further correspondence, show the estimated physical life in the report.

Using Abbreviations

Because your meaning could easily be misinterpreted, use abbreviations only when you are certain that your reader will understand them. The use of any abbreviation that is not clearly understood or is not considered as standard throughout the industry will always require a written explanation. Refer to the list of abbreviations contained in Appendix E to this book.

Documenting Discrepancies in Public Records

Include an addendum and document any differences between facts contained in your appraisal and information obtained from published data sources. This way, the reader can readily validate your material, and you can avoid further correspondence. To ensure that the addendum is not purposely removed from the report, always reference the addendum in the body of the report.

Never include information in an appraisal report that has not been verified. All the data must be verified and must be factual.

EXHIBITS AND ADDENDA TO FNMA FORM 1004—CHECKLIST

The following exhibits are required to support the Uniform Residential Appraisal Report:

1. Investment (nonowner occupied) property. Include FNMA Form 1007 and FNMA Form 216.
2. A clearly legible area map that shows the location of the subject property and all the comparable sales.
3. A perimeter diagram of the building. Show exterior building lines, with dimensions shown to the nearest $\frac{1}{2}$ foot, drawn in black ink, that identifies and shows the location of all rooms, interior walls, and interior and exterior doors. Exterior building dimensions are required; interior room dimensions are not necessary.

   The building diagram does not have to be drawn to scale; however, the drawing should closely resemble the property. For clarity, show patios and porches with broken lines. Do not stack levels or color code levels since color coding is lost in reproduction.

Draw each level separately, identify each level, and show calculations for each level separately. Show the size and location of stairwells; do not count them twice when you are defining the total gross livable area. If additions are present, identify them on the sketch. Pools, patios, covered patios, sheds, and incidental structures should be included on the diagram; however, they do not need to be drawn to scale.

Designate front, side, and rear yard setbacks. Readers will assume that the front setback is to the sidewalk unless otherwise noted, for example, to curb or to street. Show area of level pad, upslope, downslope, and any other relevant data. Indicate the direction of the view, if any, and location of economic factors that affect the value.

Examine the building sketch. Make sure all the dimensions are on the sketch, all the structures square-off, and setbacks are indicated, and recheck all the calculations.

4. Plat map with north arrow, subject street name, and nearest cross street legibly shown and the subject site clearly identified. All numbers and names on the plat map should be clearly legible. Indicate the proximity to positive and negative influences in a manner that presents a concise picture to the reviewer. If a plat map is not available, show the distance from the subject to the nearest cross street in feet or number of intervening properties on the building sketch.

5. Clear, descriptive 35mm photographs of the front and back of the dwelling and a street scene that includes the subject property in the picture. Identify all photos and identify the street scene, looking north, looking south,

and so on. Note: Most lenders require three sets of photos. Verify photo requirements with your client.

6. Photos of any detrimental conditions affecting the subject property; significant deficiencies within the subject property; extensive remodeling, upgrading, or refurbishing; outstanding yard improvements; swimming pools; views; and other significant elements of value.
7. Photographs of association-owned amenities, if applicable.
8. Interior photos as well as photos of extraordinary amenities for properties valued at $500,000. or more.
9. Photographs of the comparable sales.
10. A transmittal letter, when applicable.
11. FHLMC Form 439/FNMA Form 1004B if the form is not on file with your client.
12. Planned unit development. Include the Planned Unit Development Project Information Addendum.
13. Addenda and all other data needed to complete the report. Addenda to the appraisal report must make reference to the appraisal report and must be signed and dated by the appraiser.
14. Resume: If you are submitting your resume and samples of your appraisals, review them to make certain they are the best representation of your professional work. Make sure all the information is correct, and check the report thoroughly for omissions and mathematical errors. Only clear, legible copies should be submitted. Usually, lenders prefer sample appraisals that have been completed within the past six months.

All exhibits must be neat, uncluttered, and of a professional standard.

FHLMC Form 442, Satisfactory Completion Certificate

When an appraisal has been made "subject to" completion of the property, repairs, inspections, rehabilitation, remodeling, and so forth, the appraiser must certify that the improvements were completed in accordance with the requirements and conditions stated in the original appraisal report and that, taking into consideration current market conditions, there has been no change in the estimated market value since the date the property was originally appraised. Minor items that do not affect livability may be incomplete as long as the lender has arranged for an adequate escrow to guarantee their completion. Photos are not required unless the photos that accompanied the appraisal are no longer representative of the property.

Recertification of Value

When is a final recertification of value required? A recertification of value is utilized for two reasons: either to recertify value because an appraisal has become outdated or to certify that a required condition has been met. An appraisal can be used up to 12 months after the appraisal date, but the property value must be recertified every four months. When a final recertification of value is completed, the appraiser is stating that the property's value has not declined from the date of the original report. When an appraisal is completed "subject to" a condition, a final recertification of value is needed to signify that the condition has been met and that the value has not declined.

If the property was recently appraised, review current market data before you recertify the value. If some time has passed since the original inspection, a field inspection should be made as well. A signed statement, on the appraiser's own letterhead, is acceptable. For example, "Current market data have been evaluated. The subject property was reinspected on May 11, 1989. The property remains as described in our appraisal report dated March 28, 1989, and there has been no change in our estimate of Market Value of Three Hundred Eighty-Seven ($387,000.) Thousand Dollars."

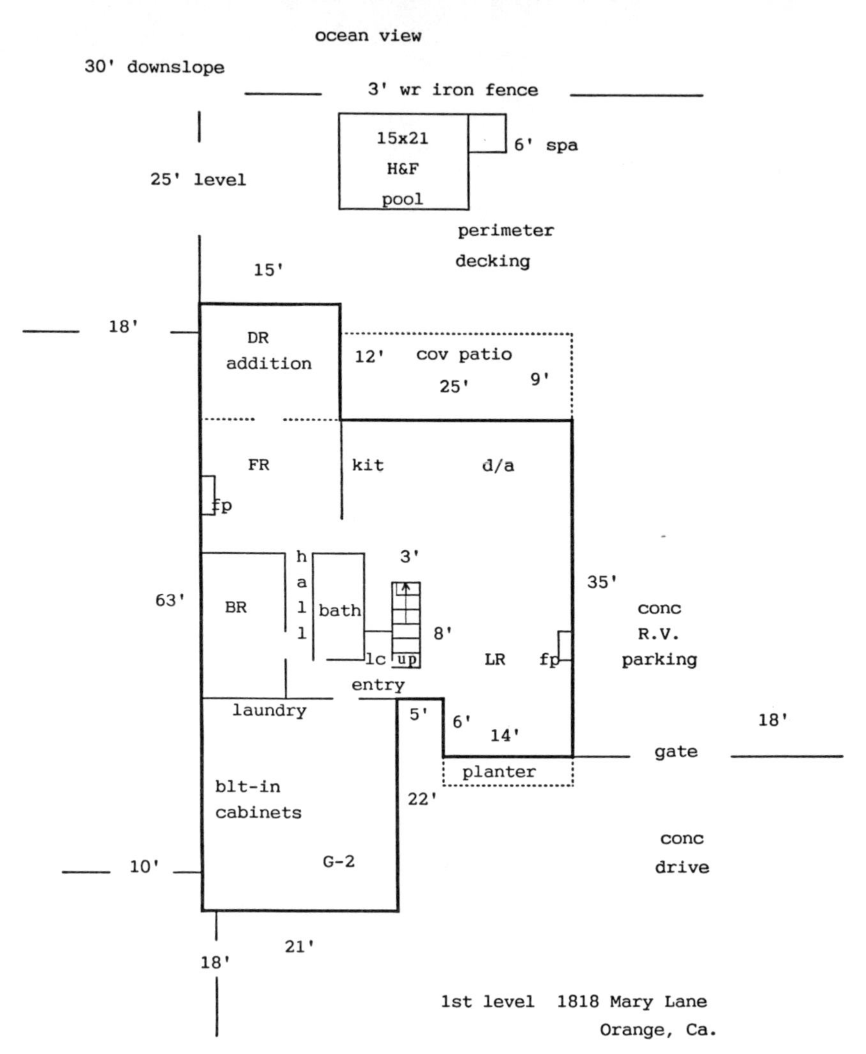

BUILDING DIAGRAM–EXAMPLE

CHAPTER 8

DESCRIPTION AND ANALYSIS OF THE PROPERTY AND NEIGHBORHOOD

As we follow the outline of the Uniform Residential Appraisal Report, we will show you how to present the written report. Answers to particular appraisal problems can usually be found under the same headings that are on the appraisal form, so you won't have to read a bunch of pages when you are looking for help. In this chapter, our discussions focus on identification of the subject and the neighborhood.

Stability of value is a major lending concern. If the appraiser does not address all the economic, sociological, political, and geographic factors that influence value, the underwriter cannot determine stability of value. To help you address all these factors in the easiest and most appropriate manner, we have included practical suggestions and sample statements to "prime the pump" when you want to say it right, but you can't get started.

Pesky little details can easily slip by unnoticed when someone or something interrupts your concentration. Therefore, we have included a number of checklists to help you avoid errors and omissions that you might otherwise overlook.

HOW TO LIST PROPERTY ADDRESSES

Street addresses require direction (n, s, e, w) and type (street, road, boulevard, or lane). Include unit numbers, as applicable. Indicate the nearest intersection when house numbers are not available. Do not spell out east, west, north, or south unless the direction is actually spelled out in the legal address.

THE RIGHT WAY TO SHOW THE CITY

When the property is located within the city limits, enter the name of the city. If the property is located in an unincorporated county area, indicate the city used for the mailing address and provide a further description in the neighborhood section. For instance, "The subject is located in an unincorporated county area with a city of Los Angeles mailing address." Mailing addresses can have a substantial influence on market value. Have you considered this in your analysis?

Names of local areas within a city or county should be shown in parentheses to distinguish between a city and a locally known area, for example, Los Angeles (Wilmington).

HOW TO PRESENT LEGAL DESCRIPTIONS

Legal descriptions can be obtained from a title company or from the owner's Grant Deed. Microfilm is not a reliable source for legal descriptions because the information might not be accurate or it might not be up-to-date. Usually, existing lot and tract numbers are changed when new housing developments are constructed. The Assessor's Parcel Number should be included (some lenders require it), but it should not be used in lieu of a legal description.

Enter lot and tract numbers. Use an addendum for a lengthy legal description. If you cannot verify the legal description, show "Please refer to Preliminary Title Report," and let the lender obtain the correct legal description.

OWNER'S, OCCUPANT'S, AND BORROWER'S NAMES

Appraisers typically file their appraisals and reference material by property address, while lenders file their loans by the borrower's name and loan numbers. Therefore, the borrower's name or loan number must be provided in the subject section of the report to enable lenders to match the appraisal with the corresponding file.

Enter the names and status of all the parties who have a significant affiliation with the property on the owner/occupant line or on the line below lender/client. For example, show "Dave Jones, owner," "Dave Jones, tenant," or "Dave Jones, borrower."

DON'T FORGET TO VERIFY OCCUPANCY

Occupancy should always be verified. If the borrower will not be occupying the property, the income approach must be incorporated into the appraisal report. Although it is not a requirement, when the property is vacant, this should be noted in the report as there is always the possibility that substantial damage could occur if the property is not being protected. For this reason, the lender might want to recheck the condition of the property before the loan is funded.

CENSUS TRACT NUMBERS

Always use six numbers for the census tract entry. For example, 45.10 should be shown as 0045.10. In remote areas where census tract numbers have not been assigned, show six zeros, that is, 0000.00. Note: This illustration refers to California census tract numbers; hence, appraisers conducting business in other states should follow local lender's requirements for inputting census tract numbers.

It is extremely critical to enter accurate census tract numbers because government officials evaluate lending policies by census tract areas.

SALES PRICE AND DATE OF SALE

Enter the sales price on the form. For "date of sale" enter the date the contracts were signed. When the appraisal is being written for purposes other than a sale, show "not applicable" (N/A) in these two spaces. Or, if the appraiser knows that the appraisal will be used for a refinance transaction, this should be indicated on the form.

Sales History

You must include a one-year sales history of the subject property. Also, if the subject is listed for sale, or has been listed for sale within the past year, pertinent data, including the length of time the property was listed, must be included in the report.

If you find there have been no transactions within the time limits set forth, the appraisal should so state.

When you appraise property that has recently sold, include the length of time the property was listed. For example, "The subject property is in escrow at a reported sales price of $175,000., which was verified by the appraiser by reviewing the Contract of Sale. The property was listed for less than one month and last transferred July 1985 for $163,000."

In the event that the appraiser is unable to obtain or verify the sales price, date of sale, past sales history, or listing information, a statement should be included explaining why the information was not available for the appraiser's review.

LOAN CHARGES AND CONCESSIONS

The lender must tell the appraiser about all financing data and sales concessions for the property that will be, or have been, granted by anyone associated with the transaction. Generally, this can be accomplished by providing the appraiser a copy of the complete, ratified sales contract for the property that is to be appraised. If the lender is aware of additional pertinent information that is not included in the sales contract, the lender should inform the appraiser.

Information that must be disclosed includes settlement charges, loan fees or charges, discounts to the sales price, payment of condominium/PUD fees, interest rate buydowns or other below-market-rate financing, credits or refunds of the borrower's expenses, absorption of monthly payments, assignment of rent payments, and nonrealty items that were included in the transaction.

Obtain a *certified* copy of the Contract of Sale, and Amendments to the Contract of Sale, from the lender, listing agent, or selling agent. If you are aware of any loan charges, concessions, or incentives furnished by the seller, enter all the relevant data in this space or in another area of the report. When the data are available, always provide the dollar amount of the loan charges or concessions.

Acknowledging Sales Concessions

On page two, in the comments and conditions section of the report, to show that you have given consideration to sales concessions, loan charges, and incentives when you arrived at your final estimate of value, include a statement, such as "The appraiser is aware that the seller is paying nonrecurring closing costs of approximately $4,000., which is typical in today's market. Appropriate consideration was rendered in concluding a final estimate of value."

REAL ESTATE TAXES AND TAX YEAR

Dated tax information or tax information that is not relative to the present value of the property is of little consequence to the lender. Lenders need current estimated taxes based on the appraised value or the sales price, whichever is greater, because this information is used to determine to what extent the amount of taxes may affect the value and marketability of the property as well as for estimating the borrower's payment schedule.

Effective Tax Rate

The effective tax rate should be included. Multiply the rate times the sales price or appraised value (whichever is greater) to determine the estimated taxes. Current tax rates should be obtained from the appropriate county assessor's office. Rather than making numerous telephone calls, it is more time effective to visit the county assessor's office personally each year, whenever new tax rates become effective, to obtain a complete list of the tax rates in each area where you typically appraise property

Special Assessments

The appraiser should identify any present or forthcoming special assessments in the subject neighborhood. A statement must be included addressing the effect of special assessments on value and marketability.

Older neighborhoods can encounter special assessments for installation, replacement, or repair of sewers, streets, sidewalks, curbs, gutters, or street lights. City officials or tax assessors can provide information relating to recent and proposed improvements in the area. It is prudent to make inquiries, even though the improvements may not require a special assessment, because a description of the improvements can provide an indication that neighborhood maintenance levels are improving.

Special assessments for maintenance of public streets, parkways, sidewalks, curbs, gutters, or sewers may also be imposed on buyers of new tract homes; therefore, always find out whether owners are liable for special assessments in addition to paying property taxes.

IDENTIFYING LENDERS AND CLIENTS

Enter the name of the originator of the report. Also, enter the status (borrower, owner, lender), if applicable. The space below lender/client can be used for identifying a client, lender, or the appraisal company name.

HOW TO IDENTIFY PROPERTY RIGHTS

The appraiser must identify the exact property rights to be appraised: leasehold or fee simple.

Leasehold Land

The "lessor" holds title to and conveys the right to use and occupy the property. The "lessee" possesses the right to use or occupy the property under the terms of the lease agreement.

There are many varieties of leasehold terms and conditions. In some instances, property that is referred to as "leased" is actually covered by a deferred purchase plan whereby the homeowner (lessee) pays the lessor "x" dollars per month until a certain specified date, at which time, the homeowner receives full title to the land. In other instances, the lessee pays rent for the use of the land until a certain specified date, at which time, the lessee has the opportunity to exercise an option to purchase the land, either for a predetermined price or at current market value, depending on the terms of the lease.

We are familiar with one particular tract where the land could be purchased for "x" dollars as of a specified date. If the land was not purchased on, or before, the specified date, the purchase price would escalate to a higher dollar amount that would, again, be valid until a certain specified date. If the land was not purchased by the second predetermined date, the land would then have to be purchased at current market value as of a predetermined date. Hence, a great variety of sales prices is exhibited in this particular tract because of the varied prices paid for the land when the options were exercised. Homeowners who did not exercise the option to purchase the land in a timely manner are having a difficult time trying to market their property, and they are finding that they have far less equity in their homes than do the property owners who purchased their land 10 or 15 years ago.

The preceding example emphasizes the importance of always examining the terms and conditions of leases because each property in a particular development could have different lease terms, rents, options, and negotiation provisions.

Appraisals of leasehold interest must include a meaningful description of the principal terms of the lease, including dollar amount of the rent, terms, options, and negotiation provisions. The appraiser should include a statement addressing the possible effect of the leasehold interest on marketability and value. Marketability can be seriously affected if the lessee must pay current market value for the land, especially when the type of improvements on the property do not warrant paying current market value for the land.

The terms of the lease can be obtained from the owner's legal documents, the lessor, participating listing or sales agent, or title companies. Real estate agents who regularly farm leasehold neighborhoods usually have copies of leases in their files.

CAUTION

Always review the "Master Lease" for lease terms because "Subleases" may not contain all of the full particulars. Comparable sales used in the appraisal report must have similar leasehold terms.

Planned Unit Developments

A "planned unit development" or PUD, as defined by FHLMC, is a development that has all the following characteristics:

1. The individual unit owners own a parcel of land improved with a dwelling. This ownership is not in common with other unit owners.
2. The development is administered by a homeowner's association that owns and is obligated to maintain property and improvements within the development (greenbelts, recreation facilities, and parking areas, and other common areas) for the common use and benefit of the unit owners.
3. The unit owners have an automatic, nonseverable interest in the homeowner's association and pay mandatory assessments.

For the purpose of this definition a condominium is not a PUD.

Appraisers must pay special attention to the location of the project, the location of the individual unit within the project, the project's amenities, and the amount and purpose of the owner's association assessment, since the marketability and value of the individual units in a project generally depend on the marketability and appeal of the project itself.

Describe the project amenities (private streets, parking, open tennis courts, common landscaped or greenbelt areas, etc.) in the addendum, "Planned Unit Development Project Information." The following information must also be provided:

1. If the project has been completed, number of phases, number of units, and number sold.
2. If the project is incomplete, planned number of phases, number of units, and number of units sold.
3. If the project is being developed in phases, total units in

subject phase, number of completed units, number of sold units, and number of rented units.

4. A description of the common elements or recreational facilities.
5. Owner's association fees per month for the unit.
6. The utilities that are included in the owner's association fees.
7. A comment about whether the unit's owner's association fees are reasonable in comparison to those for units in other projects of similar quality and design.
8. A comment about whether the project appears to be well maintained.

Homeowner's Association Dues

Show the monthly amount of the homeowner's association dues in the subject section of the report under "HOA $/Mo."

Appraisers should habitually ask property owners whether there are any common areas or association dues because these factors are not always readily apparent by visual inspection of the area. For instance, owners might be required to pay association dues for slope maintenance only, for maintenance of a small park within the development, or for storage yards provided by the association for campers and boats.

In some neighborhoods, owners are obligated to pay monthly dues to a homeowner's association that exists only to regulate the appearance of all the properties in the neighborhood. That is, changes cannot be made to any of the properties in the neighborhood with respect to colors of paint, types and colors of trim or roofs, landscaping, or yard improvements without the approval of the homeowner's association.

This situation is easily recognizable by noticing the complete uniformity throughout the neighborhood.

GENERAL DESCRIPTION OF THE NEIGHBORHOOD

Urban, pertains to cities or towns
Suburban, living in or pertaining to the outlying residential districts of the city
Rural, residential district in the country

When rural is designated, provide proximity to employment centers, availability and distance to shopping, schools, and recreational facilities; accessibility to all weather roads; and all other factors that relate to market appeal. Address other pertinent information that will enable readers to identify "vacation homes" as opposed to "full-time residences."

Percentages of Built-up Areas

Enter the percentage of lots improved with buildings. When less than 25 percent of the land is developed with residential improvements, the appraiser should explain the reasons and their effect on marketability. Get in touch with local building and planning officials to establish growth patterns.

How to Show Growth Rates

Some appraisers indicate "slow" when a property is located in an older established city with little or no vacant land available for new construction. This, usually, is a misnomer. There is, or should be, constant and uniform replacement of older buildings, which would indicate "stable" (or steady) growth patterns. "Slow" could be interpreted as an indication that there is a decline in property values because the neighborhood is not exhibiting proper maintenance and growth levels. According to some lender's guidelines, however, growth rate actually refers to population growth rather than construction of new buildings. Whenever "slow" is designated, an explanation is required.

Property Value, Demand, Supply, and Marketing Time

These three elements should be considered at the same time to avoid conflicting statements in this area of the report and in the sales comparison analysis. For instance, a conflict can arise, which would require an explanation, if "stable" was indicated and time adjustments or sales in escrow or listings were used to support an *increase* in property values.

When "increasing" property values is indicated, very current market data should be included to support your representation of increasing property values. Availability of favorable financing or a *shortage* of homes for sale (seller's market) can result in price *increases*. An *oversupply* of homes for sale (buyer's market) normally results in stabilized or *decreasing* property values. Thus, consider how each element is affected by the other when you check the different boxes. Make sure that the comparable sales data, comments regarding the comparable sales data, neighborhood description, and the subject value correspond to the marketing trend that you have indicated.

Marketing Time

Marketing time is the average time that will take to sell a property, in the same market and similar to the subject property, when it is offered for sale at a price that is close to its true market value. Ask real estate agents for their opinions of average marketing time and analyze current and historical market data to determine a marketing pattern for the area. Multiple-listing books usually show the number of days the property was listed before it sold. As you are inspecting different neighborhoods, note the occurrence and duration of "for sale" signs, which will also provide a good indication of marketing patterns.

How to Recognize Declining Market Trends

Whenever declining, oversupply, or over six months is designated, an explanation is required. When a declining trend is indicated, appraisers must provide factual and specific information to support their opinion, and they should comment on the probability of its continuance. For example, "The properties located at . . . (the appraiser should include specific addresses) reflect very poor maintenance and the yards are overgrown with weeds and littered with trash. The likelihood of a continuing declining trend is evidenced by the number of properties in the neighborhood reflecting undesirable maintenance levels."

WARNING SIGNS OF A DECLINING MARKET

Warning signs that a neighborhood may be declining are cars parked on lawns; excessive vandalism; graffiti on fences and buildings; high percentages of homes in foreclosure; an abundance of "for sale" signs in evidence; high percentages of absentee owners; high percentages of unskilled workers; workers representing only one industry; encroaching commercial, industrial, or multifamily properties; lack of or discontinuance of public amenities; poorly maintained public amenities; or evidence of uncompleted housing.

Uncompleted housing is generally a sign of a slow or

limited market. An oversupply of housing is not desirable because it indicates that houses are selling slowly with a lot of competition. Forced sales, cause by an oversupply of housing, is frequently a buyer's market situation and prices will decline accordingly.

Present Land Use Percentages

Enter the percentage of predominant land uses in the neighborhood. Include condominiums and planned unit developments with the single-family percentage. Parks, lakes, golf courses, and other similar uses may be shown under vacant land use; however, an explanatory statement should be provided in the neighborhood comments section. When there is a significant amount of vacant or undeveloped land in the neighborhood, the appraiser should include comments to that effect in the neighborhood comments section of the report to assure that the neighborhood is adequately described.

RECONCILE YOUR DESCRIPTIONS

The description of the neighborhood (in the comments section of the report) must be concurrent with the percentages shown. When the property is described as being within close walking distance to shopping or employment, do not omit a land use percentage for commercial or industrial uses. When the neighborhood is described as "mixed improved," be certain that the percentages indicated relate to your description; that is, do you mean mixed land uses or mixed architectural styles, sizes, and ages of homes?

The mix of property types in the neighborhood should be compatible. Consider whether a property located in a mixed-use neighborhood will sustain value over a long period of time. Comment on any inharmonious land uses and their effect on value and marketability.

Land use change refers to a change in the way land is being used, for example, from vacant land to built-up, from detached single-family residences to income property, residential to commercial or industrial, and so forth. Consider recent changes, as well as the potential for change.

Correlate your ratings in the neighborhood analysis (built-up, growth rate, property values, demand, supply, marketing time, land use percentage, and predominant occupancy) to changes in land use. Changes in land use should be identified, and the impact on property value and marketability should be fully described in the neighborhood comments section of the appraisal report.

How Land Use Changes Affect Property Value

Always get in touch with public officials when you appraise property in neighborhoods where there is a potential for land use changes. Changes from single-family residential zoning to other uses can be detrimental to value and should be identified. Conversely, changes in land uses can have a positive influence on value. For example, "downzoning" (new zoning laws result in a change from commercial to residential, residential income to single-family residential, or high density to low density) may halt the construction of additional apartments, commercial property, or industrial property with a resultant effect of increased demand and pride of ownership in the area accompanied by an increase in value.

Establishing Predominant Occupancy

Predominant occupancy refers to occupancy, not building types. Vacant refers to finished, but unoccupied, buildings. A check ("x") or a percentage may be used to denote occupancy.

When there is a predominance of nonowner-occupied properties in the neighborhood, or a relatively small apportionment of owners over tenants (e.g., 60 percent owners and 40 percent tenants), an explicit account of long-term stability and maintenance levels should be provided. An excessive number of tenant-occupied properties can result in rapid deterioration of a neighborhood due to the lack of pride of ownership that owner-occupied properties usually exhibit.

MAINTAIN CONSISTENCY

Predominant occupancy should be consistent with the present land use percentages. When you show tenant occupancy, don't leave the reviewer wondering whether you neglected to show a land use percentage for income property. Describe the tenant-occupied properties. Are they single-family residences, two- to four-family or multifamily income properties, commercial or industrial properties?

Determining Occupancy

Consult with real estate agents who consistently list and sell property in the subject neighborhood to determine the status of the occupants and the likelihood of change. Typically, real estate agents maintain lists of owners and occupants accompanied by comments noting the possibility of a property transfer. Owner occupancy status can also be obtained from public records (public records will show a mailing address for the owner that differs from the property address) and local homeowners.

Neighborhood Vacancy Ratio

When the neighborhood vacancy rate exceeds 5 percent, further explanation is required. What is the total estimated vacancy rate, and what factors contribute to the high percentage of vacancy? Are you referring to single-family residences, income property, stores, offices, other types of commercial property, or industrial property? Are you referring to houses that are not rented or houses that cannot be sold? Consider poor management, maintenance levels, social factors, high unemployment rate, land use changes, and other economic factors. Are the rents competitive? Is this situation curable; if so, how? Is it likely that the situation will worsen or improve? Discuss the absorption potential, supply, and demand factors.

SINGLE-FAMILY HOUSING PRICE AND AGE RANGES

Indicate the low, high, and predominant prices that represent the majority of the homes in the subject neighborhood; excluding high and low extremes, that is, if most of the homes are in the $250,000. to $265,000. range and a couple of homes sold for $240,000., omit them from the range.

Age Range and Predominant Age

The age range should reflect the oldest and newest ages of single-family residential properties; however, isolated high and low extremes should be excluded from the range. The predominant age is the one that is the most common or most frequently found in the neighborhood. The appraiser may state the predominant age as a single figure or as a range (when that is more appropriate). Appraisers should select independently the properties they use to represent the age range and predominant age, rather than merely relying on the same properties they used to illustrate the price range and predominant price.

How Price and Age Ranges Affect Marketability

The price and age range in a neighborhood relate to the marketability of a home. Marketability is usually affected to a greater extent as properties approach or exceed the higher or lower end of the age and price ranges; therefore, the ranges should reflect prices and ages *in the subject neighborhood* to define marketability and stability of value properly.

Less expensive homes can benefit by an increase in value if they are located in close proximity to more expensive homes, and price increases of more expensive homes can be affected by the close proximity of less desirable homes. Refer to the principles of progression and regression. Age and price ranges of nearby homes (located outside of the exact boundaries of the subject neighborhood) that influence value and marketability of homes in the subject neighborhood should be described in the neighborhood comments section of the report.

Always correlate the sales prices and ages of the comparables with the neighborhood price and age range. When the sales prices and ages of the comparables approach or exceed the neighborhood price and age range, an explanation should be provided.

Establishing Predominant Price

The predominant price is that which is the most common or most frequently found in the neighborhood. The appraiser may state the predominant price as a single figure or as a range (if that is more appropriate).

On more than one occasion, we have reviewed appraisals reflecting varied predominant prices even though the homes were located in the same neighborhood and the appraisals were written by the same appraiser. Varied predominant prices can be the result of the appraiser's inability to define the predominant price, an oversight on the part of the appraiser, or predominant prices that have been adjusted to coincide with the appraised value.

Appraisers should make every effort to define the predominant price realistically because lenders must consider predominant prices when they are rating the stability of value throughout the life of the loan. When the appraised value of a home lies toward the lower or middle of the neighborhood price range, it is more likely that the value will increase or at least remain constant if the neighborhood is receiving proper maintenance and there are no adverse changes in land uses. When the appraised value exceeds the predominant price, marketability may be affected because buyers looking for a higher-priced home would likely look in a neighborhood where homes are more conforming and are equal or higher in price. Consequently, greater consideration must be given to stability of value.

Dealing with Values Exceeding Predominant Price

When you appraise a four-bedroom home in a neighborhood where the majority of homes are smaller three-bedroom dwellings, state the predominant price of the three-bedroom homes. Consider the marketing period of the properties in the upper price range (in this case, four-bedroom homes) as well as past, present, and future price increases. If the marketing time is typical for the area and prices are stable or increasing, the following statement might be incorporated into the report:

"The subject value exceeds the predominant price because the neighborhood is predominantly improved with smaller three-bedroom homes. A review of market history indicates that there is sufficient demand for homes, similar in size and value to the subject, in this neighborhood; therefore, the subject is not considered to be an overimprovement for the neighborhood."

How to Handle Overimprovements

When the subject value approaches or exceeds the predominant price, and the property is an overimprovement for the neighborhood, the appraiser must form a supportable opinion relative to the necessity for, and the amount of, a deduction for an overimprovement. In other words, include sufficient market data in the report to substantiate market adjustments. You can acknowledge your consideration of overimprovements in the following manner:

"The appraised value exceeds the predominant neighborhood price because the pool, spa, and room additions are overimprovements for the neighborhood. The overimprovements have been recognized and adjusted for in the cost approach and the market analysis."

NEIGHBORHOOD ANALYSIS RATINGS

These ratings are to be based on comparison, by the appraiser, of the subject neighborhood with competing neighborhoods considering the *present and future* effect these factors have on continued market appeal for residential properties because the lender must consider stability throughout the life of the loan. Explain any changes, either favorable or unfavorable, that have occurred, or are likely to occur, and the effect on marketability as a result of the change. When you apply the ratings, do not rate the subject neighborhood with a noncompetitive area because different income groups may place more weight on some factors than others. The appraiser must explain any ratings of fair or poor.

GOOD: This rating is to be applied when the characteristics of the subject neighborhood are outstanding and superior to those found in competing neighborhoods.

AVERAGE: The elements being rated are equal to the norm found to be acceptable in competing neighborhoods.

FAIR: This rating is to be used when the factors concerned are below what is typical for comparable neighborhoods.

POOR: A rating of this nature is appropriate if the characteristics are either nonexistent or in such small supply that single-family residential values are, or may be, adversely affected.

A rating of "none" or "nonexistent" is not acceptable. If public transportation, recreational facilities, or other civic amenities are nonexistent, but this is typical for the subject neighborhood and competing properties, then "average" should be checked since the condition is typical of the subject and competing neighborhoods.

AVOID UNNECESSARY EXPLANATIONS

Two ratings in one area should be explained as your exact meaning can be confusing to the reader of the report. Correlate the ratings with the description of the subject in the neighborhood comments section of the report. When you check average and good for the general appearance of the properties in the subject neighborhood, you are indicating that the general appearance of the homes is equal to *and* better than homes in competing neighborhoods where all the homes reflect average general appearance. If this is true, include an explanation. When homes in competing neighborhoods reflect average to good general appearance as well, average should be checked because they are equal to the subject.

Always give adequate consideration to the ratings when you are filling out the form because underwriters consider every section of the appraisal, including the ratings, when they evaluate property for lending purposes and a proper evaluation cannot be made if conflicting statements are made throughout the appraisal. Consider the following examples of conflicting statements.

Example 1: In the report, the appraiser made the following comment: "The homes are superior in quality and appeal to homes in surrounding neighborhoods." However, this statement is contradicted because the appraiser indicated "average" in the neighborhood analysis ratings.

Example 2: Sales analysis comments have been known to include comments, such as "A wider than typical area was surveyed for comparable sales because the subject tract is the only development within a three-mile radius with common area recreational facilities." And the appraiser checked "average" in the neighborhood analysis ratings for recreational facilities. A rating of "good" would be indicated because of the superiority of the amenities to the surrounding, competing properties.

Make sure that ratings, sales analysis comments, neighborhood comments, the description of the subject, and all the other factors addressed in the appraisal report are interrelated. The ratings, descriptions, and analyses must be consistent throughout the appraisal report or a written explanation will be required.

Stability of Employment

Consider the number of employment opportunities as well as the variety and type of industries in the neighborhood. Also, consider proximity and accessibility to employment opportunities in other regions. Areas with only one type of industry would not be considered as favorably as those that have a broader variety of employment with greater stability.

Convenience to Employment

Contemplate the distance, both in terms of time and mileage, to employment facilities keeping in mind the economic makeup of the neighborhood. The availability, cost, and convenience of public transportation should be considered as an alternative to customary means of private transportation.

Convenience to Shopping

The appraiser should rate the neighborhood in terms of distance, time, and required means of transportation to shopping for daily necessities. Again, consider the economic makeup of the neighborhood. If the occupants cannot afford private transportation, neighborhood convenience stores should be within walking distance or be readily accessible by means of public transportation.

Convenience to Schools

Convenience to schools is a very important factor to consider. Developments that have schools within the neighborhood are usually far more desirable than neighborhoods where children have to cross major traffic streets to reach the school. If public bus transportation is required, are the children transported to local schools or to schools in a less desirable area? Are the parents responsible for transporting their children to school? Consider the time and distance to the school.

Never rely on locations of schools designated in map books because school district policies determine which school children must attend. Sometimes schools are within walking distance; nevertheless, the children are transported to distant schools. Also, the schools shown in street directories may have been closed or put to another use. Local homeowners or real estate agents can help you identify the actual convenience to schools.

Adequacy of Public Transportation

Indicate the adequacy of public transportation serving the neighborhood. Rate the adequacy and convenience to employment centers, departure centers of public transportation, shopping, and schools. When public transportation is not available in the subject and competing neighborhoods, there probably isn't any need for it, in which case, "average" would be indicated because the lack of transportation would be consistent with demand. The need for public transportation depends on the type of community as well as the desires and needs of the occupants.

Recreational Facilities

What type of recreational facilities are available and how convenient are they? Are the recreational facilities in the subject neighborhood limited as compared to those in competing neighborhoods? Neighborhoods with good recreational facilities are more likely to remain viable, because of continuing demand, than are communities without conveniently located public swimming pools, parks, and recreation centers.

A rating of "good" should be indicated when the neighborhood displays ocean, lake, wooded, or golf course orientation; association-owned facilities; or other amenities that are superior to features of competing or surrounding neighborhoods.

If there is a demand for recreational facilities, but they are nonexistent, or if existing facilities are poorly supervised or poorly maintained, a rating of "fair" or "poor" should be indicated.

Adequacy of Utilities

Rate the extent to which the utility systems (water, sewer, electricity, and gas) serving the neighborhood are adequate to fulfill the needs of the residents as compared to those of competing neighborhoods. Consideration of the utilities includes public, private (community or subdivisions), and individual. If there is a likelihood of costly special assessments for installation or repair of public or private utility systems, marketability and value may be affected. Thus, rate the neighborhood accordingly.

If property values are unaffected by the lack of sewer lines, gas, electricity, or public water at this time, are values likely to be affected at some future date? Buyers would probably discount the price to allow for the cost of installing utilities; however, the value of the property will increase once the utilities have been installed.

When you cannot find comparable sales to support adjustments for utilities, obtain actual installation costs from city or county officials. Then, use the actual cost for your market adjustments and reference your cost source.

Property Compatibility Rating

Remember, you are rating the *neighborhood* (not the property) in this section of the report. Are the majority of properties in the subject neighborhood conforming with respect to land uses, lot sizes, price ranges, building ages, and styles? If competing neighborhoods are also conforming in land uses, lot sizes, and so on, a rating of "average" would be indicated. When the subject neighborhood consists of conforming single-family residences as opposed to a competing neighborhood with mixed uses or varied building styles and ages, the subject neighborhood should be rated "good." A well-planned, association-maintained community, for example, should be rated "good" when the conformity and maintenance levels exceed those found in competing neighborhoods.

Protection from Detrimental Conditions

Are there any present or possible land uses that could affect value and marketability in the subject neighborhood? Consider proximity to income, commercial, and industrial property as well as proximity to heavy traffic streets, freeways, airports, and sources of air pollution. Are competing neighborhoods similarly affected? Has this condition, historically, been acceptable in this neighborhood? Public maintenance of sidewalks, streets, signs, street lights, and other public facilities should also be considered in this rating.

Police and Fire Protection

This rating covers the extent to which police and fire protection are adequate and equivalent to the protection provided to competing neighborhoods. Evidence of excessive vandalism and high crime rates should also be considered, because marketability and value will most certainly be affected by these factors.

General Appearance of Properties

Consider the maintenance of the structures and the yard improvements. To sustain value, older neighborhoods, particularly, should show evidence of additions, remodeling, repairs, and upgrading. The quality of these items should be in keeping with the subject neighborhood as well as competing neighborhoods. A neighborhood that does not display signs of rehabilitation, or is declining in maintenance levels, should be appropriately rated "fair" or "poor," as applicable. Fair or poor ratings should be accompanied by a detailed description and comments on the likelihood of a continuing decline in maintenance levels.

Appeal to Market

This rating is an overall summary of all the factors that affect value and marketability including location, land uses, occupancy, property compatibility, appearance of properties, and so forth. Consider long-term stability of marketability and value.

PRACTICAL SUGGESTIONS FOR WRITING NEIGHBORHOOD COMMENTS

A relatively common misconception occurs because of the design of the appraisal form; that is, since there are only four lines in the neighborhood comments section of the appraisal form, a very brief description of the neighborhood is all that is needed. Also, rather than considering marketability throughout the life of the loan, some appraisers are only concerned with the present value of the property; thus, they rate the property accordingly.

Inadequate evaluations, analyses, and descriptions make it very difficult for a reviewer or a loan underwriting officer to make a valid decision. When you appraise property in a very conforming neighborhood, a simple description of the neighborhood would be sufficient. In all other instances, make certain that complete descriptions and explanations are provided that will ensure the probability that anyone reading the report can readily make a prudent underwriting decision.

The limited amount of space on the form sometimes intimidates even the most prolific writers. If you are having this problem, experiment with writing comments, descriptions, and explanations on a separate sheet of paper. Describe the neighborhood in such a way that the reader could actually visualize it. Recompose your thoughts; make sure the commentary corresponds to your ratings in the neighborhood analysis; then transfer the information to the form. Or write the neighborhood description on an addendum, which is much easier than is struggling to compose a description that will fit neatly in the space provided. When you use addenda, the likelihood of including all the pertinent data needed to describe the neighborhood adequately will be increased.

If you have collected all the relevant information and you are still having difficulty expressing your thoughts as aptly as you wish, consider the following commentary:

Avoid vague words or those words, or statements, that could be subject to misinterpretation. Write clear, concise statements that anyone can easily understand. Ask yourself why you have made certain statements. If they are meaningless or irrelevant, eliminate them. Did you provide all the explanations, as required, from the preceding neighborhood section of the report? For instance, explanations regarding declining values, oversupply, over six month's marketing time, excessive vacancies, and fair or poor ratings?

Socioeconomic Characteristics

Did you consider and comment on the social and economic characteristics in the neighborhood that presently, or are likely to, affect the value and marketability of the property?

Keep the socioeconomic structure of the neighborhood in mind because conditions that have a negative influence in one neighborhood could have a positive influence in another neighborhood. For example, for economic or personal reasons, close proximity and easy access to employment centers, entertainment and cultural facilities, parks, shopping, and schools can be considered a definite asset to some buyers. Generally, the more affluence a neighborhood exhibits, the greater likelihood that external influences will affect value and marketability.

Adverse External Influences and Mixed Uses

Adverse external influences as well as mixed-use neighborhoods should have strong offsetting factors to sustain value and marketability. Therefore, never indicate mixed land uses, changing land uses, or adverse external influences without commenting on neighborhood acceptability and long-term stability of value and marketability.

Small neighborhood convenience stores are usually not thought of as incompatible uses; however, properties that back or side to the stores will sustain external obsolescence caused by traffic, noise, and inadequate protection from intruders.

Sometimes, homes sell at the same, or nearly the same, prices as similar properties in the neighborhood even though some type of external obsolescence is present. You will probably find, however, that the property was listed for a much longer period of time than the properties that sold unaffected by external obsolescence. Therefore, a relative adjustment should be made to compensate for the extended marketing period. Also, when there is a shortage of homes in the market, properties with external obsolescence sometimes sell for as much or sometimes even more than homes without external obsolescence due to increased demand; therefore, a deduction for adverse influences may not be relevant.

Mixed Uses: When the subject is located in a mixed-use neighborhood and the uses are found to be acceptable to typical buyers, include a comment, such as

"Apartments, commercial stores, offices, and industrial properties are interspersed throughout the neighborhood. Any adverse influences from proximity to the varied type of improvements are offset by proximity and easy access to employment centers, parks, entertainment centers, shopping, and schools. Long-term sustainment of marketability and value is evidenced by good and consistent maintenance throughout the neighborhood as well as steadily increasing prices."

Never include a simple statement that the subject is located in a "mixed-use" neighborhood without explaining what you mean by mixed use. Do you mean that the neighborhood consists of both older and newer homes? one- and two-story homes or different designs and styles? single-family residences and apartments, industrial, and commercial uses— or a combination of these elements?

External Influences: Did you describe all the adverse external influences? Did you provide a basis for any deductions for external obsolescence or lack of adjustments? Does the external obsolescence affect only the subject property or is it evidenced throughout the neighborhood? Historically, has this situation been acceptable? Are there any buffers provided to reduce the effects of negative external influences?

Land Uses: Did you address changes in land uses and their effect on value and marketability? When a residential neighborhood is changing from owner-occupied single-family residences to income property or other uses, it is likely that there will be a deterioration in maintenance levels and the general appearance of the single-family residences followed by a decline in value.

Did you describe the location and effect of toxic waste sites and landfills in the area?

Other Factors to Consider

1. Is there an excessive number of listings in the subject or surrounding neighborhoods or an excessive number of sales? If so, why? Is this situation due to inadequate maintenance of public amenities, such as streets, curbs, parkways, trees, parks, or recreational facilities? Or maybe this situation was caused by a loss of public transportation, quality and

availability of schools, rapidly increasing taxes, inadequate property maintenance, an increase in tenant-occupied property, or changes in land uses? An excessive number of listings might be caused by a seller's market situation wherein many properties are promptly listed in an attempt to make extraordinary profits.

2. If there is an overabundance of new construction in the area, find out whether the new homes are selling within a reasonable period of time. If they are not, eventually the builder may have to reduce the prices or add incentives to dispose of excess inventory. In this event, resales in the area may be affected by the discounted prices and added incentives.

3. Consider and discuss the age and life cycle of the neighborhood. Older neighborhoods should show signs of rehabilitation. Are the homes being modernized and expanded? Discuss the trend in the neighborhood—is it improving, remaining stable, or declining?

4. Discuss the characteristics of the neighborhood considering architectural styles, types of property, amenities, age, condition, and maintenance levels. Does the neighborhood consist of both one- and two-story dwellings; two-, three-, and four-bedroom homes; view-, water-, or equestrian-oriented property? Is the neighborhood particularly desirable due to larger than typical lots, estate size lots, terraced sites, rolling terrain, "single-load" streets (homes built on terraced hillsides with houses on only one side of the street), quiet residential streets?

5. If the property is located in a planned unit development, have you fully described the condition and type of common area amenities?

6. If the property is situated on leasehold land, have you addressed continuing market appeal in addition to describing the principal terms of the lease, including rent, options, and negotiation provisions?

7. Have you described the neighborhood boundaries? Since most neighborhoods are defined by a major cross street, or some other man-made or natural boundary, a reviewer might question the validity of comparables selected from outside of the apparent perimeters of the neighborhood unless you demonstrate that the subject development actually does consist of properties located on both sides of an apparent boundary line.

Anytime that there might be a question regarding your interpretation of neighborhood boundaries, describe the similarity in physical characteristics and amenities, show the boundaries of the neighborhood on a location map, and include photos to substantiate your assertion further.

8. Consider any additional information related to value and marketability that will aid the reader in making decisions.

9. If you are using canned neighborhood comments, are the comments compatible with the rest of the appraisal report?

RATING STABILITY OF VALUE

Neighborhood ratings are based on amenities that buyers consider important when they are selecting a home. Neighborhood amenities have to be considered acceptable and desirable by a large enough segment of buyers to support an active market for the property under consideration.

Some of the causes of deterioration within a neighborhood are lack of nearby employment or poor access to employment centers; inadequate or inconvenient shopping; undesirable educational facilities (not up to the levels of surrounding school districts); limited recreational facilities as compared to competing neighborhoods; a high community tax level; limited public sewers, utilities, or trash collection; poorly maintained streets; inadequate police or fire protection; incompatible or mixed uses within the neighborhood; and objectionable noise or air pollution. Eventually, these problems will result in deterioration within the neighborhood followed by slow market conditions, a high turnover rate, decreased pride of ownership, and a decline in the general market.

No matter how good a property is, it alone cannot overcome economic obsolescence in a neighborhood. When it appears that properties in the neighborhood are taking longer than typical to sell, find out why. Discuss neighborhood amenities with local owners and real estate agents, and analyze market history as well to determine the reasons for an extended marketing period and the probability of declining values.

NEIGHBORHOOD COMMENTS—EXAMPLES

Example 1: The neighborhood consists of 18- to 27-year old, average-quality, one- and two-story dwellings reflecting above-average maintenance. Many of the homes have conforming additions as well as modernized kitchens and bathrooms. Homes in surrounding neighborhoods feature varied, but pleasing, architectural styles. Maintenance levels and upgrading found in neighboring communities are comparable to those of the subject neighborhood. This community is well protected from detrimental influences by zoning and deed restrictions. Convenience to schools, shopping, employment centers, recreational facilities, and other civic amenities is good.

Example 2: This neighborhood has good proximity and accessibility to the local labor market which offers diversified employment. Prices have been steadily increasing due to locational appeal and above-average maintenance levels throughout the neighborhood. No influences that could have an adverse influence on value or marketability were noted.

Example 3: Homes in this neighborhood vary in age, size, and architectural style. Market appeal is enhanced by the well-maintained, customized appearance of the homes. Amenities include estate-size lots, fair to panoramic views, easy access to civic amenities, and proximity to employment centers via the San Diego Freeway, which is located 2 miles west.

Example 4: This is a well-established residential neighborhood improved with both older and newer custom-built homes. Newer tract-built homes are located directly north of this neighborhood. Maintenance levels range from average to very good. The appraised value exceeds the predominant neighborhood price because the subject is one of the largest custom-built homes in the immediate neighborhood, and it is situated on a much larger than typical lot for the immediate neighborhood. This is typical and common in this community because properties of this type are scattered throughout the city. Historically, marketability and value of the larger homes have not been influenced by the varied types of improvements in the immediate area. Proximity to most public conveniences is good. The Redhill Freeway, which provides ready access to outlying shopping and employment centers, is located 1 mile south.

CHAPTER 9

GENERAL DESCRIPTION AND ANALYSIS OF THE SITE AND LOCATION

Recently, a particular loan under consideration by a local lender required two appraisals. The lender questioned the validity of both appraisals because of the photographs of the pool. One set of photos revealed the top of a pine tree, which appeared to be fully grown, near the outer edge of the pool deck. The second appraiser included a picture of the swimming pool taken from the outer edge of the pool deck looking back toward the residence. The lender went to the property to make a further investigation and discovered that the back of the swimming pool and deck were actually supported by 20-foot caissons because there was a sheer drop from the outer pool deck to the ground below.

This is a good example of a lender's dilemma when the appraiser does not provide adequate and specific information in the appraisal report. The significance of providing as much pertinent information as possible cannot be overly stressed because "little details" can sometimes be critical. In this chapter, which follows the site section of the Uniform Residential Appraisal Report, we will show you how to disclose pertinent site, zoning, and location factors and how to provide satisfactory explanations, so that underwriters can make informed lending decisions.

HOW TO LIST DIMENSIONS AND SITE AREA

List the dimensions of the site and indicate whether the total represents square feet or acres. When adjustments are made for comparable or dissimilar utility in the sales comparison analysis, show the size of the level pad or usable area of the site. If you have an irregular lot with many dimensions, for example, 52.02 / 48.03 × 21.03 / 42.03 × 118 / 131.24 ft., instead of listing all of the dimensions in the appraisal, it is perfectly acceptable to show "irregular—see plat map." The site must be of a size, shape, and topography that is generally acceptable in the market area; if not, further discussion regarding the effect on value is required.

ZONING CLASSIFICATION

Verify and list the zoning classification used by the local municipality. Do not use classifications such as R-1, PD, or R/A by themselves as these descriptions tend to vary among communities; consequently, a reader from out of the area may not be able to interpret them. Show the use, or uses, that the zoning permits, for example, R-1-S (single-family residential, small lot), PDC (planned community, single-family residences and condominiums), R-2-L (two-family residential, large lot, and low-density residential), and so forth. The zoning of all the comparables used in the report should be verified as well because the comparable properties should be situated on sites with similar zoning and uses.

HOW TO CLASSIFY MIXED USES

Properties with "mixed uses," for example, single-family residential dwellings that have a business use (beauty salon, day care center, professional office, etc.) in a residential zoned area, must be given special consideration. The appraiser must consider and address the following factors in the appraisal report:

1. The property must be a single-family dwelling.
2. The use must be a legal, permissible use of the property under the local zoning requirements.
3. The property must not have any special modifications, or plans for special modifications, that would require a significant expenditure to convert back if the property were again used solely for residential purposes.
4. The use must not generate public traffic that could have a possible negative influence on the marketability and value of the subject property.

No special consideration should be given to uses other than residential uses. If the uses are detrimental to value or the uses are not legally permitted, appraisers should immediately get in touch with their client to obtain further instructions. When there are properties located in close proximity to the subject property that have mixed uses of this type, the appraiser should address the amount of foot and vehicular traffic and the influence of the traffic on the marketability and value of the subject property.

HOW TO HANDLE LEGAL BUT NONCONFORMING USES

The use of the property may not conform to current zoning regulations; however, the use may be "legal" because the use is permitted by a variance or, in some instances, a "Grandfather Clause" in zoning regulations; therefore, the property will be classified as "legal but nonconforming."

What Is a Grandfather Clause?

When the property is already in existence, and the use is viable, new zoning regulations, or changes in zoning regulations, may allow the existing use to be continued under a Grandfather Clause (or some other terminology may be used) in zoning regulations. However, the Grandfather Clause may only be in effect for a stipulated period of time, restrictions may not allow for reconstruction of the property if it is partially or completely destroyed by natural causes, reconstruction of the property may be limited to the "footprint" of the original building (exactly the way it was originally built), and certain other stipulations may have to be adhered to in order to continue the existing use, make any alterations to the building, or to reconstruct the building in the event of a natural disaster. Therefore, always discuss zoning, uses, and limitations with city officials.

Variances in Zoning Regulations

When the existing use is permitted by a *variance,* find out how long the variance will be in effect because there may be a specified time limit and the variance may be rescinded if the property is partially or fully destroyed by natural causes.

Also, find out if there are any restrictions with respect to alterations or additions.

Identifying Legal but Nonconforming Uses

Legal but nonconforming uses found in a residential neighborhood might be additions, remodeling, or structural changes that took place before zoning regulations came into existence; nonconforming setbacks; equestrian uses in a residential area; building size; number of stories; placement of the home or garage on the lot; required number of parking spaces; or two units on a single lot.

When a property has a legal but nonconforming use that cannot be continued in the event of a natural disaster, include a statement, such as "The guest house is a legal but nonconforming use under current zoning regulations; however, in the event of partial or complete destruction, current zoning regulations would not permit reconstruction of the guest house. This was confirmed by Mr. Byrd, City of Tempe Planning Department (438) 891-9087." In this instance, value could not be assigned to the guest house.

HIGHEST AND BEST USE

When you appraise a single-family residence that is situated on a lot that is zoned for other uses (income property, commercial, or industrial), you must evaluate the highest and best use of the site. Is there another use that would be more appropriate based on zoning regulations, demand, and predominant land uses in the neighborhood? Is the neighborhood exhibiting a trend or change to another use? Discuss trends and possible uses with city planning officials.

Determining Uses: Factors to Consider

The proposed use must be

1. Legally permitted by deed restrictions, environmental restrictions, and zoning regulations.
2. Physically possible; the size, shape, subsoil, and terrain of the site must allow for development to its full zoning potential.
3. Economically feasible.
4. The most profitable use of the site.

The highest and best use analysis must include two separate studies: the site as if vacant and ready to be put to its highest and best use and the property as improved. If it is not possible to achieve uses in the foreseeable future, the uses should be excluded from consideration. Don't forget about long-term leases: long-term leases may preclude development of the site.

VERIFICATION IS ESSENTIAL

Because use restrictions and zoning regulations are frequently revised, never rely on information provided by owners, real estate agents, or buyers. Always verify zoning, density, and use restrictions with city or county planning and building officials.

The following examples show you why it is important to investigate thoroughly zoning regulations, use restrictions, probable zoning changes, building codes, coastal commission reports, environmental studies, geological studies, physical restrictions, and other factors that affect the highest and best use of the site.

Example 1: The property to be appraised, for refinance purposes, was a 3,500 sq. ft. residence situated on a hilly, acreage site in a highly desirable coastal community. The owner told the appraiser that the parcel could be subdivided into five lots. The house (according to the owner) was worth $600,000., and, supposedly, the four unimproved lots could easily be sold for at least $150,000. each.

When the appraiser got in touch with city planners to find out whether the property could be subdivided, he was told that the property was located in a hazardous slide area. Consequently, the parcel could not be subdivided, and, even if the parcel could be subdivided, nothing could be built on the site because of the slippage problems. Further, the existing residence could not be rebuilt if it were destroyed by natural causes. The appraiser did not continue with the assignment because the property essentially did not have any value.

Example 2: The appraisal was for a construction loan. The owner had just paid $350,000. for the unimproved lot. He planned to grade and terrace the top of this steep lot so he could build a home with a magnificent view. The owner did not know, however, that this lot could not be graded, leveled, or terraced because building codes had been enacted to preserve the natural appeal of this community. Consequently, the lot was worthless. The effects would have been disastrous if the appraiser neglected to find out about the building restrictions and the loan were processed.

Example 3: Don't forget—"little" things can be critical: you even have to find out whether existing trees on unimproved parcels can be moved or removed. A recent appraisal was valued "subject to an oak tree permit" because the owner had to obtain a permit to remove four oak trees from the site before he could obtain a building permit. If the permit were not granted, the uses and value of the site would be substantially reduced.

Development of the Site to Full Zoning Potential

If there is a more appropriate use for the site, on the form show development of the site to its full zoning potential. If the highest and best use is for multiresidential, commercial, or industrial use, a consultation with your client would be in order because it is inappropriate to use a single-family dwelling report form if the appraiser concludes that the highest and best use of the property is a different use.

Document your opinion referencing demand and predominant land uses, the remaining economic life of the property, condition of the property, and neighborhood trends.

Multiresidential Zoning

If the zoning is multiresidential, but the present use is the highest and best use of the site, detail the reasons for your determination, such as "The highest and best use of the site is as presently improved because there is little demand, at this time, for additional income property in the subject neighborhood as evidenced by an analysis of vacancy and absorption factors." Other reasons might be "because restrictive density allowances and parking requirements limit the scope of profitable apartment development at this time" or "because the size of the site restricts alternate uses."

Anytime that you have any problems with appraising property that is nonconforming or legal but nonconforming, and you do not know how to assign value to the property, never guess! Always ask the chief appraiser at the respective lending institution how to handle the problem or discuss the situation with appraisers or underwriters with Fannie Mae or Freddie Mac.

PUBLIC AND PRIVATE UTILITIES

"Public" means the utilities are supplied, maintained, and regulated by the city or county. Further explanations regarding cost, maintenance, and continued service must be provided when the utility systems are owned or operated by the developer or a private company that is not subject to government regulation or financial assistance.

Utilities must meet community standards. Inadequate utilities to the site may result in a loss of value due to loss of site utility. Get in touch with city or county officials to find out whether utilities are scheduled for installation in the near future. Provide an explanation and a cost to cure.

Appraisers should recommend a septic tank inspection when necessary and should comment on the adequacy of wells addressing capacity and water quality. A well flow and potability test should be recommended when necessary.

If there is a cesspool on the site, verify the status of permits. When a cesspool has been properly installed in the proper location, as specified by governing agents, costs to connect to public sewers, when available, should be minimal as opposed to costs for sewer connections when the cesspool has not been properly installed.

DESCRIPTION OF THE SITE IMPROVEMENTS

Street improvements and other amenities should be of the type that are common and acceptable in the area. If any of the amenities are absent, or are in a state of disrepair, the appraiser should address value and marketability. Is there a possibility that the homeowners could face excessive special assessments for installation or repair of these amenities? State relevant costs.

Streets

Properties should front on a publicly dedicated and maintained street that meets community standards and is generally accepted by area residents. When a dwelling fronts on a street that is not typical of those found in the community, the appraiser must comment on the effect that the location has on marketability and value. State the type of surface and the condition, for example, "asphalt/good." Dirt roads should include a comment as to whether they are all-weather roads.

When access to the property is by private streets or other such right-of-way streets, describe the adequacy of access, road condition, distance to publicly maintained roads, and provisions for maintenance. Streets that are not up to public standards frequently require excessive maintenance. When the streets are not constantly maintained, the resultant effect might be lower property values.

Accessibility to the subject street should also be considered. Are roads and streets leading to the subject street well-maintained, wide, and hard surfaced? Access to the property via a steep, narrow, or curving street could be hazardous; consequently, marketability and value may be affected. Streets with relatively steep grades should have adequate concrete gutters to prevent wash from heavy rainfall.

Curbs and Gutters

Pride of ownership is more likely to be reflected in neighborhoods with curbs and gutters as opposed to neighborhoods where lawns run into the street; therefore, curbs and gutters are considered to be desirable, long range amenities. State the type and condition of the curbs and gutters.

Sidewalks

Sidewalks and well-maintained public parkways should be present at the site if it is to be competitive. State the type and condition of the sidewalks and, if applicable, publicly maintained parkways. Sometimes, the type of trees that cities provide in parkways makes a big difference in appeal, particularly when the trees are not regularly trimmed or they are messy and require constant maintenance.

Street Lights

Describe street lights as adequate, inadequate, or none. In most communities, street lights are considered to be very desirable amenities; therefore, they should be present if the neighborhood is to be competitive with surrounding neighborhoods. When there are no street lights, verify the status with public officials because there could be a forthcoming special assessment for installation of street lights. In some areas, homeowners pay a monthly service charge to the city for each street light on their property. The fees have been known to be as high as $30.00 a month, and sometimes more, per street light (acreage sites might require more than one street light). The monthly cost should be included in the appraisal report to alert underwriters to additional monthly homeowner expenses.

Alley

Indicate whether alleys are located on or off the site, public or private, paved or unpaved. Is the alley dark? Is it well maintained? Does the alley add to or detract from the value of the property?

Topography, Size, and Shape of the Lot

The topography, shape, size of a lot, and proper drainage are elements of a property that are carefully considered by a prudent purchaser. Steep slopes that cause erosion, difficulty in maintaining the yard improvements, and difficult or hazardous access to the property are generally unfavorable characteristics that the market will shy away from. A poor lot will have very little demand. When the lot is not up to neighborhood standards, describe all the conditions that contribute to a poor rating.

Consider and describe the overall utility of the site as compared to competing properties. State whether the site is level; slopes up or down from the street, sides, and rear of the site; terraced hillside; approximate square footage of the level or usable pad area; and so forth. Does the utility of the site affect the value? Furnish additional comments, as needed, in the site comments area of the report, to fully depict site utility.

Size of the Site:

State the relationship in size to the neighborhood, for example, typical, larger than typical, or smaller than typical. When the size is not typical for the neighborhood, provide further commentary. Make certain that your comments are consistent with the lot sizes of the comparables shown on page two of the form.

Shape of the Lot:

Describe the shape, for example, rectangular, irregular, oblong, or flag lot. Provide explanations in the site comments section when the value of the property is affected by the shape of the lot. When the shape of the lot is nontypical for the neighborhood, state whether the shape has any effect on marketability and value.

Does the shape of the lot affect proper orientation of the structure on the site? Does the shape of the lot affect utility of the site? A flag-shaped lot can provide better views and additional privacy depending on the orientation of the structure on the site.

Setbacks and Zero Lot Lines:

Discuss setbacks, if applicable. Houses that are located too close to the street are usually less desirable than are homes that are set farther back from the front property line. Properties that feature "zero (or offset) lot lines" can be very desirable. Typical tract dwellings have a 5-foot setback on each side of the house. In a zero lot line situation, one side of the dwelling will be constructed right on the lot line, which leaves a setback on the opposite side of the house that is twice as wide as typical; therefore, site utility and privacy are generally enhanced.

Drainage

Drainage must be away from the improvements to avoid the collection of water in or around the dwelling unit or other improvements. Enter the direction of the drainage and state whether drainage is adequate or inadequate. Note areas of excessive dampness, standing water, and low areas. A termite inspection should be recommended when there are signs of excessive dampness or inadequate drainage. A geology report, or an inspection by a professional soils engineer, should be recommended when there is evidence of erosion, slippage, or slide activity. Are there any soils conditions on adjoining or nearby properties that could affect the subject property? A rating of "inadequate" requires an explanation.

View Amenities

Provide a brief description of the view, if any, and the effect it has on value, for example, ocean—excellent, mountain—average, and so forth. Explain specifics of views under site comments.

DON'T OVERLOOK THIS

When you rate the subject's view as well as when you are considering adjustments for views, don't forget to consider the permanency of the view. Is it possible that the view could be partially or completely obstructed by landscaping, trees, or future construction in the area? If so, market appeal and value should be adjusted accordingly.

Landscaping and Driveway

Rate the landscaping based on neighborhood standards and indicate average, superior, inferior, none, professional, and so forth. Describe the condition and extent of the landscaping and other yard improvements under site comments or additional features.

Indicate the type of surface and condition of the driveway. Are the materials and condition typical for the neighborhood? Is the driveway long enough and wide enough to provide adequate utility and off-street parking? Consider the convenience with respect to the slope of the driveway as well as possible hazardous ingress and egress. Driveways with inlaid brick or other decorative materials should be rated for added appeal and additional cost because they are quite expensive to install.

APPARENT EASEMENTS AND DETRIMENTAL CONDITIONS

Describe any easements, encroachments, or detrimental conditions. If appropriate, show "typical utility easements" or "no title records provided." Roadway easements require a further explanation; describe the roadway easement and the effect on value.

Easement

An easement is the right or interest in the land of another that entitles the holder thereof to some use, privilege, or benefit (such as to place power poles, pipelines, roads thereon, or travel over, etc.) out of or over said land.

Encroachment

When a building, a wall, a fence, or other fixture encroaches upon (overlaps) the land of an adjoining owner, there is said to be an "encroachment," provided such adjoining owner has not consented thereto.

Restrictions

"Private deed restrictions" are restrictions that may have been imposed on the property by former owners restricting the use and development of the land. "Public restrictions" are restrictions on the use of the land that are imposed by laws, such as zoning laws, building codes, fire ordinances, and health codes.

FEMA FLOOD HAZARD AREAS

The federal government has placed responsibility for determining if a property is in a flood hazard area upon the appraiser. The appraiser and lender will be held liable for any damage occurred during a flood if the information is incorrectly reported.

When a property is located in a special flood hazard area—zones A, AE, AH, AO, A1-30, A-99, V, VE, or VI-30— flood insurance is required. If the land is in the hazard area, but the improvements are not, flood insurance is not required. When the appraiser determines that a property is located in a special flood hazard area, the appraiser must indicate on the appraisal report form the map or community panel number, date of the panel, and the specific flood zone.

When the property is not located in a special flood hazard area, show "no" and indicate the map or community panel number and date of the panel. Under site comments, include a statement, such as, "The subject is not located in a flood hazard area: flood zone B, panel no. 060212-0019A, effective 9/14/79, per City of Anaheim." When the area has not been mapped by governing agencies, enter "not mapped."

Maps and information can be obtained by sending a self-addressed large envelope and list of maps wanted to Federal Emergency Management Agency, Flood Map Distribution Center, 6930 (A-F) San Tomas Road, Baltimore, Maryland 21227-6227. Or telephone 800-638-6620 (for the continental United States), or 800-492-6605 (for Maryland only), or 800-638-6831 (for Alaska, Hawaii, Puerto Rico, and the Virgin Islands).

Flood hazard information can sometimes be obtained from local planning departments.

SITE COMMENTS AND REVIEW OF VALUE FACTORS

Describe apparent easements, encroachments, special assessments, adverse external influences, and any other positive or negative influences that affect value and marketability.

Check the plat map and location (area) map. Are there any possible adverse influences indicated on the plat map or location map that should be explained? Many times plat maps or location maps indicate the presence of freeways, major highways, airports, or other adverse influences; yet explanations have not been provided in the appraisal report. In most cases, the appraiser has not mentioned these items because they do not influence the property in any way; however, possible adverse influences should always be addressed because reviewers have no way of knowing whether these elements have an adverse influence unless you tell them. For all they know, these items could have been overlooked by the appraiser.

Reporting Geological Hazards

In California, problems of this type fall into two general categories: (1) danger of slippage, subsidence, or heaving causing structural damage or loss due to topography or soil conditions and (2) danger to structures because of proximity to or location actually on an active earthquake fault.

If, upon inspection of a property, the appraiser is concerned about the location in a problem area, he or she should require a report from an expert in these matters, for example, a soils engineer's report, a geological report, or both. Sometimes a structural engineer's report should also be required to make certain that any problems noted in the other reports are overcome by the design of the foundation or structure of the improvements.

Special Assessments

A "special assessment" is a tax levied upon property to pay its proportionate share of a public improvement or service. The likelihood of a special assessment can be evidenced by the lack of public utilities and off-site improvements or the need to repair existing improvements. If this is the case, get in touch with public officials to ascertain the status of current or future special assessments. Special assessments can also be imposed on individual owners for maintenance or repair of privately owned streets, off-site improvements, and utilities. Explain any present or forthcoming special assessments and their impact on value.

Flood Control Channels

When a flood control channel is located on or near the site, state whether it is concrete lined or unlined (dirt lined) and its impact on value and marketability. Unlined flood control channels have been known to collapse during heavy storms, thereby causing extensive flooding. In most instances, any adverse influence from the proximity to a flood control channel is offset by the additional privacy provided from the open space; that is, many people prefer a flood control channel to having another house in proximity. Ask property owners for their reactions.

How to Classify Air Traffic

When airports are located in the vicinity of the subject property, note the flight pattern, type of aircraft, and the number of flights. This information can be obtained from airport traffic personnel. When aircraft originate from a military base, military officials usually will not divulge any information; therefore, discuss noise levels with local property owners.

Occasionally, a reviewer will look at a map book or a location map and discover that there is an airport in proximity to the subject property; however, the appraiser has not referenced the airport because it does not represent an adverse influence. Remember, a reviewer who has not made a physical inspection of the property has no way of knowing that. Hence, always describe the proximity to the airport and state whether the property is under the flight pattern. If the home is not under the flight pattern, include a comment, such as, "The Ontario Airport is located 2 miles northwest; however, the property is not under the flight pattern and there is no evidence of any adverse effect on marketability or value caused by the subject's proximity to the airport."

When the property is located under the flight pattern, historically, the proximity to the airport may be tolerated by inhabitants of a particular neighborhood, with little or no adverse influence on value and marketability. Discuss noise levels and make adjustments for external obsolescence when indicated. A study of market history and the length of time it typically takes to market property in the subject neighborhood should disclose the relevancy of an adjustment. If the air traffic is limited to small private planes, ask local property owners and real estate agents whether there are any negative reactions to the proximity of the airport.

How to Classify Railroad Traffic

Get in touch with the "dispatcher" to find the number of trains scheduled per day and the time of day that trains pass through the area. Ask nearby property owners for their opinions of noise levels. Describe the rail traffic in the report noting the number of trains per day or night, the noise levels, and the impact on marketability and value.

SUMMARY

1. As you are writing the report, think about change. What is changing and what are the changes leading to?
2. Did you verify the zoning and uses? Did you consider the size, shape, and topography of the lot?
3. Did you overlook any geological hazards or toxic environmental influences?
4. Have you considered and commented on all the locational influences that might affect marketability and value, such as proximity to apartments, condominiums, or industrial property; to commercial property (taverns, restaurants, amusement places, animal shelters, etc.) that generates a lot of noise and activity; nearby vacant land; and to high-tension power lines, heavy traffic streets, traffic signals, and bus stops?
5. Are positive and negative influences confined to the subject property, or are they evident throughout the neighborhood? Are buffers provided? If so, describe them. Are noise levels audible on the interior as well as the exterior?
6. Have you provided a basis for any adjustments; that is, did you include comparable sales or a study of market history that support your determination? If you feel that the external influences do not affect value and marketability, describe your findings. For example, "These conditions, historically, have been accepted by the local marketplace and have little or no adverse influence on marketability or value."
7. Show the location of all the positive and negative influences on the plat map, the location map, or the building diagram. Provide photos, as applicable.

CHAPTER 10

GENERAL DESCRIPTION AND ANALYSIS OF THE IMPROVEMENTS

This chapter covers the descriptions and analysis of the improvements in the order of their occurrence on the Uniform Residential Appraisal Report form.

Financing concessions, overimprovements, additions, poor condition of the property, and functional obsolescence often cause major appraisal problems; therefore, our objective is to show you why, when, where, and how these factors should be addressed in the appraisal report. The following tips and checklists will also help you avoid problems with incomplete, inaccurate, and conflicting descriptions that sometimes find their way into appraisal reports.

NUMBER OF UNITS ON THE SITE

The FNMA Form 1004 should be used for single-family residential property and planned unit developments. This form should also be used for properties that have a "true" guest house and two-family properties if the value of the second unit is relatively insignificant in relation to the total value of the property, in which case, "two units" should be indicated.

NUMBER OF STORIES

List the number of above-grade floors of finished living area. This should be the same number indicated on the room list and the same number used to calculate the gross living area in the cost approach.

When the second story of the dwelling does not extend the full width or depth of the house, or only half the area can be used as livable floor area, the number of stories should be shown as "1 $\frac{1}{2}$." A split level home should be shown as "two-story split level" or "three-story split level," depending on the number of levels. Basements or attics should not be included in the number of stories; they should be calculated separately.

TYPE OF RESIDENTIAL UNIT

Show detached or attached. There are single-family residences in some communities that are sometimes referred to as (1) attached single-family residences, (2) duplex-style single-family residences, or (3) fourplex-style single-family residences. They are all single-family residences in every respect except that they are built adjacent to each other (attached or duplex style), or they are located in a four-unit building (fourplex style).

In many instances, the dwelling units look like they have a common wall; however, each residence may have its own exterior wall with a 4- to 6-inch (typically) airspace between the walls of the two separate living units. In some instances, the only "common wall" is between the garages of the adjacent units.

The type of construction should be fully explained in the appraisal report. Provisions for maintenance of any common walls or other common areas should be provided. At least two comparable sales that have been similarly constructed should be included.

DESIGN AND STYLE OF THE IMPROVEMENTS

Do not use the builder's model name. Describe the structure using local terminology, such as conventional (a stock-built or tract home), Spanish, colonial, Cape Cod, saltbox, Tudor, ranch style, contemporary, split level, or trilevel.

EXISTING IMPROVEMENTS

When appropriate, enter "yes." Show "N/A" if the subject is proposed or under construction. When the dwelling is under construction, but it is almost finished, check the "existing" box on page one and check the box "subject to repairs, alterations, inspections or conditions listed below" on page two. Under comments and conditions of appraisal on page two, list the items that require completion, for example, "Subject to installation of appliances and flooring." This enables the lender to project a more precise funding date for the loan.

HOW TO HANDLE PROPOSED UNITS AND UNITS UNDER CONSTRUCTION

The appraisal must be made "subject to completion" and an estimated date of completion should be provided.

Building Plans

When you appraise custom-built homes, the building plans should be initialed and dated by the appraiser. A statement should be included to identify the plans that were reviewed by the appraiser. For example, "The appraisal report and value conclusion are contingent upon completion of the proposed improvements in accordance with the plans and specifications prepared by (include architect's name) with a last revision date of (insert date of last revision) which have been initialed and dated by the appraiser." The date the land was purchased, the purchase price, and the builder's cost estimates should be included, as applicable. These requirements do not apply to appraisals of homes in new tract developments.

Photos of Uncompleted Construction

Include photos of the uncompleted structure. When you are appraising a home under construction in a new tract development, rather than including a photo of a vacant lot, include a photo of a completed model home that is the same plan as the subject. If you are including copies of building plans for proposed properties, include a copy of the front elevation.

ACTUAL AGE OF THE STRUCTURES

Show the actual age of the structures. When the dwelling has been newly constructed, make sure that the building permit has been finalized or that a Certificate of Occupancy has been issued. Include permit numbers and the source of your information in the report.

EFFECTIVE AGE OF THE STRUCTURES

Show a specific figure or a small range.

The effective age is the "years of age" indicated by the condition and utility of the structure. The relationship between the actual age and the effective age of a property is a good indication of its condition, that is, when the house has been properly cared for, rehabilitated, or modernized, the effective age is reduced.

The effective age should approximate the actual age unless the residence has been well maintained through the years or has undergone remodeling or renovation. The effective age should be based on the extent of maintenance, remodeling, or renovation. When a dwelling has had better than average maintenance, rehabilitation, or modernization, the effective age will be less than the actual age. When a dwelling has been completely gutted, modernized, or remodeled, the appropriate effective age might be "effectively new." The effective age could be greater than the actual age if the property has been poorly maintained. Make certain that the descriptions of the interior and exterior of the property do not conflict with the actual and effective ages of the dwelling.

How Architectural Obsolescence Affects Effective Age

Do not overlook the possibility of "architectural obsolescence" or the quality of construction when you estimate an effective age. The architectural design may be such that there is very limited market appeal for the property, in which case, the effective age should be adjusted accordingly. If the quality of construction is poor, the effective age of the property would, most certainly, be affected.

Cosmetic Improvements and Value

Never let "cosmetic" improvements (superficial improvements to the dwelling) or furnishings influence your judgment when you are evaluating property and defining the effective age. Your primary concern should be to rate elements in the property that contribute to long-term stability of value, such as structural soundness; condition and quality of the foundation, roof, exterior and interior walls and finishes; plumbing, electrical, and heating equipment; and kitchen and bath equipment.

Neighborhood Relationship to Effective Age

In addition to considering the condition of the subject property at this time, to determine its useful life, the appraiser must consider the neighborhood. Even though the subject property has been well maintained, renovated, or modernized, when a neighborhood is declining to a point where all the homes may be replaced by encroaching multifamily income property, commercial or industrial development, or other uses that are detrimental to value, the demise of utility most likely will be brought about by neighborhood or environmental changes that should be reflected in the remaining economic life of the property.

1. Correlate the effective age with the amount of depreciation in the cost approach. Is the dollar amount of depreciation appropriate?

2. When an inappropriate effective age is selected, and there is inadequate commentary, an underwriter might misinterpret the information to mean that there is substantial depreciation present that may affect the terms of the loan.

3. When there is a wide distinction between the actual age and the effective age, you must justify your opinion. That is, fully explain the extent of modernization, renovation, and maintenance levels. Provide costs, as applicable, to support provide further support.

4. You wouldn't compare a new home to a 20-year-old home; therefore, you shouldn't compare an effectively new home to a 20-year-old home. Sales comparables should always be similar in effective age to the subject. If a home is "effectively new," the sales should have been comparably updated and remodeled or sales of newer homes should be used for comparison purposes.

EXTERIOR DESCRIPTION OF THE IMPROVEMENTS

Common types of foundations are concrete slab, cinder or concrete block, brick, field stone, treated wood, wood blocks or sills, and piers or posts on concrete footings. The three basic forms of foundations are poured concrete or concrete slab, basements, and pier and beam. Pier-type foundations support the structure on several posts or piers. An inspection by a structural engineer should be recommended for dwellings with pier-type foundations.

In the absence of a continuous perimeter foundation, the appraiser must comment on the type of foundation present, its compliance with local building codes, its sufficiency to support the subject structure, and the acceptability in the marketplace.

Exterior Walls

Indicate the type of material used for the major portions of exterior wall finishes; describe other finishes under additional features. Common types of wood siding are clapboard, log cabin, shiplap, and board and batten. Several years ago, an imitation wood siding was introduced, which is a horizontal siding consisting of masonite or hardboard; hence, if appropriate, show masonite or hardboard siding.

Other types of exterior finishes are stucco, masonry, asbestos or asphalt shingles, aluminum siding, vinyl siding, clay bricks, or brick and stone. When the siding is brick or stone, specify whether it is solid masonry or veneer to provide an indication of quality.

Roof Surface

Specify the materials used and, if applicable, the quality and condition. Recommend a roofing inspection when signs of deferred maintenance, such as curled, broken, cracked, or missing shingles; debris on the roof; or water stains on the ceiling have been noted.

Common types of roofing materials are rolled asphalt (laid down in strips that overlap), tar and gravel, rock, asphalt shingles, wood shingles, wood shakes, aluminum "shingle-shakes," clay tile, slate, stone/steel (imitation Mission Tile), and Mission Tile.

Gutters and Downspouts

Indicate the material (typically aluminum or wood) used for both. Show the location (front and/or rear) of the gutters. When there are no gutters, specify the width of the overhang. Did you check the site grading around the foundation walls for adequate drainage?

Window Types

Describe the type of window and the materials for the major portion of the structure, for example, wood double hung, metal casement, steel swing-out, or aluminum sliding. Decorative windows, such as bay windows or garden windows, should be described under additional features.

FOUNDATION

Indicate the type of foundation. When there is more than one type of foundation, show the percentage of each type of foundation in the appropriate space.

Dampness: When there is evidence of excessive dampness, show yes; describe the extent of the dampness elsewhere in the report; and, if appropriate, recommend an inspection.

Settlement: A structural inspection should be required when possible major structural damage is evidenced by uneven floors, walls, or ceilings; large foundation cracks; or sagging roof trusses. A structural inspection should also be required when the building rests on pier-type foundations. Clear, descriptive photographs of any damage should be included with the report.

Infestation: Always recommend an inspection by a licensed pest control contractor when there is evidence of water damage; dry rot; or the presence of termites, carpenter ants, or other wood-destroying insects. The appraiser must comment on the effect on value and marketability when there is evidence of structural damage, dry rot, dampness, or wood-boring insects.

BASEMENT

Show the square footage area of the basement based on exterior dimensions. Indicate the percentage of this area that is finished and describe the type of finishes. When there is an outside entry, describe the type of entry. When value is given to finished basement rooms, there should be sufficient ventilation and light to provide good healthy living space. Include photos when additional value is assigned to finished basement rooms.

INSULATION

The appraiser should make every effort to determine the presence of insulation and particularly to determine the presence of urea-formaldehyde and asbestos insulation—which are described in Chapter Six.

Reporting Unhealthy Insulation

Urea-formaldehyde and asbestos insulation have been designated as possible health hazards; therefore, if the appraiser has reason to believe urea-formaldehyde or asbestos insulation is present, the lender should be notified immediately and a full description should be provided. If known, always include the date of installation.

Rating Adequacy of Insulation

If available, always indicate the "R" factor. The appraiser should indicate an overall rating under "adequacy" using the terms high, adequate, or low. These same terms should be used on page two to describe special energy-efficient items in the sales comparison analysis or the appraiser can specifically list the items on page two. When value is assigned to energy-efficient items, they should be specifically described, for example, solar hot water heating system, weather-stripping, insulated ducts, insulated hot water heater, double- or triple-paned windows, building designs that minimize energy use, and so forth. If relevant, include owner's costs of these improvements.

When to Use the Energy Addendum Residential Appraisal Report

If adjustments are substantial, the appraiser may wish to include the optional FHLMC Form 70A, "Energy Addendum Residential Appraisal Report." This is an optional report designed to assist appraisers in describing the energy efficiency and estimating the value of energy-saving items when there is insufficient market data available to provide a basis for adjustments.

How to Classify Energy Ratings

Energy efficient items should be assigned an overall rating of high, adequate, or low. The FHLMC Form 70A could be used to develop the rating. Generally, a dwelling must contain features from each of the following three major categories to receive a "high" rating.

1. *Insulation and Infiltration.* Insulation or infiltration barriers should have adequate "R" factors:
   a. Insulation in ceilings, roofs, or attic floors that are over conditioned spaces, in exterior walls, under floors that cover unheated area, around slabs, around heating or cooling ducts, or pipes that run through unconditioned spaces, around the sill area and around the water heater.
   b. Caulking or weatherstripping around window and door areas and at the sill area.
   c. Special fireplace devices or features, such as combustion-air and flue dampers, and a fire door.
   d. Sealing of the sole plate and penetrations of the exterior shell.
   e. Dampers for exhaust fans.
2. *Windows and Doors*
   a. Double- or triple-paned windows or storm windows.

   b. Storm doors or insulated doors.
3. *Heating and Cooling Systems.* New efficient heating and cooling systems or appropriate modifications to an existing system.
   a. *New efficient systems* include items, such as a high-efficiency oil or gas furnace with an Annual Fuel Utilization Efficiency (AFUE) rating of 80 percent or higher, a high-efficiency heat pump with a Seasonal Energy Efficiency Ratio (SEER) measure of 9.0 or greater, and a central air conditioner with a SEER rating of 9.0 or greater.
   b. *System modifications* include items, such as a flame retention oil burner, vent dampers for oil and gas furnaces, pilotless (electronic) ignition for gas furnaces, a secondary condensing heat exchanger for gas and oil furnaces, zoned heating and/or air conditioning, automatic setback thermostats, and solar equipment or design.

ROOM LIST—FNMA FORM 1004

Typically, areas *below* grade level must be considered as a basement; however, there are occasions when deviations from instructions may be necessary to illustrate clearly the design of the residence, assign proper costs, and facilitate making appropriate adjustments in the sales comparison analysis. Of course, any deviations from instructions must be accompanied by proper explanations.

Why You Should Use the Same Levels of Adjustment

Homes that are built on terraced hillsides sometimes have one or more floors of actual (not basement) living area below grade. The comparable sales could have one or more floors of living area below grade, or none, depending on the design of the structures. Suppose you included only the above-grade square footage as the total gross living area for the subject. Would this relate to the total gross living area that is shown in public records for the comparable sales? Remember, you have to *use the same levels of adjustment* between the comparable sales and the subject. Therefore, list the rooms in a fashion that makes the most sense with relationship to the subject and comparable sales. Explain what you did and why it was necessary. List the first level of actual living area as level 1, then go on to level 2, and so forth.

How to List the Number of Rooms

For typical homes, enter the number of each type of room on each level. Room counts must match those depicted on the building diagram and the room count of the subject property in the sales comparison analysis section of the report. Show a trilevel home as level 1, level 2, and level 3.

When a portion of a room is used for another purpose, do not include the second use in the total room count; that is, when part of the living room is used as a dining area, do not enter an "x" under dining; enter "area" to illustrate the difference and do not include the dining area in the room count. A "dining room" is a separate room or an area of sufficient size that it could effectively be divided into another room.

When a portion of a room is used as an office, den, sewing room, and so on, describe the areas elsewhere in the report and do not include these areas in the room count. If they actually are separate rooms, list them under "other" and include them in the room count. Always consider the added value of any additional rooms in the sales comparison analysis because buyers will often pay more for a home with a bonus room, recreation room, den, or dining room.

Laundry rooms: The laundry should not be included in the total room count even though it may be a separate room unless the room definitely adds value to the home and you will be considering the value in the sales comparison analysis, in which case, the room should be precisely described and the additional value should be documented. In some homes, laundry rooms are almost as large as some bedrooms, and they have a multipurpose use, for example, a portion of the room can be used as an office or a sewing room.

Counting the Number of Bathrooms:

one-fourth bath	one fixture—a sink or a toilet
one-half bath	two fixtures—a sink and a toilet
three quarter bath	three fixtures—a sink, toilet, and a stall shower or tub
full bath	three fixtures—a sink, toilet, and a tub/shower combination; or four fixtures— a sink, toilet, separate tub, and separate stall shower

Note: Show "3/4 bath" on the building diagram, for clarity, but count it as "one bath" for the room count.

Functional obsolescence should be noted when there is only one bathroom as well as when there is not at least one-half bath on each floor of livable area. Homes with only one bathroom should not be compared to homes with two bathrooms because there is normally a wide variance in prices.

DESCRIPTIONS OF INTERIOR FINISHES

Describe the floor coverings in the major portion of the residence, which is typically carpet. Floor coverings in other areas of the dwelling (kitchen, bath, foyer) should be described under additional features. Marketability and appeal can be drastically reduced by undesirable colors of flooring, different grades of flooring throughout the residence, or mixed types and colors of carpet and flooring throughout that do not blend well with each other or the wall finishes. All these situations should be considered because a buyer may have to replace the floor coverings throughout the residence to enhance the overall appeal of the home. Consider the cost of replacing the floor coverings as well as market standards.

Wall Finishes

Describe the wall finishes in the major portion of the residence, which are typically drywall or plaster. When both plaster and drywall are present, this may be an indication that there is a room addition or, perhaps, the dwelling may have been rehabilitated or remodeled.

DON'T FORGET TO RATE MARKET APPEAL

Market appeal can be affected by different colors of painted walls throughout the residence, undesirable colors of painted walls or wallpaper, bold wallpaper patterns, uncoordinated wall coverings (wall coverings do not match throughout the dwelling), and multiple layers of paint or wallpaper. Consider the acceptability of these conditions in the subject's particular neighborhood. If appropriate, consider the cost and make adjustments for refinishing the walls.

Adequacy of Trim and Finishes

This particularly refers to the adequacy of the trim and finishes with relationship to the type of home and other homes in the subject and competing neighborhoods. Rate the interior finishes as inferior, typical, or superior to competing properties.

Bath Floors and Wainscot

Typically, bath floors are ceramic, vinyl or asphalt tile. Carpet or rugs that are not permanently installed should not be included in the description.

Wainscoting is ceramic tile, plastic, or marlite panels placed above, or around, the perimeter of a tub or shower to prevent water damage. Newer, average-quality homes usually have one-piece fiberglass tub and shower combinations.

Interior Doors

The type of doors found in the major portion of the dwelling should be described. The type of doors and the materials relate to the quality of construction of the dwelling itself; therefore, the type of interior doors should be given due consideration.

Rating Quality:

To clarify quality, doors could be described as stock hollow-core doors to indicate fair quality, medium-grade hollow-core doors to indicate average quality, veneered hollow-core doors to indicate good quality, and hardwood veneer or solid wood for better-quality residences, if, in fact, these are the type of doors found in the residence.

Rating Quality of Interior Surfaces

Each of the preceding elements under surfaces should have a surface rating; that is, you should state the condition of the elements. The definitions of good, average, fair, and poor to be applied to the surface ratings (condition) are the same as those set forth in the neighborhood analysis section of the report. The appraiser must explain any ratings of fair or poor.

Surface improvements in excess of neighborhood standards should be rated as overimprovements for the neighborhood. When the surfaces have not received proper maintenance and updating, in keeping with the subject and competing neighborhoods, the property should be regarded as an underimprovement and appropriate adjustments for repairs or updating should be considered.

Number and Kinds of Fireplaces

Specify the material (Palos Verdes stone, brick, used brick, brick veneer, masonry, simulated marble) and the number of fireplaces. If fireplaces are an important feature of the home or they have hearths and mantels, which indicate quality, provide a more detailed description under additional features.

Heating Equipment

When the type of heating, unvented heating, or lack of heating is a possible health or safety hazard to the occupants, the appraiser should explain the status of the heating in detail and appraise the property "subject to inspection and correction of inadequate heating."

Different types of heating systems are forced-air furnace; gravity furnace, floor or wall furnace, electric baseboard (heating units occupy space ordinarily taken by the baseboard); hot water, gas or steam baseboard; hot water, steam or gas radiators; radiant floor; electric ceiling radiant; and heat pumps.

Cooling Equipment

Types of cooling are central air conditioning, wall or window air conditioning, evaporated, combination forced-air heating and cooling units, and heat pumps. Easily removable types of air conditioning units (typically window units) should be considered as personal property; therefore, describe the unit and indicate "no value assigned." If you omit the description of the unit you may have to provide a letter of explanation at a later date because someone may wonder why value was not assigned to the air conditioner.

Kitchen Equipment

Enter an "x" or the number of appliances. Free-standing ranges, ovens, refrigerators, dishwashers, and microwave ovens should be considered as personal property; hence, they should not be included. If items of personal property are included in the sales price, the items should be considered as a sales concession with corresponding deductions from the sales price. Refrigerators should be included if they are actually built-in.

Assigning Value to Attics

Include photos and a full description when value is assigned to finished attic areas. Value cannot be assigned to finished attic areas unless proper finalized permits are on file with governing agencies. Finished attic areas should have proper light, heating, and ventilation as well as normal ceiling height. "Scuttle" refers to an opening in a ceiling, with a removable cover, that provides access to the attic.

AUTOS AND PARKING REQUIREMENTS

The availability and type of parking must conform to zoning regulations and neighborhood standards. When the garage has been converted without permits, the appraiser should assign garage value only as well as including and adjusting for costs to convert the structure to its legal and intended use. When a garage has been constructed on a lot without permits, and it has been placed in a location that does not conform to zoning regulations, it may have to be moved or torn down.

When most of the homes in the subject and competing neighborhoods have two-car garages, a one-car garage would be "functionally obsolete." A rating of "inadequate" requires an explanation. When there is no garage or carport on the site, the appraiser must provide further commentary regarding marketability. For example, "There is no covered parking on the subject site which is typical and common in the subject neighborhood; hence, marketability is not affected." Find out whether covered parking or on-site parking is required by local zoning regulations.

Classifying Interior Garage Finishes

Describe electric garage door openers and interior garage finishes under additional features or in an addendum. Consider neighborhood standards before assigning value to finished interior walls, built-in workshops, shelves, lighting, built-in storage cabinets, and so forth. Typically, the market does not recognize full return of the costs to install these items.

Outside Entries into the House or Basement

Entry from the garage into the house or basement should be rated based on neighborhood standards. Homes usually have greater appeal and utility when there is direct access from the garage into the dwelling, particularly when laundry facilities are located in the garage. Direct access to a basement also provides greater utility. Outside entry does not refer to the main (overhead) garage door, it refers to a "man-door" (a door by which persons enter and leave). When there is no outside man door entry to the garage, to avoid leaving blank spaces, which may be questioned, insert an asterisk in the "outside entry" box and include this statement under additional features: "The garage has an overhead door; however, there is no man-door for outside entry."

ANALYSIS OF THE IMPROVEMENTS

The rating factors of good, average, fair, and poor are to be based on comparison by the appraiser of the subject property with competing properties considering the effect these factors have on continued market appeal for residential properties. The ratings must be consistent with the subject's description and the sales comparison analysis. The property ratings indicate how the subject property compares to competing properties with respect to quality and soundness of construction, convenience of living, and appeal to the market. All these factors have a major effect upon the marketability of any single-family property. When the property is being appraised "subject to," make certain all the descriptions and ratings are consistent with the condition the property will be in when the repairs or other property improvements are completed.

Explanations Required by Lenders

The appraiser must explain any ratings of fair or poor. Typically, when three or more elements in the appraisal are rated fair or poor, the loan will be declined; hence, make sure that any fair and poor ratings are appropriate.

An explanation must accompany two ratings for one item because this can be confusing to the reader who is trying to interpret your implications. A rating of average to good might be indicated for condition and could be explained as follows: "The subject property reflects overall good maintenance and is comparable to other properties in the neighborhood with the exception of the floor coverings, which are beginning to show signs of wear; therefore, the condition has been rated as average to good."

How Improvement Ratings Are Affected by the Neighborhood

Consider the age of the dwelling and the neighborhood in which the subject property is located when you are assigning ratings. The electrical and plumbing may not be up to today's standards; however, if the dwelling is functional for its era, does not present any hazards to the occupants, and conforms to other properties in the neighborhood, the property rating should be "average." Also, the room sizes, number of closets, layout, and utility may be adequate and acceptable in one neighborhood and quite the reverse in another neighborhood. If these conditions are acceptable by neighborhood standards, the rating should be "average."

Requirements for Reporting Detrimental Conditions

The use of ratings does not preclude an appraiser from reporting the detrimental condition of improvements even if the condition is also typical for competing properties. Any condition that may affect the value or marketability of the subject property must be reported to assure that the appraiser adequately describes the property. For instance, the appraiser should note whether a property is characterized by deferred maintenance or a lack of updating even though the same condition applies to competing properties in the neighborhood.

Quality of Construction

Consider the quality of workmanship throughout as well as the quality and durability of materials used in all components of the building. When the quality of the home is good and the quality of competing properties is equally good, the subject's rating should be "good." If the subject's quality is good, but the quality of the competing properties is average, the subject property might be an overimprovement for the neighborhood. Make certain that ratings of fair or poor have been reflected in the effective age of the property.

Condition of Improvements

The appraiser is to rate the condition of the building and is to take note of all aspects of physical depreciation including deferred maintenance and report these in the comments section. Include an itemized list and total cost of the repairs needed to raise the property to neighborhood standards.

Room Sizes and Layout

Rate the layout as to the extent to which it facilitates easy access to all rooms without interfering with the intended use of other rooms.

Rating consistency:

Privacy of sleeping areas should be considered. While the location of bedrooms might be considered to be objectionable, if the layout is consistent with competing properties, the subject should receive a rating of "average." Many older homes do not have hallways; thus, access to bedrooms is directly from the living room or, sometimes, from the kitchen. A statement should be included, such as, "The appraiser has considered the absence of hallways and the direct access to bedrooms from the living room. This condition is consistent with layouts in the neighborhood, is accepted by typical buyers, and has little, if any, adverse influence on value or marketability."

Functional obsolescence:

When a room is arranged one before the other (access to one room is through another room), the arrangement is referred to as "tandem." In most cases, when you must walk through one room to get to another room, the layout would be considered functionally inadequate; however, this depends on the use of the room and the flow of traffic through the room as well as neighborhood compatibility. Many times this situation can be corrected by putting the room to another use, installing a door, or adding a hallway.

Other factors to consider:

Is there sufficient wall area to permit suitable furniture groupings? Are the rooms adequate in size throughout the dwelling? Can the furniture be arranged so that it is not too close to sources of heat? Are the stairs, doors, and hallways adequate in width? Are there too many stairs or are they overly steep? Are there adequate toilet or bath facilities on each floor?

Functional obsolescence must be taken into consideration when a rating is less than average and should be reflected in the cost approach and the market analysis. If functional obsolescence is present, is it curable? How can it be cured and what is the cost? Perhaps a bath or hallway can be added, doors installed, walls moved or removed, or possibly the rooms could be put to a more functional use.

Closets and Storage

Rate the adequacy and convenience of closets and general storage as compared to competing properties. This is an important item that can have a substantial effect on livability and marketability and should, therefore, not be ignored by the appraiser. In addition to considering storage within the dwelling, rate the available storage areas in the basement, attic, and garage as well as exterior storage facilities.

Energy Efficiency

Rate the energy-efficient elements with relationship to neighborhood standards and typical buyer's reactions to the presence or absence of energy-efficient items.

Adequacy and Condition of Plumbing

Consider the number, style, and condition of the plumbing fixtures, the materials used for piping, and the condition of the piping as well as the proper operation of any on-site water or septic systems. If the plumbing is consistent with competing properties, but is substandard, rate the property as "fair to average." Include an explanation, such as, "The number of plumbing fixtures is substandard as compared to today's standards; however, this condition is common and acceptable in the subject and competing neighborhoods." The effective age of the property should be adjusted accordingly.

Adequacy and Condition of Electrical Equipment

This rating includes the adequacy of electrical service available within the structure, the number and location of outlets and switches, the quality and condition of the wiring, and the adequacy and style of the lighting fixtures. A split rating should be handled in the same manner presented under plumbing.

Adequacy and Condition of Kitchen Cabinets

Rate the adequacy of the amount of kitchen storage space in relation to the likely number of occupants of the dwelling as well as consistency with the neighborhood. The style, quality, and condition of the cabinets are also factors to be considered when applying a rating.

Compatibility to Neighborhood

This rating is to indicate the extent to which the amenities, size, age, price, architectural design, and construction of the subject property conforms to the neighborhood. Appropriate adjustments should be made in the market analysis when the property is nonconforming.

Appeal and Marketability

Consider the market appeal and demand for the subject property based on all the factors presented in the report. Provide an explanation if there is any reason why the subject would not sell within the period specified in the neighborhood section under marketing time.

Estimated Remaining Economic Life

Enter the estimated remaining number of years over which the improvements can be expected to make a contribution to the value of the property. This should coincide with generally accepted total economic life estimates as well as the estimated depreciation. Many lenders limit the term of the mortgage based on the appraiser's estimate of remaining economic life; that is, if the appraiser specifies an remaining economic life of 25 years, the lender may make a loan based on 20 years or less. Therefore, make every effort to select an appropriate figure.

Show a specific figure or a small range. Deduct the estimated effective age from an economic life new of the improvements to find the remaining economic life. Economic life new, based on a national average, is 75 years, which is a generally accepted economic life estimate; however, the figure used for economic life new should be suitable for the area in which you are appraising.

Estimated Physical Life

Remaining physical life appears on the Uniform Residential Appraisal Report because it is a HUD (Department of Housing and Urban Development) requirement. It is not required for Fannie Mae. The appraiser should report the physical life as "N/A" (not applicable) unless the appraisal is for HUD purposes or the client requires an estimated physical life.

ADDITIONAL FEATURES, MODERNIZATION, AND REHABILITATION

All the entities that are assigned value in the cost approach and are considered in the sales comparison analysis must be precisely described. Include age, size, construction materials, and condition to provide a basis for costs and adjustments. Also include a summary of the owner's costs for improvements, if relevant.

A full description of all the improvements that contribute to value of the subject property is very important because the reader must be able to comprehend readily how you arrived at your costs and adjustments; that is, to state simply that there is a pool, without describing the age, size, construction materials, condition, or type and amount of decking does not provide a basis for a cost of, say, $25,000., and it does not provide a basis for a commensurate adjustment in the sales comparison analysis.

When the structures are 20 to 25 years old or more, there should be signs of rejuvenation of the improvements up to modern standards. This may be evidenced by additions to existing structures, extensive remodeling and repair, new kitchens, or new bathrooms. Lenders usually look at properties more favorably when the homes have been modernized and rehabilitated because the remaining economic life is proportionately extended and these expenditures usually reflect a strong neighborhood with an increasing price trend.

AN IMPORTANT REMINDER

The reader does not have any way to validate the appraiser's property ratings unless appropriate commentary is included describing the extent of modernization or rehabilitation. A gross lack of thoroughness, which indicates a poorly prepared appraisal, is easily recognized when the description of the property, alleged condition, and improvement analysis ratings do not relate to the appraiser's estimate of the actual and effective ages of the home and no commentary is included to clarify conflicting illustrations. We cite the following examples:

Example 1: The subject is 30 years old and an effective age of 25 years is shown. The condition of the exterior, interior, plumbing, and electrical are rated good; however, the appraiser has not stated whether any of the components of the property have been replaced or repaired or whether the dwelling has been rehabilitated, remodeled, or modernized.

The reader is left to wonder: Why is the condition rated good if the dwelling hasn't been brought up to current market standards? Is the house in good condition only because cosmetic improvements have enhanced the appearance of the property? Is the good condition the result of major rehabilitation, updated plumbing or electrical equipment, or other modernization? If so, why doesn't the effective age reflect the improvements to the property? Then again, maybe the property is really only in average condition?

Example 2: In other instances, descriptions of different components of construction (window type, roof, exterior and interior wall finishes, bath wainscoting, kitchen equipment) have been included that do not relate to the age of the home; yet, there are no comments regarding modernization, additions, remodeling, or refurbishing.

For example, the subject home was constructed in 1945. The following finishes and equipment are described in the appraisal: wood casing *and* aluminum sliding windows, fiberglass wainscoting, forced-air heating, built-in range and oven, dishwasher, disposal, and vinyl flooring. It is apparent that some type of revitalization has taken place or, possibly, there is an addition; however, no commentary has been provided to clarify the descriptions that conflict with the subject's age.

These examples are not extreme cases. Conflicting and insufficient illustrations occur frequently enough to cause real concern to lenders. An underwriter cannot be expected to second-guess the appraiser's meaning. An appraisal is supposed to be "self-contained," which means that the appraiser must provide enough descriptive information to enable the reader to arrive readily at the same conclusions as the appraiser.

Reconciling Your Descriptions

Review your descriptions giving due consideration to the actual and effective ages when you are describing finishes and condition as well as when you are assigning improvement analysis ratings. Explain all the details of remodeling, modernization, rehabilitation, and additions in a manner that will enable an underwriter to make an informed and appropriate decision.

How to Classify Personal Property

Occasionally, appraisers question the inclusion of certain improvements, such as sheds, storage structures, patio covers, or above-ground spas in the value of the property. Ask yourself the following questions: Is the element permanently affixed to the property or should it be considered as personal property? Does it have permits? Could you assign a remaining economic life? Would it even have value if it was depreciated? Is it insurable? Would a buyer actually pay more for the property if this element was included? What would you use as a basis for adjustments in the sales comparison analysis?

Assigning Value to Insignificant Improvements

Consider age, cost, construction materials, utility, and condition. Improvements that do not contribute to the value of the property should not be assigned value. They should also be looked upon with respect to a possible negative influence on value and marketability with corresponding adjustments to reflect the cost of removing any negative influences on value.

Consider patio covers or storage sheds, for example,

which, in some instances, would be better described as an assemblage of a number of cheap building materials imitating a patio cover or storage shed. An observant appraiser would not assign $500., $1,000., or even greater adjustments to "amenities" that are cheaply or haphazardly constructed or improvements that are in poor condition simply because they exist. Often, the value of the property will be enhanced by the removal of such items. Consider the item with respect to neighborhood standards as well as considering the quality and condition. Would a buyer actually pay an additional $1,000. or $2,000. (or whatever figure is supposedly applicable) for this item? In reality, would an adjustment for the cost of removing the item be more appropriate?

Anytime that there are any outbuildings (buildings other than the main structure or residence) or other improvements on the property that are hazardous, fully depreciated, or poorly constructed, the appraiser should include costs to remove the item from the property. For example, it might be appropriate to include costs for removing swimming pools that are in a state of disrepair, old garages or guest cottages that have deteriorated and have little or no value, dilapidated storage buildings, piles of wood (which can bring on termite infestation), other items stored on the property, overgrown trees that are too close to the structure (which could cause structural damage), trees that have heavy and overgrown root systems (which could damage main sewer lines from the house to the street), or fencing that is in a state of disrepair.

PREFERRED METHODS FOR DEALING WITH ADDITIONS

Any component of a property that does not conform to zoning regulations *cannot be assigned value*. Governing authorities have the right to have an unapproved addition or conversion dismantled; therefore, value cannot be considered.

However, before you automatically exclude any improvements that could add value to the property, report your findings to your client because they may want to put the appraisal in abeyance until proper permits are obtained and finalized.

Garage Conversions

Garage conversions should be considered only as covered parking if there is a zoning violation. Costs to convert the garage to its original intended use should be included and appropriate adjustments should be made, that is, deduct the cost to convert the garage to its original use from each comparable in the sales comparison analysis (in the space designated for garage descriptions and adjustments). State whether the garage door is in place and operable; if not, include a cost to install the garage door.

A legal garage conversion could be documented in the following manner:

"A 9- by 20-ft. section of the garage has been converted to an office with a half-bath and a french door to the front entry porch. According to zoning officials, the garage conversion, although not permitted, is not a code violation as the garage doors are in place and operable and two garage stalls are available for parking."

Kitchen Facilities: Zoning Compliance

Kitchen facilities in guest quarters, free-standing recreation rooms, mother-in-law quarters, or other structures that may be classified as a second unit may have to be removed for the property to be consistent with zoning regulations because two units are seldom permitted on an R-l (single-family residential) zoned lot. It is always possible that the second unit has been classified as a legal use or a legal but nonconforming use because of a Grandfather Clause in zoning regulations or a variance may have been granted; however, since zoning regulations and uses are subject to constant revisions, conformity to *current* zoning regulations must be ascertained for every property appraised.

Building Regulations and Permits

All significant changes from the original structure must be described in the appraisal report, and the appraiser must consider and comment on the legality, conformity, quality, and functional utility. The actual permits do not have to be attached to the appraisal; however, the appraiser must designate the status of finalized building permits as well as stating the source of his or her information. An owner's declaration regarding permits is not acceptable; the permits must be verified with city officials.

Just because a conversion, addition, or other violation of zoning regulations has been in existence a long time doesn't mean that it presently is (or ever could be) labeled a legal use and there is no guarantee that the city will not, at some time, require the property owner to either bring the structure up to current code requirements or remove it.

How Code Violations Are Discovered

Building inspectors don't ordinarily go out looking for trouble; however, if they find improvements that are not to code, they will usually make certain that the situation is rectified. For example, city officials have been known to make owners restore garages to their original intended use, tear down garages or additions that did not conform to building codes, tear down and rebuild concrete block wall fencing that did not have proper reinforcing rods, remove the kitchen in second units, and so forth. In many instances, great financial losses to owners could have been avoided by spending a relatively insignificant amount of money to obtain a building permit.

Ask city officials how they uncover code violations because each city varies in procedure. In some cities, when a property changes hands, a "Truth in Sales" document must be obtained from the city and filled out by the owner. Any improvements made to the property, including additions, must be listed. If the buyer waives the document in writing an inspector will not go to the property. If the buyer does *not* waive the document, an inspector will go to the property and all code violations will have to be corrected and permits will have to be obtained for any previously nonpermitted work that has been done.

Sometimes code violations are made known to city officials when parking congestion becomes a problem or when complaints are filed by parties that become aware of code violations. Governing officials may then be compelled to force owners to comply with zoning regulations, thereby, in many instances, producing an undesirable effect on the value of the property. Don't try to second guess what the city might or might not do because the lender is depending on you to report factual data—finalized permits are either on file or they are not.

Problems Created by Discrepancies in Public Records

It has been common practice to assume that permits have been finalized for a property when the present square footage of the property is the same as the total square footage depicted in the assessor's records. Building department officials, who were contacted for clarity regarding the similarity in square footage, stated that the assessor is probably picking up the size of the dwelling, including additions, from reported "Changes in Ownership" (a document buyers are required to submit when property changes ownership) and not from permits as there were no permits on file for the particular properties in question. This illustrates one more reason for verifying permits.

Does Everything Need a Permit?

All the changes that are made to the original property usually require permits, including installation of new heating equipment, plumbing and electrical equipment, hot water heaters, new driveways, fencing, roofs, enclosed patios, patio covers, decks, swimming pools, spas, remodeling, and structural changes. Building codes change over the years; therefore, changes must coincide with today's building requirements. Legitimate contractors always obtain permits. When an element has been added or a structural change has been made that has not been permitted, the item was probably built, installed, or changed by the owner or an unscrupulous contractor; consequently, code violations could be present.

Always verify permits with the building department, or ask owners for copies of building permits. Get in touch with your client to obtain further instructions when you are informed of an alleged permit that you are unable to verify. When you call to verify permits, do not simply ask whether a permit has been issued for a certain item. Permits may have been taken out; however, the permits might not have been finalized because a building inspector was not completely satisfied with the work and made certain stipulations that were never attended to.

PERMITS MUST BE FINALIZED

Building permits are not acceptable unless they have been finalized; therefore, the pertinent question to ask is: "Have the building permits been *finalized?*" Some cities issue a "Certificate of Occupancy" instead of a finalized building permit.

How to Handle Nonpermitted Additions

Nonpermitted additions (including any outbuildings, such as sheds, storage buildings, and garages) should always be described in the appraisal report, and the dimensions of the additions or outbuildings should be shown on the building diagram. Show "no value assigned" on the building diagram and in the appraisal report. Describe the quality, size, condition, and conformity to the subject property as well as competing properties. If applicable, when the addition appears to be up to code, a second value, "if permits are obtained," should be provided in the comments section on page two of the appraisal.

How to Handle Permitted Additions

Permitted additions should be explicitly described and the location and dimensions of the addition should be clearly illustrated on the building diagram. Discuss the consistency in size, design, quality, and utility with the original structure and competing properties in the neighborhood. Include permit numbers, date, and source of information.

DEPRECIATION FACTORS

Discuss the relationship of any property improvements to the commensurate adjustments or the reasons why an adjustment was not appropriate. Adjustments in the sales comparison analysis and interrelated allowances reflected for functional obsolescence should be defined by evaluating the effect of the improvement on the subject's property value considering consistency in size, design, quality, and utility to the subject property as well as considering consistency with competing properties in the neighborhood.

Comment on unusual floor plans, inadequate equipment, and lack of amenities that are expected by buyers in this particular neighborhood. These factors limit value and market appeal and are important to the underwriter in determining the property's suitability for long-term financing. Over- and underimprovements deserve special comments. Overimprovements represent a higher risk than do typical properties in the neighborhood because their construction cost may be greater than their market value. Since cost and value can be quite different, the appraiser's value conclusion should reflect and be consistent with market information. Properties that are nonconforming generally do not hold their value to the same extent as conforming properties.

The Importance of Rating Consistency

All the improvements must be reviewed for their consistency including additions; interior and exterior upgrading, renovating, and modernization; and yard improvements, such as landscaping, patio covers, decks, spas, and swimming pools. When a property is overimproved, based on neighborhood standards, it is unlikely full dollar value will be returned because buyers will look to a more conforming neighborhood for a similar property. To market an overimproved property, the cost of the overimprovement would have to be discounted to arrive at a value consistent with other properties in the neighborhood. The amount of the discount (adjustments) should be determined by a thorough market analysis.

Do not overlook the income levels of the occupants when you are considering consistency based on neighborhood standards. For example, little or none of the cost of a swimming pool could be retrieved in a neighborhood where income levels prohibit the luxury of owning or maintaining a swimming pool. The presence of any amenity has to be appealing to enough purchasers to create active demand. If active demand is nonexistent, the amenity should be considered as "inconsistent" with the neighborhood and relevant adjustments should be reflected in the market analysis and the cost approach for "functional obsolescence."

In some cases, as much as, or even more than, the cost of an improvement will be returned in exchange for improving the property to neighborhood standards. This occurs when the economic standards of the neighborhood demand extensive upgrading, landscaping, yard improvements, and swimming pools and when the majority of homes in older neighborhoods have additions, remodeling, renovating, or upgrading. In either case, a statement should be included illustrating why an adjustment was not called for. Comparable sales with like improvements should be included to provide a basis for your conclusions.

Older properties that are overimprovements for the neighborhood are generally considered to be high-risk situations because older neighborhoods usually have a tendency to decline in value unless they are located in areas of high demand; therefore, consider this situation when you are making your comments.

An old dwelling located in an area that generally consists of newer homes is usually acceptable if it can be demonstrated that the property can be, or has been, modernized to conform to the neighborhood. If the property is an underimprovement and the neighborhood is in great demand, the chances are relatively strong that there will be an active market for the underimproved property because some people will desire to live in this particular neighborhood; however, they may not be able to afford the typical dwelling.

REPAIRS AND OVERALL VALUE

Rate the property considering compatibility to the neighborhood. What elements would have to be repaired or replaced to market the home in the subject neighborhood? When you are relating the condition of the property to other homes in the neighborhood, remember that even the homes that are purported to be in good condition will surely have some items that require cleanup or repair as it's nearly impossible to maintain a home to 100 percent perfection at all times.

How to Deal with Minor Repairs

When minor repairs are needed and the condition is typical and acceptable in the neighborhood, it would not be necessary to expand on items that do not significantly affect marketability, value, or the security of the loan. Small cracks in windows, dripping faucets, torn screens, and other minor homeowner-type repairs should be obvious to the buyer and are usually not detrimental to the overall value of the property.

APPRAISED VALUE: AS IS OR SUBJECT TO

For existing property, appraise the property in an "as is" condition except when it is evident that the health, safety, or security of the occupants is threatened or when there is evidence of current or potential structural damage. Requirements for repairs or inspections are then stipulated. The appraiser must list specific items and include estimated costs for correction of these items. The final estimate of market value should then be made "subject to inspection and satisfactory correction of . . ." (list each item).

Considerations of Health, Safety, and Security of the Occupants

Some of the items that could affect the health, safety, and security of the occupants are broken windows, exposed wiring, unvented heating units, broken or inadequate heating or plumbing equipment, broken railings, and broken steps. Smoke alarms should be tested because some cities will not permit property transfers unless the smoke alarms are in working order.

When the property is in need of maintenance or repair, but is otherwise acceptable security for a loan and the property is otherwise consistent with the neighborhood, it should be appraised on an "as is" basis and the curable physical depreciation should be reflected in the market value estimate. Depreciation conditions should be represented in the effective age, remaining economic life, estimate of depreciation in the cost approach, and appropriate adjustments should be provided in the sales comparison analysis. Include an itemized list and a total estimated cost of all repairs needed that influence the value of the property and are needed to place the home in good marketable condition.

GENERAL MARKET CONDITIONS AND SALES CONCESSIONS

The appraiser must provide specific sales or financing concession data for the subject property and record the types of financing prevalent in the subject market and must comment on the effect on marketability and value. Common special conditions are seller-assisted financing, loan discounts, builder's incentives, special occupancy provisions, refunds, absorption of monthly payments, apportionment of rent payments, and the inclusion of personal property.

If the subject is located in a speculative market area that has experienced dramatic price fluctuations relative to regional norms, the appraisal must also include sales histories of the comparables.

Canned statements or computer-generated statements in

this area should be avoided due to the variances in types of financing in different market areas and the likelihood of change, which sometimes can be very rapid, in the general marketplace.

Financing Statements—Examples

Statements regarding financing might read as follows:

Example 1: Conventional financing at market rates is the most prevalent type of financing in the subject's marketing area at the present time. A few transactions have reflected seller-assisted financing in the form of Second Trust Deeds; however, little, if any, impact on value can be related to this form of financing under current market conditions.

Example 2: Financing for the subject's marketing area consists of mostly conventional loans, both fixed and variable rates, with plus or minus 80 percent loan to value ratios, and spread over 30 years with occasional 15-year notes.

Example 3: Typical financing for the subject's marketing area is conventional with 5 percent to 25 percent cash down payments. Marketing time is considered to be good.

Description of the Property—Examples

When the property is conforming in all respects and is well maintained, comments might read as follows:

Example 1: The improvements are well maintained and are consistent with neighborhood standards. There are no apparent physical, functional, or external inadequacies present that could affect value or marketability.

Example 2: The subject conforms to the neighborhood and the competition with respect to age, type of property, design, construction materials, and functional utility. The condition of the property is above average.

Example 3: The property has been appropriately rehabilitated and modernized over the years and is in keeping with competing properties. There are no apparent physical, functional, or external inadequacies present that could affect value or marketability.

Example 4: Within the past four years the dwelling has been completely modernized and refurbished. The refinements include top-quality ceramic tile flooring in the kitchen, dining area, baths, entry, and hall as well as top-quality wall coverings throughout; high-quality carpeting in the living room and bedrooms; and a new range/oven, dishwasher, and microwave oven. The remodeling and upgrades are not considered to be overimprovements because the majority of homes in the area have been similarly upgraded.

SUMMARY

At this point, pause for a moment to reflect on your evaluation of the neighborhood, site, and the improvements. Always remember that lending institutions are in the business to make loans. Therefore, although you are responsible for reporting all the facts as you see them as well as never withholding pertinent information, at the same time, you should not go overboard and be overly severe when you are describing the neighborhood and the subject property.

Are you actually looking at the neighborhood and the subject property from the viewpoint of a typical buyer for this type of home in this particular neighborhood or are you allowing your personal opinions to overrule your judgment? Eliminate any "prejudicial" (conceived without proof or competent evidence, but based on what seems valid to one's own mind) opinions, statements, and descriptions as well as any inconsequential data that do not relate to the neighborhood or property description, the final estimate of market value, or value and marketability throughout the life of the loan.

Explain any variations between your physical measurement of the subject structures and site and the assessor's (or other data source) total square footage as well as any other information that is shown in public records, which you have verified as being incorrect.

ILLUSTRATIONS: POOR UTILITY AND FUNCTIONAL OBSOLESCENCE

The following two illustrations are presented to demonstrate poor layout, poor utility, and functional obsolescence.

Example 1 is a poorly designed house with a lot of wasted space. Not only is the house poorly designed, but the problem is compounded by the dining room addition. Study the example and note the following deficiencies:

1. Occupants must walk through the living room or kitchen to reach the dining room.
2. The living room does not allow for desirable furniture placement due to walk-through traffic, placement of the fireplace, and open entrances from the hallway.
3. The den is too small and too open to have good utility.
4. Approximately 350 square feet of livable area is wasted because of the oversized and impractical hallway.
5. Storage in the hallway is placed poorly.
6. Wasted space in the master bath is caused by two separate entries.
7. Poor placement of laundry and storage exists in the ga-

rage; occupants must walk around the storage area to reach the laundry facilities.

Example 2 is also a poorly designed house that exhibits functional obsolescence, such as

1. Entry directly into the living room; occupants must walk through the living room to reach all the other rooms in the house, resulting in much walk-through traffic and little room for desirable furniture placement.

2. Convenience to laundry is poor; access is through one of the bedrooms or via an outside entry.

3. The dwelling exhibits functional obsolescence because it only has one bathroom.

4. The home has inadequate storage areas.

5. There is no separate dining room and only a very small dining area in the kitchen.

FUNCTIONAL OBSOLESCENCE, Example No. 1

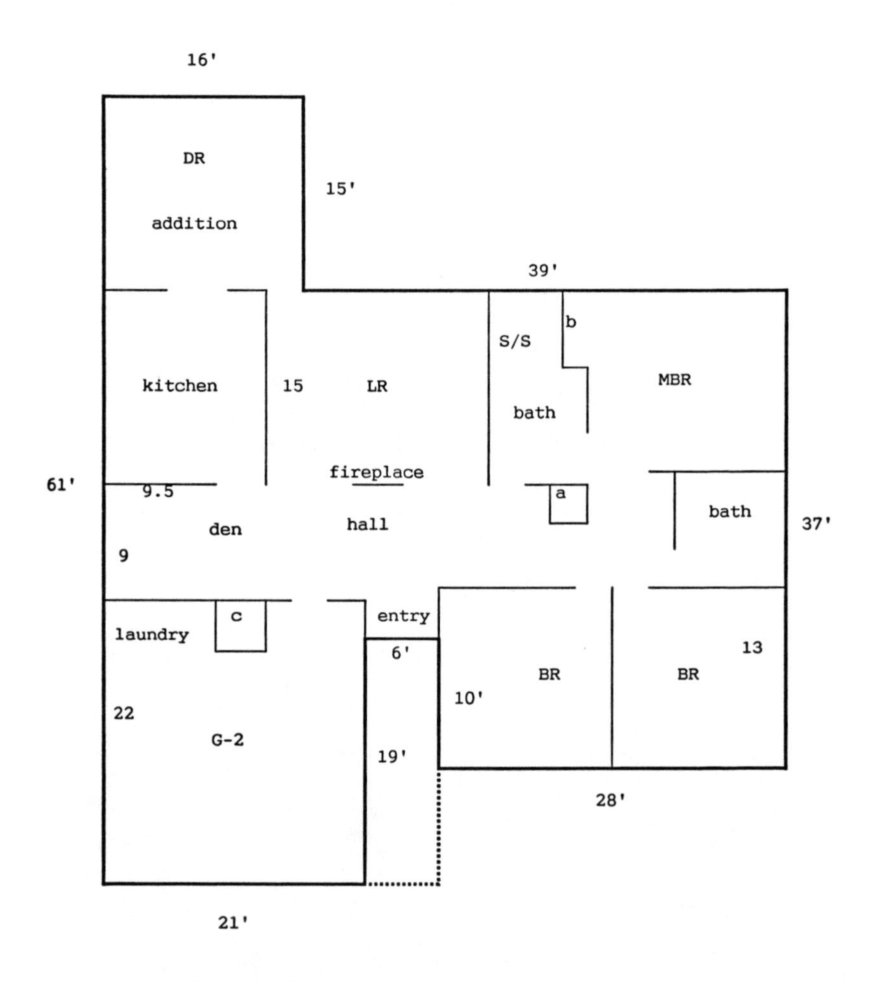

a - interior storage
b - walk-in closet
c - garage storage

FUNCTIONAL OBSOLESCENCE, Example No. 2

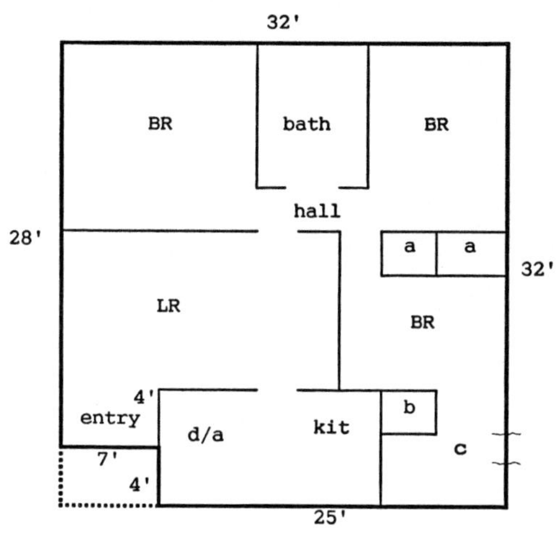

a - closet
b - storage
c - laundry

CHAPTER 11

THE COST APPROACH TO VALUE

This chapter provides specific instructions for estimating building costs, depreciation, and site value.

The "reproduction cost" is the cost of reproducing the subject structure, and other components of the property, using the same materials and workmanship, and the same layout, at current prices. Adjustments for condition and obsolescence should be made under depreciation.

The cost approach can be a reliable indication of value if the property is new, or if it is relatively new with little depreciation, and meaningful land sales are available. The cost approach is a less reliable indication of value when a property is older and depreciation is difficult to estimate.

When you appraise older structures containing obsolete materials or unusual functional features, it might be difficult, if not impossible, to estimate reproduction cost with any reasonable degree of accuracy. In such cases, replacement cost can be used; however, appraisers must specifically state that they are using replacement costs, and they must include a detailed description of the materials and the quality of materials from which the estimate of replacement cost was established. Any functional deficiencies that are eliminated by using replacement costs, rather than reproduction costs, must be fully described.

ADVANTAGES OF THE COST APPROACH

The cost approach, if properly prepared, can be beneficial as a reinforcement to the sales comparison approach to value. The cost approach can also be beneficial for a number of other reasons, particularly as a defense against errors made in other areas of the appraisal report. Precision in executing the cost approach is extremely important when you appraise property for tax appeals—to estimate damage losses caused by slippage problems, to determine the highest and best use of the site, and to determine feasibility in relation to a renovation program—and other occasions when it is important to segregate land values, building values, and depreciation factors.

The ability to estimate accurately building costs, costs of extras and amenities, and garage costs; to assign value to site improvements; and to assign dollar estimations accurately to elements of depreciation will enable you to extract definitive land values. Accurate land values are extremely critical because there will be many occasions when you will be called upon to provide preliminary estimates of value.

Sometimes lenders, or clients, request preliminary estimates of value to determine the feasibility of the transaction to avoid expending a good deal of time, effort, and money on a pointless undertaking. If you do not have sufficient knowledge of costs and land values, and you are unable to render a reasonable estimate of value readily, your client will most certainly question your lack of experience and expertise. Put forth the effort to become very proficient with the cost approach because your clients will always feel more confident when they know they can depend on you to provide accurate building costs, land values, and reasonable preliminary and final estimates of value. The benefits far outweigh the effort because you will also be able to write a precise appraisal in a minimal amount of time.

When comparable sales data are limited or nonexistent in the subject neighborhood, estimated values by the cost approach (if properly prepared) can be used as a guide to begin your research as well as validating estimated values by the market approach. A comprehensive knowledge of costs and land values is also needed to authenticate owner's and builder's alleged building and land costs. Additionally, local lenders, underwriters, and reviewers are usually familiar with costs and land-to-building ratios in given areas (or they might use the costs provided in cost manuals to validate the entire cost approach); therefore, they will surely recognize misstated costs and land values. Consequently, they may question the validity of the entire appraisal.

You can quickly estimate rough values if you make a note of the land-to-building ratio every time that you write an appraisal. For instance, in "Circle City" the land value is typically 40 percent of the total property value. You have estimated a depreciated value of the improvements of, say, $84,000. Divide $84,000. by 60 percent (100 percent less 40 percent land value leaves 60 percent for the improvements) to find the estimated value, which is $140,000.

Because land sales are not always available, you should be familiar with typical land-to-building ratios so you can define realistic land values. Make certain, however, that you consider view and location amenities as well as the overall lot size when you are estimating land values.

USING THE COST APPROACH TO ELIMINATE ERRORS

The cost approach should be resolved before you attempt to determine the income and market values because this practice will help to illuminate possible discrepancies in the report.

Each value should be determined on its own merit, and each value should corroborate the other. The indicated values by the cost approach, income approach, and the market approach do not have to be the same, but they should be reasonably close. If the values are not within a close range, look for possible errors and omissions. Check the cost approach to make sure costs have been assigned to all the elements of value and all items have been appropriately depreciated. Check the arithmetic in the cost approach and the sales comparison analysis. Make certain that you have not overlooked any elements requiring adjustments, check the adjustments again to make sure that they are reasonable, and look for plus signs where there should be a minus sign and vice versa.

OBTAINING COST ESTIMATES

Cost estimates can be obtained from cost manuals published by several reputable organizations, appraiser's files, and local building contractors. Cost manuals not only include instructions for determining costs; they also contain a variety of other useful information, including pictorial illustrations. These illustrations can be very helpful when you are attempting to define the age, type, and quality of different structures.

Whenever you are appraising property where rooms have been added or there is evidence of remodeling, upgrading, replacement of any type of equipment, new flooring, new wall or window coverings, or yard improvements that have been recently installed (including landscaping, patio covers, enclosed patios, swimming pools, spas, block wall fencing, and concrete driveways), always ask owners to define their costs because this is a very effective way to learn local costs of many different types of improvements.

HOW TO CALCULATE BUILDING SIZES

Building dimensions must be accurate to the nearest half foot, and they must be the same as the dimensions indicated on the building diagram. Include finished gross livable area only. Always recheck the subject's description on page one and page two to make certain the total gross livable area is consistent throughout the report.

Calculate finished and unfinished basement and attic areas separately. Stairs are usually not considered as livable area; however, you should always use the same levels of adjustment. Therefore, inclusion of the stairs in the gross livable area should be considered on a case basis; that is, if the gross livable area of the comparable sales includes the stairs, you should include the stairs as well, so you will be using the same levels of adjustment.

Why Consistency Is Important

If you do not use the same levels of adjustment, your value could be distorted. For example, suppose you deducted a 5 ft. × 10 ft. of 50 sq. ft. stairway from the subject dwelling and the square footage of the comparable sales included the stairways? If you were making size adjustments of $35. per square foot, you would be making a $2,000. adjustment that might not be appropriate. Since you have no way of knowing, in most instances, whether the size of the comparable sales includes the stairways, the only method you can use to determine whether a deduction for stairs is appropriate is by analyzing the indicated value of the subject for each of the comparables. If the indicated values do not appear to be making sense, it may be due to the adjustments for size. Explanations should be provided if you do not deduct the stairs or adjustments are not made for variances in size.

Considerations Given to Hillside Property

Hillside properties deserve special consideration. For Fannie Mae purposes, any living area that lies below the position of the front door is typically considered "below grade." This property is kept separate from the above-grade, or main-level, living area and is usually valued independently. The rationale for this requirement has to do with the lower building costs usually associated with lower levels or basements. However, when you define the gross livable area of hillside properties, make certain that you use the same levels of adjustment between the comparables to the subject. The subject could have one or more floors of actual (not basement) livable area below grade, and the comparable sales could have one or more floors of actual livable area below grade or none. If the total gross livable area of the subject includes only the square footage above grade level—will this figure actually relate to the gross livable area of the comparable sales? Always check the sizes of each comparable sale while you are in the field to make certain that you will be using the same levels of adjustment.

HOW TO PRESENT BUILDING CALCULATIONS

Show all of the calculations in the building sketch area of the form, on the building diagram itself, or on a separate addendum. The dimensions should not be shown in inches; always use decimals, for example, 12 ft., 6 in. should be shown as 12.5 or 12.50. Show calculations for the garage separately, show calculations for each floor and the total of each floor separately, and indicate the final total gross livable area. The following format is recommended:

26.0 ft. × 35.5 ft.	=	923.00 sq. ft.
4.0 ft. × 7.0 ft.	=	28.00 "
−6.5 ft. × 15.0 ft.		−97.50 "
Total 1st floor	=	835.50 sq. ft.
22.0 ft. × 29.0 ft.	=	638.00 "
−7.0 ft. × 9.0 ft.	=	−63.00 "
Total 2nd floor	=	575.00 sq. ft.
Total GLA	=	1,410.50 sq. ft.
Garage 25.0 ft. × 20.0 ft.	=	500.00 sq. ft.

HOW TO ESTIMATE BUILDING COSTS

Following instructions provided in a cost manual, select a base cost applicable to the subject size and quality. Always remember that costs provided in cost handbooks represent average costs; therefore, the costs should be refined to represent the particular property and the particular area in which the property is located. When a residence being valued obviously falls between two qualities, a suitable cost may be interpolated from the basic cost levels.

Next, add adjustments for the type of roofing, type of flooring, number of plumbing fixtures, appliances, fireplaces, and so on. The indicated value by the cost approach will be distorted if you neglect to consider the cost and quality of these items when you define the cost of the residence. Use the following checklist to avoid overlooking elements of value that should be added to the base cost of the dwelling:

1. Exterior wall trim or finishes: define the additional cost based on the amount, type, and quality of common brick, brick veneer, face brick, stone, aluminum siding, wood siding, or shingle siding.
2. Adjustments for the type and quality of roofing material.
3. Number and type of plumbing fixtures in kitchen and baths.
4. Number and type of fireplaces; costs of hearths and mantels.
5. Number, type, and quality of range/oven, dishwasher, disposal, microwave oven, and other kitchen equipment.
6. Recessed lighting.
7. Built-in vacuum system, intercom system, and security system.
8. Type and quality of heating and cooling systems.
9. Type and quality of floor coverings.
10. Types of wall finishes and window coverings.
11. Types and quality of interior and exterior doors and other wood finishes.
12. Type and quality of kitchen and bath cabinetry.
13. Built-in storage units, bookshelves, bars, wetbars, and any other upgrades.

Costs for the preceding components can be found in cost handbooks under "square foot costs" or in the "segregated costs" section of the handbook. Base costs and segregated costs can also be defined based on the appraiser's knowledge of costs. Some or all of the items might be classified as overimprovements to the property; however, they must be considered when you estimate the reproduction cost new of the dwelling. If any of the components of the property are overimprovements, an appropriate adjustment should be made in the depreciation category.

After the adjustments have been applied to the basic cost, apply current cost multipliers and then refine the costs to arrive at a local cost level by applying local cost multipliers. Refer to Appendix A, Example: Cost Calculations.

Estimating Building Costs for Unique Property

When you appraise unique properties, a segregated cost method might be more appropriate and base costs could require further refinement. Certain building designs, customizing, property located in outlying areas, inaccessible locations, hillside locations, and construction with excessive foundation costs can result in costs above or below those considered as the norm in cost handbooks. Labor is usually cheaper in outlying areas resulting in less cost to build; however, the cost of labor could be offset by the additional cost of transporting materials to the site. Access to and from the job and the neighborhood itself can play an important part in the cost of labor and material. When you assign costs, make sure that the costs are appropriate with respect to the architectural design and location of the property as well as considering quality, customizing, and upgrading.

When you appraise nontypical property, obtain cost estimates from local contractors familiar with the type of property and the location of the property. Whenever you have the opportunity to appraise proposed construction, keep a file copy of the estimated construction costs projected by various builders for future reference because this is a good way to learn how to estimate costs for custom-built homes and unusual properties. When appropriate, comment on higher than typical costs due to the unique characteristics of the property.

Why Cost Estimates Should Be Rounded

Always round cost figures to the nearest dollar or half-dollar (whichever makes the most sense) because it is unrealistic to calculate *estimated* costs to cents. For example, square foot costs of $45.61/sq. ft. should be appropriately rounded to $45.50, $45.00, or $46.00.

Additional Considerations: Extras

List all the elements that require separate consideration and costs, such as finished attic, basement, finished basement, swimming pool, spa, sauna, or recreation room. All the elements that are assigned a cost in the cost approach must be specifically described in the appraisal report and the quality, type of materials, condition, age, and size of the elements must be identified because it would be impossible to assign appropriate costs if these factors were not considered. Additionally, the quality, type of materials, condition, and age must be reckoned with when you are estimating depreciation.

When you are listing extras, be specific. For example, indicate swimming pool and perimeter decking when the decking is included in the cost of the pool. This way, the reader does not have to wonder whether the decking is included in the cost of the swimming pool, included in the site improvement category, or, perhaps, the cost of the decking might have been overlooked.

Special Energy-Efficient Items

Enter the costs of special energy-efficient items. Specific descriptions must be included in the appraisal report. Include itemized costs when available and appropriate. If the costs are substantial, the appraiser might want to include the optional FHLMC Form 70A "Energy Addendum Residential Appraisal Report" to provide a basis for costs and adjustments.

Porches and Patios

Explain the reasons for nontypical costs; that is, are you assigning costs for a covered porch; covered patio; brick, concrete, or flagstone patio; enclosed patio; wood deck; or a covered entry?

Garages and Carports

Sometimes appraisers list the area of the garage as, say, 220 sq. ft. while descriptions throughout the report depict the garage as a "two-car garage." Therefore, always make sure that the description of the garage is consistent throughout the report. Approximate garage sizes are one-car garage, 200 sq. ft., two-car garage, 420 sq. ft., three-car garage, 630 sq. ft.

Calculate the cost of the garage. For attached and built-in garages, deduct the cost of common walls and common roofs. Make sure the costs reflect finished walls, built-in cabinets, built-in shelves, insulation, electric garage door openers, or other elements of value when these items are present. Describe amenities that are assigned value in the body of the report or in an addendum so reviewers can readily validate the costs.

New or Proposed Construction

When you appraise custom-built homes that are new, under construction, or proposed, an itemized list of the builder's projected construction costs should be included with the appraisal and the costs must be validated by the appraiser. Also include the cost of the land and the date the land was purchased when this information is available. If land costs are not relevant or the costs are not available, provide an explanation.

Adjusting Base Costs

The base cost of the dwelling and the land must be adjusted to reflect extraordinary costs of development due to locational or other influences, such as location within the city; hillside locations; accessibility to the site; residential street improvements; connections to public utilities; excavation costs; fill; pilings or unusual foundation costs; or removal of existing structures, trees, rocks, and shrubs.

Add contractor's profit and overhead, as applicable. Overhead, soft or indirect costs, and contractor's profit are usually not included in a general contract for construction. Consider architectural, engineering, and consulting fees; cost of plans; plan checks; insurance and taxes during construction; interest on land costs and construction loans; title changes; feasibility studies; loss of reasonable return on the investment until anticipated occupancy is obtained; and marketing costs. Builder's profit and soft (indirect) costs can typically add 15 to 25 percent, or more, to basic labor and material costs depending on the type of building, the extent of the marketing effort, the length of time it takes to complete construction, and construction interest charges at the time.

When you define projected builder's costs, segregate the costs applicable to the improvement from those applicable to the land. Also, if the owner paid, say, $300,000. for the land, either with or without on-site or off-site improvements, you should not automatically use the purchase price (cost) for the land value in the cost approach. The value of the land should be the value that is indicated *by the market* regardless of what the owner paid for it.

When you appraise new, proposed, or uncompleted custom-built homes; always be careful not to confuse the concept of cost with the concept of value.

When and How to Include Cost Sources and Land Sales

When the cost approach is given the greatest consideration in defining a final estimate of value, the source of the cost data and comparable land sales must be included. For example, provide the following information (which can be presented in the building sketch area of the report): "For cost information, the appraiser has used the Marshall-Swift Valuation Service as a basis for determining construction costs for the subject dwelling."

State whether the comparable land sales are finished or unfinished sites and make adjustments, as applicable. The land value in the cost approach should represent *finished* lot value, including grading, street improvements, connection to utilities, and so forth.

TOTAL ESTIMATED COST NEW

Reconcile the costs assigned with the description of the subject property to make certain that all the components of the property have been considered. Items frequently overlooked are cost adjustments for upgrading, number of fireplaces, air conditioning, security systems, interior garage finishes, and extraordinary exterior wall finishes.

PROCEDURES FOR ESTIMATING DEPRECIATION

Accrued depreciation is the loss from the upper limits of value resulting from physical depreciation, functional obsolescence, or external (economic) obsolescence. The appraiser is called upon to observe, in detail, the physical, functional, and external influences associated with the appraised property to formulate a studied projection of depreciation. The precision of the appraiser's estimate is directly related to the subject property. The problem involves identifying the causes of depreciation and assigning a proper rate of depreciation.

Physical Depreciation

Physical depreciation is the loss in value inherent in the structure itself as a result of wearing out or deterioration of the structure. It results from the interaction of several elements, including age and deferred maintenance

Curable and Incurable Physical Depreciation

"Curable" physical depreciation occurs because of deferred maintenance, such as painting, minor carpentry, plumbing and electrical repairs, roof repairs, replacing worn flooring, and other homeowner-type repairs. "Incurable" physical depreciation is the physical wearing out of the structure as well as major repair work that is not economically feasible to undertake, that is, if the cost to cure exceeds the value it adds to the property, this would imply that the condition is incurable. Incurable physical depreciation also refers to other items that are currently not practical or feasible to correct, such as furnaces or roofing that have not reached the end of their economic life.

If there is an extensive amount of curable physical depreciation present that affects the value of the property, an itemized list of repairs and an estimated total cost of the repairs should be included. Corresponding adjustments should be reflected in the sales comparison analysis.

How to Estimate Physical Depreciation Based on Economic Life

There are several methods that can be used to define a dollar amount of physical depreciation. One commonly used method, when appraising a single-family residence for lending purposes, is "physical depreciation based on economic life," which is similar to "straight line depreciation" except it is based on economic life instead of physical life. For this method to be effective, careful consideration must be given to the economic life estimate. Following is an example of estimating physical depreciation based on economic life:

Effective age	10 to 12 years
Remaining economic life	50 to 53 years
Total life span:	60 to 65 years

Ten years divided by 60 is 17 percent; 12 years divided by 65 years is 18 percent. Depreciation should be in the range of 17 to 18 percent. Multiply the dollar amount of the total estimated cost new by the percentage estimate of depreciation to find the dollar amount of depreciation.

Why You Should Refine Estimates of Depreciation

This age/economic life concept is frequently used because it is simple. However, the problem with this method is that the percentage derived includes all three causes of depreciation—physical, functional, and external. Therefore, the percentage estimates derived from this method should be adjusted to account for functional and external obsolescence that is deducted separately. The appraiser may, for example, reason that a total depreciation estimate of 17 percent is made up of 11 percent for physical depreciation, 4 percent for functional obsolescence, and 2 percent for economic obsolescence for the particular property being appraised. The appraiser should always relate the percentage derived to the particular structure being appraised and adjust the percentage of depreciation accordingly—based on his or her experience and judgment.

How to Extract Percentage Rates of Depreciation from the Market

A percentage rate of depreciation, which also includes all three causes of depreciation, can be extracted from the market when there are a sufficient number of sales available. To determine an estimate of depreciation, analyze several sales of properties that are similar in characteristics to the subject property. Subtract the land value of the comparable sale from the sales price to determine the value attributed to the improvements. Next, subtract the indicated improvement value from the total estimated reproduction cost new of the comparable sale to define a dollar amount of depreciation. Divide the dollar amount of depreciation by the reproduction cost new of the comparable to derive a percentage figure of depreciation.

Using Cost Handbooks to Estimate Depreciation

Cost handbooks contain tables, based on experience surveys, that can be used to estimate depreciation. Always check the tables that you are using to see if they are based on economic or physical life. The tables in the *Residential Cost Handbook,* published by Marshall and Swift, are based on economic life. Functional obsolescence is included in the depreciation tables. Any information obtained from outside sources, including the material contained in cost handbooks, must be authenticated and the data evaluated for interrelationship to the subject property.

Defining Functional Obsolescence

Functional obsolescence is a loss in value caused by deficiencies in utility, inadequacies, poor or nonconforming architectural styles and designs, and excess. Consider curable and incurable functional obsolescence separately and provide explanations for clarity.

"Curable" obsolescence is measured by the cost to cure. Obsolescence that is not profitable or feasible to cure is termed "incurable." The feasibility of curing obsolescence, and the dollar amount of obsolescence used for any adjustments, should be related to the market; that is, will the market return all or some of the cost to cure? For example, if it cost $4,500. to add a garage and the market return was $3,500., it would not be economically feasible to add the garage. If the figures were reversed, the obsolescence inherent in the property, due to inadequate parking facilities, would be termed curable.

The dollar amount of *curable* functional obsolescence can be measured by the excess cost of adding the item to the existing structure over the cost of incorporating it in the reproduction cost. For example, the cost of installing a bath at the present time is $6,000. The cost of installing the bath at the time the house was originally constructed was $4,500. Hence, the dollar amount of curable functional obsolescence is $1,500.

The dollar amount of *incurable* functional obsolescence can be measured by the difference between the cost, less depreciation, and the amount returned by the market. For example, the cost of a swimming pool is $20,000. and market studies show that homes with similar pools sell for $10,000. more than comparable homes without pools; hence, the market adjustment is $10,000. To find the amount of functional obsolescence, subtract the market adjustment and depreciation from the cost in the following manner:

Cost of swimming pool	$ 20,000.
Less : Percentage of depreciation applied to cost new (say, 20%)	– 4,000.
Less: Market adjustment	– 10,000.
Functional obsolescence	$ 6,000.

An outline similar to this example should be presented in the report to demonstrate the manner in which the adjustment for functional obsolescence was obtained.

Estimating the Dollar Amount of External Obsolescence

External obsolescence is a reduction in market value caused by factors external to the property, such as encroachments; excessive taxes; deterioration in the quality and accessibility of schools, shopping, or community facilities; loss of public transportation; undesirable proximity to commercial or industrial property, power lines, freeways, traffic streets, or toxic waste sites; or any other adverse environmental hazards or nuisances.

To estimate the effect of any external influences and to find the dollar amount of external obsolescence, examine variations in sales prices of homes in the subject neighborhood and, if appropriate, competing neighborhoods, with and without the particular external influence in question. When recent comparable sales data are in short supply, or nonexistent, the appraiser can make a judgment decision, based on his or her knowledge and experience in analyzing similar property, rating the effect of the influence (inconsequential, positive, or negative) on the subject property and the entire neighborhood.

Sometimes appraisers make a deduction for external obsolescence in the depreciation category as well as deducting an additional amount from the land value for the same external influence. In most cases, economic obsolescence should not be attributed to the improvement value *and* the land value. Before making dual deductions for external obsolescence, consider whether the adverse effect on value actually affects the improvement value, the land value, or both because appropriate statements, explaining the basis for your deductions, must be included in the appraisal report.

Reconciliation of Depreciation

Show the percentage and the dollar amount of depreciation on the form. In addition to providing complete descriptions of depreciation conditions on page one of the report, provide a brief explanation of the deductions made for functional and external obsolescence in the building sketch area of the report or in an addendum to the report. Make certain that corresponding adjustments have been made in the sales comparison analysis.

SITE IMPROVEMENTS "AS IS"

Estimate the cost of each component part of the site improvements included in your description of the property. Then, enter the depreciated ("as is") value on the form.

Bushes, flowers, shrubs, and trees can range from small immature vegetation to fully grown, very exotic, and very expensive; therefore, costs should reflect the age, size, and type of plantings. Have you considered the particular type of ground cover or lawn when you were estimating costs? Have you estimated costs based on the type of material as well as the quality of the yard improvements? The linear feet of fencing, the width and depth of the driveway, type of materials and size of planters and other yard improvements?

DON'T FORGET ABOUT THE SIZE OF THE SITE

Have you considered the *size of the site* with relationship to the costs? Minimal site improvement costs for a larger than typical site is obvious evidence of lack of thoroughness on the part of the appraiser.

Minimal site improvements (landscaping, sidewalks, fencing) usually run about $1.00/sq. ft. Typical, depreciated, site improvements are in the $2.00 to $2.50/sq. ft. range. Five dollars per square foot, or more, is not unreasonable for extensive site improvements and landscaping.

Overimprovements and Repairs

Further explanations should be provided when site improvements are considered to be overimprovements for the neighborhood. If repairs or replacements are needed to bring site improvements up to neighborhood standards, include an itemized list and an estimated total cost of the repairs. Adjustments for overimprovements, underimprovements, or repairs should be reflected in the sales comparison analysis.

Site Improvements: Planned Unit Developments

For planned unit developments, when site improvements are owned in common, under the category "site improvements, as is," include the unit's pro-rata share of value of amenities in the cost of site improvements and provide an explanation in another area of the report.

How to Estimate Site Value

Since there are seldom any residential land comparables available in built-up areas, the allocation (or extraction) procedure is the most common method used for valuing land for single-family residential purposes. By analyzing a sufficient number of sales in given areas, the appraiser can establish a ratio of land value to the total value of the improvements, that is, subtract the value of the improvements from the total value of the property to find the approximate value of the land. If the land value ratio is excessively high, this may be an indication that the present use is not the highest and best use of the land.

Land Estimate Using an Abstraction Technique—Example Comparable 6

Address: 4831 West Street, Laguna Beach	
Sale/ listing price:	$1,190,000.
Deduct for negotiation	119,000.
Deduct building cost: 4,500 sq ft × $77.50	348,750.
Deduct garage: 500 sq ft × $16.00	8,000.
Deduct extras	15,000.
Deduct landscape and site improvements	20,000.
Remainder equals land value	$ 679,250.
Location adjustment .	.13
Estimated subject land value	$ 767,552.

When you are using this method, make certain that the sales comparables being analyzed to determine land value are very similar to the subject property and the resultant value truly represents the subject lot size. Also, be certain that you consider the amenities, for example, proximity to ocean, lakes, or golf courses.

Documenting Speculative Land Values

Include land sales whenever the value appears to be speculative. Adjust land sales, as needed, to represent finished site value, that is, add costs for grading, street improvements, utilities, wells, septic systems, and so forth.

When the land value exceeds 30 percent of the total value, provide an explanation, such as

Example 1: The subject is located in a neighborhood with strong demand because of the convenience to schools, shopping centers, and local employment centers. Locational appeal and the small size of the dwelling contributes to a higher than typical ratio of land to building, which is common for this neighborhood.

Example 2: The land value ratio is typical for the neighborhood, which is entirely built up. As land has become increasingly scarce, the value of the land has been increasing.

Example 3: The subject property is located in a prestigious, high-demand neighborhood in which the ratio of land to building is higher than in less desirable areas. The subject's land-to-building ratio is common for this neighborhood.

CAUTION

Never misrepresent building costs to simulate a lower land value in an attempt to keep the land value within a certain ratio. Appraisers should always attempt to be as accurate as possible with land costs because the value of land in proportion to the value of the total property is an important underwriting consideration.

How to Present Land Sales

The market value of the land is estimated based upon the sales and asking prices of other properties that possess similar physical characteristics. Consideration is given to the desirable locational features of the site, dimensions and shape, topography, access to and from the site, immediate and adjacent uses, soil and subsoil conditions, drainage, utility of the site, private and public use restrictions, easements, public utility service, environmental influences, and the sales price, date of sale, and terms of the transaction.

For presentation of land sales data, a format similar to the example provided in Appendix B, Example: Land Sales is recommended. When a number of comparable sales are included in the appraisal report, the appraiser should include a "spread sheet" or summary of the salient features of the comparable sales, for example, comparable number, address, zoning, size, sales price, unit price, and adjusted unit price.

INDICATED VALUE BY THE COST APPROACH

The indicated value by the cost approach is an estimate; therefore, it should be rounded to the nearest $100. or the nearest $500.; for example, round $1,285,700. to $1,286,000.

CHAPTER 12

PRESENTATION AND ANALYSIS OF THE COMPARABLE SALES

This chapter deals specifically with procedures for presenting, documenting, and adjusting market data. As we continue to follow the format of the Uniform Residential Appraisal Report, we will show you the easiest and most effective ways to list the information that you have gathered, how to handle cash equivalency, the quickest and best ways to make market adjustments, and how to tell your readers what you did and why you did it.

THE RIGHT NUMBER OF SALES TO USE

At least three comparables must be closed sales. The appraiser must include a statement confirming that the sales are, in fact, closed sales. Document numbers should be used to show that the sales have recorded.

Sometimes document numbers are not available even

though the sales have actually closed. For example, property situated on leasehold land will not be shown as a recorded sale with a document number if the land has not changed hands. When land contracts are used in lieu of purchase money mortgages, the title does not change hands until the mortgage debt has been paid in full. There are numerous other reasons why closed sales are not recorded until some months later. When document numbers, proof of ownership changes, or recording dates are not available, explain the circumstances and provide some other data source, so readers can verify the closing dates of the sales. For example, list the real estate agent's name and telephone number; escrow officer's name, telephone number, and the escrow number of the sale; or buyer's or owner's names and telephone numbers.

More than three closed sales should always be evaluated and included in the appraisal report when

1. you are appraising higher-priced property.
2. the sales have other than conventional financing.
3. property values are increasing or decreasing.
4. the appraised value differs from the sales price (is either higher or lower).
5. when the market data are so dissimilar to the subject that large or numerous adjustments are applied.

Most lenders require a minimum of five comparable sales for properties valued at $500,000. or more.

Why You Should Eliminate Redundant Sales

Occasionally, simply because appraisers have reviewed several sales, they will incorporate all of them in the appraisal report even though some of the sales are of little consequence with respect to providing a sound basis for the adjustments or adding support to the concluded value. Redundant sales, included in this manner, only confuse and complicate the issue because underwriters and reviewers have more sales to evaluate and many questions can arise regarding the inclusion of meaningless market data. The more sales that are included, the greater the likelihood that errors will be made. Do not confuse *quantity* with *quality;* include only three *appropriate* sales unless one or more of the previously mentioned conditions exists, in which case, include only those sales comparables that actually are relevant.

Using Additional Market Data

When an appropriate number of sales have been incorporated in the appraisal report and you wish to reference additional pertinent market data without making formal adjustments or including photos, present the sales information in an addendum or in the comments section of the report. Consider the ensuing representation:

"147 Ash Street, located opposite the subject, is in escrow at a reported sales price of $178,000. with conventional terms. 843 Lemon Street, two blocks south, has a pending offer of $182,000. with conventional terms. Both properties are equivalent to the subject in size, age, and condition and lend additional support to my concluded value."

This practice also eliminates questions from reviewers who might ask why certain sales were not included in the report.

ARM'S-LENGTH TRANSACTIONS

Do not use sales that are not "bona fide arm's-length transactions." If the sales have been forced for any reason, such as a foreclosure, tax sale, the liquidation of an estate, divorce settlement, or employee transfer, or if the principals are related, the sale might not be an arm's-length transaction. Refer to the definition of market value.

How to Use Listings in the Market Analysis

Do not automatically discount listing prices by the agent's typical percentage rate of commission to find an approximate selling price. Adjustments derived in this manner seldom relate to the market because real estate agents do not determine a probable sales price and then add on the exact dollar amount of their commission to find a listing price. Agents usually know the approximate amount that typical buyers discount from the listing prices; therefore, the listing prices will be adjusted accordingly to leave room for negotiation. When listings are used for additional supportive data, review market history in the area to find the dollar amount that listing prices are usually discounted to arrive at a sales price. Then, adjust and document the listing accordingly. For example,

Comparable No. 5 is a current listing in the subject development. The 1.5 percent reduction from the list price is based on the average selling price discount in this neighborhood:

Comparable	List Price	Selling Price	Discount
No. 1	$337,000.	$333,000.	−1.2%
No. 2	$340,000.	$335,000.	−1.5%
No. 3	$350,000.	$350,000.	−0.0%
No. 4	$389,000.	$385,000.	−1.0%

Don't forget to review the type of financing that was offered in listings that you use in your reports. If the owner or agent believe that the property might sell with special terms, they might increase the listing price to compensate for special financing terms or concessions. A financing adjustment might be warranted if the listing price appears to be inflated because of the type of financing or concessions offered by the owner.

When listings are presented in the report, the appraiser must make a complete analysis of the listing, include a photostatic copy of the listing, and provide an explanation supporting its use.

HOW TO MAKE VALUE ADJUSTMENTS

The subject is the standard against which the comparable sales are evaluated and adjusted. Comparable sales are adjusted to the subject property. When an item in the comparable property is *superior* to the subject, a *minus* adjustment is made. When an item in the comparable property is *inferior* to the subject, a *plus* adjustment is made to bring that item equal to the subject.

Most lenders view the use of "similar" or "equal" with disfavor. In fact, some lenders will not accept appraisals when these terms have been used to describe items in the sales analysis section of the report. The appropriate descriptive terms to be used are good, average, fair, or poor (which are related to the subject in the same manner as described in the neighborhood section of this book), superior, or inferior. Lenders prefer these terms because it makes it easier for them to relate the comparable sales to the subject property.

Requirements for Comparability

External influences, inadequacies, and amenities may or may not influence the sales prices of property in the subject's particular neighborhood; therefore, the only valid and effective method of determining whether there should be an adjustment is by analyzing sales prices of similar neighborhood properties, with and without the item in question, every time a different property is appraised.

The appraiser must provide a basis for all the adjustments to the comparable sales; that is, an adjustment for a swimming pool should be supported by reference to at least one sale (two sales are preferable) of a like property with a swimming pool. If market data available are insufficient to provide a basis for adjustments, the appraiser can make a judgment decision. Adjustments based on the appraiser's experience are usually acceptable if they are realistic and typical, and the reader can easily follow the appraiser's logic. Explanations must be provided. For example,

"There have been no recent sales of comparable homes with swimming pools in the subject neighborhood or competing neighborhoods. The market adjustment for the swimming pool is based on market history and the appraiser's experience in assigning value adjustments in this neighborhood."

Using Rules of Thumb

Rules of thumb can be used, for your own purposes, as a starting point in your analysis; however, adjustments based on rules of thumb must always be refined to reflect typical buyers' reactions in the subject's particular neighborhood. Habitual use of rules of thumb, such as "x" amount of dollars for traffic street locations, variations in lot sizes, number of fireplaces, size of garages, air conditioning, swimming pools, and patios is a very easy way to arrive at unfounded and erroneous estimates of market value.

When appraisers apply rules of thumb by rote, they typically overlook economic factors. For example, the market value of swimming pools, garages, fireplaces, and extra baths can differ substantially in varied neighborhoods depending on the income levels, needs, and desires of the occupants. When houses are in short supply and demand is high, buyers sometimes overlook any number of external influences or undesirable features within the property; hence, "typical" adjustments may not be appropriate. To illustrate this point, during a high-demand period when houses sold as fast as they were listed, houses that backed to heavy-traffic streets sometimes sold for much higher prices than did houses in the interior of the development.

Whenever you are assigning adjustments, ask yourself: What difference does the presence or absence of the factor under consideration make in the sales price of the property in the PRESENT, LOCAL MARKET?

Determining the Relevancy of Market Adjustments

When new homes are sold by the developer, sales prices are usually not discounted even though the property has an unfavorable location or some other inadequacy. As a matter of course, appraisers always question the relevance of making adjustments for inadequacies when they are appraising a resale of a newer home—the developer did not discount the price for the inadequacies; hence, why should the appraiser discount the price? New homes sell because they are new and because developers usually offer very attractive financing programs; thus, inadequacies in the property itself and adverse external influences may be ignored by the buyers. However, when the homes are resold, unless there are some very compelling reasons to purchase the property, prudent buyers are usually unwilling to accept inadequacies without discounting the price of the property. Therefore, the only way to determine the relevancy of adjustments is by evaluating current market data.

WATCH OUT FOR THIS

Some appraisers feel impelled to make an adjustment for every variance observed when they are equating a sale to the subject property. Applications of automatic adjustments, without relating the adjustments to neighborhood standards and current market conditions, usually results in overly inflated values, particularly when the adjustments are applied to lower-priced properties. If a 90 percent or 95 percent loan was being considered for a property, an error of a couple of thousand dollars could eliminate most of the lender's equity in the property.

Window or wall air-conditioning units of little value, small patio slabs, minimal-quality patio covers, free- standing metal fireplaces, built-in workbenches, small fire rings, barbecues, storage units, fair-quality carports, and other inconsequential items typically do not warrant separate adjustments. Minor improvements that do not have permits and have little or no influence on value or marketability should be eliminated, or a statement should be included indicating that value was not assigned to the item due to age, quality, condition, or lack of permits.

When to Bracket Sales

Sales comparables are usually not acceptable when they reflect a predominance of plus or minus adjustments because this situation suggests a forced value. Most underwriters will question the validity of the sales when there are across-the-board adjustments (each comparable sale has a plus adjustment for the same item or a minus adjustment for the same item). To avoid these situations, bracket the sales, that is, define a value conclusion that is representative of the middle of the range by incorporating some sales in the report that are secondary to the subject and some that are superior to the subject.

Basing Market Adjustments on Cost

Adjustments should not be based on the actual cost of the items in question. The actual cost of improvements, such as upgraded items in new tract homes, a new roof, or the cost to cure deficiencies in the property could be used for a guide to define the adjustments or to set the upper limits for any adjustments; however, the actual adjustment must be based on the contributory value of the item in the subject's particular marketing area.

How to Round Market Adjustments

Although value adjustments must be based on market evidence, any adjustments are still, at best, estimates. Therefore, all value adjustments should be appropriately rounded. Do not use dollar amounts, such as $225., $250., $340., or $1,050. Round all the adjustments, with the exception of adjustments for gross living area, to the nearest $100. or $500., whichever is realistic and makes the most sense.

Upgrades in New Tract Homes

When you appraise new tract homes, always round the dollar amounts of the upgrades and relate the dollar amount of the adjustments to the overall added value to the property as evidenced by the market because the market may or may not support the actual cost of the upgrades. Are the upgrades an overimprovement for the neighborhood? Sometimes appraisers make adjustments for the exact dollar amount of upgrades, and the final estimate of value is exactly the same as the sales price; then, the buyer adds another $50., $75. or some other insignificant amount, in upgrades. Consequently, the appraisal must be rewritten, which usually results in a great loss of time and money for everyone concerned. Appraisals would seldom have to be rewritten if the adjustments are based on market conditions, appropriately rounded, the final estimate of value is based on the most relevant sales, and the final estimate of value is appropriately rounded.

Rounding Gross Living Area Adjustments

When you assign adjustments for variances in gross livable area, round the adjustments to the nearest $100. or $500. For example, the comparable sale is 113 sq. ft. larger than the subject and the market indicates an adjustment of $25.00/sq. ft. or $2,825., which should be rounded to $2,900. or $3,000. When your calculations result in a dollar amount of $2,225., the adjustment should be rounded to $2,000. or $2,200. It does not make sense to be overly exact when you are assigning a dollar amount for gross livable area adjustments since you have physically measured the subject property whereas the comparable properties were measured by someone else. Many appraisers show the dollar per square foot adjustment under "comments on sales comparisons." For example, "Gross living area adjustments were made at $25.00/sq. ft., rounded to the nearest $500."

Using the Same Levels of Adjustment

Always use the same levels of adjustment for each comparable. When you adjust for variances in lot size based on $2.00/sq. ft. for one comparable, all the comparables should be adjusted on a basis of $2.00/sq. ft. Round the adjustments to the nearest $100. or $500. When specific dollar amounts of adjustments are assigned for differences in room count, bathroom count, number of garage spaces, type of heating, air conditioning, fireplaces, and so forth, use the same level of adjustments for all the comparables. When you make adjustments for variances in ages of homes, use the same basis for each comparable. All the gross living area adjustments should be based on the same price per square foot. Explanations are always required when there are any deviations in the levels of adjustment.

How to Make Market Adjustments

When you make adjustments, always consider adjustments for the least subjective items first. Making adjustments in this manner should provide insight into the dollar amount for more subjective items. Make sure that all adjustments are typical and realistic because you must provide a basis for adjustments as well as providing reasons for adjustments.

Explanations Required by Lenders

The appraiser must comment on the reasons for not using more similar comparables when the following situations appear in the appraisal report:

1. Adjustments are not supported by a like property.
2. Individual items have excessively high or higher than normal adjustments (in most cases this relates to location, view, condition, and lot size adjustments).
3. Adjustments are lower than typical.
4. The comparables have a predominance of plus or minus adjustments.

5. Adjustments are made across-the-board.
6. Number of adjustments is excessive.
7. An item that apparently should have an adjustment is not adjusted.
8. All the sales have other than conventional financing.
9. Market data are very dissimilar to the subject.
10. Comparable sales are located outside of the subject neighborhood.
11. Comparable sales are over six months old.
12. Comparable sales do not represent the same zoning and use as the subject property.
13. Total adjustments for a comparable exceed 15 percent of the sales price.
14. Gross adjustments exceed 25 percent of the sales price. (The value of the gross adjustment is determined by adding all the individual adjustments without regard to plus or minus signs.)

It is mandatory that the appraiser complete the analysis of each property characteristic, or item, on the form. If not, an explanation is required.

HOW TO HANDLE FINANCING CONCESSIONS

All sales must be adjusted, as applicable, to a cash or cash equivalency basis. Do not adjust the comparables to the subject. Each comparable should be adjusted to the market (to itself) *at the time of the sale of the comparable property.*

The appraiser must show the form of financing and as many details as possible, including cash down, loan amount, interest rate, and second trust deeds. When financing information is not available, the appraiser must explain why it is not available. The appraiser's explanations must indicate that an earnest effort was made to obtain financing information; if not, the explanations would not be acceptable.

FHA/VA Transactions

Points are a fee that the *buyer,* or borrower, typically pays to the lender for the purpose of obtaining a loan. Loan fees (or points) for conventional financing vary per lender, and points are usually adjusted according to current market conditions. Points for VA or FHA transactions are normally $1.00 per $100.00 of the mortgage funds extended, that is, a 1 percent discount.

Comparables that sold with FHA or VA financing are usually not acceptable unless appropriate downward adjustments have been made to reflect any loan discount points paid by the *seller.* Even though the points paid by the seller are considered to be typical for the market area, the appraiser must still evaluate the effect on market value and make appropriate financing adjustments as indicated by the market. Adjustments for FHA and VA financing can be derived from the market by comparing sales with conventional financing to sales with FHA or VA financing or an adjustment can be based on the typical amount of points paid at the time of the sale. Current FHA and VA points, market rates, and other financing information can be obtained from local lenders, loan agents, or real estate agents. When adjustments for FHA or VA financing are not warranted, provide an explanation.

Rating Builder's Incentives

Cash rebates, furniture packages, builder's incentives, seller financing, special occupancy provisions, loan discounts, absorption of monthly payments, apportionment of rent payments, or personal property included in the sales price are considered to be "concessions," and appropriate adjustments must be made. You cannot ignore these items and state that they have no effect on the value just because the financing or concessions are "common and typical" for the market area. The financing concessions might be prevalent in the market area; however, concessions and special financing can result in inflated sales prices. Therefore, adjustments must be made, based on the increase in the sales price, as determined by the appraiser.

Unfavorable Financing

An upward adjustment might be appropriate to reflect unfavorable financing. For example, when interest rates decline to a low or favorable level, the resultant effect is typically a "seller's market" followed by correspondingly increasing prices. Thus, if a home sold for $250,000. at 15 percent interest, the same home would probably sell for much more if interest rates fell to 10 percent because there would be a higher demand. Consequently, the sale with the unfavorable financing at 15 percent interest should be adjusted upward to correlate with the sales price of the home that sold at a higher price.

ADJUSTING SALES FOR CASH EQUIVALENCY

The adjustment for cash equivalency is the difference between the sales price of a property that sold with incentives, concessions, or special financing as opposed to the sales price of a property that sold with conventional financing at market rates (not necessarily for cash).

Adjusting for cash equivalency means that you must determine whether the sales price of the property was inflated because the owner gave the buyer some type of incentive, premium, or concession, such as furniture, gifts, cash remuneration, upgrades at a discounted price or no cost, deferred down payment, deferred payments, interest rate buydowns, buyer's nonrecurring closing costs paid by the seller, or below market interest rates.

Reasons for Seller Financing

Financing adjustments are sometimes used as a scapegoat; that is, an adjustment for cash equivalency is thrown in simply to equate one sales price to the other. Just because below-market financing or concessions are part of a sales transaction does not mean that the price was inflated accordingly.

Why do some sellers provide financing or concessions? To effect a fast sale, to avoid having a sale recorded that could cause the owner to pay substantial capital gains taxes, to obtain a higher price, to market a problem property, to enable a marginal property or buyer to qualify for a conventional loan, to increase the appeal of the loan to a seller as an investment, to market the property when interest rates are so high that properties are not selling at a reasonable price and within a reasonable period of time, or to market the property when the buyer does not have the funds to make the necessary or required down payment.

Suppose the sellers want to market their property more quickly. The property would only sell in less time if the financing or concessions were more beneficial to the buyer in terms of interest rate, monthly payment structure, down payment, or other respects than the terms offered, or available, for comparable properties. If sellers increased their prices as well as offering special financing terms, they would be defeating their purpose. To justify an increase in price and still market the property instantly, the financing terms offered by the sellers would have to be well below market rates or more favorable to the buyer for other reasons, such as inability of the buyer to qualify for conventional financing, deferred down payment, or little or no down payment.

Assume that the sellers are providing special financing for investment purposes. If the sellers carry the mortgage on the property, they will usually try to increase the asking price by the projected dollar amount that the mortgage loan would have to be discounted in order to convert it readily to cash. Sellers can sometimes command a higher sales price if they provide special financing at below-market costs. For example, inflated asking prices may be completely ignored by buyers who are more concerned with the amount of money they have to put down on the property or the amount of the monthly payment than they are with the asking price.

Prudent, well-qualified buyers, however, would probably not go along with inflated asking prices. If the buyer knows that the sellers are making a profit on the interest on the loan payments as well as making a profit by increasing the price of their property, they would attempt to discount the price in an effort to balance the profits between the buyers and sellers. Therefore, it would be unlikely that the sellers could raise the price in addition to providing special financing.

The preceding examples were presented to demonstrate that seller financing does not always result in price increases. The sales price may or may not be affected by special or creative financing, depending on the motives of the buyer and seller, the type of property, the marketing era, the dollar amount of the loan affected by the special or creative financing, conditions of the sale, the type of concession, the terms of the financing, and the interest rate. It could be to the seller's advantage to finance the purchase of the property; therefore, the special financing might not have created an increase in the sales price. In fact, a transaction could reflect a discounted sales price as well as below-market or special financing.

Cash Equivalency and Mathematical Calculations

Dozens of articles have been written explaining the meaning of "cash equivalence," and a number of methods for defining the dollar amount of adjustments for cash equivalency have been established. Some of the methods entail complex mathematical calculations as a basis for determining the dollar amount of an adjustment for cash equivalency.

For tables and mathematical calculations to be effective, the appraiser must determine the length of time the loan discount will affect the property as well as all the terms of the seller financing, such as interest rate, presence or absence of balloon payments, actual down payment, amount of and payoff period of deferred down payments, and any other terms or concessions that may be relevant. When an adjustment is made using tables or calculations based on the loan reaching its full maturity, this usually results in an excessive adjustment for below-market financing because buyers typically do not retain the property until the loan reaches full maturity or the property might be refinanced if more favorable interest rates become available.

Mathematical calculations appear to have more significance in application when they are related to large income property, industrial and commercial property, or large land transactions than when they are related to single-family residences because (1) there are too many variables that must be perceived and dealt with; (2) it is difficult and sometimes impossible to obtain complete financing information from buyers, sellers, and agents; and (3) it is perceived that the typical buyer and seller will not peruse cash equivalency tables or complicated math calculations to arrive at a listing or selling price.

Using Market Data for Cash Equivalency Adjustments

When you are appraising single-family residences, the relevancy of adjustments and the dollar amount of market adjustments can usually be determined by comparing the sales prices of the comparables that reflect special or creative financing with the sales prices of properties that exhibit typical financing, that is, 10 percent or 20 percent down at market rates. Adjustments should not be calculated on a mechanical dollar-for-dollar cost equal to the seller's cost of the concession. The amount of the negative adjustment should reflect the difference between what the comparable sales sold for with concessions and what they would have sold for without concessions.

The appraiser must compare the terms of each individual transaction to the rates and terms of institutional financing at the time of the sale of the comparable property. In other words, if one sale is being compared against another to define an adjustment, they must both have sold at approximately the same time for the apparent dollar amount of the adjustment to be realistic. The amount of the negative adjustment to be made to comparables with financing concessions should equal any increase in the sales price of the comparable that the appraiser determines to be attributable to the concessions. Because every property and every transaction is unique, it would be irresponsible to assign the same dollar amount to each comparable. Each sale must be analyzed on its own merit to determine whether an adjustment is warranted and to define the dollar amount of any adjustments.

If you are appraising a property in an area where there are no comparable sales available that exhibit institutional financing, make a thorough study of the sales history in the neighborhood to find out whether creative financing has resulted in increased sales prices. Consult with several real estate agents to solicit their opinions regarding potentially inflated prices. Additionally, in this instance, mathematical calculations should be employed to determine the relevancy of and the dollar amount of adjustments for cash equivalency.

Using Loan Payments for Cash Equivalency Adjustments

When there are no sales of conventionally financed properties to use for comparison purposes to determine cash equivalency adjustments, the appraiser could use a cash equivalency technique wherein the buyer's monthly payments are compared to monthly payments at market rates. If the buyer's actual monthly payment is unknown, the interest rate, loan amount, and payoff period must be established to estimate the dollar amount of the buyer's monthly payment. Once these factors have been determined, use an amortization schedule to find the dollar amount of the monthly payments.

In the following example, the property was purchased for $330,000. with a down payment of $80,000. The buyer assumed a first mortgage of $250,000. at 13 percent interest with a remaining term of 23 years. The buyer's actual monthly payments are $2,766. Market rates, at the time, were 15 percent. A $250,000. mortgage at 15 percent for 23 years commands monthly payments of $3,230. Hence,

$$\$2{,}766. \div \$3{,}230. = .8563 \text{ or } 85.63\%$$

Multiply the amount of the first mortgage by this percentage to find the adjusted value:

$$\$250{,}000. \times 85.63\% = \$214{,}075.$$

Add the down payment to the adjusted value of the first mortgage to find the cash equivalency value of the property:

$$\$214,075. - \$80,000. = \$294,075.$$

The dollar amount of the cash equivalency adjustment is $35,925. ($330,000. - $294,075. = $35,925.), rounded $36,000.

The preceding representation is a simple method for defining cash equivalency adjustments. When you use this method or any other method where mathematical formulas are used, always refine the result, based on your judgment, to reflect buyer and seller motivation in the subject's market.

A thorough investigation of the financing terms of a comparable sale may reveal reasons to eliminate the comparable altogether if the terms cannot be delineated and adjusted to correlate with market value, as defined. Sales that are not truly representative of the market should be eliminated because undocumented and subjective adjustments must be avoided. What motivated the seller to provide incentives or financing concessions? Why was the sales price discounted or increased? Are the reasons related to the market? Are these factors represented throughout the report?

The foregoing observations represent only a condensed rendition of factors pertaining to financing and cash equivalency adjustments. Therefore, appraisers should carefully study and adhere to guidelines and requirements for financing adjustments set forth by the Federal Home Loan Bank Board, Freddie Mac, Fannie Mae, and institutional lenders.

If you were asked to provide explanations, could you illustrate the method that you used to define casn equivalency adjustments? If not, you should attend classes and seminars presented by the professional appraisal organizations and study all the articles in professional appraisal journals that illustrate different methods for defining cash equivalency adjustments.

HOW TO PRESENT YOUR MARKET ANALYSIS

Show the exact street number and name on the form. Include unit numbers, if applicable. Always include Street, Avenue, Lane, Circle, and so on, for the subject *and* the comparables. Include the name of the city when the comparables are located in a city that differs from the subject's city. If an address has not been assigned to the property, identify the property by its legal description. Some lenders require Assessor's Parcel Numbers for all the comparables as well.

The reputation of an area or neighborhood can have a tremendous influence on property values; therefore, the subject and the comparable sales must have the same mailing address, that is, the same city or community. If not, an explanation is required.

Listing the Proximity to Subject

List the proximity in terms of lots, blocks, or miles, and indicate the direction, for example, north, south, east, or west. In urban or suburban areas, the comparable sales should be located in the same neighborhood. In rural areas, comparable properties may be acceptable even if they are located several miles from the subject property. Include map book page and grid numbers when the comparables are located more than a short distance away from the subject property.

If the neighborhood has been properly defined in the body of the report, the reader should be able to recognize immediately the relationship of the location of the comparables to the subject neighborhood. Explanations are required any time that the comparables are located outside of the subject neighborhood; therefore, provide reasons why it was necessary to extend your search for comparable sales. Explain the relationship of the alternate neighborhood to the subject neighborhood addressing similarities in appeal. Include sales in escrow, sales history, or listings from the subject neighborhood to add further support to your value conclusion when some or all of the comparable sales are located outside of the subject neighborhood.

Price per Square Foot of Gross Living Area

The price per gross living area of each comparable should be in the range of the subject's price per square foot. An excessive variance, either high or low, is an indication that the sale is not really comparable to the subject. Unreasonable variances should explained by the appraiser.

Always use the sales price to find the price per square foot for the subject when the subject is a sale. The price per square foot for the subject should be extracted from the final value when the subject is not a sale.

Data Sources

Most lenders require two legitimate data sources for each comparable. "Personal inspection" or "microfiche" are not acceptable data sources. Document numbers can be used as a data source; however, document numbers and "public records" do not count as two data sources since document numbers are obtained from public records. Document numbers should be referenced by the appraiser to establish verification that the sale actually closed and recorded. You may use "Appraiser's Files" for one data source if you appraised the referenced property.

Include multiple-listing numbers when data are obtained from multiple-listing services. Names and telephone numbers should be referenced when data sources are agents, owners, or buyers. When the information has been obtained from a published source, show the month and the year of the publication. Real estate sales agents and all other parties that may benefit from the sale or appraisal of the subject property are not acceptable data sources unless verification can be provided by a disinterested third party.

Reporting Requirements for Date of Sale

The appraiser should provide the date of the sales contract and the settlement or closing date for each comparable sale. Unless the appraiser believes that the exact date is necessary to understand the adjustments, only the month and year of the sale need to be reported. If the appraiser does not report both the contract date and the settlement or closing date, he or she must identify the reported sale date as either the contract date or the settlement or closing date. If the appraiser reports the contract date only, he or she must state whether the contract resulted in a settlement or closing.

Generally, the appraiser should use comparable sales that have been settled or closed within the last 12 months. However, the appraiser may use older comparable sales as additional supporting data if he or she believes that it is appropriate. The appraiser must comment on the reasons for using any comparable sales that are more than 6 months old. The appraiser may use the subject property as a fourth comparable sale or as supporting data if the property previously was sold (and closed or settled). If the appraiser believes that it is appropriate, he or she also may use contract offerings and current listings as supporting data.

For sales to be reliable indications of current market

value, the sales should have been executed *and* recorded within the 6-month period. Recorded sales are past evidence of value because the actual signing of sales agreements could have taken place many months previous to the date that the sales actually recorded. To establish *current* market value, appraisers should consider the actual date that the sales contracts were signed in addition to noting the date the sale closed or recorded.

How You Will Benefit by Using Current Sales

In most cases, the 6-month limit refers to 6 months from the date the loan is funded, not 6 months from the date the appraisal was written. When sales are incorporated in the appraisal that are 6 months old, or close to it, at the time the appraisal is prepared, by the time the loan funds, the sales might be dated and they might have to be supplemented or replaced, in which case, you might find it difficult, if not impossible, to locate additional market data that will support your final estimate of value. If the appraisal has to be rewritten because the comparable sales are dated, and the value is lower than the estimate of value stated in the original appraisal, the entire transaction might be voided. Any time an appraisal has to be explained or rewritten, your credibility and expertise are questioned; therefore, it is always expeditious to use market data that are as recent as feasibly possible.

How to Confirm Market Trends

When there is little activity in the local market and the comparables are older than six months, or there is evidence that values are increasing or decreasing, include at least two current listings or sales in escrow. If you only include one sale or listing, you will not provide sufficient market evidence that prices are increasing or decreasing. When values are increasing or decreasing, in the absence of current sales in escrow or listings, include an analysis of market history to support your conclusions. Or discuss values with knowledgeable real estate agents and include supportive commentary in the appraisal report accompanied by names and telephone numbers of the real estate agents.

If you are appraising a new tract home, and there has been a recent price increase, include a sale in escrow as well as a closed sale in the subject development to document the price increase or include sales brochures to document price changes from phase to phase.

How to Make Time Adjustments

Time adjustments should be supported by recent sales or sales in escrow. If three sales are used, and only one sale is recent, this will not provide adequate support for time adjustments for the two older sales. Always include at least two sales in escrow and two listings, or one of each. Time adjustments should be consistent with your description of neighborhood value trends. Time adjustments can be defined in the following manner:

Market history has shown that prices have been increasing at the rate of 8.5 percent per month over the past several months. The property sold seven months ago for $595,000. Hence,

$595,000. × .0085 = 5057.5 × 7 months = $35,403.
Time adjustment, rounded = $35,000.

When and How to Make Location Adjustments

Provide an overall rating for the subject and a comparison rating for the comparables using the suggested terms of excellent, good, average, fair, poor, superior, or inferior. If you wish to expand on these terms to emphasize the reasons for any adjustments, show avg/trf (average traffic street location), fair/bks comm (fair location backs to commercial property), good/CDS (good location on cul-de-sac street), and so forth. All location adjustments must, however, be specifically described in the comments section, or in an addendum, when the relevancy of the adjustments is not readily apparent.

Make adjustments for the differences between the subject and the comparables. The adjustments must be consistent with the descriptions of the subject and the neighborhood that are presented on the first page of the report. Did you refine the adjustments to represent neighborhood standards and current market conditions? When external obsolescence has been acknowledged in the neighborhood section of the report and the cost approach, when appropriate, make certain that corresponding adjustments have been made in the market analysis.

Does the proximity to the subject shown in the sales comparison analysis relate to the location adjustments or lack of adjustments? When the comparable sales are located outside of the subject neighborhood, explain why it was necessary to extend your search for comparables outside of the neighborhood perimeters.

The comparable sales should represent the same zoning and uses as the subject. Property situated on leasehold land, land zoned for equestrian use, or land zoned for income, commercial, and other nonsingle-family residential uses must be compared to property with like zoning and uses. Waterfront property, view-oriented property, security-gated communities, and planned communities should also be compared to like property.

Hard and fast rules, or rules of thumb, should particularly be avoided when adjustments for location are being considered, because economic influences and buyer's attitudes in particular markets can nullify so-called typical adjustments. Consider the following circumstances:

1. When there are a limited number of properties listed, buyers might have to put up with any number of undesirable factors and pay top dollar as well if they are intent upon purchasing a home within a certain time period.

2. Desirability of a corner lot versus an interior lot must be considered on a case basis; it depends on buyer's attitudes in each distinct neighborhood. Some people prefer corner lots because of the additional air space and privacy from neighboring property. A corner lot might be less desirable than an interior lot because traffic is heavier. Some buyers might be willing to pay a high premium for a corner lot, cul-de-sac lot, alley-serviced site, or a site at the end of a dead-end street if they need extra space for recreational vehicle or boat parking and storage, especially in cities that do not allow recreational vehicle or boat parking on city streets, or sometimes, not even on private driveways. Buyers sometimes pay premiums for interior lots because they believe that the location is safer (access to the property by prowlers is more difficult) or they might simply enjoy the closeness of neighbors.

3. Locations on cul-de-sac streets or dead-end streets may or may not be more desirable depending on buyer motivations, traffic patterns, parking congestion, and even the width and length of the street. And, depending on the particular neighborhood, there may or may not be excessive traffic from cars turning around on cul-de-sac or dead-end streets.

4. Adjustments for traffic noise from feeder streets into a tract or neighborhood must be considered on a case basis

because the traffic count could be very light, depending on neighborhood occupancy and the layout of the streets within the development.

Site and View Adjustments

Split the site and view adjustments to provide clarity for the reader—do not lump both adjustments together. When you need more space, show the description and adjustments in one of the spaces below or use an asterisk and provide further explanations in the comments section. When there are differences in lot sizes between the subject and comparables and you are not making any adjustments, include an explanation or, for example, show "6,580/comp utility."

Provide the actual area of the subject site and the comparables in square feet or acres. Be consistent. If the size of the subject lot is shown in square feet, show the comparable lot sizes in square feet as well. The actual lot sizes of the comparables must be shown; the use of similar or other terms is not acceptable.

Describe the view in a manner that enables a reviewer to easily follow the reasons for your adjustments. For example, indicate the lot size and view as 6,540/none; 6,540/good; 6,540/ocean; or 6,540/wooded for the subject and 6,540/avg; 6,540/sup; 6,540/inf for the comparables.

Factors to be considered under "site/view" include view, overall size of the lot, shape of the lot, level pad size, utility, orientation of the house on the lot, topography, accessibility, utilities, drainage, easements, and encroachments as well as any other positive or negative elements that influence the value and marketability of the subject and comparable properties.

Do not make adjustments for variances in lot sizes without evaluating all the site factors that influence value and marketability—particularly utility. The overall lot size of the comparable sales could be greater or less than the subject lot size; however, can the site be put to the same or similar use as the subject site (comparable utility) even though the overall sizes vary? If so, lot size adjustments should reflect similarities in utility. Does the shape of the lot provide greater or less buyer appeal, site utility, or superior setbacks from the street or neighboring properties? Does the shape of the lot, topography, or orientation of the house on the lot provide more privacy or greater protection from environmental or external influences?

The best utility is when the house is oriented on the lot in a manner that provides the maximum amount of open land area that can be used for private enjoyment of the house itself and the land. When a dwelling is situated too close to the front property line, private enjoyment and overall livability might be adversely affected. The shape of the lot or the topography might prohibit installation of a swimming pool, play equipment, patios, or other outdoor recreational facilities; hence, an adjustment for inferior utility might be in order.

Flag lots might be more or less desirable depending on the orientation of the home on the site. Zero, or offset, lot lines are generally more appealing due to greater utility and privacy. Homes situated on single load streets, gently sloping terrain, hillside sites, and terraced lots usually have more esthetic appeal, more privacy, and, sometimes, better views.

Because of the extreme variances in premiums paid for views, overall lot size, lot utility, and other site factors in different neighborhoods, a sufficient number of sales must be analyzed and included in the report to isolate and provide support for site and view adjustments. Lot size adjustments must be consistent: use the same level of adjustment for each comparable. Do not arbitrarily make adjustments for small variances in lot sizes unless you can show that the adjustments are realistic by referencing like properties. Unless the reasons are obvious, all site and view adjustments must be explained in the comments section.

Adjustments for Design and Appeal

There are no absolute standards that can be used to measure value differences in design and appeal because buyers' opinions of what constitutes desirable architectural design vary to the same extent that architectural styles vary. Typically, however, values increase in direct relationship to the refinements of architectural details. Adjustments for design and appeal are usually highly subjective and should be avoided whenever possible. Appraisers should be exceedingly careful not to let their own preferences influence their judgment when they are evaluating design and appeal. Adjustments for design and appeal must be explained in the comments section.

Because there is such a wide variance in market appeal, contemporary homes should not be compared to homes featuring more traditional styling. Do not compare one-story homes to two-story homes or two-story homes to split-level, trilevel, or three-story homes unless sufficient recent market data are available to provide a basis for any adjustments.

Consider the resemblance of the comparables to the subject from the viewpoint of the typical buyer within the applicable price range. Factors to be considered are architectural design, number of stories, orientation of the improvements on the lot, attractiveness of landscaping and yard improvements, interior design and appeal, and special features. The architectural design of the house should conform to the neighborhood and amenities. For instance, a modern style house would look out of place in an older neighborhood or more rural setting, a contemporary-style home might look out of place in a wooded area, and so on. If the property does not conform to the neighborhood, an adjustment is warranted.

Do not make adjustments for differences in roofing materials unless you have actually derived a basis for the adjustment from the market. Consider the age, quality, and condition of the roof in addition to evaluating market appeal, for example, it wouldn't make sense to make an adjustment for "superior" roofing materials if the roofs were older or in need of repair or replacement. Shake roofs might be undesirable to some buyers because of known fire hazards; therefore, the buyers might discount the price of the home to allow for costs to replace the roof. If the roofing materials do not conform to the predominant type of roofing in the neighborhood, an adjustment for a "misplaced improvement" might be valid.

Adjustments for functional obsolescence for misplaced improvements, underimprovements, or overimprovements should be made under the design and appeal category. Only factors that affect the utility of the home should be considered under functional utility.

Adjustments for additions, upgrading, remodeling, or rehabilitation would not be appropriate if the effect is greater conformity to the neighborhood. When the subject property or the comparable sales have additions, or they have been rehabilitated or remodeled, loan underwriters and review appraisers will expect to see related adjustments; therefore, appraisers should always explain the absence of adjustments in addition to explaining reasons for adjustments. When appropriate, in the comments section, explain that the improvements represent greater conformity to the neighborhood. Always include comparable sales that substantiate your conclusions.

Adjustments for Quality of Construction

Indicate the subject's overall quality rating commensurate with the rating on page one of the report. Rate the comparables to the subject with respect to quality of materials and workmanship throughout. If the quality of construction varies considerably between the subject and the comparables, appraisers should evaluate their selection of comparable sales because homes located in the same or similar neighborhoods typically do not vary in quality. Explanations for quality adjustments must be provided in the comments section.

When assigning a quality rating, the appraiser should evaluate the type and quality of framing, roof, interior and exterior finishes and trim, doors, hardware, kitchen equipment and finishes, bath fixtures and finishes, plumbing, and electrical equipment. Also, note the type and placement of windows, depth of roof overhang, and quality of the parking structure.

Variances in quality of any of these items within the subject property might indicate the presence of an addition, rehabilitation, or modernization, in which case, the quality of the improvements should be conforming to the subject and the neighborhood. If they are not, a corresponding adjustment for an overimprovement or underimprovement should be considered. For example, if the subject has been modernized with better-quality materials than those originally found in the home to the extent that the home is overimproved for the neighborhood, the quality rating might be shown as "average-good." When the comparable sales are not similarly improved, the rating of the comparable sales should be shown as "average," and appropriate adjustments for the subject's overimprovement should be assigned for the differences in quality. The dollar amount of the adjustment should be based on market studies; however, if market data are unavailable, the appraiser could make a judgment decision which should be accompanied by proper explanations.

Actual and Effective Ages

Show the actual age or the effective age, whichever is more suitable to the appraisal problem. If the subject property has been rehabilitated or modernized, the effective age of the structure would probably have more relevance; thus, the effective age should be shown, for example, "Eff: 17 yrs." If you are stating an effective age for the subject, an effective age should be shown for the comparables as well. Always be consistent when you are writing your descriptions.

Effective age does not include physical curable deterioration; therefore, adjustments for physical curable deterioration should be made in the condition category. For example, the dwelling may be effectively 15 years old overall; however, if it is in need of carpet, paint, or some other homeowner-type repair, an adjustment should be made under condition to reflect the market return of the items under consideration.

Do not methodically assign adjustments for age. Differences of a few years in age are seldom noticed by buyers because most people generally think of houses as old, older, 20 or 30 years old or so, nearly new, new, and so forth. Also, buyers are usually more concerned with design, appeal, quality, and condition (does it need a new roof, a lot of repair, cleanup, or modernization?) of the property than the actual age.

Adjustments for variances in age should be derived from the market; however, if sufficient market data are not available for comparison purposes, adjustments for age can be based on a percentage of the reproduction cost new of the subject dwelling. Based on his or her judgment and experience in appraising homes in the subject's marketing area, the appraiser may decide to use an age adjustment based on 1 percent per year. For example,

Assume the reproduction cost new of the subject property is $84,000. and the difference in age between the subject and the comparable is 12 years.

$$1\% \times \$84{,}000. = \$840. \times 12 \text{ years} = \$10{,}080.$$

Hence, the adjustment for the difference in age is $10,080., rounded $10,000.

Houses that are 20 to 25 years old or more should be

showing signs of rejuvenation up to modern standards. If there is no indication that rehabilitation or modernization has taken place, this might point to a decline in neighborhood values. Reconcile your descriptions: do the actual ages of the subject property and the comparable sales relate to the neighborhood description on page one of the report? Does the subject's age relate to the description of the dwelling, the effective age, remaining economic life, and physical depreciation shown?

How to Document Adjustments for Condition

Incurable physical depreciation, which is inherent within the property (physical wearing out of the structure), is represented in the age of the house. Curable physical depreciation, such as deferred maintenance, should be represented under the category of condition.

Adjustments for condition should be consistent with the effective age of the property as well as the dollar amount of curable physical depreciation shown in the cost approach. That is, if you are indicating a large adjustment for condition, the actual and effective age of the property should be within a close range. Also, the dollar amount of adjustments for condition should be less than the dollar amount of depreciation shown in the cost approach because the total amount of physical depreciation shown in the cost approach should represent both curable and incurable depreciation.

Large adjustments for condition should be explained and should be accompanied by an itemized list of needed repairs to bring the subject property or comparable property up to good marketable condition. Explanations should give readers an indication that the amount of the adjustment is reasonable. For example, "Comparable 2 sold in need of interior paint, new flooring, and new window coverings throughout."

WATCH OUT FOR THIS

Large adjustments are sometimes shown for condition that are unrealistic and inappropriate. For example, the subject is an average-quality dwelling containing 1,400 sq. ft. of livable area. An $8,000. adjustment was made for condition. The appraiser indicated that the property needed exterior and interior paint, new kitchen and bath flooring, and new carpet throughout. In this instance, it appeared that the appraiser had picked a figure out of the sky, possibly in an effort to achieve a certain value.

If this amount of money were spent for painting, installation of new carpet throughout, and installation of new kitchen and bath flooring in an average-quality, 1,400-sq. ft. dwelling, this would amount to a gross overimprovement because, typically, costs would be in the range of $3,500. to $5,000., at best. Furthermore, the market normally does not return investments on a dollar-for-dollar basis; therefore, adjustments for condition must be refined to reflect buyer's attitudes in the subject's current market.

When a house has been repaired or rehabilitated, it will not be worth any more than similar houses that have sold in comparable condition regardless of the actual dollar amount spent for refurbishing the property. Hence, you cannot simply add up the cost of repairs and use the total cost for an adjustment for condition. At least two comparable sales of similar homes, in comparable condition, should be included to provide a basis for any adjustments. Always make certain the dollar amount of the adjustments relates to the quality and size of the home under consideration.

Suppose the subject property has a new $3,500. roof, a new $1,000. concrete driveway, and new concrete block wall fencing that cost $2,500. There are no recent, recorded sales with similar improvements in the subject or competing neighborhoods. Would you have to include dated sales, sales in escrow, listings, or market history studies to provide a basis for your adjustments? Not necessarily, if the adjustments are prudent. However, you should at least review historical market data to determine the effect similar improvements have on market value to assign a reasonable dollar amount for any adjustments. If appropriate, include a statement such as, "Adjustments for the subject's new roof, concrete drive, and block wall fencing are based on market history in the neighborhood as well as the appraiser's judgment and experience."

Above-Grade Room Count

To provide a distinction among the factors, split the dollar amount of the adjustments, for example, show "10,000. BR, 2,500. BA, or 6,500. GLA." Always use the same levels of adjustments for each comparable sale.

The following examples are provided to illustrate the manner in which deceptive values can be reached when the original design and layout of the subject and comparable properties have not been taken into consideration:

Example 1: The subject is a 1,300 sq. ft. dwelling that originally contained three bedrooms and a den. The owner added a closet in the den, thereby incorporating a fourth bedroom into the structure. Hence, the subject was described, in the appraisal report, as a four-bedroom house. Two of the comparables described in the report were 1,325 sq. ft. three-bedroom houses. The appraiser did not explore the probability of a similar room count (that is, three bedrooms and a den) with somewhat similar utility, which was evidenced by the similarity in gross living area. Thus, an inappropriate upward adjustment was made because the comparable houses contained "only" three bedrooms. When the sales were verified, the reviewer discovered that the comparable sales actually consisted of three bedrooms and a den; hence, the relevancy of the adjustments was questioned.

Example 2: In the report, the subject was described as a "four-bedroom home." One of the comparables was shown as a "six-bedroom home," and the appraiser made a minus adjustment for the two additional bedrooms. Although the square footage shown in the appraisal report for the comparable property varied somewhat from the subject, photos of the subject and the comparable property, as well as further research conducted by the review appraiser, clearly indicated that both houses originally contained four bedrooms and a bonus room, and they were, in fact, identical plans. However, the listing depicted the comparable sale as a six-bedroom house because the bonus room was converted into two bedrooms. The foregoing situations usually occur because

1. Data sources do not list all the individual rooms.
2. Permits were not issued; therefore, public records do not contain updated information.
3. Information provided by data sources was not current or accurate.
4. The appraiser did not explore the possibility that modifications to the original structure might have taken place.
5. The appraiser did not verify the information through a second source.
6. The data were verified through a second source; however, the appraiser did not conduct a definitive investigation of the comparable property.

Are adjustments of this nature relevant? The two extra bedrooms could be converted back to a bonus room by removing the closets and dividing wall at a relatively small cost. Likewise, the four-bedroom home could be restored to its original state by removing a closet at little cost. Should an adjustment be made to reflect the cost to restore the rooms to their original status? Or should you apply a plus adjustment for the bonus room and a minus adjustment for the two extra bedrooms? Would a buyer actually pay $4,000. more for a home with two extra bedrooms if a wall and closets could be installed for $1,000.? Or should the homes be considered as comparable in utility (which would probably make more sense) with no adjustment? Make all the other adjustments first. Next, compare the indicated values of all the comparables to each other, and the subject, to determine whether adjustments for differences in room count is evident or appears to be relevant.

Differences in sales prices attributed to variances in room count should be determined by a thorough analysis of neighborhood market data; however, it is unlikely that there would be an adequate number of recent sales available with similar conversions that would establish a basis for the adjustments. Consequently, a determination may have to be based on the appraiser's experience and judgment. A logical explanation for the adjustment, or lack of an adjustment, must be provided in the comments section.

Some appraisers never make adjustments for the total room count, or different types of rooms, because they believe that any differences in room count, or types of rooms, are reflected in adjustments for overall size. This unfounded conjecture illustrates the importance of thoroughly analyzing market data, and more than three sales, in the subject's particular neighborhood to determine reasons for price differentials because the appraiser might discover that two properties, which are identical in size, as well as number of bedrooms, actually have completely different floor plans and utility.

Suppose, for example, there are two different three- bedroom plans, each containing 1,300 sq. ft., in the subject neighborhood. Plan 1 features three large bedrooms, a utility room, and a small dining area. Plan 2 has smaller bedrooms and no utility room; however, it features a formal dining room. Historically, in this tract, homes with a formal dining room have sold for $3,000. more than homes with larger bedrooms. In other neighborhoods, the reverse could be true. Or there might not be any difference in prices.

Most buyers specifically look for homes that have full dining rooms, dens, studies, recreation rooms, ample-size bedrooms, and utility rooms. And buyers are usually willing to pay more for homes that specifically satisfy their needs. Hence, the total number of rooms, and types of rooms, should not be ignored simply because the appraiser does not believe that there is a need for adjustments or because the form only lists "total, bedrooms, and baths."

Appraisers should consider the *actual* total number of rooms (rather than simply adding the living room and kitchen to the bedroom count of the comparable sales to find a total room count), the different types and uses of rooms, and the layout of the comparable properties, as well as analyzing the subject property, to define functional utility properly.

At least two comparable sales with the same room count and similar types of rooms should be included to provide a basis for adjustments. For clarity, room counts might be shown as "8-4-DR-BR-3" or "6-3-DN-2." Reasons for adjustments can usually be readily perceived by reviewers when the room count is presented in this manner. When the reasons for the adjustments are obvious, an explanation does not have to be provided.

Because of the wide variance in prices between one- and two-bedroom homes and homes that contain three or more bedrooms, one- and two-bedroom homes should only be compared to like property. Adjustments for the number of baths should be extracted from the market. Dwellings with only one bath should only be compared to similar property unless an adequate number of sales are included that will provide a basis for adjustments for the number of baths.

Gross Living Area Adjustments

Gross living area adjustments must relate to the neighborhood or location of the property as well as the quality, size, design, and features of the subject property and the comparable sales. All the comparables should be adjusted at the same price per square foot. When they are not, an explanation must be provided. Gross living area adjustments should be appropriately rounded.

Gross living area adjustments should have some relationship to the cost of the property, that is, type of property, design, size, quality, and upgrading; however, the square foot adjustment is *not* derived from, or based on, the price per square foot cost to build, the price per square foot of the depreciated value of the improvements, or the indicated value by the cost approach. And the square footage adjustment is *not* based on the price per gross living area of the comparable sales. The only appropriate way to determine the price per square foot adjustment is by using the "paired sales method" of extracting the relevant amount of dollar adjustments from the market.

Pay close attention to the price per square foot adjustments whenever you are writing an appraisal. After you have appraised a number of properties in a given area, you should then have the ability to define gross living area adjustments quite accurately without analyzing numerous paired sales. For example, typical gross living area adjustments in one given area might be $12. to $15./sq. ft. for small, fair-quality homes, $20. to $25./sq. ft. for average-quality, medium-sized homes, or $30. to $35./sq. ft. for better-quality, larger homes.

Always make sure, however, that the adjustments are refined to reflect neighborhood standards because a "typical" $25.00/sq. ft. adjustment that is appropriate in one neighborhood might be totally out of order in another neighborhood. Don't forget to correlate the adjustments to the quality, size, design, and features of the particular properties as well.

Make certain that you are using the same levels of adjustment between the subject and the comparables. Does the total gross living area of the comparable sales, which has been obtained from outside sources, relate to the gross livable area of the subject, which has been physically measured? To avoid making inappropriate adjustments when the comparable sale is the same plan as the subject, use the subject's physical measurements for the comparable property rather than the total square footage reported by an outside source.

Adjustments for less than 100 sq. ft. are questionable with respect to relevance. If the subject was physically measured by the appraiser, and the square footage of the comparables was obtained from an outside source, adjustments for insignificant variances in square footage wouldn't make sense because two appraisers taping the same property will not always define exactly the same square footage. Additionally, the market might not reflect an adjustment for size. Do buyers actually recognize small variances in square footage and adjust their offering prices accordingly?

Basement and Finished Rooms Below Grade

Describe basements and finished rooms, below grade, for the subject and the comparables. If there are no basement, partial basement, or rooms below grade, this should be indicated.

Sales of similar properties should be included to provide a basis for any adjustments. Compare the adjustments to the depreciated cost of the basement or finished rooms to avoid overstating the amount of any adjustments.

How and When to Adjust for Functional Utility

Rate utility with respect to the neighborhood as follows:

Good:	Superior to other homes in the neighborhood
Average:	Equal to the norm found in the neighborhood
Fair/Poor:	Below typical for the neighborhood

The functional utility rating refers to room sizes, layout, and overall livability. The appraiser should assign a rating of good, average, fair, or poor that is consistent with the improvement analysis ratings on the first page of the report. Comparison ratings of good, average, fair, poor, superior, or inferior should be assigned to the comparables, and pertinent adjustments should be made to represent the market's reaction to any differences.

When the subject's description or the cost approach indicates functional obsolescence that is not accompanied by relative adjustments, an explanation is required. When a large amount of depreciation for functional obsolescence is taken in the cost approach, the subject property should not be rated as average or good.

When the subject is an over- or underimprovement, or a misplaced improvement, a relative adjustment should be made in either the design and appeal classification or under functional utility, depending on the reason the home is designated as underimproved, overimproved, or a misplaced improvement. When the home has good functional utility, but doesn't "belong" in the neighborhood, the adjustment should be reflected in the design and appeal category. When overall livability is affected, the adjustment should be made under functional utility.

Compared to today's standards, many older homes lack good functional utility or display functional obsolescence due to poor design, undesirable floor plans or poor layouts, an inadequate number of bathrooms, or outdated equipment. Many newer homes, including homes selling at the present time, exhibit functional obsolescence. Functional obsolescence found in recently constructed homes includes rooms that are too small, entry directly into the living room, lack of convenient hallways and stairs, spiral wrought iron stairways (which usually lead to loft or sleeping areas) that are too narrow for practical use, access to other rooms through the living room or other living areas, very little or no dining area in the kitchen, room design not allowing for suitable furniture arrangements, family rooms that are too close to bedrooms, inadequate storage and closet space, or poor window placement that inhibits good cross ventilation.

Consider the price range as well as the needs and desires of typical occupants of the homes in the subject's particular neighborhood. In lower-priced neighborhoods, most deficiencies are usually overlooked by buyers. In higher-priced neighborhoods, homes with inadequacies might be difficult to market, and prices may have to be discounted substantially to market the homes within a reasonable period of time. When new homes are initially sold, many deficiencies might be endured by buyers because the deficiencies are offset by other compelling reasons to purchase the property.

Conformity to the neighborhood and *marketability* are the two key words to remember when you are assigning a rating or are considering an adjustment for functional utility or functional obsolescence. Although there may be many apparent deficiencies in the property, if the property conforms to the neighborhood, or appeals to a sufficient number of typical buyers to impart normal marketability, and there is evidence of long-term sustainment of value, functional utility should be rated as "average." Include sales of like properties to substantiate your conclusions.

Since most neighborhoods are made up of homes that were built during similar time periods, and similar types and styles of homes are usually found in the same neighborhood, you will find that adjustments for functional utility are seldom warranted. In fact, probably the only occasions when adjustments might be warranted is when you are appraising a poorly planned custom-designed home or when additions are poorly planned.

When you appraise a home with a tandem addition, or poorly designed addition, it is usually difficult, if not impossible, to find comparable sales that exhibit similar deficiencies. Real estate agents are usually your best source of information under these circumstances because you couldn't determine functional obsolescence from a visual inspection of the exterior of the comparable sales.

In the event that there are no sales that display similar obsolescence, consider the feasibility of curing the obsolescence and the dollar amount to cure; for example, add a hallway or doorway, remove or add a wall, and so forth. If the obsolescence is curable, use the dollar amount to cure the deficiency for functional utility adjustments.

Inconsequential adjustments should be omitted; therefore, if the costs to cure are insignificant, omit them and include an explanation. When there are no comparable sales available to provide a basis for adjustments and you are unable to assign a cost to cure the deficiency, to avoid making overly subjective adjustments, consider employing the following method for defining an adjustment for incurable functional obsolescence.

In this example, the subject has a 12 ft. x 18 ft. or 216-sq. ft. family room addition. In the reproduction cost new, a cost of $52.00/sq. ft. has been assigned to the total gross livable area of the dwelling (which includes the family room), and a rate of 17 percent has been assigned for physical depreciation. An analysis of market data in the subject neighborhood has evidenced a justifiable price per square foot adjustment, for variances in gross living area, of $20.00/sq. ft. A fairly reasonable adjustment can now be defined by subtracting the market adjustment for the size of the family room from the depreciated cost of the family room, for example,

Cost of family room: 216 sq. ft. × $52.00/sq. ft.	= $11,232.
Less: 17% depreciation	−1,909.
Depreciated cost of family room	$ 9,323.
Price per square foot market adjustment is $20.00 per sq. ft.; hence, $20.00 x 216 sq. ft.	= −4,320.
Loss attributed to functional obsolescence	$ 5,003.

Thus, $5,000., rounded, might be used for a dollar amount of functional obsolescence in the cost approach, and an adjustment of $5,000. might be appropriately used for functional utility in the market analysis. Always make sure, however, that the adjustments relate to market history as well as current comparable sales included in your analysis.

Reasonable estimations of dollar loss in market value resulting from poor architectural design and appeal or functional inadequacies displayed in some custom-built homes can seldom, if ever, be extracted by direct market comparison because sales of similar properties are usually nonexistent. Sometimes, real estate agents can provide some insight into the problem if they know the extent of typical discounts for nonconforming properties in the area or they have knowledge of equitable offers to purchase the property in question.

If feasible, an alternative means to define dollar adjustments, in an attempt to refrain from making highly speculative adjustments when you are appraising a poorly designed custom-built home, might be to estimate the dollar amount to correct the deficiencies in the property.

If you have exhausted all the procedures recommended and you are unable to provide a basis for adjustments by any other means, you might be compelled to make a judgment decision, in which case, include relative statements explaining the situation.

Heating and Cooling

Specify the type of heating or cooling equipment, or the lack thereof, for the subject property and each comparable. Rate the differences in heating and cooling systems with respect to their capacity to heat or cool the entire home or only certain areas of the home.

Homes that are comparable in age, quality, and location usually have the same type of heating systems. Any dissimilarities would indicate possible modernization or rehabilitation; has the home been modernized or rehabilitated throughout?

Make an adjustment based on the cost to cure when there are no safe sources of heat or the heating system is inadequate. When appropriate, appraise the property "subject to installation of an adequate heating system" or "subject to satisfactory repair of existing equipment."

Before you assign adjustments for air conditioning, consider the necessity of cooling and neighborhood standards. Central air conditioning could be an overimprovement when temperate climatic conditions do not warrant a cooling system. For example, do you think a buyer would actually pay $1,000., or more, for a home with air conditioning that is located 2 miles from the ocean? Consider the income levels of the occupants. Central air conditioning would be a misplaced improvement in neighborhoods where buyers could not afford to pay for the cost of running the unit, in which case, adjustments should be modified accordingly. When air conditioning is an expected item in the neighborhood, an appropriate adjustment reflecting the added value of an air-conditioning unit might be warranted.

Always relate adjustments to the size of the dwelling. For example, adjustments for air-conditioning units in smaller homes will usually be $1,000. to $3,000. while costs and adjustments for larger homes, over 2,000 sq. ft., will be $3,000. to $6,000., or more, depending on the size and number of air-conditioning units.

Consider the depreciated value and market appeal of window and wall air-conditioning units before you automatically assign adjustments. Are they really worth a $500., or greater, adjustment? Window or wall air-conditioning units that are not permanently attached to the structure should be considered as personal property; therefore, descriptions of these items should accompanied by a statement that "no value was assigned as the item is considered to be personal property."

Garages and Carports

The dollar amount of the adjustments should reflect the need, desire, and requirements for parking within the subject neighborhood. The adjustments should not represent the cost of construction of a parking structure; adjustments must be based on local market appeal. Buyers in more affluent neighborhoods are usually willing to pay more for additional garage space than are buyers in lower-income neighborhoods. If the garage has been converted to an illegal use, the dollar amount of the adjustment should reflect the cost to convert the structure to its original intended and legal use.

Do not overlook relative adjustments for garages that

are larger than typical in width or depth, finished garage interiors, built-in cabinets, built-in storage areas, workshops, insulation, and other elements of value. Have these improvements been described in the body of the report and have they been considered in the reproduction cost? Larger than typical adjustments require an explanation.

Patios and Porches

Do not make adjustments for improvements that are substandard in quality, condition, and conformity to the norm. Improvements of this nature sometimes have more of a negative than a positive influence on value and marketability; therefore, you might have to consider the cost of removing the item. Relevancy to overall value should always be examined before you arbitrarily assign adjustments. If an element adds no value or detracts from the value, state the reasons for your opinion, and, if applicable, itemize costs to remove the item.

Yard Improvements

Consider the size of the lot and the estimated cost and present worth of the yard improvements as well as the condition of the yard improvements when you relate the comparables to the subject.

An appraiser's carelessness can easily be evidenced in adjustments for yard improvements. Consider the case of an appraiser who assigned a $5,000. adjustment for landscaping in the sales analysis section of the report while the depreciated cost of the improvements in the cost approach was only $3,000. Always correlate adjustments to the cost approach. Refine the adjustments to reflect neighborhood standards and include detailed descriptions and explanations so readers can readily validate your conclusions.

Swimming Pools

The economic makeup of a neighborhood substantially influences the worth of a swimming pool. In lower-priced residential neighborhoods, a swimming pool may have a negative influence on marketability because the typical buyer cannot afford the additional burdens of maintenance and higher taxes. At the opposite end of the spectrum, a swimming pool is usually an expected item in higher-priced neighborhoods; therefore, adjustments will usually be higher. Above-ground pools and spas should be considered as personal property with no value assigned.

Neighborhood appeal, materials and quality, age and condition of patios, enclosed patios, covered patios, pools, spas, and yard improvements should be addressed before you assign dollar amounts of adjustments. The contributory value should be measured in the market by a comparison of sales with and without the item in question. Adjustments that vary from the norm have to be explained. For example, "The subject swimming pool is older and reflects below-average maintenance and condition; therefore, adjustments were modified accordingly."

Special Energy-Efficient Items

Evaluate the market value (not the cost) of solar water heating, solar pool heating, insulation, double-paned windows and sliding glass doors, and other energy-efficient items. The adjustment should be based on an analysis of comparable properties with and without the items in question. In the event that adequate comparables are not available, the appraiser may develop an analysis of the present worth based on the estimated savings in utility costs. To do this, the appraiser may use a procedure similar to the one used in Part II of the Energy Addendum—Residential Appraisal Report, FHLMC Form 70A.

When large adjustments are made, itemize the items assigned value. Terms, such as standard, typical, superior, or inferior might be appropriately used if the items under consideration (insulation, weatherstripping, automatic setback thermostats, or electronic ignitions) do not significantly affect the value and no adjustments or only modest adjustments are made.

Adjustments for Fireplaces

Be careful when you use rules of thumb: adjustments should be based on type, quality, market appeal, and standards. The dollar amount of the adjustment for fireplaces could be $1,000., $3,000., or as high as $5,000. for each fireplace. Are fireplaces an expected item in the subject neighborhood or an overimprovement? List the number of fireplaces. When larger or smaller than typical ($1,000. to $3,000.) adjustments are made, explanations should be provided.

Examine the photos of all the comparable sales. Have you overlooked any fireplaces that are evident in the photos?

Other, Kitchen Equipment, and Remodeling

The items under this heading are to be reported for the subject property and the comparable sale whether or not adjustments are being made. "Kitchen equipment and remodeling" is shown on the form simply to illustrate some of the more common features that should be described in the report; therefore, the appraiser should not feel constrained to consider only the physical features shown. Describe and assign adjustments for any other improvements that affect value and marketability.

The type, cost, and materials of kitchen equipment; cabinetry; countertops; flooring; bath finishes; plumbing equipment; and so forth should relate to the age, style, and quality of the dwelling. Variances in quality and types of finishes usually reflect partial or full modernization, remodeling, or the presence of additions. At least two sales should have comparable remodeling or modernization to provide a basis for any adjustments. If there are no like sales available, this might be an indication that the subject is overimproved for the neighborhood.

When appliances are not built-in (free-standing ranges, microwave ovens, refrigerators), they should be considered as personal property, with no value assigned.

CHAPTER 13

RECONCILIATION AND FINAL ESTIMATE OF VALUE

In this chapter, which follows the format of the Uniform Residential Appraisal Report, we will show you the final steps of the appraisal process:

- Analyzing market data
- Writing market analysis comments
- Completing the income approach
- Reconciling the data
- Estimating the final value

HOW TO DEFINE THE ESTIMATE OF MARKET VALUE

Market value should always be defined in accordance with the most current standards set forth by governing agencies. The data contained in the appraisal report, and the type of form, must also conform to the most current standards set forth by governing agencies. In the event that you are confronted with conflicting standards, the highest standards should always prevail.

The final estimate of market value must be based on the definition of market value provided on FHLMC Form 439/FNMA Form 1004B, revised July 1986. This form must be included with the appraisal report or be on file with the client.

RECONCILING NET ADJUSTMENTS

Total the adjustments for each comparable. Add or subtract the total adjustments from the sales prices shown for each comparable to arrive at an indicated value of the subject property.

It is expected that the indicated values will not be identical for all properties; however, a definite pattern should be evident, and the values should fall within a reasonable range, if not, further analysis of the comparable sales is indicated.

ANALYSIS AND RECONCILIATION OF THE COMPARABLE SALES

1. Errors in arithmetic can have a substantial effect on the final concluded value. Review the mathematical accuracy of all the adjustments. Have the adjustments been correctly added or subtracted from the sales price of the comparables? Is there a plus sign where there actually should be a minus sign, or vice versa?

2. Do the indicated values relate to the indicated value by the cost approach? If not, determine the reasons for any variations. Review the arithmetic in the cost approach. Are costs, percentages of depreciation, value of site improvements, and the land value realistic? Did you overlook any elements of value in the cost approach?

3. When the comparables do not adjust out evenly, examine the reliability of your data sources. Perhaps the size, age, or some other element of value was misrepresented or omitted.

4. Are the properties selected as comparables sufficiently similar to the subject property? If the adjustments are excessive, reconsider whether the comparable property is truly comparable, if not, replace it with a sale that provides a better indication of the subject's value.

5. Has an item needing an adjustment been overlooked or an item of comparison omitted?

6. Have you, perhaps, been too stringent or too generous when you were assigning the adjustments? Examine the adjustments made between the subject property and the comparable sales. Refine the adjustments to reflect buyer's attitudes in the subject market.

7. Have the adjustments been appropriately rounded to the nearest $100. or $500.? Eliminate meaningless adjustments. Adjustments for items valued at less than $500. are, in most cases, unrealistic. Insignificant items of value are usually attended to when values are appropriately rounded.

8. If the indicated value of a comparable sale doesn't appear to make sense, this may be the result of an inappropriate adjustment for condition if the comparable property was refurbished after the sale recorded.

9. Review all the descriptions and ratings. Has superior been indicated when inferior was meant, good rather than average, or two-car garage instead of three-car garage? Have any of the numbers in the sales comparison analysis or cost approach been transposed or incorrectly written?

10. Make sure that adjustments have not been made in more than one category and the adjustments have been made in the appropriate category.

Occasionally, appraisers do not follow a logical pattern when they are making adjustments. The reasons for this might be attributed simply to an oversight on the part of the appraiser or an attempt to obtain a higher market value or, perhaps, the appraiser was so overly impressed with the property that excessive adjustments were made. For example, we have reviewed appraisals where adjustments were made in the category of design and appeal because the subject was upgraded and modernized; therefore, according to the appraiser, it had more appeal than the comparables. And another adjustment was made for condition because the subject had been upgraded and modernized; therefore, it was in better condition than the comparables. Additionally, a third adjustment was made for modernization. Obviously, the value was overstated because the subject and comparable sales were not evaluated in a proper manner and the sales were not really comparable.

INDICATED VALUE BY THE SALES COMPARISON APPROACH

Never average the indicated value to the subject represented by the comparables to arrive at the subject's market value. Each sale merits serious and special consideration. Generally, the sales with the least amount of adjustments, either in dollars or number of items designated, are deemed the best indicators of market value; however, you must also consider the financing of the comparable properties. The greatest consideration should be given to the sales that are most relevant to a value that represents cash equivalency.

Market value may or may not be the same as the subject's sales price. Market value is established by the most representative sales; it is not established by the sales price of the subject property.

If you are appraising a new tract home, one of the comparable sales should be located in the subject development and at least one of the comparables should be located outside of the subject development. There are no requirements for giving the greatest consideration to the comparable sale that is located in the subject development. As previously stated, the value is established by the most representative sales, not by the sales price of the subject property, in which case, the comparable sales located outside of the subject development might justify a higher, or even a lower, value than the comparable sale that is located in the subject development. This is the reason why appraisers must analyze comparable sales located outside of the subject development: to justify the subject's sales price or to show that the sales price is not supportable in the market. This is particularly important when builders offer sales concessions. Always notify your client immediately when the sales price is not supportable in the market.

Never assign a value that is exactly the same as the sales price of a new tract home, for example, $105,200. Based on the indicated value represented by the most comparable sales, round the concluded value to the nearest $500. or $1000. In the first place, values should always be rounded. Second, if the buyer adds an insignificant number of upgrades, the appraisal may not have to be rewritten because the value is too precise.

COMMENTS ON SALES COMPARISONS

While this is probably the most well-read and the most important part of the appraisal, this section of the report does not always get the attention it deserves. In a misguided effort to be concise, some appraisers do not give their readers enough information and supporting detail. Consequently, their readers cannot make intelligent underwriting or investment decisions.

If the type and quality of the information is within the scope of lender's guidelines and the market adjustments are all self-explanatory, it is not necessary to make a statement about every one of the sales. If the information is not self-explanatory, however, the relationship of the comparable sales to the subject property should be clearly demonstrated. Present a brief summary of all the relevant factors that led to your conclusion. Let your readers know that you have considered all the sales that were reasonably comparable and that the most comparable sales were used in your report.

Brief comments, such as comparable 1 has a superior view, comparable 2 has a supcrior location, or sale 3 has been modernized, should not be used, particularly when large adjustments are made. Highlight the reasons why you included the sales and how you arrived at your market adjustments. Your reasons for presenting the particular comparable sales and the reasons for the adjustments must be readily discernable to the reader. Attach an addendum, if needed, but be specific.

Consider the strength and weaknesses of the comparable sales when you are making your comments. Describe the condition and features of the comparable sales. Do they have room additions, upgrading, new paint, modernization, new carpet? What is the exact extent of the modernization and upgrading? Are repairs needed? What kind of repairs? What is the dollar amount of the repairs? Why is the view or location superior? Why does the lot have inferior utility?

All the subjective adjustments must be thoroughly explained, and all the controversial items receiving adjustments (location, site, view, design, appeal, quality, functional utility, or condition) should be explained in detail and should be accompanied by adequate supportive data.

The appraiser should indicate the comparables that have been given the greatest weight in arriving at market value and a final estimate of value.

Read your comments. Do they make sense? Consider the reader's dilemma when the appraiser describes the location of a sale as "twelve blocks from the subject" in the comments section while the proximity of the same sale is shown as "same project" in the body of the report and the location map depicts yet another location that is 1 mile outside the subject neighborhood. Always correlate your commentary with the description of the subject and comparable properties as well as with the neighborhood description.

SALES COMPARISON COMMENTS—EXAMPLES

Example 1: Comparable 3 is a dated sale; however, due to the lack of overall market appreciation in the area, as evidenced by the listings and sales in escrow, it is considered to be a valid indicator of current market value. Comparable 2 would have sold for the same price without any sales concession; therefore, no financing adjustment was required.

Example 2: Comparables 1, 4, and 5 are dated sales; however, they are considered to be valid indicators of current market value because the market has remained stable in this area as evidenced by comparables 2 and 3.

Example 3: There have been no recent closed sales of similar properties with swimming pools in the subject neighborhood; therefore, market data have been obtained from an alternate neighborhood that exhibits similar characteristics and proximity to desired amenities.

Example 4: The subject is located in phase IV. There has been a $4,000. increase in the builder's prices since sale 1, located in phase III, sold; therefore, this sale reflects a $4,000. time adjustment. Sale 4, located in phase IV, is in escrow and reflects recent price increases.

Example 5: Comparable 1 is the only recent recorded sale of a three-bedroom home in the subject or competing neighborhoods. The subject property contains three larger than typical bedrooms and a family room. The utility of the subject dwelling is considered to be comparable to sales 2 and 3, which are four-bedroom homes without family rooms; therefore, no adjustment was made for the bedroom count.

Example 6: All sales presented were taken from the subject's marketing area. They are closed and documented and are believed to be the most comparable at time of inspection. Sales 1 and 2 have a location adjustment because they back up to a major street and experience excessive residual traffic noise. Greatest consideration was given to comparable No. 3; it is most similar in characteristics to the subject.

To avoid redundancy, we have not included statements in all the foregoing examples identifying the comparable sales that were given the greatest consideration in defining market value or statements indicating that all the sales were closed and recorded; however, these statements should always be included in your appraisal report.

INDICATED VALUE BY THE INCOME APPROACH

If the mortgagor will occupy the subject property, show "not applicable" (N/A). When the mortgagor is not going to occupy the property (the property will be used for investment purposes), the appraiser must complete the income approach to value, substantiated by rent comparables.

The appraiser must complete the "Single-Family Comparable Rent Schedule" (FNMA Form 1007) and include the form with the report. Also, FNMA Form 216, Operating Income Statement, shall have the appraiser's comments section completed by the appraiser. The remainder of this form should be completed by the lender prior to the appraisal request and submitted with the request to the appraiser. When the appraiser is relying on the income approach, he or she must attach the supporting comparable rental and sales data, and the calculations used to determine the gross rent multiplier, as an addendum to the appraisal report form.

When the property is rented, or leased, at the time of the appraisal, use actual rents if the rents are close to market rents and when there is a long-term lease on the property. If the rents are low and you feel that the rent should be raised to market levels, use market rents to estimate the value by the income approach. Include a statement identifying the actual rent and the reasons why you feel the rent should be increased. The monthly rent used to determine the value, whether actual or economic (market) rent, must be substantiated by your rental survey. If the property is in a rent-control area, address rent-control policies and ordinances and their effect on rentability and marketability.

The gross rent multiplier should be extracted from the market by analyzing sales prices and rents of comparable properties. To find the gross rent multiplier, divide the sales price by the gross rent. Several properties should be analyzed in this manner. Gross rent multipliers, like indicated values to the subject derived from comparable sales, are never determined by means of averaging several multipliers. Select a suitable gross rent multiplier based on the properties that are the most similar to the subject property.

If the subject property is furnished, select a gross rent

multiplier from an analysis of properties that are comparably furnished. When the subject property will be rented unfurnished, only unfurnished properties should be considered in your analysis.

To determine the indicated value by the income approach, multiple the total monthly rent by the gross rent multiplier; for example,

$850./month × 135 GRM = $114,750., rounded $115,000.

Discuss vacancy and rental stability. If the property is not rented or leased, include a supported estimate of the time it will take to rent the property. A typical statement might read as follows: "The absorption period of one month is based on rental surveys in the subject neighborhood and interviews with property owners and managers, real estate agents, and appraiser's files. Rental absorption rates are indicated on rental comparables where available. Most of the homes, when rented at close-to-market-level rates, reflected absorption periods from as little as one week for well-located, well-maintained properties, to two months for less desirable properties. We found the typical absorption period to be one month."

Rent comparables can be obtained from local property owners as they can usually point out the rental properties in the neighborhood. Also, survey rental advertisements in local newspapers and consult with local real estate brokers who are familiar with the neighborhood rental rates.

VALUE AS IS—VALUE SUBJECT TO

Check the appropriate box to indicate whether the subject property is appraised "as is" or whether the appraisal is based on certain repairs, alterations, or other conditions to achieve the estimated value. Provide an itemized list of the repairs and a total dollar estimation for the repairs. Make sure these items have been taken into consideration in the market approach as well as the cost approach.

If the property being appraised is proposed construction, or it is under construction, indicate that the value is "Subject to satisfactory completion per approved plans and specifications, and per description contained in this report." (Make certain that you show "approved" plans and specifications.) Provide an estimated completion date. When you appraise custom-built homes, the plans should be dated and initialed by the appraiser. The name of the architect and the date the plans were approved, or the last revision date, should be shown.

When you appraise property with a partially completed addition, or incomplete modernization or renovation, unless the lender has specifically requested otherwise, appraise the property "subject to satisfactory completion of . . . (list the work that needs to be completed)" and, if appropriate, "subject to finalized permits." Include an itemized list and a total cost of the work that needs to be completed.

Appraisals should always be made subject to repairs when the deficiency is structural, when there is strong potential to cause structural damage, or where there are items present that could affect the health or safety of the occupants. All other appraisals, except for property that is proposed or under construction, should be appraised "as is" unless the lending officer has specifically requested that the appraisal be made "subject to."

When there are a substantial number of repairs, include an itemized list and a total cost of the repairs needed, and appraise the property "as is." Also, show a "value when repairs have been completed" in the "comments and conditions of appraisal" area of the report.

COMMENTS AND CONDITIONS OF APPRAISAL

Itemize, in detail, any recommended repairs, inspections, or other conditions that should be brought to the reader's attention even though these conditions may have been addressed on page one of the report. Unless the repairs or inspections are related to structural damage or affect the health and safety of the occupants, the repairs or inspections should be "recommended" instead of "required," unless the lender specifically requests otherwise. If you are requiring or recommending an inspection, always include the word "satisfactory," for example, "subject to a *satisfactory* soils engineer's report." Otherwise, a report or inspection might be obtained, though it might not be acceptable or satisfactory.

If there are any items in the "Certification and Statement of Limiting Conditions" that do not apply, this should be so stated. Or a statement could be included, such as "Certification and Statement of Limiting Conditions attached to this report apply."

FINAL RECONCILIATION OF VALUE ESTIMATES

The correlation of the data compiled and the indication of value is the final step of the appraisal process. The data have been gathered and analyzed for the purpose of judging the typical reactions of the typical purchaser of similar properties in this market.

The three basic approaches to value have varied degrees of applicability, depending on the circumstances. The cost approach is significant when the improvements are new or nearly new and fully utilized. The income approach indicates the amount at which a prudent investor would receive an appropriate return on an investment in the subject property. The sales comparison approach, or market approach, reflects actual prices paid for similar properties. The appraiser should study the significance and validity of each approach to value and present justification for the value selected as the final estimate of value.

When you appraise single-family residences, the market approach is usually given the greatest consideration in arriving at a final estimate of market value. The cost approach to value is the estimating of the cost to reproduce new a specific improvement with one of like utility, less depreciation, and plus the estimated land value. The cost approach to value is usually given the least weight because single-family residences are seldom purchased on the basis of cost.

It should be emphasized that the final reconciliation is not an averaging process nor is it a narrowing of the range of value estimates. Reconciliation is the weighing of all the facts presented in the report; reconciliation of the differences by reasoning; and arriving at a final estimate of value that is logical, sound, and defensible.

The indicated values by the cost approach, income approach, and the market approach can all be different, but they should be within a reasonable range. The final value does not have to be identical to the market value or the approach that was given the greatest consideration; however, the final estimate of value should be reasonably close to the value given the greatest consideration in arriving at the final value estimate. If the final value is the value indicated by the cost approach, the source of cost factors and comparable land sales should be included.

FINAL RECONCILIATION COMMENTS—EXAMPLES

Example 1: The market approach to value is based upon the principle of substitution and is deemed the most reliable indicator of current value. The cost approach was calculated using the "Marshall and Swift" cost guidelines and is supportive of the market approach.

Example 2: The market approach is considered the most indicative of buyer and seller attitudes in the current marketplace and is given the greatest weight in the final value conclusion. Because the subject property is unique, the cost approach was also weighted heavily in arriving at an estimated market value.

FINAL ESTIMATE OF MARKET VALUE

The final estimate of value is an opinion based on the appraiser's experience, knowledge, professional judgment, and a complete and unbiased analysis of the subject neighborhood, the subject property, and the comparable sales. Appraisers must completely disassociate themselves from the final valuation result. The final estimate of value must be sound, reasonable, and defensible and supported by factual market data.

The final estimate of value is precisely that—an estimate. Hence, to remove any suggestion or unjustified assertions of excessive accuracy or mathematical precision, values should be appropriately rounded, typically, to the nearest $500. Expensive, or very expensive, properties might be appropriately rounded to the nearest $1,000. or $5,000.

It is not considered to be within the appraiser's depth of knowledge to "second-guess" the market. If the sales indicate a value that is lower, but within close tolerance of the subject sales price, it is not unreasonable that the appraiser's final value estimate would be the same as the sales price of the property, particularly when speculative or substantial adjustments have been made.

Significant differences between the sales price and the final estimate of value must be explained when the final estimate of value is lower or higher than the sales price. A statement to the effect that the subject appears to have sold under (or over) market is not sufficient. The appraiser must address specific reasons for the variance in value and price. Some of the reasons you might find for differences between sales prices and appraised values are as follows:

1. The property was listed and sold by a broker from out of the area or by an agent who was not familiar with local property values.
2. The sales price was discounted to effect a 30-day escrow because the owner was transferred out of the area.
3. The property was sold by an owner who was unfamiliar with property values in the area.
4. The property was sold by an owner, and the sales price was discounted to allow for the absence of a real estate commission.
5. The property sold based on a lease option with a predetermined sales price below current market value.
6. The transaction was a forced sale.

CERTIFICATION AND STATEMENT OF LIMITING CONDITIONS

This box must be marked regardless of whether the actual form is attached or on file with the lender. Include the date, if applicable, that FHLMC Form 439/FNMA Form 1004B was filed with the client. Unless the form is on file with the lender, it should always be included with each appraisal.

If the appraisal requires additional limiting conditions, the appraiser may add these to Form 439/1004B. Include the form with the report. If an addition or deletion to the Certification and Statement of Limiting Conditions is made, the appraiser must reference the changes in the "reconciliation" section of the report.

EFFECTIVE DATE OF VALUE ESTIMATE

The date can be stated as either the date the property was inspected or the date the appraisal was prepared. The date of the value estimate, however, should approximate the date the property was inspected to reduce the likelihood of any material changes in the market between the time the property was inspected and the date the appraisal was written.

APPRAISER'S SIGNATURE

The appraiser who physically inspected the subject and the comparables, analyzed the data, and prepared the report *must* supply the signature on the left side of the form. If the firm's principal or another appraiser assisted, then more than one signature is appropriate on the left side of the form. If the principal did a desk review, with or without a field review, then that appraiser's signature should be on the right-hand side of the form. Trainees receiving training and guidance from the principal should sign the report in the appropriate place: on the left side of the form.

It is unethical for the principal or someone else to sign the report on the left unless all the preceding requirements have been met. Not only is it unethical, but it constitutes a fraud in that the signing appraiser is certifying to certain conditions.

ADDITIONAL REQUIREMENTS FOR APPRAISALS

1. The appraiser must include a one-year sales history of the subject property. If there have been no transactions within the past year, this should be noted in the appraisal.
2. If the subject property is listed for sale, or has been listed for sale within the past year, include pertinent listing data.
3. If the subject property has recently sold, include the length of time the property was listed.
4. Include applicable permit numbers and sources of verification.
5. Include verifiable evidence of closed sales.
6. For properties valued at $500,000., or more, include two additional comparables in addition to the normal three, additional photographs of the interior and exterior to illustrate property amenities further, and an addendum more fully describing the improvements.
7. For properties valued at $750,000., or more, most lenders require a narrative-style report.
8. All exhibits and forms must be dated and identified and have an *original signature*. Copies, if there are any, must be legible and have an *original signature.*
9. Any corrections or changes on the form must be initialed by the appraiser, particularly in the flood-zone area and the date of the appraisal. *Never* use correction fluid or correct the values by the different approaches to value, particularly the final estimate of value. When a correction is made to the final estimate of value, the appraisal will have to be resubmitted.

10. All appraisals must have the appraiser's name and appropriate state classification typed on the report. Appraiser's designations should be typed on the report, as applicable. Appraiser's telephone numbers (including area code) and tax identification numbers are also required by many lenders.

SUMMARY

The significance of producing an appraisal that strictly adheres to Fannie Mae, Freddie Mac, Federal Home Loan Bank Board, and institutional lender's guidelines as well as to the standards set forth by professional appraisal organizations cannot be overly stressed.

The appraiser's role is to provide the lender, or client, with an adequately supported estimate of value and a complete, accurate, and unbiased description of the neighborhood, subject property, and comparable properties. The appraiser must always remain free of any outside influences in the valuation process. Every appraisal should be presented in a manner that reflects a true representation of the appraiser's skill, knowledge, good judgment, and integrity.

Reevaluate the appraisal. Is it totally self-contained; will third-party readers of the report be able to understand your logic, reasoning, judgment, and analyses fully? Will they be able to make a prudent underwriting decision? In other words, if you had not visually inspected the property, could you make a sound lending decision based on the information contained in the report?

Is there any pertinent information that has been withheld? Does the appraisal contain a complete, accurate, and unbiased description of the neighborhood, subject property, and comparable sales? Is your estimate of market value adequately supported? Review the soundness of the value conclusion drawn from the adjusted sales prices of the comparable properties.

Put the appraisal aside for a day; then go back and examine the report once more for inconsistencies throughout the report, blank spaces that have not been filled in, arithmetic errors, missing adjustments, and any other errors or omissions.

Uniform Residential Appraisal Report—Example

Property Description & Analysis

UNIFORM RESIDENTIAL APPRAISAL REPORT

File No. TEST 21

SUBJECT

Property Address 321 S. Sunshine Drive | Census Tract 0045.10
City Sunville | County Orange | State Ca. | Zip Code 72846
Legal Description Lot 4 Blk 6 Tract 3475 APN: 345-09-5786
Owner/Occupant Smith, John (owner) | Map Reference 34 A-6
Sale Price $ refinance | Date of Sale N/A
Loan charges/concessions to be paid by seller $ N/A
R.E. Taxes $ 687.00 | Tax Year 1988/89 | HOA $/Mo. -0-
Lender/Client R & B Mortgage Company
Appraiser: R. H. J. Appraisal Corp.

Property Rights Appraised: [X] Fee Simple [ ] Leasehold [ ] Condominium (HUD/VA) [ ] De Minimis PUD

LENDER DISCRETIONARY USE
Sale Price $ ______
Date ______
Mortgage Amount $ ______
Mortgage Type ______
Discount Points and Other Concessions ______
Paid by Seller $ ______
Source ______

NEIGHBORHOOD

LOCATION	[ ] Urban	[X] Suburban	[ ] Rural
BUILT UP	[X] Over 75%	[ ] 25 - 75%	[ ] Under 25%
GROWTH RATE	[ ] Rapid	[X] Stable	[ ] Slow
PROPERTY VALUES	[X] Increasing	[ ] Stable	[ ] Declining
DEMAND/SUPPLY	[X] Shortage	[ ] In Balance	[ ] Over Supply
MARKETING TIME	[X] Under 3 Mos.	[ ] 3 - 6 Mos.	[ ] Over 6 Mos.

NEIGHBORHOOD ANALYSIS	Good	Avg	Fair	Poor
Employment Stability	[ ]	[X]	[ ]	[ ]
Convenience to Employment	[ ]	[X]	[ ]	[ ]
Convenience to Shopping	[X]	[ ]	[ ]	[ ]
Convenience to Schools	[X]	[ ]	[ ]	[ ]
Adequacy of Public Transportation	[ ]	[X]	[ ]	[ ]
Recreation Facilities	[ ]	[X]	[ ]	[ ]
Adequacy of Utilities	[ ]	[X]	[ ]	[ ]
Property Compatibility	[ ]	[X]	[ ]	[ ]
Protection from Detrimental Cond.	[ ]	[X]	[ ]	[ ]
Police & Fire Protection	[ ]	[X]	[ ]	[ ]
General Appearance of Properties	[X]	[ ]	[ ]	[ ]
Appeal to Market	[ ]	[X]	[ ]	[ ]

PRESENT LAND USE %		LAND USE CHANGE		PREDOMINANT OCCUPANCY		SINGLE FAMILY HOUSING PRICE $(000)	AGE (yrs)
Single Family	85	Not Likely	[X]	Owner	[X]	234 Low	15
2-4 Family	10	Likely	[ ]	Tenant	[ ]	260 High	32
Multi-family		In process	[ ]	Vacant (0-5%)	[X]	Predominant	
Commercial	5	To:		Vacant (over 5%)	[ ]	250 -	25
Industrial							
Vacant							

Note: Race or the racial composition of the neighborhood are not considered reliable appraisal factors. COMMENTS: Mixed improved neighborhoood consisting of conforming, one and two story single family residences & scattered, small residential income properties. Maintenance levels are above average. The Sunville Airport is two miles west; however, this neighborhood is not under the flight pattern and no adverse influences are noted. Schools, shopping, & other public amenities are within walking distance.

SITE

Dimensions 80 x 100
Site Area 8000 Sq.Ft. | Corner Lot No
Zoning Classification R-2 (multi-family) | Zoning Compliance Yes
HIGHEST & BEST USE: Present Use Yes | Other Use See site comments

UTILITIES	Public	Other
Electricity	[X]	
Gas	[X]	
Water	[X]	
Sanitary Sewer	[X]	
Storm Sewer	[X]	

SITE IMPROVEMENTS	Type	Public	Private
Street	Asphalt/average	[X]	[ ]
Curb/Gutter	Concrete/average	[X]	[ ]
Sidewalk	Concrete/average	[X]	[ ]
Street Lights	Adequate	[X]	[ ]
Alley	None	[ ]	[ ]

Topography	Level
Size	Typical for nbhd.
Shape	Rectangular
Drainage	Appears adequate
View	None
Landscaping	Typical for nbhd.
Driveway	Concrete
Apparent Easements	Typical utility
FEMA Flood Hazard	Yes* No X
FEMA* Map/Zone	060213004C/Zone C*

COMMENTS (Apparent adverse easements, encroachments, special assessments, slide areas, etc.): *9/16/82. The highest & best use of the site is as presently improved as restrictive parking requirements limit the scope of additional development at this time. There are no apparent adverse influences present.

IMPROVEMENTS

GENERAL DESCRIPTION		EXTERIOR DESCRIPTION		FOUNDATION		BASEMENT		INSULATION	
Units	One	Foundation	Concrete	Slab	Yes	Area Sq. Ft.	-0-	Roof	None [ ]
Stories	One	Exterior Walls	Stucco	Crawl Space	No	% Finished	N/A	Ceiling	R-11 [X]
Type (Det./Att.)	Detached	Roof Surface	Shake	Basement	No	Ceiling	N/A	Walls	None [ ]
Design (Style)	Conv	Gutters & Dwnspts.	2' O.H.	Sump Pump	No	Walls	N/A	Floor	None [ ]
Existing	Yes	Window Type	Al/sliding	Dampness	None noted	Floor	N/A	None	N/A [ ]
Proposed	No	Storm Sash	None	Settlement	None noted	Outside Entry	N/A	Adequacy	Med'm [ ]
Under Construction	No	Screens	Yes	Infestation	Inspection recommended due to age of home.			Energy Efficient Items:	Auto set-back thermostat
Age (Yrs.)	1963	Manufactured House	No						
Effective Age (Yrs.)	13-15								

ROOM LIST

ROOMS	Foyer	Living	Dining	Kitchen	Den	Family Rm.	Rec. Rm.	Bedroom	# Baths	Laundry	Other	Area Sq. Ft.
Basement												
Level 1	X	X	X	X				3	2	X		2,000
Level 2												

Finished area above grade contains: 6 Rooms; 3 Bedroom(s); 2 Bath(s); 2,000 Square Feet of Gross Living Area

INTERIOR

SURFACES	Materials/Condition	HEATING		KITCHEN EQUIP.		ATTIC	
Floors	Carpet/good	Type	FAU	Refrigerator	[ ]	None	[ ]
Walls	Drywall/good	Fuel	Gas	Range/Oven	[1]	Stairs	[ ]
Trim/Finish	Average	Condition	Avg.	Disposal	[1]	Drop Stair	[ ]
Bath Floor	VAT/good	Adequacy	Avg.	Dishwasher	[1]	Scuttle	[X]
Bath Wainscot	Ceramic/good	COOLING		Fan/Hood	[1]	Floor	[ ]
Doors	medium grade hollow core	Central	None	Compactor	[ ]	Heated	[ ]
		Other	None	Washer/Dryer	[ ]	Finished	[ ]
		Condition	n/a	Microwave	[1]		
Fireplace(s)	used brick # 1	Adequacy	n/a	Intercom	[ ]		

IMPROVEMENT ANALYSIS	Good	Avg	Fair	Poor
Quality of Construction	[ ]	[X]	[ ]	[ ]
Condition of Improvements	[X]	[ ]	[ ]	[ ]
Room Sizes/Layout	[ ]	[X]	[ ]	[ ]
Closets and Storage	[ ]	[X]	[ ]	[ ]
Energy Efficient	[ ]	[X]	[ ]	[ ]
Plumbing-Adequacy & Condition	[ ]	[X]	[ ]	[ ]
Electrical-Adequacy & Condition	[ ]	[X]	[ ]	[ ]
Kitchen Cabinets-Adequacy & Cond.	[X]	[ ]	[ ]	[ ]
Compatibility to Neighborhood	[ ]	[X]	[ ]	[ ]
Appeal & Marketability	[X]	[ ]	[ ]	[ ]
Estimated Remaining Economic Life	50 - 52 Yrs.			
Estimated Remaining Physical Life	55 57 Yrs.			

AUTOS

CAR STORAGE:							
Garage	[X]	Attached	[X]	Adequate	[X]	House Entry	[X]
No. Cars 2	Carport [ ]	Detached	[ ]	Inadequate	[ ]	Outside Entry	[ ]
Condition Average	None [ ]	Built-in	[ ]	Electric Door	[ ]	Basement Entry	[ ]

COMMENTS

Additional features: Common brick exterior trim, 10' x 20' covered patio, above-ground spa (personal property; no value assigned to above-ground spa), sprinkler system; front & rear, perimeter grapestake fencing.

Depreciation (Physical, functional and external inadequacies, repairs needed, modernization, etc.): Kitchen and both baths were recently modernized including all new equipment, flooring, & countertops. Many of the homes in this neighborhood have been comparably modernized; therefore, no functional obsolescence is noted. There are no apparent physical inadequacies present.

General market conditions and prevalence and impact in subject/market area regarding loan discounts, interest buydowns and concessions: Prevalent financing consists of mostly conventional loans, both fixed and variable rates, with plus or minus 80% loan to value ratio, & spread over 30 years with occasional 15 year notes. Subject has not been listed or transferred in the past year.

Freddie Mac Form 70 10/86 | This form was produced on Richard Heyn and Associates' LaserForm system (800) 234-URAR | Fannie Mae Form 1004 10/86

Uniform Residential Appraisal Report—Example

Valuation Section **UNIFORM RESIDENTIAL APPRAISAL REPORT** File No. TEST 21

Purpose of Appraisal is to estimate Market Value as defined in the Certification & Statement of Limiting Conditions.

COST APPROACH

BUILDING SKETCH (SHOW GROSS LIVING AREA ABOVE GRADE)
If for Freddie Mac or Fannie Mae, show only square foot calculations and cost approach comments in this space.

GLA	1.00 x	53.00 x	1	=	53
•	5.00 x	25.00 x	1	=	125
•	2.00 x	31.00 x	1	=	62
•	3.00 x	35.00 x	1	=	105
•	22.50 x	50.00 x	1	=	1125
•	20.00 x	26.50 x	1	=	530
•		Total Sq. Ft.		=	2000

The land to value ratio is typical for the area. This value has been abstracted from the market analysis.

ESTIMATED REPRODUCTION COST-NEW-OF IMPROVEMENTS:

Dwelling 2,000 Sq. Ft. @ $ 55.00	= $	110,000
Sq. Ft. @ $	=	
Extras Included in base	=	
	=	
Special Energy Efficient Items	=	400
Porches, Patios, etc. Covered patio	=	3,000
Garage/Carport 400 Sq. Ft. @ $ 16.00	=	6,400
Total Estimated Cost New	= $	119,800
Less Depreciation — Physical 15,574 / Functional / External	= $	-15,574
Depreciated Value of Improvements	= $	104,226
Site Imp. "as is" (driveway, landscaping, etc.)	= $	12,000
ESTIMATED SITE VALUE	= $	125,000
(If leasehold, show only leasehold value.)		
INDICATED VALUE BY COST APPROACH	= $	241,200

(Not Required by Freddie Mac and Fannie Mae)
Does property conform to applicable HUD/VA property standards? [ ] Yes [ ] No
If No, explain:

Construction Warranty [ ] Yes [X] No
Name of Warranty Program
Warranty Coverage Expires

SALES COMPARISON ANALYSIS

The undersigned has recited three recent sales of properties most similar and proximate to subject and has considered these in the market analysis. The description includes a dollar adjustment, reflecting market reaction to those items of significant variation between the subject and comparable properties. If a significant item in the comparable property is superior to, or more favorable than, the subject property, a minus (-) adjustment is made, thus reducing the indicated value of subject; if a significant item in the comparable is inferior to, or less favorable than, the subject property, a plus (+) adjustment is made, thus increasing the indicated value of the subject.

ITEM	SUBJECT	COMPARABLE NO. 1		COMPARABLE NO. 2		COMPARABLE NO. 3	
Address	321 S. Sunshine Dr.	2040 Star Avenue West		1628 Delwest Avenue		2086 Haven Avenue	
Proximity to Subject		3 blocks northwest		7 blocks north		8 blocks east	
Sales Price	$242000.A/V		$ 248,000		$ 237,000		$ 241,000
Price/Gross Liv. Area	$ 121.00 ¢	$ 115.89 ¢		$ 119.70 ¢		$ 117.56 ¢	
Data Source	Personal Insp	Title Co/CMDC 5/88		Title Co/CMDC 5/88		Title Co/App. Files	
VALUE ADJUSTMENTS	DESCRIPTION	DESCRIPTION	+(-) $ Adjustment	DESCRIPTION	+(-) $ Adjustment	DESCRIPTION	+(-) $ Adjustment
Sales or Financing Concessions		Conv 80% LTV		Conv 78% LTV		Conv 80% LTV	
Date of Sale/Time	N/A	Rec.4-21-88		Rec. 4-27-88		Rec. 5-18-88	
Location	Cnr/RV access	Cnr/RV access		Int/none	+3,000	Cnr/RV access	
Site/View	8000/none	8100/none		7900/none		8000/none	
Design and Appeal	Conv/Good	Conv/Good		Conv/Good		Conv/Good	
Quality of Construction	Average	Average		Average		Average	
Age	Eff. age: 15	Eff. age: 15		Eff. age: 14		Actual: 12	
Condition	Good	Good		Inferior	+2,000	Good	
Above Grade Room Count (Total / Bdrms / Bath)	6 / 3 / 2	6 / 4 / 2.5	-3000*	6 / 3 / 2		6 / 3 / 2.5	-1,000
Gross Living Area	2,000 Sq. Ft.	2,140 Sq. Ft.	-3,500	1,980 Sq. Ft.		2,050 Sq. Ft.	
Basement & Finished Rooms Below Grade	None Document No:	None 048732		None 049731		None 060832	
Functional Utility	Average	Average		Average		Average	
Heating/Cooling	Gas FAU	Gas FAU		Gas FAU		Gas FAU	
Garage/Carport	2 Car Garage	2 Car Garage		2 Car Garage		2 Car Garage	
Porches, Patio Pools, etc.	Zoning R-2 Covered patio	Zoning R-2 Covered patio		Zoning R-2 None	+500	Zoning R-2 Covered patio	
Special Energy Efficient Items	Auto set-back thermostat	Equal		Equal		Equal	
Fireplace(s)	1 used brick	1		1		1	
Other (e.g. kitchen equip., remodeling)	Mod. K & bath built-ins	Mod. K & bath built-ins		Mod. K & bath built-ins		Inferior built-ins	+5,000
Net Adj. (total)		[ ] + [X] -	$ 6,500	[X] + [ ] -	$ 5,500	[X] + [ ] -	$ 4,000
Indicated Value of Subject			$ 241,500		$ 242,500		$ 245,000

Comments on Sales Comparison: * $3,000. Room adjustment/Comp 1: -2000/BR & -1000/baths. GLA adj. rate: $25/sq.ft. Comp 1 is the only recent neighborhood sale with R.V. access. Comp No. 3, located in a nearby, competing neighborhood with similar market appeal, also has R. V. access.

INDICATED VALUE BY SALES COMPARISON APPROACH $ 242,000

INDICATED VALUE BY INCOME APPROACH (If Applicable) Estimated Market Rent $ N/A /Mo. x Gross Multiplier N/A = $ N/A

RECONCILIATION

This appraisal is made [X] "as is" [ ] subject to the repairs, alterations, inspections, or conditions listed below [ ] completion per plans and specifications.

Comments and Conditions of Appraisal: Certification & Limiting Conditions attached to this report apply. All of the comparables were weighed equally in arriving at a final estimate of value.

Final Reconciliation: The market approach to value is based upon the principle of substitution and is deemed the most reliable indicator of current value. The cost approach is supportive of the market approach.

This appraisal is based upon the above requirements, the certification, contingent and limiting conditions, and Market Value definition that are stated in
[ ] FmHA, HUD &/or VA instructions.
[X] Freddie Mac Form 439 (Rev. 7/86)/Fannie Mae Form 1004B (Rev. 7/86) filed with client 19 [X] attached.

I (WE) ESTIMATE THE MARKET VALUE, AS DEFINED, OF THE SUBJECT PROPERTY AS OF June 4 19 88 to be $ 242,000

I (WE) certify: that to the best of my (our) knowledge and belief, the facts and data used herein are true and correct; that I (we) personally inspected the subject property, both inside and out, and have made an exterior inspection of all comparable sales cited in this report; and that I (we) have no undisclosed interest, present or prospective therein.

Appraiser(s) SIGNATURE Review Appraiser SIGNATURE [ ] Did [ ] Did Not
NAME Appraiser's name/Class IV (if applicable) NAME Inspect Property

Freddie Mac Form 70 10/86 Fannie Mae Form 1004 10/86

CHAPTER 14

CONDOMINIUMS, COOPERATIVE UNITS, AND PLANNED UNIT DEVELOPMENTS

Our explanations and discussions in this chapter follow the order of the entries on the Condominium Form (FHLMC Form 465), Addendum A (project analysis), and Addendum B (budget analysis).

A number of items listed on the single-family form are the same items that are found on the condominium form; therefore, to avoid redundancy, we have addressed only the specific requirements for condominiums, planned unit developments, and cooperative units in this chapter.

Condominiums and planned unit developments are generally appraised in the same manner as single-family residences, and the same principles and requirements that apply to writing single-family residential appraisal reports also apply to condominiums and planned unit developments. For appraisals of condominiums or planned unit developments, however, in addition to describing and analyzing the neighborhood, the appraiser must also analyze and describe the characteristics of the project.

HOW TO DIFFERENTIATE A CONDOMINIUM FROM A TOWN HOUSE

What is the difference between a condominium and a town house? A condominium unit is a one-family dwelling located in a condominium project. A condominium unit may be part of a high-rise building, an attached row house, or even a single- family detached residence. However, in every case, the individual owners hold title to units in the project along with an undivided interest in the real estate that is designated as the common area for the project.

In the vast majority of cases, a condominium owner acquires a fee simple interest in a cubicle of airspace and the interior surfaces of the walls, floors, ceilings, and windows that define the airspace. The underlying land and virtually all the rest of the structure that houses the condominium unit, as well as the common area facilities (which can include private streets, clubhouses, swimming pools, tennis courts, greenbelts, and so forth), are owned in tenancy in common with other owners in the development.

"Town house" is not a legal term. The term describes a residential development in which individual dwellings are in very close physical proximity, sometimes separated only by party walls. It is conceivable that a residential development utilizing the town house design could be legally structured as a condominium. For the most part, however, this is not done. Town houses generally do not have other units above or below, do not have more than two walls that are common with adjacent units, and always have individual exterior entries. Appraisers sometimes refer to "town house design" when condominiums are comprised of more than one story.

Town houses normally fall under the "PUD classification." In a planned unit development (PUD), each individual owner has fee title to the structure and the land underlying the structure. A planned unit development, which can consist of one- to four-family dwellings, is one that consists of common property and improvements that are owned and maintained by an owner's association, corporation, or trust for the benefit and use of the individual units within that parcel of land (common property), and such association, corporation, or trust requires automatic, nonseverable membership of each individual unit owner, with mandatory assessments.

In some instances, a condominium regime may exist within a planned unit development. These are usually large projects where the developer has established condominium regimes covering only the living unit structures and the land they stand on, while all green areas, recreational facilities, parking, and street areas have been deeded to a "Master PUD Association" for repair and maintenance.

Other terms commonly used by developers, lenders, and management companies are the following:

Single Regime: Refers to the type of HOA (homeowner's association) established for a condominium or PUD project in which the entire project is considered as the one and only phase. Usually found in smaller projects.

Multiple-Regime: Several homeowner's associations within one project. In larger projects, multiple-regimes are used to create more manageable, less cumbersome entities to oversee the common elements within a section or phase in the parent project.

Umbrella Association: A "Master Homeowner's Association" composed of member associations within a multiple-regime project and created to administer to the common problems of each member homeowner's association.

Phasing: The process employed by condominium/PUD developers whereby a project is developed in stages; each stage consisting of a group of units that may or may not be operated as separate regimes.

Declaration of Ownership

Declaration of Ownership—also known as Declaration; Master Deed; Public Deed; or Conditions, Covenants, and Restrictions (CC&Rs)—is the legal document establishing the condominium regime. The declaration will generally include the legal description of the property; description of the individual units; description of the common elements; provision to create an owner's association; and miscellaneous provisions setting forth the unit owners rights to sell, mortgage, rent, insure, remodel, decorate, or dissolve.

Public Subdivision Report

The "Public Subdivision Report" usually contains full descriptions of condominium projects and planned unit developments. When you schedule appointments, ask owners whether they can locate their copy of the CC&Rs, Public Subdivision Report, or other legal documents that will help you describe the project. When project information cannot be obtained from the owner's legal documents, obtain the description of the project from city planning officials or the homeowner's association.

HOW TO APPRAISE CONDOMINIUMS AND PUD UNITS

Use the URAR form and the FHLMC Planned Unit Development Project Information Addendum for planned unit developments.

Technically, the lender is supposed to complete the portion of the form "to be completed by lender"; however, this is seldom done. Therefore, the appraiser must complete all the information that has not been provided by the lender, including information relating to financing terms. If the lender did not provide a copy of the sales contract and the appraiser is not aware of the financing terms, this should be noted in the report. The project name and phase number *must not* be omitted. This information can usually be obtained from the homeowner's association, owner's legal documents, or city planning departments. When specific "instructions to appraiser" have not been provided, show "Estimate Market Value," or other purposes, as applicable, in the space provided. Although the form does not specifically call for these data, provide the assessor's parcel number and tract number in this area of the report.

Present Land Uses

Indicate the percentages of present land uses making certain that the total equals 100 percent. Include PUD properties with single-family percentages. Correlate the percentages with the neighborhood description, potential for additional condo/PUD units in the area, percentage built-up, and the growth rate.

Predominant Price and Age Ranges

The appraiser should be aware that with many investors, the *loan amount* requested may not exceed the predominant price stated unless it is explained in the comments section that predominant prices in the neighborhood are increasing, or explain that the subject is not considered to be an overimprovement for the neighborhood. Provide supportable reasons for your conclusions.

Potential for Additional Condominium and PUD Units

Correlate your comments with the neighborhood description, present land use, growth rate, percent built-up, demand and supply, and marketing time. Consider the following examples of typical comments:

1. The surrounding area is virtually 100 percent developed.
2. There is considerable land available for development to the east which will probably be developed over the next several years.
3. There is potential for additional units on a large vacant parcel to the north and nearby parcels improved with older, tear-down single-family residences.
4. The area is entirely built-up, and no significant increase in competing condominium projects is anticipated.

Neighborhood Ratings

Neighborhood ratings are to be based on comparison of the subject neighborhood to competing neighborhoods. Ratings of fair or poor must be explained. Consider and explain any changes, either favorable or unfavorable, that have occurred, or are likely to occur, and the effect on marketability and long term stability of value as a result of the change.

Distance to Civic Amenities

Indicate the distance to public transportation, employment centers, and other civic amenities from the project in terms of blocks or miles. If the items are nonexistent, show none, but indicate "average" if the lack of the amenity is typical for the area. If the amenity is needed but not available, a fair or poor rating, accompanied by an explanation, should be indicated. A good rating for grammar schools should be indicated when schools are in proximity and children do not have to cross major traffic streets to reach the school or good public transportation to schools is provided.

DEFINING THE SITE, LOT DIMENSIONS, AND LOCATION

When the appraised property is a condominium, and the underlying land is owned in tenancy in common with other owners in the development, show the total acreage of the entire project, for example, "Total project 5.3 acres."

Project density is obtained by dividing the total number of units in the project by the total acreage; for example, 86 units divided by 8.198 acres is 10.49 units per acre.

Listing Zoning Classifications

Verify and list the zoning classification used by the municipality. Show the uses that the zoning permits; for example, PDC (planned community), PD 1 (planned development, specific plan), HR (high-rise overlay), or R-3 (1 unit/1,000 sq. ft).

Off-Site Improvements

Off-site improvements refers to site improvements within the project. The appraiser should comment on the condition of the off-site improvements, particularly when maintenance levels are below average or inadequate.

Private streets are usually indicated by special symbols in map books, or the incidence of private streets can be determined by a review of owner's legal records or from the owner's association, city public works departments, or city planning departments.

Project Ingress/Egress, Topography, Size/Shape, and View

Rate the safety and convenience of ingress and egress as good, adequate, or inadequate. When access to the unit is inadequate, describe the inadequacy. Describe the topography of the project and the unit's view. For condominiums, show "condominium" for the size/shape factor.

Drainage and Flood Conditions

If there are any drainage problems, specifically describe the problem in the comments section or in an addendum. For example, "Leak in subterranean parking area from main pipe over garage No. 119. Slight adverse effect on marketability is noted."

Even though the form does not specifically call for the community panel number, date of the panel, and zone, always include this data under site comments.

Site and Location Comments

Describe easements, encroachments, adverse conditions, positive marketing influences, views, and other pertinent value factors. Describe the location of the subject unit in the project and, if applicable, the precise location in the building. Is the subject's location superior, equal to, or inferior to other units in the project and competing projects?

DESCRIPTIONS OF THE PROJECT IMPROVEMENTS

For existing projects, show the year in which the project was built. If the project was constructed in several phases over a number of years, describe the different phases, number of units in each phase, and the year that each phase was built.

Original Use of the Unit

Show the original, intended use of the structures, for example, condominium, single-family residence, or apartments.

Condominium Conversions

Part II of FHLMC Form 465—Addendum A must be completed by the appraiser if the project is in the process of conversion or if the conversion process was completed less than two years. The appraiser must verify conformity of the conversion to zoning regulations and requirements for rehabilitation work for both units and common areas. Indicate the status of completion and finalized permits or Certificates of Occupancy. The extent of the rehabilitation work should be fully described in the report.

The condition of the units and project, and the extent of rehabilitation work, must be considered in the market data analysis. When the apartments (condominium conversions) have been completely modernized, rehabilitated, or refurbished, and they are effectively new or near new, use comparable sales that have been recently constructed or are comparable in effective age. For example, if the apartments were originally constructed in 1972, and they were rehabilitated to the point where they are effectively new, and comparables were used that were built in 1972 that were not rehabilitated, an adjustment for condition would be in order. However, it is unlikely that a basis for an adjustment for condition could be established, and, if the dollar amount of the adjustment could be established, the adjustment would probably be excessive. Hence, it makes more sense to use sales that are close in effective age.

Proposed Units and Units Under Construction

Include the estimated date of completion. Appraise the property "Subject to satisfactory completion per approved plans and specifications, and per description contained in this report."

Correlate descriptions of proposed, new, or uncompleted projects with the neighborhood description considering percentage built-up, growth rate, property values, demand and supply, marketing time, percentage land use, changes in present land use, price and age ranges, and potential for additional units.

Differentiating Row Houses from Town Houses

Row houses differ from town houses in that they are usually individually built as single residences without common walls or other structural systems, such as the foundation or roof. This type of row house has finished side walls, or blind walls, between residences, and the living area is usually entirely on the second level with the garage located on the ground level.

The term "row house" is often used to describe condominiums or town houses that are lined up in a row; that is, there are several units in a line or building. Other types of buildings are high-rise (multiple stories) or low-rise (a few stories) condominium complexes, stacked units, attached duplex-style units, or detached units.

Primary Residence, Second Home, or Recreational Use

Primary residence refers to year-round owner-occupied units or tenant-occupied units that do not reflect "seasonal rents." Second home or recreational refers to units where the intent is to occupy the property only certain times of the year.

How to List the Number of Units

When the project is entirely completed, enter the total number of phases in the project and total number of units in the project. For number sold, include closed sales and sales to bona fide purchasers who are legally obligated to close. Estimates, or totals designated "plus or minus," are not acceptable. The total number of units and phases must be verified.

If the project is planned or under construction, show the total number of planned or projected phases, total number of units in all the phases, and the number sold.

Units in Subject Phase:

Enter the number of units in the subject phase, the total number completed, and the total number sold in the subject phase. This information can usually be obtained from the developer, owner's legal documents, homeowner's association, city planning department, or real estate agents.

Number of Units Rented:

The appraiser must include the number of tenant-occupied units in the subject project; the terms "unknown" or "unavailable" are not acceptable. Never provide guesstimates because the number of units rented is an important underwriting factor. An excessive number of nonowner-occupied units can have a tremendous effect on marketability and long-term stability of value.

If the number of units rented is in excess of 5 percent of the total units in the project, the appraiser should provide further explanations addressing maintenance levels, marketability, and probability of sustainment of value. For example, "Twenty percent of the units in the project are rented; however, the project is well maintained, there is no outward evidence of an excessive number of rental units, and the number of units rented does not appear to have any negative effect on marketability or value."

The number of units rented can be obtained by interviewing property managers, owners in the project, real estate agents who regularly farm the project, from the homeowner's association, or from title company records (which usually indicate mailing addresses for owners that differ from the project address when the units are nonowner occupied).

Number of Units for Sale:

Obtain the total number of units for sale from the project sales office; correlate this figure with the preceding totals shown for complete units, incomplete units, and units in the subject phase. For older projects, count the number of "for sale" signs in the project or use multiple-listing books to find the number of units listed for sale. An accurate count should be referenced because an oversupply of units for sale can affect marketability and value. Consider demand and supply, marketing time, and sustainment of value.

Project Classification

When you appraise condominium and PUD projects, the following are two classifications that you should note on the appraisal report:

Type E: Established PUD projects in which control of the owner's association has been turned over to the unit purchasers.

Type F: New PUD projects that are still under the control of the developer.

Security Features

List all the security features including dead-bolt locks, automatic garage door openers, locked security entrances to the project, and monitored security entrances. The comparable sales should have the same or similar security features because security is a very important marketability and value factor. Communities with monitored security entrances should not be compared to properties without security guards unless realistic and reasonable adjustments can be determined by market evidence.

Elevators

Enter the number of elevators, adequacy to service the number of units, and condition. Elevator-serviced buildings should not be compared to buildings without elevators.

Vertical Soundproofing

Typically, vertical soundproofing consists of double-stud walls, two hour walls, or party walls with a 1-inch airspace and insulation between the walls, which might be briefly described in the report as "dbl stud walls & R-30." If you are unable to verify the type of soundproofing, the terms "good,"' adequate,' or "typical" could be used.

Horizontal Soundproofing

Sometimes insulation is installed between the floors; however, two-story or "town house"-style units typically do not have horizontal soundproofing. Stacked units usually have lightweight concrete between floors, sound boards, or insulation. Discuss noise levels with the occupants. When soundproofing is inadequate, consider the long-term effect on marketability and value.

Parking Facilities

The total number of parking spaces should include the number of garage spaces, number of subterranean parking spaces, carports, open spaces, and guest spaces.

Ratio:

Divide the total number of parking spaces by the number of units to find the ratio. For example, 187 spaces divided by 86 units is 2.17 spaces per unit.

Type:

Include a description of all the different types of parking facilities available in the project, for example, show garages, carports, open spaces, or subterranean parking.

Guest Parking:

Include the number of spaces assigned and held for guest parking only. The use of "unknown" or "unavailable" requires an explanation. Never provide guesstimates for the number of guest spaces because projects should have an adequate number of guest parking spaces in order to be considered desirable and competitive. The comparable sales should have a similar ratio of total parking spaces and guest spaces; if they do not, appropriate adjustments should be considered. Spaces should be physically counted in smaller projects. For larger projects, a breakdown of types of parking can be obtained from city officials or the homeowner's association.

Common Elements and Recreational Facilities

List all the commonly owned elements and recreational facilities in the project. Include an addendum if necessary. If any of the common elements have not yet been completed, provide the stage of the construction and the estimated date of completion. Consider the maintenance levels of the common areas and adequacy of common area facilities with relationship to the total number of units in the project. Commonly owned elements, such as green areas, parking spaces, laundry facilities, and recreational facilities should be consistent with the nature of the project, and they should be competitive in the marketplace. Provide concise comments describing any positive or negative conditions that influence value and marketability.

Leased Common Elements and Recreational Facilities

In the event any of the common elements, recreational facilities, or parking areas are leased to or from the owner's association, the appraiser must document this and provide an addendum to the appraisal report addressing rental terms and options.

HOW TO RATE THE PROJECT

The project ratings are to be based on comparison, by the appraiser, of the subject project with competing projects considering the effect these factors have on present and continued market appeal.

Location of the Project

Is the location comparable to competing projects? Correlate the project rating with neighborhood ratings. Describe positive and negative influences in the neighborhood section of the report, site section, or in an addendum.

General Appearance, Amenities, and Density

Consider the design and appeal of the units as well as the design and attractiveness of the arrangement of the buildings, common areas, amenities, and recreational facilities in the project. Are the amenities and recreational facilities competitive with other nearby projects? Does the subject project have a higher density than competing projects? If so, address marketability and appeal, demand and supply, marketing time, and long-term sustainment of value.

Classifying the Unit Mix

Does the number of one-, two-, or three-bedroom units in this project compare to the unit mix in other projects? Does the unit mix conform to market standards and demand? Consider the number of stories in the building, number of one- and two-story units, the number of stacked units, and the size of the units. Are these factors compatible with market appeal, demand, and competing projects?

Condition of the Improvements

This refers to the interior and exterior of all the buildings, common areas, amenities, and recreational facilities in the entire project. There should be evidence of an ongoing program of maintenance and repairs. When maintenance levels are below average, and especially when major repairs are needed, the appraiser should provide a detailed list of the items needing repair, that is, type of repair (roofs, patios, stairs, railings, plumbing, laundry facilities, streets, parking facilities, or recreational facilities) and building numbers and locations of buildings needing repair. Are the dues adequate to service the project? Is is possible association funds are being misappropriated? Is it likely that the owners will be faced with substantial special assessments for repairs? If appropriate, address these factors in the appraisal report.

Appeal to Market

This rating is an overall summary of all the other ratings. Provide further explanations for any fair or poor ratings. Can these conditions be corrected? If so, in what manner? Is it feasible? And what is the estimated cost? Will marketability and value be enhanced if these conditions are corrected?

INCLUSIONARY ZONING RESTRICTIONS

When a condominium project is located in an area with "inclusionary zoning restrictions," which provide affordable housing for low- and moderate-income people, the appraiser should get in touch with city or county governing officials to find out whether there are any restrictions for renting and selling the property. Include this information in the report and provide names and telephone numbers of governing officials for confirmation.

DESCRIPTION OF THE INDIVIDUAL UNIT

Indicate the same number of floors that are shown on the room list. The actual floor level on which the subject unit is located should be described in the comments area of the report or in an addendum.

Unit Livable Area

For units in condominium projects, interior perimeter unit dimensions are required instead of exterior building dimensions. Remember, in most condominium projects, the walls are owned in tenancy in common with other owners in the development. Exterior building dimensions should be employed for PUD projects. In all cases, use the same level of measurement between the subject unit and the comparable sales.

How to Measure Condominiums

Study the design of the building to determine the division of the units. Typically, the dividing walls are midway between two windows or midway between two entry doors. Then, tape the exterior dimensions of the condominium structure and subtract the depth of the walls.

If you are appraising a unit that is difficult or impossible to measure, dimensions can usually be obtained from plans on file at local planning or building departments. A visit to the local planning department is well worth the time invested because you can assemble neighborhood data, zoning information, project descriptions, and dimensions at the same time.

Parking for Unit

Always verify the number of spaces owned or assigned with the owner or homeowner's association. Usually, one or more garages, carports, or subterranean spaces are owned; however, the owner may have access to an additional parking space that is assigned or leased. If any of the parking spaces are leased or rented, include the terms and the amount of rent in the appraisal report.

Unit Rating

The rating factors are to be based on comparison by the appraiser of the subject unit with competing properties considering the present and future effect these factors have on continued market appeal. An explanation should accompany any ratings of fair or poor.

Estimated Effective Age and Remaining Economic Life

Both blanks have to be filled in for each factor. When the property is new or nearly new, the effective age might be shown as "new-0" years or "0-1" year.

ANALYSIS OF THE BUDGET—PAGE TWO OF FHLMC FORM 465

The budget analysis must be completed in its entirety, in detail, by the appraiser. The use of "unknown" or "not available" is unacceptable. Inadequate or low ratings must be accompanied by a suitable explanation from the appraiser.

Unit Charges

When there is more than one association, for example, a master association and a subassociation, or a multiple-regime, provide a concise description of each association, names and telephone numbers of each association, and a breakdown of the association dues. Dues for master associations and subassociations should not be lumped together. If the unit charges appear excessive or insufficient to maintain the project satisfactorily, provide further commentary.

Utilities

The number and kind of utilities included in unit charges are important marketing and underwriting factors; therefore, always verify this information with the owner or the owner's association. In the market data analysis, weigh the type and number of utilities included in unit charges for the comparable properties as compared to utilities included in unit charges for the subject project. If applicable, assign adjustments and provide a basis for the adjustments.

Fees Other than Condominium and PUD Charges

Additional fees, or rents, are sometimes assessed for extra parking spaces, extra storage areas, security guards, use of swimming pools, and so forth. State the purpose and amount of the fees.

Identification of the Management Group

The name, address, area code, and telephone number of the homeowner's association must be provided for all projects less than four years old. In all other cases, provide the name of the management group, owner's association, or management agency.

Condominium and PUD Documents

Do not show "none" unless you have actually reviewed the condominium or PUD documents and have reached that conclusion. If you have not had the opportunity to review the documents, a statement might be included, such as "Condo/PUD documents were not available for the appraiser's review." If the appraiser is aware of any detrimental, unusual, or undesirable conditions or restrictions, this information should be presented in the appraisal report.

Insurance Requirements

The appraiser should state whether the project has hazard and flood insurance coverage. Representatives of the homeowner's association can usually tell you whether the project has "blanket" hazard and flood insurance policies.

KEY ELEMENTS OF THE COST APPROACH

For condominiums, indicate "N/A" (not applicable).

One item often overlooked by appraisers is the cost of parking structures because the form does not have a space for this entry. To provide clarity, add a line above the reproduction cost new of the unit to show costs for the parking structure if it is actually owned and not leased or assigned. If assigned or leased, the value of the parking structure should be included in "pro-rata share of value of amenities."

Depreciation

Correlate elements of depreciation with the subject's description, neighborhood description, project description, and market data analysis.

Land Value

Obtain land value in the same manner established for single family residential property—by abstraction from the market.

Value of Amenities

Estimate the total depreciated cost of the amenities of the entire project. Divide the total estimated cost by the total number of units to find the subject's pro-rata share of the amenities. Or consult with developers or homeowner's associations to ascertain the dollar amount of owner's pro- rata share of value of amenities. With experience, the appraiser should be able to provide a reasonably accurate estimate without making numerous mathematical calculations.

MARKET DATA ANALYSIS

For new or recently converted condominium projects, the appraiser must compare the subject property to other properties in its general market area as well as to properties within the subject subdivision or project. This comparison should help demonstrate market acceptance of new developments and the properties within them. Generally, the appraiser should select one comparable sale from the subject subdivision or project, one comparable sale from outside the subject subdivision or project (do not include outside sales that were sold by the same developer affiliated with the subject tract), and one comparable sale, that can be from inside or outside of the subject subdivision or project as long as the appraiser considers it to be a good indicator of value for the subject property. In selecting the comparables, the appraiser should keep in mind that sales or resales from within the subject subdivision or project are preferable to sales from outside the subdivision or project as long as the developer or builder of the subject property is not involved in the transactions. When there has been a recent price increase, include a sale in escrow as well as a closed sale in the subject development to document the price increase, or include sales brochures to document price changes from phase to phase.

The outside sales should be as similar to the subject project as possible in location, views, design, appeal, amenities, density, age, size, and condition to avoid making subjective or unsupportable adjustments. Similarities in locational appeal should be aptly described when outside sales are used.

The following excerpt was taken from Fannie Mae guidelines: "For units in established condominium or PUD projects (those that have resale activity), the appraiser should use comparable sales from within the subject project if there are any available. Resale activity from within the subject project should be the best indicator of value for properties in that project. If the appraiser uses sales of comparable properties that are located outside of the subject neighborhood, he or she must include an explanation with the analysis."

Price per Gross Living Area

A reasonable range should be evident or an explanation should be provided. Question whether the sale is actually comparable if the price per gross living area differs substantially from the other sales or the subject's price per gross living area.

Location: The Prime Factor for Variances in Prices

Location is the prime factor for variances in prices in condominium and PUD projects. Each project, and each unit within the project, should always be evaluated on a case basis because location factors that have a positive influence on marketability and value in one project could have negative, little, or no influence on marketability and value in another project depending on the particular location of the project and buyer's attitudes in that particular market. Location factors that should be considered are as follows:

- Generally, the fewer common walls, floors, and ceilings shared with adjacent units, the more desirable the location is.
- End units usually command premiums because they share fewer common walls and they typically have more airspace, better ventilation, better views, and easier accessibility.
- Buyers sometimes prefer the first level because there are no stairs to climb and access is more convenient; however, second-level units might be more desirable because there are no units above the unit, there is less noise, and views are usually superior.
- First-level units fronting to waterscaping, lakes, golf courses, greenbelts, or other desirable amenities usually command higher premiums than do other units because owners of the former have convenient access to the amenities as well as good views. In this instance, premiums usually vary according to the particular location on the lake, golf course, or greenbelt. Typically, the highest premiums are paid for units that front to desirable amenities and prices keep decreasing as the buildings are lo-

cated farther away from the amenities. In a terraced hillside situation, upper-level units usually command the highest premiums when they have view locations.

- Traffic streets may present little or no adverse influence on marketability and value, or, in some cases, traffic streets could have a positive influence on value and marketability because there is added open air space and appeal as compared to a location on the interior of the development where there is less open space, less privacy, and more congestion. Convenience to the unit and convenience to on-street parking are other factors to consider when you are evaluating traffic street locations.
- Locations close to community parks, swimming pools, tennis courts, or recreation buildings could be undesirable due to less privacy, more congestion, and noise. In some instances, however, people prefer the convenience to recreational facilities, and they enjoy being a part of the activities.
- Stacked units (one unit over the other) are always less desirable than are one- or two-story units; hence, they should not be compared to one- and two-story units.
- A lot of foot traffic back and forth in front of a unit can be detrimental to value due to noise and lack of privacy.
- Condominiums located in high-rise and low-rise buildings usually have location premiums per floor level and per location in the building as well as view premiums.
- Units close to laundry facilities are usually less desirable due to congestion, foot traffic, and noise.
- Locations in the interior of the project are sometimes dark, less private, and more congested; hence, interior locations may have less appeal than locations on the perimeter of the project.

- Proximity to commercial property or nonconforming property might be more or less desirable depending on the location of the project and needs and desires of the occupants.
- Poorly designed units with inadequate ventilation and natural lighting or units located in buildings with dark interior hallways exhibit functional obsolescence; therefore, adjustments should be appropriately considered.

Rating Locational Appeal:

As evidenced by the preceding illustrations, location adjustments in condominium/PUD projects are seldom "typical," and they are usually not determinable by simply analyzing a few sales.

Always drive through the entire project or analyze the entire high- or low-rise building to determine the likelihood of location adjustments. When recent market data do not provide a basis for adjustments, study market history or, if possible, obtain the original sales prices from a title company or the developer. Study the variances in sales prices to see if a pattern can be established for location premiums paid when the project was new. Also, get in touch with real estate agents, who are familiar with the subject project, when you need help.

Do not use the terms "similar" or "equal" to describe the location of the comparable sales. More appropriate descriptive terms are good, average, fair, poor, superior, or inferior. Or show the floor level that the units are located on in the building or show front unit, end unit, middle unit, opposite pool, or waterfront.

Garages and Carports

Before you automatically assign adjustments, verify ownership of the parking facilities in the subject project and the comparable projects. Are the parking facilities owned, assigned, leased, or rented? Evaluate the total number of spaces available in the project as well as the total number of guest spaces, and, if applicable, make adjustments.

Common Elements

List all the common elements; if they are extensive, show "refer to page one." It may seem rather picky; however, a few lenders have been known to request letters of explanation when all the common elements are not listed in this space.

When you assign value to privately owned swimming pools, spas, patios, or other privately owned yard improvements, describe the improvements on the first page of the report, or in an addendum, and list and adjust for the improvements in the "other" category to distinguish privately owned amenities from common elements.

Monthly Assessments

A letter of explanation is required when "unknown" or "not available" is indicated. Monthly assessments can be obtained from owners, homeowner's associations, real estate agents, or multiple-listing books. When listings of the subject unit or comparable units are not available, check listings of other units in the project to find the amount of the monthly assessment.

Rate the monthly assessment of the comparable property to the subject. If the assessments appear excessive or inadequate, provide further commentary.

INCOME APPROACH TO VALUE

Complete the income approach in the same manner recommended for single-family residences when the unit is or will be nonowner occupied.

RECONCILING THE DATA

Correlate your statements, descriptions, and values, making certain that consistency is evident throughout the report. Eliminate meaningless commentary and data. Have you provided all the required explanations? Recheck all the numbers for accuracy, check the arithmetic, and recheck your adjustments.

If you are using Fannie Mae forms that reference the obsolete form 1004B, mark through the 10/78 date and write in July 1986.

ADDITIONAL REQUIREMENTS FOR PLANNED UNIT DEVELOPMENTS AND CONDOMINIUMS

1. The appraiser must include a one-year sales history of the subject property. If there have been no transactions within the past year, this should be noted in the appraisal.
2. If the subject property is listed for sale, or has been listed for sale within the past year, include pertinent listing data.
3. If the subject property has recently sold, include the length of time the property was listed.
4. Include applicable permit numbers and sources of verification.
5. Include verifiable evidence of closed sales.
6. For properties valued at $500,000. or more, include two additional comparables in addition to the normal three, additional photographs (interior and exterior) to illustrate property amenities further, and an addendum more fully describing the improvements.

7. For properties valued at $750,000. or more, most lenders require a narrative-style report.

8. All exhibits and forms must be dated, identified, and have an *original signature.* Copies, if any, must be legible and have an *original signature.*

9. Any corrections or changes on the form must be initialed by the appraiser, particularly in the flood-zone area and the date of the appraisal. *Never* use correction fluid or correct the values by the different approaches to value, particularly the final estimate of value. When a correction is made to the final estimate of value, the appraisal will have to be resubmitted.

10. All appraisals must have the appraiser's name and appropriate state classification typed on the report. Appraiser's designations should be typed on the report, as applicable. Appraiser's telephone numbers (including area code) and tax identification numbers are also required by many lenders.

EXHIBITS AND ADDENDA TO FHLMC FORM 465

1. Investment properties: Include FNMA Form 1007 and FNMA Form 216.

2. A clearly legible area map that shows the location of the subject property and all of the comparable sales.

3. Plat map with north arrow, subject street name, and nearest cross street legibly shown and the subject site *clearly* identified. All numbers and names on the plat map should be clearly legible. If a plat map is not available, or if the plat map does not depict the exact location of the unit, submit a sketch showing the location of the

subject property in the project and the number of intervening buildings to the nearest cross street. Identify the cross street, the subject street, and include a north arrow. Many projects have a directory of buildings and street layouts at the entrance to the project. A clear photo of the directory can be used as a substitute for a plat map.

4. For units in condominium or cooperative projects, the sketch of the unit must indicate interior perimeter unit dimensions rather than exterior building dimensions. Generally, the appraiser must also include calculations to show how he or she arrived at the estimate for gross living area; however, for units in condominium or cooperative projects, the appraiser may rely on the dimensions and estimate for gross living area that are shown on the plat. In such cases, the appraiser does not need to provide a sketch of the unit as long as he or she includes a copy of the plat with the appraisal report.

   A floor plan sketch that indicates the interior room layout is required if the floor plan is functionally obsolete, resulting in a limited market appeal for the property in comparison to competitive properties in the neighborhood. Show privately owned patios, yards, decks, pools, and garages on the sketch. Common areas, amenities, or recreational facilities should not be included in the diagram.

5. Clear, descriptive 35mm photographs of the front and back of the subject property and a street scene that includes the subject property in the picture. When the units are "back to back" and you are unable to take a rear photo of the subject unit, include an explanation. Identify all photos and identify the street scene, for example, looking north, south, east, or west. Note: Most lenders

require three sets of photos. Verify photo requirements with your client.

6. Include photos of any detrimental conditions affecting the subject property, significant deficiencies within the project or subject property, and extraordinary amenities or features of the subject property that are assigned value, such as views, positive locational influences, extensive upgrading, privately owned swimming pool, spa, and extensive yard improvements.
7. Include photos of major common area recreational facilities.
8. For properties valued at $500,000., or more, include interior photos as well as photos of extraordinary amenities.
9. Photos of the comparable sales.
10. If applicable, include a transmittal letter.
11. Include FHLMC Form 439/FNMA Form 1004B, as applicable.
12. Part I of the Project Analysis, FHLMC Form 465—Addendum A must be completed by the appraiser if less than 70 percent of the individual units in the project have sold.
13. Part II of FHLMC Form 465—Addendum A must be completed by the appraiser if the project is in the process of conversion or the conversion process has been completed less than two years.
14. Analysis of Annual Income and Expenses/Operating Budget, FNMA Form 1073 or FHLMC Form 465—Addendum B must be completed if the homeowner's association has been controlled by the owners for less than two years and/or developer control has not been terminated. Get in touch with the participating lender to find out

which form is required: FNMA Form 1073 or FHLMC Form 465.

15. All exhibits must be neat, uncluttered, and of a professional standard. All addenda and forms must have an original signature.

HOW TO APPRAISE COOPERATIVE UNITS

A cooperative is similar in many respects to a condominium; however, in the cooperative form of ownership, a corporation holds title to the residential project and sells shares of stock that give the purchasers the right to occupy the individual units in the project. The owners of stock in the cooperative development pay a proportionate share of the interest and real estate taxes paid by the corporation.

Purchasers of cooperative units are required to buy a certain number of stock shares for the unit. Subsequently, the purchaser is granted a long-term lease on the individual unit, known as a "proprietary lease." In essence, the proprietary lease renders benefits equivalent to outright ownership. Each month thereafter, the purchaser of the unit makes a rent payment to the corporation which is his or her proportionate or pro-rata share of the blanket mortgage payments. The purchaser also pays his or her pro-rata share of operating and maintenance expenses for the common areas, for example, a monthly maintenance and expense fee.

COOPERATIVE UNITS ARE EVALUATED AND WRITTEN UP IN THE SAME MANNER AS CONDOMINIUMS WITH THE FOLLOWING EXCEPTIONS:

Because there are so few cooperatives in existence, the market is generally uninformed with respect to their characteristics, financing is sometimes difficult to obtain because many lenders do not provide financing for cooperatives, cooperatives are in direct competition with condominiums which are typically easier to finance, and the condominium concept is easier for buyers to understand. Hence, buyers are usually reluctant to enter into the cooperative form of ownership.

Appraisers must comment on the acceptability of cooperatives in the market area and address any effect that this has on marketability and value, particularly when cooperative ownership is new to the area and there is evidence of buyer resistance to this form of ownership. The appraiser can usually effectively demonstrate the acceptance of this form of ownership by evaluating and including sufficient market data in the appraisal report to support his or her conclusions. The comparable sales should be selected from similar types of cooperative projects with equivalent common amenities and recreational facilities.

When the property is located in a new or recently converted cooperative project, the appraiser must include at least one closed sale from within the project and at least two closed sales from competing projects. Include two closed sales from within the project and one outside sale when the subject is located in an established cooperative development. Two data sources must be included in the report.

The sales should be similar cooperative units; however, if there are no sales of cooperative units available, the appraiser can use sales of condominium units. The appraiser must explain why these sales were used as well as making appropriate adjustments if the market indicates a preference for condominium units. Include additional market data from within the project and sales from competing projects (sales in escrow, dated sales, or an analysis of sales history) to add further support to your conclusions.

When you evaluate a cooperative unit, you must estimate the market value of the cooperative interest. The cooperative interest is the ownership interest of the shares that are attributable to the cooperative unit—excluding the unit's pro-rata share of the blanket mortgage's debt service. The pro-rata share of the blanket mortgage payments that are attributable to the unit are determined by dividing the number of the unit's shares by the total number of project shares.

First, determine the estimated market value of the unit in the same manner as a condominium. Show the estimated market value on the form. Then, define the market value of the cooperative interest in an addendum. For example,

Estimated market value, as encumbered by blanket mortgage	$108,000.
Less: Unit's pro-rata share of blanket mortgage payments, as of 10/7/88	–18,000.
Estimated market value of cooperative interest	$ 90,000.

Additional requirements for appraisals of cooperative units are as follows:

1. The appraiser must use reliable sources to obtain data on the cooperative project, the individual subject unit, and the comparable properties and indicate the name of each source on Form 1073 or in an addendum.

2. The appraiser must certify in the appraisal report that the pro-rata share of the blanket mortgages on the real estate have not been included in the market value estimate of the cooperative interest of the unit.

3. The appraiser must comment on the adequacy and reasonableness of the cooperative corporation's budget, including the working capital, replacement reserves funds, and any other factors that might result in an increase of the subject unit's debt service.

4. The appraiser must include the amount of the subject unit's blanket mortgage payment as well as the monthly maintenance and expense fees.

5. Describe the types of stock shares and indicate the number of shares assigned to the subject unit.
6. The name of the lienholder and the lien position of all project financing must be included.
7. Reference any tax abatements or exceptions that are attributable to the unit and their remaining term and provisions for escalation of real estate taxes. The dollar amount by which the taxes will increase and the year in which the increase will occur should be shown. If appropriate, include the following statement: "There are no excessive taxes or possible tax escalations attributable to the subject unit."
8. If the appraiser is aware of any mechanic's liens that have been filed against the project, this information should be referenced in the appraisal report.
9. Submit a perimeter diagram of the unit showing interior dimensions. Include an area map, plat map, subject photos, photos of common area recreational facilities, photos of the comparables, photos of other positive and negative influences, sales history of the unit, and FHLMC Form 439. FNMA Forms 1007 and 216 must be included for nonowner-occupied property.

REQUIREMENTS FOR ADDENDUM A AND ADDENDUM B

FHLMC FORM 465: Addendum A—Project Analysis
FHLMC Form 465: Addendum B—Analysis of Annual Income and Expenses (Budget)
Typically, Part I of the Project Analysis (Addendum A) must be completed by the appraiser if less than 70 percent of the individual units in the project or section (phase) have been sold to bona fide purchasers who have closed or who are

legally obligated to close. Multiple purchases of condominium/PUD units by one owner in a project are to be counted as one sale to determine if this sales requirement has been met. The subject's section (phase) may be combined with other completed, sold, and occupied sections (phases) to meet this requirement, provided all are under a common owner's association.

Part II of FHLMC Form 465—Addendum A must be completed by the appraiser if the project is in the process of conversion or the conversion process has been completed less than two years.

Analysis of Annual Income and Expenses/Operating Budget (Addendum B) is not required if the developer control has been terminated and the homeowner's association has been controlled by the unit owners for two or more years.

PROJECT ANALYSIS—PAGE ONE, ADDENDUM A

The information contained in Addendum A should always be kept current; therefore, when you appraise additional units in an ongoing project, rather than rewriting the entire Addendum A, present any significant changes or updated information in the comments section. When the lender requests updated data or a certification that there have or have not been any significant changes, this information can also be presented in the comments section.

The following illustrations are presented in the same order that they are listed the form:

Section I—Project Analysis

The project analysis must be completed in its entirety by the appraiser. Explanations will be required when there are any blank spaces or omissions.

Indicate the full project name, actual street address or

major cross streets that identify the location, city, zip code, and the phase number of the unit. For subsequent appraisals in the project, make certain that the phase number and other information is appropriate.

If the project is not completed, discuss the proposed overall development or conversion plan and stage of completion including the number of sections, units, and recreational facilities per section, and the estimated completion date of each section.

Example 1: Phase I, consisting of 59 units, is complete with the exception of installation of floor coverings. Phase II, consisting of 47 units, is currently under construction with a scheduled completion date of August 31, 1989.

Example 2: The subject 88-unit development, including the common elements, was entirely completed as of February 23, 1989.

1. Describe the common elements and recreational facilities, and comment on their adequacy and condition. For example, "The Villa Clairmont Community Association will provide exterior maintenance of the units and maintenance of carports, greenbelts, and private streets. The Villeurbanne Master Association will provide maintenance of all recreational facilities, which will include two swimming pools, two spas, two bath houses, one recreation room, and one landscaped area. The scheduled completion date of the recreational facilities is August 31, 1989. The proposed common areas and recreational facilities will be adequate, consistent with the nature of the project, and competitive in the marketplace."

2. Are the recreational facilities available for use by individuals other than unit owner's and guests? If yes, comment as to the effect on marketability. Always review the owner's legal documents or ask homeowner's association representatives whether the recreational facilities can be used by nonowners and guests. If there are any unusual or undesirable restrictions regarding the use or availability of recreational facilities, provide further commentary, and address the effect on marketability and value.

3. Storage space. Storage space is an important marketing factor for condominium and PUD units; hence, always describe storage facilities. Show the type and location of the storage facilities and rate the adequacy. For example, "Secured storage closets are located in the patio area of each unit and assigned, secured storage areas are located in the subterranean parking garage. Storage space is adequate and consistent with competing projects."

4. Laundry facilities. Specify the type, location, and adequacy of laundry facilities. Address the added appeal with respect to competing projects.

5. Trash removal. Is trash removal the responsibility of the homeowner's association or the city? How many trash bins are there and how convenient are they to the units? Is trash removal service provided on a timely basis? Are the trash bins overflowing, unsightly, a health hazard, and detrimental to marketability?

6. Parking facilities. Describe the parking facilities noting the total number of spaces, type, number of guest parking spaces, and ratio or number of spaces per unit. Are the parking spaces owned, rented, or leased? Address the adequacy of parking, condition, and consistency with competing developments.

7. Soundproofing material. Describe any vertical or horizontal soundproofing, for example, party walls, two hour walls, double-stud walls, insulation, lightweight concrete, or sound boards. Comment on the adequacy of the soundproofing. If the soundproofing is inadequate, consider and comment on the long-term effect on marketability and value.

PROJECT ANALYSIS—PAGE TWO, ADDENDUM A

List the number of units, total room count, gross livable area, price range, price per square foot, monthly association dues, number planned, number sold, and number completed for each separate plan or unit type. If the development is small, describe the entire development. For larger developments, only the subject's phase might be included in this analysis. In any case, clearly indicate the number of the phases included in this analysis. For appraisals in ongoing projects, this information should be continuously updated.

1. Discuss sales performance to date (per phase/section), if applicable. The appraiser should consider and comment on the absorption rate of the entire project or the current phases in the project. Is the absorption rate consistent with competing projects in the area? Address the reasons for a lower than typical absorption rate, that is, why are the units selling slowly? Consider location, design and appeal, size of the units, quality, amenities, recreational facilities, amount of association dues, prices, and availability of financing.

A typical comment might be, "The first phase sold out completely in March 1989, on a reservation basis. During construction of the units, there were several fall-outs and resales. As of this date, 13 units in Phase I remain unsold. Phase II, consisting of 47 units, was released for sale April 25, 1989. The total overall absorption rate for Phases I and II is 7.07 units per month, which is competitive for the subject's market area."

2. Estimated absorption time. Show the total number of unsold units in either the entire project or the subject's phase, whichever is most meaningful. Correlate the total number sold with totals referenced in the preceding sections of the project analysis. Indicate the phase numbers incorporated in the total number of unsold units.

The estimated absorption time for the unsold units is established by the appraiser's experience and judgment giving due consideration to the present absorption factor, absorption rates of competing developments, demand for housing in the subject's market area, appeal and marketability of the project, price range, and availability of favorable financing.

3. Comment on any unit types on which sales appear to be

slow. Discuss marketability of the different types of units with a sales representative. If applicable, describe the units that are selling slowly and provide apparent reasons for market rejection of the particular units. Has the developer considered any changes that would enhance market appeal? When there are no marketing inconsistencies, include a statement, such as "All of the units appear to be selling at a comparable rate."

4. Discuss project density as it compares to others in the area from a standpoint of marketability. Compare the development to similar projects in the area. The project density for competing developments can be obtained from sales representatives of the developer, public records, or city planning officials. Typical comments might read as follows:

Example 1: This development has a much higher density than nearby projects. However, the units are superior in design and appeal, amenities, and recreational facilities in relation to competing projects; consequently, the units are selling at a faster and more consistent rate.

Example 2: This project has a lower density than competing developments in the area. The nearby "Eveningsun" tract, constructed by Sunwood Homes, consists of 142 units with a density of 13.69 units per acre. Other nearby projects range in density from 12.02 to 15.81 units per acre.

Example 3: This is a well-planned development with much lower density than competing town house projects.

12. State the approximate number of units currently for sale by the developer in prior phases. If more than one prior phase, list for each phase. List the unsold units by phase number. For example, "Phase I: six units, Phase II: three units, Phase III: eight units."

Or describe the project in the following manner: "The development consists of three phases of 182 units. Only three model units in Phase I and eight units in phase III remain unsold at this time." Or, if appropriate, show "none." Correlate these data with other sections of Addendum A.

13. Discuss any rental or sales concessions being offered; if none known, so state. The appraiser should describe, in this space, or in an addendum, all the financing programs offered by the developer. When there are a number of different financing programs available, list only the most prevalent financing programs. Rate the financing programs offered by the subject developer to competing developments. A typical comment might be

"Buy down program: The buy down rate for the first year to 13.9 percent is 3 percent, and 2 percent to 14.9 percent for the second year. This practice is common in today's market as evidenced by a personal survey made of competing condominium projects in the area."

In this case, include an addendum listing financing programs offered by competing developments.

14. If the developers plan to retain any unsold units for rental, discuss number, voting rights, and comparability of unit charges; if none, so state. When the developer is retaining unsold units for rental purposes, the appraiser should address sustained marketability and value of the development. If the developer subsequently discounts the price of the units, will marketability and value of other units in the project be affected?

15. Describe nearby competition including sales prices, rate of sales, and sellout time. For example, "The area directly north consists of vacant, rolling terrain, which is scheduled for development of view-oriented town houses in the near future. The nearest competing development is the "Saratoga" condominium development, constructed by Georgetown Development Company, which is located 3 miles south. Prices range from $106,990. for 982-sq. ft., 2-bedroom, 1 1/2-bath units to $122,990. for 1,224 sq. ft., 3-bedroom, 2-bath units. Sales began April 12, 1989. One hundred fifty-nine units have been released for sale out of a total of 178; 135 units have sold for an absorption rate of 7.94 units per month."

16. Describe potential for additional condo/PUD units in nearby areas, considering land availability, zoning, utilities, and apartments subject to conversions. This is an important factor to consider with respect to future marketability and value of the subject units. Discuss the effect on value and marketability generated by proposed condominium projects, planned unit developments, and condominium conversions that might be in direct competition with the subject project. Locations of planned projects, and the names of the developers, can usually be obtained from city planning officials.

17. General comments including any probable changes, in the economic base or neighborhood which would either favorably or unfavorably affect condo/PUD sales. Describe proximity to employment centers; types and variety of employment; probability of continued or increasing employment opportunities; and convenience to schools, shopping, transportation, and freeways. Discuss detrimental conditions, general appearance of properties, appeal, marketability, and property compatibility. General comments might read as follows:

Example 1: The economic base is stable and no changes are anticipated. This development has convenient proximity to local employment centers, shopping, schools, and other civic amenities.

Example 2: Demand for condominium projects and planned unit developments in the area should remain strong and continue to improve due to citywide commercial and industrial development taking place, which will provide additional employment opportunities and convenience to local shopping centers.

Example 3: The general economic trend in the area is improving as a result of increasing employment opportunities, a recently completed freeway system, which provides easy access to outlying employment centers, and city-funded redevelopment in neighboring communities. There are several new shopping centers in the immediate area and other civic amenities are conveniently located.

Section II—Project Analysis

This section must be completed by the appraiser when the project is in the process of conversion or the conversion process has been completed less than two years.

The appraiser should verify zoning compliance and the exact extent of the requirements for the apartment conversion with city planning officials. Do the requirements for approval of the conversion specify total rehabilitation of the units, partial rehabilitation, new wiring, new plumbing, new roofs, new appliances, interior and exterior paint, added recreational facilities, repair of existing recreational facilities, added parking spaces, or different types of parking facilities? Use an addendum if necessary, but list all the city requirements.

Discuss the stage of completion and the condition of the improvements. When appropriate, recommend inspections by soils engineers, geologists, roofing inspectors, electrical inspectors, mechanical engineers, or termite inspectors. Discuss positive and negative marketing factors. Correlate your data with the appraisal report of the individual condominium unit presented on FHLMC Form 465.

AVOID ERRORS AND OMISSIONS

Review the entire Addendum A making certain all the statements are consistent throughout and are consistent with the appraisal report of the individual condominium or PUD unit.

Always keep the original copy of the Addendum A. Submit a legible copy to the lender with an original signature on each copy. This way, the information can be easily updated on the original form and better copies can be made for subsequent submissions

ANALYSIS OF ANNUAL INCOME AND EXPENSES, ADDENDUM B

FHLMC Form 465—Addendum B is not required if the developer control has been terminated and the homeowner's association has been controlled by the unit owners for two or more years. If required, this form must be completed in full by the appraiser with the exception of the Seller/Servicer's section of the form and the certification by the homeowner's association representative.

A copy of the budget can usually be obtained from the tract sales office. If not, a copy of the budget can be obtained from the homeowner's association. When the information provided in the budget is incomplete or erroneous, or you are having difficulty interpreting it and filling out the form, homeowner's association representatives should be able to help you. If the homeowner's association is uncooperative, a friendly call to the sales representative, developer, or lender will usually bring prompt results because it is in their best interest to effect a timely closing of the transaction.

Before you begin to fill out the form, look for mathematical errors and omissions in the association's budget. Find out whether the budget pertains to the entire project or only the specific phase in which the subject is located; then, enter this data on the form in the appropriate space. More often than not, many items will be listed in the budget that are not specifically listed on the form. In this event, include some of the miscellaneous expenses with other expenses; however, keep them under the proper heading, for example, administrative expenses, operating expenses, or repairs. Or cross out one or more of the items listed and insert another item, for example, cross off "snow removal" and add roof repair.

All the items on the form are usually not shown in homeowner's association budgets, and an expense does not have to be shown for every item on the form. However, the appraiser should evaluate the budget making certain that items are included that should be included. For example, when there is a management firm, there should be a management fee; if there is a pool, a dollar amount for maintenance and repairs of the pool should be included in the budget. If replacement reserves are not included in the budget, cost estimates should be obtained from the homeowner's association and entered on the form. The appraiser should state whether the budget appears to be realistic and adequate to maintain the project.

Remember to convert monthly expenses to annual expenses. The expenses can be rounded to the nearest dollar. The total annual expenses and replacement reserves should be within a reasonably close range to the project's annual income from condo/PUD charges and other income. If not, further explanation is required. Get in touch with your client if there appears to be a problem with inadequate funds.

Retain the original form; forward a legible copy to the homeowner's association representative for signature; then include a signed copy with the appraisal report. Because lenders usually require original signatures, send several copies to the homeowner's association representative for signature, so the additional forms will be readily available for future use.

CHAPTER 15

HOW TO CONDUCT EFFECTIVE APPRAISAL REVIEWS

Reviewers should maintain the same professionalism and same high standards that are expected from appraisers; they should refrain from "nit-picking," and they should remember that the measure of a good appraisal is *quality* not quantity. Pay close attention to explanations and carefully review the report for infractions, but be professional; do not make a production out of every insignificant infraction when you write your review.

Appraisers should fill in all the blanks, use proper English and proper sentence structure, and spell all the words correctly; however, these items should not be the reviewer's major concern. The reviewer's major concern should be the overall presentation. Does the report contain factual, verified data? Can you arrive at the same conclusion as the appraiser based on the description of the neighborhood, property, and analysis of the market data contained in the report? Is the value valid and adequately supported by market data?

REVIEW PROCEDURE—CHECKLIST

Use the following checklist for reviewing appraisals. Highlight errors and refer to them when you are writing a review.

1. Copy the report so comments and corrections can be noted on the report as you proceed.
2. Is the property history of ownership included?
3. If the property rights are leasehold, does the appraisal contain a leasehold analysis? Are the comparable sales situated on leasehold land?
4. If the subject is located in a PUD project, the project must be appropriately described and monthly association dues and the utilities included in the owner's association fees must be noted. Are the comparable sales located in a PUD development, as required? Did the appraiser include the FHLMC Planned Unit Project Information Addendum?
5. Does the present land use add up to 100 percent? Does the neighborhood description refer to land uses that are not included in this percentage?
6. Review all the arithmetic. Look for errors in math, missing numbers, and transposed numbers.
7. Blank spaces and items labeled "not applicable" or "unavailable" should be accompanied by appropriate explanations.
8. Examine the building diagram for errors and omissions. Square-off all the structures. Add up the setbacks and check the lot size. Does the lot size indicated on the diagram coincide with the lot size shown in the report? Are there any apparent encroachments?
9. Check the flood hazard data. Are map numbers, dates,

and designated zone numbers referenced? Corrections in the "yes" and "no" area should be initialed by the appraiser.

10. Verify the zoning and highest and best use of the site. Is the highest and best use adequately and appropriately described? If a legal but nonconforming or nonconforming use is indicated, did the appraiser address legally permitted, physically possible, economically feasible, most profitable use of the site? Can the property be rebuilt if partially or fully destroyed? In what manner?

11. Check the plat map. Is the site description accurate? Is the description consistent throughout the report? Did the appraiser properly evaluate the size of the site, utility, topography, shape, orientation, location, and amenities? Are these elements reflected in the market data analysis, land value, and final estimate of value? Examine the photos. Are there any positive or negative site influences that were overlooked by the appraiser?

12. If private streets are indicated, did the appraiser reference maintenance levels and provisions for maintenance?

13. Verify the interior and exterior description of the property. Examine the photos for obvious omissions in the subject's description and description of the comparable sales. Review internal consistency. Do the descriptions correspond to data contained in addenda to the report, sales comparison analysis, cost approach, and building diagram?

14. Do the descriptions of the exterior, interior, surfaces, heating, plumbing, kitchen equipment, and bath finishes relate to the actual and effective age of the subject? Are the property ratings supported by adequate commentary? Have explanations been provided for fair or poor

ratings? Check the photos. Do the characteristics of the property correspond to the subject's age?

15. Was the property appraised subject to completion if it is proposed, under construction, or in the process of rehabilitation or modernization? If appropriate, did the appraiser recommend or require final inspections? If repairs are needed, did the appraiser provide a list of the repairs and estimated costs?

16. Were all the elements of curable and incurable functional obsolescence addressed in the subject's description, market analysis, and cost approach? Does the building diagram display evidence of functional obsolescence that was not explained?

17. Study the building diagram and photos for evidence of additions. If there are any apparent additions that have not been described in the report, call the local building department to find out if there are any permits on file. If the appraiser has referenced additions, modernization, remodeling, or rehabilitation, does the effective age reflect the condition of the property? Are the comparables similar in effective age, size, and condition? Did the appraiser address conformity, appeal, and quality of construction throughout the appraisal? Did the appraiser indicate that finalized permits were verified? Is there any evidence of nonpermitted improvements or additions that are included in the final estimate of value?

18. Did the appraiser present a comprehensive, but concise description of the neighborhood that provides insight into those factors that have positive or negative influences on the appraised property's value and marketability? Did the appraiser provide a precise indication of value trends in the neighborhood?

Correlate the neighborhood ratings to the neighborhood comments. Were all the required explanations provided for external influences, mixed uses, vacant land uses, land use changes, predominant occupancy, fair or poor ratings, declining values, oversupply, excessive vacancy? Examine internal consistency.

19. Does the subject value or the sales prices of the comparables exceed the predominant age and price? Did the appraiser provide appropriate explanations?

20. Study a local map book, the location map, plat map, and photos. Are there any elements of external obsolescence that the appraiser did not mention, such as airports, railroads, traffic streets, freeways, landfills, dumps, flood control channels, rivers, vacant land, commercial or industrial property, condominium developments, or apartments? If any of these elements are present, were they considered in the cost approach and market analysis?

21. Examine the cost approach. Is it complete? Are the costs realistic? Is the site value realistic considering the size of the lot and the amenities? Were all the required explanations for obsolescence factors and land value provided? Is the percentage of physical, functional, and external depreciation reasonable? Does the percentage of depreciation relate to the effective age and condition of the property? Are all the elements of depreciation reflected in the market analysis?

    Is the total gross livable area of the structure consistent throughout the report? Is the description of the parking structure consistent throughout the report? Does the dollar amount of the site improvements represent a cost new rather than depreciated costs? Does the cost relate to the dollar amount of adjustments in the market analysis? That is, the dollar amount of the adjustments should be less than the cost new and the depreciated cost of the element in question, if not, an explanation should be provided.

22. If the greatest consideration in arriving at a final estimate of value was given to the cost approach, did the appraiser include land comparables and a source of costs? Do the land comparables support the subject land value? Are the sales recent and located in proximity to the subject? Do they represent finished land value? Are the descriptions adequate? Do the land sales represent cash equivalency? If applicable, did the appraiser include the builder's land costs and proposed construction costs?

23. Check the accuracy of the proximity of the comparable sales to the subject. Are the comparable sales located within the neighborhood? If not, did the appraiser provide appropriate explanations?

24. Are two data sources referenced? If the property is located in a new development, did the appraiser include at least one inside and one outside sale? Verify the descriptions of the comparable sales. Do the sales have similar zoning, land uses, and locational influences? Are the sales recent? Did the appraiser display logic in his or her selection of market data? Did the appraiser include document numbers or other evidence that the sales are closed?

25. Review each item in the market analysis for adjustments that might have been overlooked. Are plus adjustments indicated where there should be minus adjustments or across-the-board adjustments? Are all the sales adjusted upward or downward? Did the appraiser bracket the sales appropriately? Did the appraiser apply the same levels of adjustment for each comparable for room

count, gross living area adjustments, lot size, view, locational influences, garage, heating and cooling equipment, fireplaces, and kitchen equipment? Do the adjustments for yard improvements relate to the size of the lot? Are the adjustments consistent with the descriptions presented on page one of the report? Are the adjustments typical, excessive in number, excessive in dollar amount, less than typical, reasonable? Do the total adjustments exceed 15 percent? Do the gross adjustments exceed 25 percent? Did the appraiser provide all the required explanations?

26. Does the market data adequately provide a basis for the adjustments? Did the appraiser illustrate the relationship of the comparables to the subject and present a thorough, consistent, and convincing market data analysis? Are the sales comparison comments adequate? Do they relate to the neighborhood description?

27. Check the price per gross living area of the comparables and the subject. Is the range reasonably close? Are the indicated values to the subject within close range? If not, why not?

28. Does the final estimate of value include any personal property? Did the appraiser make appropriate adjustments for financing concessions?

29. If the appraised property is a condominium or PUD, is Addendum A or B required? If so, did the appraiser provide a definitive analysis of the project and budget?

30. Is the income approach required? If so, was the income approach completed properly? Did the appraiser include FNMA Form 1007 and FNMA Form 216? Are the forms complete? Did the appraiser present a suitable analysis of the rent comparables?

31. Check the "as is" and "subject to" boxes. Did the appraiser overlook any requirements for completion of the improvements, repairs, or inspections?

32. Did the appraiser present justification for the value selected as the final estimate of value, that is, which approach to value was given the greatest consideration? Is the explanation appropriate?

33. Is the final estimate of value valid and adequately supported by the market data? Look for corrections in the date and final estimate of value.

34. Did the appraiser sign the appraisal? Did the appraiser include all the required documentation, such as location map, plat map, building diagram, limiting conditions, certification, and addenda? Were the photo requirements met? Do the photos adequately depict the subject property and comparable sales? Was the appraisal report and documentation presented in a professional manner?

UNIFORM STANDARDS OF PROFESSIONAL APPRAISAL PRACTICE

In developing a review appraisal, the appraiser must observe the following requirements in the "Uniform Standards of Professional Appraisal Practice."[1]

"Standard 3: In reviewing an appraisal and reporting the results of that review, an appraiser must form an opinion as to the adequacy and appropriateness of the report being reviewed and must clearly disclose the nature of the review process undertaken."

---

[1]The material that follows is taken from The Appraisal Foundation, copyright ©1987 by The Appraisal Foundation. All rights reserved.

"Standards Rules Relating to Standard 3—S.R.3-1: In reviewing an appraisal, an appraiser must observe the following specific guidelines:

(a) Identify the report being reviewed, the real estate and real property interest being appraised, the effective date of the opinion in the report being reviewed, and the date of the review.
(b) Identify the scope of the review process to be conducted.
(c) Form an opinion as to the adequacy and relevance of the data and the propriety of any adjustments to the data.
(d) Form an opinion as to the appropriateness of the appraisal methods and techniques used and develop the reasons for any disagreement.
(e) Form an opinion as to the correctness and appropriateness of the analyses, opinions, and/or conclusions in the report being reviewed and develop the reasons for any disagreement."

"S.R.3-2: In reporting the results of an appraisal review, an appraiser must

(a) disclose the nature, extent, and detail of the review process undertaken.
(b) disclose the information that must be considered in S.R.3-1(a) and (b).
(c) set forth the opinions, reasons, and conclusions required in S.R.3-1(c),(d), and (e).

No pertinent information shall be withheld."

"S.R.3-3: In reviewing an appraisal and reporting the results of that review, an appraiser must separate the review function from any other functions."

HOW TO SUMMARIZE REVIEW APPRAISALS

All the preceding standards should be addressed in the review; however, a review report should be simple and straightforward. Appraisers should not sign the report being reviewed. A review summary, such as the following, accompanied by brief explanatory comments, a cover letter, and the review appraiser's limiting conditions, certifications, and qualifications is recommended. Enter an "x" or "n/a" (not applicable) in each space, as applicable.

REVIEW SUMMARY—EXAMPLE

REVIEW SUMMARY

Appraisal Section	Adequate	Omissions	Inadequate
1. Property identification	( )	( )	( )
2. Property history	( )	( )	( )
3. Neighborhood data	( )	( )	( )
4. Site/ lot data	( )	( )	( )
5. Zoning/ highest/ best use	( )	( )	( )
6. Subject improvements	( )	( )	( )
7. Improvement diagram	( )	( )	( )
8. Area calculations	( )	( )	( )
9. Cost approach	( )	( )	( )
10. Comp sales selection	( )	( )	( )
11. Description of comps	( )	( )	( )
12. Analysis of market data	( )	( )	( )
13. Income approach	( )	( )	( )
14. Selection of rent comps	( )	( )	( )
15. Analysis of income	( )	( )	( )
16. Analysis of expenses	( )	( )	( )
17. Selection of cap rate	( )	( )	( )
18. Final reconciliation	( )	( )	( )
19. Subject photos	( )	( )	( )

20. Comparable photos	( )	( )	( )
21. Plat map	( )	( )	( )
22. Location map	( )	( )	( )
23. Limiting conditions	( )	( )	( )
24. Certification	( )	( )	( )
25. Required addenda	( )	( )	( )
26. Leasehold analysis	( )	( )	( )
27. Discount analysis	( )	( )	( )
28. Absorption study	( )	( )	( )
29. Other: qualifications	( )	( )	( )
30. Overall reliability and accuracy	( )	( )	( )

ADVANTAGES OF PROPER COMMUNICATION

No one likes to have his or her work criticized, especially by reviewers who seem to know less about appraising than you do. (How many appraisers will concede that reviewers know more than they do?) In all situations, however, you should always remain professional in manner and accept the reviewer's comments as constructive criticism that is a part of the learning process. Once an appraiser becomes hostile or defensive, the issues are seldom resolved in a manner that is beneficial to the appraiser. Rather than disagreeing with the reviewer's opinions, support your conclusions with market evidence in a matter-of-fact, professional manner, or admit your mistakes, thank the reviewer for pointing out your shortcomings, and make every effort to provide supplemental supportive data or make corrections as quickly as possible so the transaction can be completed in a timely manner.

CHAPTER 16

NARRATIVE APPRAISAL REPORT

A narrative appraisal report should provide not only the facts about the property, the appraisal should also illustrate the reasoning by which the appraiser has developed the estimate of value. The appraiser should guide the reader through the report beginning with stating the purpose of the appraisal followed by a thorough, but concise description of the neighborhood (and region, if applicable), subject property, and comparable properties. The appraiser should include statements and conclusions showing the relationship of the presented data to the appraisal problem, reasonable supporting documentation, and a final analysis that clearly demonstrates the appraiser's logic and judgment in arriving at the final estimate of value.

A narrative appraisal report should be an excellent demonstration of the appraiser's professionalism. Therefore, the appraiser should not employ "Chamber of Commerce, boilerplate, computer, or vacuum cleaner" techniques whereby the reader must sift through pages and pages of descriptions, technical jargon, theory, or mathematical calculations that actually have no bearing on the property or value. Computer-generated or boilerplate statements should not be included unless they have been correlated to the appraised property.

By eliminating all the filler, meaningless descriptions, and meaningless market data, and by maintaining consistency of methodology and valuation factors throughout the report; the need for a lot of lengthy explanations will be eliminated because the reader will be able to relate the data and analyses to the appraised property readily, comprehend your logic, and concur with your conclusions.

REQUIREMENTS FOR NARRATIVE APPRAISAL REPORTS

1. TITLE PAGE: Identify the written matter, for example, "Appraisal Report of a Single-Family Residence." Include the complete address of the property; complete name and address of the client; date of the valuation; and the appraiser's name, address, and designations.

2. LETTER OF TRANSMITTAL: Identify the real estate being appraised and define the purpose and function of the appraisal. Include a reference that the letter is accompanied by a complete appraisal report or supported by material in the appraiser's files, statement that the inspection of the property and necessary investigation and analyses were made by the appraiser (certification of value), conditions (as is or subject to), date of valuation, and the final estimate of value.

   Unusual or exceptional property features, appraisal techniques, limiting conditions, or assumptions should also be addressed in the transmittal letter. Although it is not a requirement, a brief description of the improvements should be included in the transmittal letter. Some appraisers prefer to include certifications, assumptions, and limiting conditions in the letter of transmittal rather than incorporating this data in the body of the report or in the addenda section.

3. TABLE OF CONTENTS: List all the main topics of the appraisal report with page numbers. Make sure the section headings, or main topics, are in proper order and the pages are numbered correctly.

4. PHOTOGRAPHS OF THE PROPERTY: Include only the front photo in the body of the report; include the balance of the photos in the addenda section.

5. SUMMARY OF IMPORTANT FACTS AND CONCLUSIONS: Include location, client, owner of record, legal description, assessor's parcel number, census tract number, site description, zoning, highest and best use, flood hazard zone, improvement description, date of valuation, appraised value, property condition, occupancy (owner, tenant), property history, current taxes, and effective tax rate. Include gross annual income and net annual income for income-producing property.

6. PURPOSE OF THE APPRAISAL: Identify the reason for the appraisal assignment, for example, "to estimate fair market value."

7. DEFINITION OF VALUE: Quote an accurate and meaningful definition of market value and document the definition by reference to the source.

8. IDENTIFICATION: Identify the borrower's and/or owner's name, street address, and legal description of the property.

9. TAX AND ASSESSMENT ANALYSIS: Provide current tax information including the dollar amount of the taxes,

assessed value, and tax rate. Include special assessments, if applicable. Discuss the likelihood of changes in tax rates and the resultant effect on value and marketability.

10. FUNCTION OF THE APPRAISAL: Define the use of the appraisal, for example, transfer of ownership, dissolve partnership, financing purposes, feasibility study, or for inheritance tax purposes.

11. SCOPE OF THE APPRAISAL: The term "scope of the appraisal" means the extent of the process of collecting, confirming, and reporting data. Consider the extent of your investigation of the property, neighborhood, comparable sales and rentals, plans and specifications, and other factors paramount to the appraisal problem.

12. DATE OF VALUATION: Show the effective date of the appraisal.

13. INTEREST APPRAISED: Indicate fee simple, leasehold, partial rights, or limited rights. Identify other encumbrances such as easements, mortgages, or special occupancy or use requirements. Explain the relationship to the defined estimate of value.

14. CASH EQUIVALENCY: Discuss cash equivalency adjustments, common concessions, and typical financing available in the area. When estimating market value, the appraiser must include a statement defining whether the estimate is expressed in terms of cash, terms equivalent to cash, or other precisely defined terms.

15. VALUATION OF PROPERTY: Identify the techniques or approaches to value that are being employed in appraising the property.

16. OCCUPANCY AND VACANCY ABSORPTION: For income-producing properties, discuss present and projected occupancy and vacancy factors.

17. REGIONAL AREA DATA AND ANALYSIS: Consider locational influences, political/governmental influences (tax rates, planning, zoning), economic trends (employment, stability of employment, other economic enterprise, community services, and regional resources), and sociological factors (population data and growth statistics, composition, education, recreational facilities, and cultural facilities). A regional description should be included only when it is useful in measuring the future marketability of the property, its economic life, the stability of its location, or area trends. The appraiser must include a statement of conclusions showing the relationship of the presented data to the appraisal problem.

18. NEIGHBORHOOD DATA AND ANALYSIS: Present a clear, concise description of the neighborhood addressing positive and negative locational influences; taxation levels; percent built-up; growth rate; supply and demand; marketing time; property compatibility; age and general appearance of properties; appeal to market; convenience to employment centers and commercial amenities; predominant type of development; population change; owner/tenant ratios; and quality and availability of schools, transportation, and recreational facilities. Include a statement of conclusions showing the relationship of the presented data to the appraisal problem.

19. SITE ANALYSIS: Describe the site noting dimensions, area of the site, topography, soil and subsoil conditions, utilities and services, streets, curbs, gutters, landscaping, conformity, ingress/egress, drainage, easements, and positive and negative site influences.

20. ZONING: State zoning and uses, public and private restrictions, and conformity to zoning. If applicable, discuss possible changes in zoning.

21. HIGHEST AND BEST USE: Define "highest and best

use'' and indicate the highest and best use of the land as though vacant and/or highest and best use of the property as improved.

22. IMPROVEMENT ANALYSIS: Provide a concise description of the physical characteristics of the property including actual age, effective age, remaining economic life, condition, gross improved area, functional utility, amenities, and external influences. Address marketability and stability of value.

23. DIRECT SALES COMPARISON APPROACH: Include only those sales that are pertinent to the appraisal problem. Three good sales are far more meaningful than a dozen sales that lend little or no support to the final value conclusion. The description of the sales should be adequate, but concise. Reference the price per square foot of total improved area as well as any other meaningful units of comparison, such as price per room, price per unit, or gross rent multiplier. Provide justification and support for any adjustments, reconciliation of the data, and indicated value. When there are a number of sales, summarize the data on a chart or spreadsheet.

24. INCOME ANALYSIS: Include an income analysis if the subject is or will be an income-producing property. The appraiser should explain and justify the actual and forecasted gross income, net income, vacancy factors, expenses, and capitalization rate. Include rent and sale comparables, with actual or inputed capitalization rates, that justify your conclusions and indicated value. Appraisals of existing income-producing properties should also contain a summary of actual annual operating statements accompanied by an identification of the source of this information.

25. COST APPROACH: Include an estimate of replacement cost or reproduction cost new; physical, func-

tional, and external depreciation; source of costs; site valuation accompanied by supportive land sales; reconciliation; and indicated value.

26. RECONCILIATION AND FINAL VALUE ESTIMATE: Provide a concise reconciliation of the previously presented data considering the strengths and weaknesses and appropriateness of the data and the approaches to value, income, market, and cost. Include the property condition (as is or subject to) and the date of the value estimate.

    If the property is proposed or under construction, the appraiser should include a "market value as is on appraisal date," a "market value as if complete on appraisal date," and "prospective future value upon completion of construction." For income-producing properties, the appraiser should include an estimate of "prospective future value upon reaching stabilized occupancy." Refer to Federal Home Loan Bank Board "Rules and Regulations" for additional details of market value requirements.

27. EXPLANATIONS: Explain any departures from standard procedure. A statement should also be included when required documentation is not available.

28. PRESENTATION: The presentation should be well organized, well documented, and professional in appearance. Check the report for errors and omissions, particularly review numbers, calculations, dates, and value conclusions.

29. ADDENDA AND EXHIBITS:
    a. Detailed statistical data
    b. Leases and lease summaries
    c. Certification, assumptions, and limiting conditions
    d. Qualifications of the appraiser
    e. Maps: regional map and/or neighborhood map iden-

tifying locations of the subject, comparable sales, and comparable rental properties

f. Plot plan identifying location of the improvements, adjacent and cross streets, alleys, dimensions, easements, and other pertinent data

g. Building diagram, drawn to scale, with exterior dimensions and setbacks

LETTERS OF ACCEPTANCE

Letters of acceptance should reference the following data:

1. Identification of the real estate being appraised.
2. The complete agreement of appraiser and client as to what the assignment entails; therefore, explain the purpose of the appraisal so it is clearly understood.
3. Definition of the type or style of appraisal report, for example, letter of opinion, form-style, or narrative-style.
4. Definition of the type of real estate to be valued.
5. For protection from unwarranted uses of the appraisal, definition of the intended use of the appraisal, for example, feasibility study in relation to renovation program, management decisions, tax appeal, or to arrive at the essential security offered for a proposed mortgage loan. If the appraisal is not to be used for mortgage loan purposes, the letter should so state.
6. To protect yourself from assertions that the client would not have requested the appraisal if he or she had been informed of the contingencies and limiting conditions, inclusion of a copy of "Contingent and Limiting Conditions" with the letter of acceptance. Have the client sign

and return the copy as a part of the contract. If the client refuses to sign, you should decline the assignment.

7. Inclusion of the projected date of the initial inspection of the property and estimated completion date.
8. Inclusion of the amount of the fee.
9. Request for any documentation needed from the client for completion of the assignment.

ACCEPTANCE LETTER—EXAMPLE

Date

Client's name, title
Company name
Complete address

RE: (borrower's name, subject property address, and/or legal description)

Dear :

This is a letter/contract sent to you for the purpose of confirming the details of your request and authorization for a narrative-style appraisal of the above-referenced property.

As I understand, the purpose of the appraisal report is to estimate the Market Value of the Fee Simple Interest of the subject property. The function of the appraisal will be to aid in a feasibility study in relation to a renovation program. It is also my understanding that the appraisal will not be used for mortgage loan purposes.

As I indicated in our telephone conversation, I will begin inspecting the property on February 5, 1989, having the report completed four weeks thereafter. The fee for the appraisal is twelve hundred dollars ($1,200.00).

In order to complete the assignment, please provide the

following documentation: complete legal description, approved set of blueprints, and scheduled contractor's fees.

A copy of "Contingent and Limiting Conditions," which will be included in the appraisal report, is attached. Please sign the form, retain a copy for your files, and return the original signed copy to me.

If these terms and conditions are acceptable to you, please acknowledge by signing and returning this letter along with the fee of $1,200. I am looking forward to working with you on this assignment. Thank you for the opportunity to be of service to your company.

Respectfully,

(signature)
Appraiser's Name, Title

(signature)

Client's Name, Title

NARRATIVE APPRAISAL REPORT—EXAMPLE

Appraisers should develop a format, similar to the following illustration, for presentation of narrative-style appraisal reports, and use it consistently, so time and energy can be concentrated on content and analysis rather than layout or style. To avoid redundancy, only the most pertinent factors are represented in this example. To provide a variety of examples, the following illustration contains excerpts from several actual appraisals; however, names, places, and descriptions are fictitious.

The following hypothetical example of a narrative-style appraisal report is presented to provide a general outline of a narrative report for a conforming single-family residence. The sample statements should be expanded upon, by the appraiser, to the extent that the reader of the report can readily comprehend how the appraiser arrived at his or her conclusions.

APPRAISAL REPORT

OF

A SINGLE-FAMILY RESIDENCE

LOCATED AT:
7574 Highland Avenue
Santa Maria, California

PREPARED FOR:
Robert M. Jones, President
Santa Maria Mortgage Company
7854 Brookline Street, Suite 809
Pacific Heights, California 98765

As of: January 31, 1988

PREPARED BY:
Appraiser's name, designations
Appraiser's Business Address

SAMPLE TRANSMITTAL LETTER

Date
Client's name, title
Company name
Address
RE: (borrower's name, subject property address, and/or legal description)

Dear: ______________

In response to your authorization, I have made an inspection and analysis of the above-referenced property, neighborhood, and sales of similar property which has enabled me to form an opinion of Market Value.

The improvements consist of a 15-year-old, 2,800-square- foot, well-maintained, single-family residence featuring extensive landscaping improvements, swimming pool, tennis court, and a panoramic white-water ocean view.

Based on the investigation and analyses, and on my experience as a Real Estate Appraiser, it is my opinion that the property described herein has a Market Value of the Fee Simple Estate, As Is, as of January 31, 1988, amounting to

EIGHT HUNDRED FIFTY THOUSAND DOLLARS
($850,000.)

The narrative report that follows sets forth the results of our investigation and analyses; pertinent facts about the area, subject property, and comparable data; and the reasoning leading to the conclusions set forth.

Respectfully,
(signature)

____
Appraiser's name, designations

TABLE OF CONTENTS—EXAMPLE

The following example illustrates many of the elements that are usually contained in a narrative appraisal. Refer to this list to make sure that you didn't omit anything.

TABLE OF CONTENTS

Summary of Salient Facts and Conclusions ... iv
INTRODUCTION ... 1
Purpose of the Report ... 1
Definition of Value ... 1
Property Identification ... 2
Tax and Assessment Analysis ... 2
Function of the Appraisal ... 2
Date of Valuation ... 3
Interest Appraised ... 3
Cash Equivalency ... 3
Valuation of Property ... 3
Occupancy and Vacancy Absorption ... 4
DEMOGRAPHIC DATA ... 5
City Data ... 5
Climate ... 5
Shopping ... 5
Education ... 6
Hospitals and Health Facilities ... 6
Recreational and Cultural Facilities ... 7
Governmental Facilities ... 7
Airport and Public Transportation ... 8
Economic Trends ... 8
Transportation ... 8
Agricultural Activity ... 9
Industrial Activity ... 9
SITE DATA ... 10
Site Analysis ... 10

Zoning 11
Highest and Best Use 11
IMPROVEMENT DESCRIPTION 12
Market Data Analysis 15
Market Data 18
Market Value Conclusion 20
INCOME APPROACH 22
Rental Analysis 22
Comparable Rental Data 23
Conclusion of Economic Rent 25
Rent Schedule 26
Analysis of Income and Expenses 28
Capitalization Process 30
COST APPROACH 32
Land Valuation 33
Land Sales 34
Land Value Conclusion 35
Summary of Cost Estimate 35
RECONCILIATION
AND FINAL VALUE ESTIMATE 38
Limiting Conditions 40
Certification of Appraiser 41
Qualifications of Appraiser 42

APPENDIX

Exhibit A—Photographs of Subject Property
B—Photographs of Comparable Sales
C—Photographs of Comparable Rentals
D—Metropolitan Area Map
E—Neighborhood Map
F—Building Diagram
G—Statistical Neighborhood Data
H—Lease Summary

SUMMARY OF SALIENT FACTS AND CONCLUSIONS

Thomas Guide Reference:	41 B-4 (Santa Maria County).
Location:	7574 Highland Avenue Santa Maria, California.
Client:	Santa Maria Mortgage Company.
Owner of Record:	James M. and Maria L. Smith.
Borrower:	Same.
Legal Description:	Lot 75 Tract 5986.
Assessor's Parcel Number:	4586-09-0987.
Census Tract Number:	0045.10.
Flood Hazard Zone:	Not in flood zone. Flood Zone B, Panel No. 090212-0019A, effective 9/14/79.
Site Description:	130 ft. × 180 ft. or 23,400 sq. ft., level midblock site.
Zoning:	R-1 (single-family residential).
Improvements:	15-year-old, 2,800 sq. ft. SFR, tennis court, pool, panoramic white-water ocean view.
Highest and Best Use:	As presently improved.
Date of Valuation:	January 31, 1988.
Appraised Value:	$850,000.
Property Condition:	"As Is."
Occupancy:	Owner.
Property History:	According to public records, the last recorded transfer of the subject property was 10/12/78 for $558,000. with conventional terms.
Current Taxes:	Tax year 1988–89: $7461.16
Effective Tax Rate:	1.0987
Assessed Building Value:	$355,000
Assessed Land Value:	$325,000
Total Assessed Value:	$680,000

PURPOSE OF THE REPORT

The purpose of this appraisal is to set forth the data, analysis, and conclusions relative to the opinion of Fair Market Value of the existing single-family residence located at 7574 Highland Avenue, Santa Maria, California.

The opinions set forth are subject to the premises, assumptions, and limiting conditions listed on the following pages.

DEFINITION OF MARKET VALUE

The definition of Market Value, as defined by (appraisers should reference their source) is as follows: (the appraiser should include an appropriate definition of market value).

PROPERTY IDENTIFICATION

James M. and Maria L. Smith, Owners
7574 Highland Avenue
Santa Maria, County of Santa Maria, California
Legal Description: Lot 75, Block A, Tract 5986, Map Book 26, Page 71 and 72.
(Note: If the legal description is lengthy, it may be placed in the addenda section of the report.)

TAX AND ASSESSMENT ANALYSIS

Assessor's Parcel Number:	4586-09-0987.
Tax Year:	1988-89.
Current Taxes:	$7471.16.
Tax Rate:	1.0987.
Tax Increase:	1.2% total full value change per year for the past several years.
Building Value:	$355,000.
Land Value:	$325,000.

Total Assessed Value: $680,000.
Special Assessments: None noted.

FUNCTION OF THE APPRAISAL

This appraisal will be used for mortgage loan purposes

DATE OF VALUATION

January 31, 1988

INTEREST APPRAISED

The property appraised is described as a Fee Simple Title. "Fee Simple Title" is defined as

"A title that signifies ownership of all the rights in a parcel of real property subject only to limitations of the four powers of government."[1]

CASH EQUIVALENCY

A cash equivalency analysis has been considered appropriate where necessary with the sales data employed in this report. In those cases where the appraiser was not able to verify comparable data or financing, the sales were assumed to be typical market transactions. Typical sales terms generally consisted of a cash payment and financing for the balance of the price. Mortgage terms were at current interest rates with various payoff schedules. Financing generally consisted of an underlying first mortgage and either a second mortgage or a wraparound mortgage with the property as security. Since the market data in this report represent current market transactions with no abnormal financing in most of the sales analyzed, no adjustment for a cash equivalency was warranted.

---

[1] *The Dictionary of Real Estate Appraisal,* 2nd ed. Chicago, Illinois: American Institute of Real Estate Appraisers, 1989), p. 120.

VALUATION OF THE PROPERTY

In valuing the property, I have used the three conventional techniques of real estate valuation: cost, income, and market. (Or in valuing the property, I have used two conventional techniques of real estate valuation: cost and market. The income approach is not considered a good indicator of value as properties of this nature are typically not purchased for their income-producing capabilities. Thus, the income approach was not utilized in this report.)

OCCUPANCY AND VACANCY ABSORPTION

(If the property is or will be tenant occupied, the appraiser should discuss vacancy and absorption factors.)

DEMOGRAPHIC DATA

(The appraiser should describe regional, neighborhood, or city data, as applicable. Refer to items 17 and 18 in "Requirements for Narrative Appraisal Reports" and refer to the "Table of Contents" example for topics of discussion.)

SITE ANALYSIS

Location:	Interior site located on the south side of Highland Avenue in the highly desirable "Highland Heights" district of Santa Maria.
Dimensions:	130 ft. × 180 ft. or 23,400 sq. ft.
Topography:	Level at street grade.
Shape:	Rectangular.
Soil:	No soil engineering test reports were provided to the appraisers.
Drainage:	Drainage for the site is considered adequate. No adverse conditions were noted.

Streets:	Property fronts to a 38-ft.-wide, asphalt-paved, public street. Streets, curbs, gutters, sidewalks, street lights, and parkways are well maintained. Ample parking is available on both sides of the street.
Ingress/Egress:	Good. No adverse conditions noted.
Utilities:	All public utilities are presently connected to, and in use, at the site.
Easements:	Typical utility easements. A title report was not provided to the appraisers.
Zoning:	R-1, single-family residential, minimum lot size 20,000 sq. ft.
Conformity:	The site is typical in size for the neighborhood and is considered to be conforming.

HIGHEST AND BEST USE

In common appraisal practice, the concept of highest and best use represents the premise upon which a value estimate is based. The determination of highest and best use is the result of the appraiser's judgment and analytical skill. The use determined from analysis represents an opinion, not a fact to be found.

"Highest and best use" is defined as follows: "The reasonably probable and legal use of vacant land or an improved property, which is physically possible, appropriately supported, financially feasible, and that results in the highest value."[2]

It is to be recognized that in cases where a site has existing improvements on it, the highest and best use may very well be determined to be different from the existing use. The existing use will continue, however, unless and until land value in

---

[2]Ibid., p. 149.

its highest and best use exceeds the total value of the property in its existing use.

Four considerations are imposed upon a site in the estimation of highest and best use:

1. Possible Use: What uses of the site in question are physically possible?
2. Permissible Use (Legal): What uses are permitted by zoning and deed restrictions on the site in question?
3. Feasible Use: Which possible and permissible uses will produce the highest net return or the highest present worth?
4. Highest and Best Use: Among the feasible uses, which use will produce the highest net return or the highest present worth?

After analyzing present developments in this area and the subject site itself, the appraiser is of the opinion that the highest and best use of the subject site is as presently improved, a single-family residence that meets the requirements of existing zoning and conforms to similar uses in the neighborhood.

IMPROVEMENT DESCRIPTION

(The appraiser should provide a concise description of the physical characteristics of the property including actual age, effective age, remaining economic life, condition, gross improved area, materials of construction, electrical and mechanical equipment, functional utility, yard improvements, amenities, external influences, and other pertinent factors.)

MARKET APPROACH

The Market Data Approach (also known as the Sales Comparison or Direct Sales Approach) is a method of estimating market value by comparing the subject property to data obtained from the relevant marketplace. Such data ideally result from sales transactions of properties similar in type and market location to the subject, though volatile markets or limited data may require the inclusion of asking and offering price data from property listings.

Application of this approach requires an understanding of the equilibrium in the marketplace between supply and demand for similar properties. In the reasonable presence of such equilibrium, market data will tend to indicate a good relationship between prices paid for similar properties in accordance with the principle of substitution.

This approach is most applicable to properties for which there exists a reasonably active and balanced market, similarity among properties, and reasonable economic stability in the marketplace. To the degree these features are absent, adjustments are made to the comparable sales to reconcile the observed differences. The following steps are taken in applying this approach:

1. Research the relevant market to obtain and verify information about sales transactions, listings, and offerings of properties similar to the subject.
2. Qualify prices asked, offered, or paid as to terms of sale, motivating forces, and bona fide nature.
3. Determine relevant units of comparison and compare significant attributes of comparable properties with the subject, among which are timing, financing terms, conditions of sale, location, physical characteristics, and income characteristics.
4. Consider all dissimilarities in terms of probable effect on sales price, and adjust the comparable upward for inferior conditions and downward for superior conditions to

remove the effect of such differences on the comparative price of the subject.

5. Reconcile the multiple-value indications into a single opinion of value of the subject property.
6. Deduct the present value loss resulting from rent-up period for proposed properties or from encumbrances of long-term, below-market leases.

MARKET DATA ANALYSIS

We have gathered and analyzed information pertaining to the sales of similar single-family residences in the subject market area. The comparables presented in this report were the best and most recent to be found. The market summary that follows discloses the results of our investigation.

MARKET DATA

(Appraisers should provide an adequate, but concise, description of the comparable sales and/or provide a chart or spreadsheet summarizing the salient characteristics of each comparable sale, for example, comparable number, address, date of sale, sales price, size, price per square foot, other meaningful units of comparison, amenities, and brief comments relating the market data to the subject.)

MARKET VALUE CONCLUSION

(Appraisers should provide a summarizing statement of their market data analysis and conclusions referencing reasons for assigning more weight to one comparable than another and referencing those factors that were given consideration in arriving at a conclusion of market value.) For example, the adjusted comparable price range is from $795,000. to $930,000. Comparable 1 was given the greatest weight and consideration as of the closed sales; it required the least adjustments and is located within the subject's "Highland Heights" neighborhood.

It is our opinion that the preceding data adequately bracket the overall value range of the subject property. Based on a physical review and inspection of each comparable, the indicated value of the subject property is estimated at $850,000.

INDICATED VALUE BY THE MARKET APPROACH:
$850,000.

INCOME APPROACH

The income approach is not considered a good indicator of value as properties of this nature are typically not purchased for their income-producing capabilities. Thus, the income approach was not utilized in this report.

Note: When the appraised property is an income-producing property, the appraiser should include rent comparables, analysis of comparable rentals, conclusion of economic rent, rent schedule, analysis of income and expenses, and capitalization process.

COST APPROACH

The cost approach is based primarily on the principle of substitution, which affirms that no prudent investor will pay more for property than the amount for which a comparable site can be acquired and upon which improvements with equal desirability and utility can be constructed.

The application of this approach is limited by other influences, including the supply of and demand for comparable sites and external factors, such as zoning policies, financing and construction industry price levels, and labor availability.

The approach is most applicable when appraising relatively new properties with little or no accrued depreciation and when construction services, materials, and financing are reasonably available at reasonable rates. In applying this approach, the following steps are taken:

1. Estimate the value of the land as though vacant and available for development to its highest and best use. Generally, this estimate is based on a separate market data approach applied to vacant land, though residual or extraction approaches may be required in the absence of suitable or sufficient data.
2. Estimate the reproduction or replacement cost of improvements as new, including all components of replacement as well as indirect and direct costs and developer profit.
3. Estimate all the elements of accrued depreciation.
4. Deduct total accrued depreciation from the reproduction or replacement cost new of the improvements, resulting in an estimate (depreciated reproduction or replacement cost) of the contribution of the cost of improvements to the total value by this method.
5. Add the depreciated reproduction or replacement cost, including the cost of site improvements, to the previously determined land value to obtain the final estimate of value.

LAND VALUATION

To determine the market value of the subject lot, we gathered and analyzed data pertaining to sales of other similar parcels of land in Santa Maria. For the greatest degree of comparability, we concentrated our search on parcels located within the "Highland Heights" district of Santa Maria.

The following sales summary outlines the results of our investigation.

LAND SALES

(The appraiser should present an adequate, but concise, description of the land sales and/or a chart or spreadsheet summarizing the salient characteristics of each sale.)

LAND VALUE CONCLUSION

Certain elements of comparability include general location, immediate environmental influences, zoning, availability of street improvements, land size, shape, topography, and site prominence. The date of sale and marketability of each sale were also considered. Marketability is the practical aspect of selling a property in view of all the elements constituting value and certain economic and financing conditions prevailing as of the date of the sale.

The sales summary presented on the preceding page outlines the results of our investigation.

The land data ranged from $13.00 to $17.25 per sq. ft. Based upon an analysis of the most comparable data, it is our opinion that the subject site has a present-day market value of $14.00 per sq. ft., as follows:

23,400 sq. ft. × $14.00/sq. ft. = $327,600.
Say $328,000.

SUMMARY COST ESTIMATE

(The appraiser should provide an outline of the estimated replacement or reproduction cost new for the subject property accompanied by a reconciliation and indicated value.)

Replacement Cost Estimate

The following costs are based upon costs derived from Marshall and Swift Valuation Services and those obtained by the appraisers from builders of similar properties.

Living Area ______ sq. ft. × $______/sq. ft.	$______
Garage Area ______ sq. ft. × $______/sq. ft.	______
Fireplaces (included in base)	______
Driveways and walks	______
Landscaping	______
Pool, spa, and decking	______
Total estimated costs	$______
Less: Depreciation	
Depreciated improvement value:	$______
Add: Land value	
Total estimated value	$______
Say	$______

RECONCILIATION AND FINAL VALUE ESTIMATE

From the approaches utilized in this report, the following indicators have been drawn:

Cost approach $862,000.
Market approach $850,000.
Income approach (N/A)

The cost approach was not heavily relied upon in the final value estimate because the cost approach is not a direct market measurement and properties of this type are seldom purchased on the basis of cost. Also, the cost approach is a less reliable indicator of value due to the difficulty in estimating accrued physical depreciation.

The market approach involved comparing the subject property to other comparable properties that are located in the same general area. The market approach produced a wide range of values due to locational and physical differences between the comparables; however, the final estimate of value is well bracketed and well supported by recent market data. Hence, the market approach was given the greatest consideration in arriving at a final value estimate.

The income approach is not considered a good indicator of value as properties of this nature are typically not purchased for their income-producing capabilities. Thus, the income approach was not utilized in this report.

Based on the investigation undertaken, the analyses made, and our experience as real estate appraisers, we have formed the opinion that, as of January 31, 1988, subject to the assumptions and limiting conditions set forth in this report, the estimated fair market value, as is, of the subject property is

EIGHT HUNDRED FIFTY THOUSAND DOLLARS
($850,000).

The concluded value represents cash or cash equivalent terms.

■ ■ ■ End of Report ■ ■ ■

APPENDICES

APPENDIX A

Example—Cost Calculations

BASIC RESIDENCE COST:

	2,000 sq. ft. × $34.84/sq. ft.	= $ 69,680.
Square Foot Adjustments		
Wood shake roof	2,000 sq. ft. × $ 0.85/sq. ft.	= +1,700.
Hardwood floors	120 sq. ft. × $ 3.97/sq. ft.	= + 476.
Wall furnace	2,000 sq. ft. × $ 0.89/sq. ft.	= −1,780.
Plaster interior	2,000 sq. ft. × $ 0.81/sq. ft.	= +1,620.
Common brick exterior trim	(appraiser's estimate)	+1,100.
Central A/C	2,000 sq. ft. × $2.05/sq. ft.	= +4,100.
Upgraded wall coverings, drapes	(appraiser's est.)	+4,000.

<u>Lump-Sum Adjustments</u>

Single, one-story, fireplace	+1,700.
Built-in range/oven, gas	+ 635.
Garbage disposer	+ 165.
Range hood and fan	+ 155.
Dishwasher	+ 440.
Porch, open with steps, 100 sq. ft. × $6.44/sq. ft. =	+ 644.
Subtotal residence cost:	$ 84,635.
Current cost multiplier 1.02 × local multiplier 1.23 × subtotal of all building improvements ($84,635.) =	$106,183.
Attached stucco garage 400 sq. ft. × $11.36/sq. ft. =	4,544.
Deduct for common wall: 20 linear ft. × $25.72/ft. =	−514.
Add for finished walls: 80 linear feet × $12.35/ft. =	+ 988.
Subtotal garage cost: $5,018.	
Current cost multiplier 1.02 × local multiplier 1.23 × subtotal garage cost ($5,018.) =	$ 6,296.

HENCE:

Use $53.00/sq. ft. for residence cost ($106,183. divided by 2000 sq. ft. = $53.09, rounded $53.00) and $16.00/sq. ft. for garage cost ($6,296. divided by 400 sq. ft. = $15.74/sq. ft., rounded $16.00).

APPENDIX B

Example: Land Comparable

LAND COMPARABLE 1

Location/Address:	NEC Fairview Street and Mountain Avenue, Santa Fe (Map Code 82-F-5)
Assessor's Parcel No:	4503-48-3098
Zoning and Uses:	R-1, single-family residential, minimum 20 ft. front, 5 ft. side, and 25 ft. rear setbacks
Size and Shape:	75 ft. × 130 ft. or 9,750 sq. ft. rectangle
Soil and Subsoil:	Typical; adequate for zoned uses
Contour:	Level and at street grade
Public Utilities:	Water, gas, electric, telephone, sanitary sewer, storm sewer
Street and Sidewalk:	38-ft.-wide asphalt street, curbs, gutters, and sidewalks
Locational Influences:	Corner, view of mountains, heavy-traffic street
Sales Price:	$109,000.
Unit Price:	$11.18/sq. ft.
Terms of Sale:	25 percent down, 1st TD Seller $81,750.
Cash Equivalency:	$109,000. −5,500. CE Adjustment $103,500. or $10.62/sq. ft.
Recording Date:	7/11/87 (Document No. 009087)
Data Source:	Appraiser's files and public records
Remarks:	Similar physical characteristics and location, two miles southwest, older tear-down SFR on the site

APPENDIX C

Example: Area Computations

The area of a house is found by dividing it into convenient shapes. To find the area of an irregular shape, the usual procedure is to divide the area into smaller areas of common shapes such as rectangles, triangles, and squares. Compute the areas separately; then add them together as illustrated.

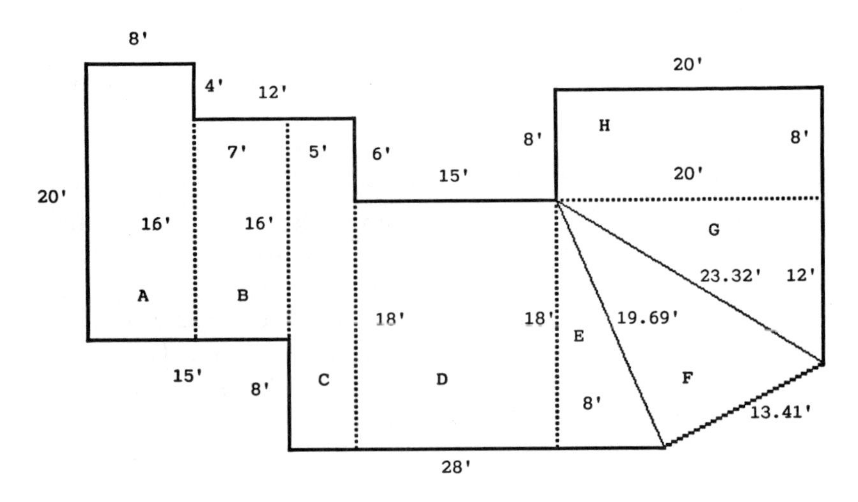

Calculations:

(A)	8 × 20	=	160
(B)	7 × 16	=	112
(C)	5 × 24	=	120
(D)	15 × 18	=	270
(E)	1/2 (8 × 20)*	=	80
(F)	1/2 (13 × 20)*	=	130
(G)	1/2 (12 × 20)	=	120
(H)	8 × 20	=	160
	Total		1,152 sq. ft.

The preceding procedure for defining and calculating irregular areas has been presented in various real estate textbooks. This procedure is very precise; however, it is not practical, nor is it necessary, to divide areas E, F, and G into triangles. Consider the following example:

(A)	8 × 20	=	160
(B)	7 × 16	=	112
(C)	5 × 24	=	120
(D)	15 × 18	=	270
	20 × 26	=	520 (areas E, F, G, and H)
	1/2 (6 × 12)	=	- 36 (triangle at lower right corner of house)
	Total:		1,146 sq. ft.

This procedure results in a variance of only 6 sq. ft., which will not affect the appraised value of the property.

*13.41, rounded 13; 19.69, rounded 20

APPENDIX D

Principal Information Sources

For (1) call city or county, (2) city, (3) county, (4) state, (5) federal, (6) local agency

BUILDING AND SAFETY, Department of (1) building permits, land uses, building codes, soil and subsoil

CHAMBER OF COMMERCE (2) area development trends, statistics, population

COMMUNITY DEVELOPMENT AGENCY (1) area development trends, redevelopment

CONTRACTORS (6) building costs

ENGINEERING DEPT (1) verify lot dimensions

HIGHWAYS OR STREETS, Department of (1) traffic count, maintenance

HOUSING AND COMMUNITY DEVELOPMENT AGENCY (1) area development trends, redevelopment, rent control

HOUSING AND COMMUNITY DEVELOPMENT, Department of (4) manufactured housing, mobile homes

HOUSING AND URBAN DEVELOPMENT, Department of (5) major programs of housing and urban development, urban renewal, low-rent public housing, rent control, municipal planning

PARKS AND RECREATION DEPARTMENT (1) community facilities

PLANNING COMMISSION (1) land uses, zoning maps, area development trends, zoning, flood and earthquake data, special assessments, building plans, lot dimensions

PUBLIC WORKS, Department of (1) sewers, storm drains, flood control channels, lot dimensions

RAILROADS (6) listed under specific railroad; ask for "dispatcher" for rail traffic and time schedules

REDEVELOPMENT AGENCIES (1) area development trends, redevelopment
SURVEYOR (3) location and names of new streets, lot dimensions
TAX ASSESSOR (3) taxes, tax rates, special assessments
TITLE COMPANY (6) recorded sales data, plat maps, legal description
TRANSIT DISTRICT (1) public transportation
WASTE MANAGEMENT AGENCY (3) landfill sites, dumps

APPENDIX E

Abbreviations

Abbreviations may be used to save time and space; however, never use abbreviations that are not standard throughout the industry or abbreviations that might be misinterpreted. The following abbreviations are commonly used by appraisers:

aggr	aggregate
A/S	aluminum sliding
amt	amount
apt	apartment
A/T	asphalt tile
ASMP	assumption
avg	average
BBQ	barbecue
bsmt	basement
BR	bedroom
b/c	broom closet
bldg	building
blt-in	built-in
C/P	carport
csmt	casement
CE	cash equivalence
CTNL	cash to new loan
C/I	cast iron
C/A	central air
C/T	ceramic tile
c/l	chain link
comb	combination
comm	commercial
comp	comparable
C/S	composition shingle
conc	concrete
condo	condominium

conv	conventional
co-op	cooperative
CCM	current cost multiplier
CU	comp utility
det	detached
D/A	dining area
DR	dining room
DW	dishwasher or drywall
DHW	double hung windows
D/S	downspout
D/B	drainboard
D/S	drain/splash
Eff	effective
elec	electric
elev	elevation
encl	enclosure
E/O	external obsolescence
evap	evaporated cooler
FR	family room
F/S	fee simple
FG	fiberglass
FP	fireplace
FF	floor furnace
FAU	forced-air unit
F&S	frame and stucco
FR FT	front foot
F&R	front and rear
F/O	functional obsolescence
G-1	one-car garage
G-2	two-car garage
GDO	garage door opener
G/D	garbage disposal
HB	hardboard
HW	hardwood
H&F PL	heated and filtered pool
HPL	heated swimming pool

HOA	homeowner's association
H/F	hood and fan
HWH	hot water heater
impvmts	improvements
inf	inferior
kit	kitchen
L/L	land lease
ldry	laundry
LH	leasehold
l/c	linen closet
lino	linoleum
LR	living room
M/W	microwave oven
MT	Mission Tile
mtg	mortgage
NH	neighborhood
OH	overhang
PV	palos verdes (stone)
pkg	parking
PUD	planned unit development
pl	plaster
P&S	pool and spa
prefab	prefabricated
PV	present value
R/O	range and oven
RE	real estate
rec rm	recreation room
RV	recreational vehicle
rehab	rehabilitation
REL	remaining economic life
S/P	sales price
SP	service porch
shgl	shingle
SOT	shower over tub
SFR	single-family residence
s/g	sliding glass (door/window)

SS	stainless steel
S/S	stall shower
SF	square foot
sup	superior
T/G	tar and gravel
TH	town house
T/C	trash compactor
T/D	trust deed
VRM	variable rate mortgage
VAT	vinyl asbestos tile
WI	walk-in
WF	wall furnace
W/R	wardrobe
W/SH	wood shake
W/S	wood shingle
WD/S	wood siding
WR IR	wrought iron

APPENDIX F

Checklist—Subject And Comparable Sales

Address________________________Agent ____________
Telephone ____________MLS No.________Date________
Roof: Type______Age______Width/Overhang __________
Condition________________Recommend Inspection _____
Exterior Walls: Finish __________Condition __________
Exterior Trim: Common Brick__Brick Veneer__Used Brick__
Wood Siding ____Alum Siding ____Shingle ____Other _____
Linear Feet/Siding________Height _____ Condition ____
Placement of House__Steep Steps to Entry __No. of Steps __
Drainage/Grading: Subject ________________________
Drainage/Grading: Adjacent Property _______________
Settlement/Structural Damage/Cracks in Walls/Foundation
____________________________Recommend Inspection ___
Dry Rot/Termites____________ Recommend Inspection ___
Condition: Windows ______Doors ______Screens ________
Addition: Date/Permit No. _________________________

____

Interior Walls: Finish _____________________________
Condition ______________________________________
Floors: Finish ___________________________________
Condition ______________________________________
Baths ____Kitchen ______Basement ______Garage ________
Attic Finishes ___________Ceiling Height ____________
Bsmt Finishes________________Ventilation ___________
Floorplan/Functional Utility _______________________
Width: Doors/Halls/Stairs ______Conformity of Decor __

____

Electric: Amps/Volts ____No. of Outlets____Adequacy____
Cross Ventilation ____________________Storage ________
Modernization: Kitchen ____________________________
Modernization: Baths ______________________________

Rehabilitation: Wiring ____ Plumbing _____ Heating ______
Rehab: Dwelling ______________________________________
Date/Permit No. __________ Upgrades/Owners Costs _____
____
Overimprovement/Underimprovement __________________
Photos/Upgrades,etc.? _______________________________
Interior Garage Dimensions _____ Garage Built-ins _______
Other ____
____
____

APPENDIX G

Checklist—Subject And Comparable Sales:

SITE IMPROVEMENTS AND AMENITIES

Address ______________________________ Agent __________________

Telephone ______________ MLS No. ________ Date __________

Driveway: Concrete __Asphalt __Dirt __Ribbon __Other___

____

Width ________ Turning Radius ______ Grade ____________

Ingress/Egress_________________ Condition _____________

Walkways: Covered __Brick __Concrete __Flagstone ______

Wood ____Other ____Condition ____________________

Retaining Walls _____________________________________

Sprinklers: Multihead/No. Heads/Front ___Side ___Rear __

Planters: Location/Materials ___________________________

Fountain______Pond ________Courtyard ______________

Other ____

Fencing: Conc Blk__Grapestake ____Wood ____Picket ____

Stone___Wr. Iron ____Split Rail ____Gates/Type/No. _____

Linear Feet: Fencing ____________Condition ___________

Lawn/Trees/Shrubs/Plants: Type/No./Condition ________

____ Cost _______

____

Patio: Covered ________Open ________Enclosed _________

Condition __________Cost ________Permit No. __________

Swimming Pool: Gunite ____Vinyl ____Fiberglass __Age ___

Size ____Condition ________Cost ____Permit No. ________

Decking/Amt/Type ___________________________________

Spa: Type ________In-Ground __Above-Ground __Size ____

Age ______Condition ______Cost ______Decking _________

BBQ ____________Fire Ring __________Other ____________

Barn: Type/Age/Size/Condition/Permit No. ____________

____

Corrals _______________Storage Sheds _______________

Other Outbuildings __________________________________

Sauna ________Cabana ________Tennis Court ________
Lighting: Pool/Yard/Tennis Court ________________
External Obsolescence ____________________________
Views ____
All Bldgs Squared Off____Photos: Views/External
Obsolescence and Amenities _______________________
Lot Size/Shape/Utility/Topography ________________
____
Lot Size and Building Size Same as Public Records? _______
Other ____
____

APPENDIX H

Checklist—Neighborhood Description: external Obsolescence, Environmental Deficiencies

Address____________________Date ________________
Airport: Location/Noise ____________________________
Air Pollution: Cause/Location ________________________
Alleys: Maintenance/Lighting ________________________
Public ____ Private ________Access ____Width _______
Community Recreational Facilities: Type/Location _______
____
Adequate ____ Condition ______Public ____Association ____
Conversion of Bldgs to Incompatible Uses _______________
____
Density/Excessive Dwelling Unit/Overcrowding __________
____
Dumps/Toxic Waste Sites ____________________________
Flood Control Channel: Lined/Unlined/Location ________
____
For Sale Signs: Number/Duration ____________________
Agent's Names/Phone No./Property Address ____________
____
____
____
Freeway___________________Buffers________________
Graffiti: Location ________________________________
Ingress/Egress to NH _____________________________
Maintenance Levels/Deferred Maintenance: Addresses _____
____
____
Mixed Uses (Conformity): Type/Location _______________
____
Buffers ____

Obsolete Buildings ____________________
Parkway/Curbs/Gutters/Maintenance____________________
Railroad: Location/No. Trains/Time/Buffers____________________
Stop Signs/Bus Stops/Location____________________
Streets: Deficient/Unsafe/Congested____________________
Streets: Heavy Traffic/Street Name/Location____________________
Buffers____________________
Power Lines: Location____________________Buffers____________________
Schools: Proximity____________________Shopping____________________
Vacant Land/Location/Zoning/Proposed Use____________________
____
Other ____________________
____________________Photos Taken?__________

APPENDIX I

Glossary

accrued depreciation Actual depreciation from the time of construction to the date of the appraisal.

acre A measure of land, approximately 206 ft. × 206 ft. in area; 43,560 sq. ft.

amenities Conditions of agreeable living or beneficial influences arising from the location or improvements: satisfaction of enjoyable living derived from the home.

appurtenance A word employed in deeds, leases, and so on for the purpose of including any easements or other rights used or enjoyed with the real property, which are considered to be so much a part of the property that they pass to the grantee under the deed conveying the real property.

arm's-length transaction A transaction in which both seller and buyer act willingly, are under no pressure to act, and both have knowledge of the present conditions and fu ture potential of the property.

assessments A tax levied upon property to pay its proportionate share of a public improvement or service.

backfill The gravel or earth replaced in the space around a building wall after foundations are in place.

balloon payment The final installment payment on a note that is greater than the preceding installment payments and that pays the note in full.

baseboard A board along the floor against walls and partitions to hide gaps.

baseboard heating Heating in which the radiant heating element is located at the base of an interior wall; sometimes referred to as electric baseboard heat.

batten Small thin strips covering joints between wider

boards on exterior building surfaces; sometimes referred to as board and batten.

bearing wall A wall that supports a floor or roof of a building.

bona fide In good faith, without fraud.

building codes Federal, state, or local laws that set minimum construction standards.

built-up roof A roofing material applied in sealed, waterproof layers, where there is only a slight slope to the roof.

buydown A loan that has been bought down by the seller for the benefit of the buyer. Additional discount points are paid to a lender in exchange for a reduced rate of interest on a loan, which may be for all or only a portion of the loan term.

caissons Poured-in-place concrete pilings.

cantilever A projecting beam or joist, not supported on one end, used to support an extension of the structure.

casement A window sash that opens on hinges at the vertical edge.

casing Door and window framing.

cesspool A pit that serves for storage of liquid sewage which is disposed of through seepage into the surrounding soil.

chair rail A protective wooden molding on a wall around a room at the level of a chair back.

cistern A tank to catch and store rain water.

clapboard A long thin board, thicker on one edge, overlapped and nailed on for exterior siding.

clerestory window Vertical windows, or a series of vertical windows, set above the primary roof line.

cluster housing Detached dwelling units grouped fairly close together, generally leaving open spaces as common areas.

conditions Restrictions created by a qualification annexed to the estate by the grantor of a deed, upon breach of wnich the estate is defeated and reverts to him.

cove lighting Concealed light sources behind a cornice or horizontal recess which direct the light upon a reflected ceiling.

crawl space A shallow, unfinished space beneath the first floor of a house which has no basement. Also a shallow space in the attic, immediately under the roof.

deferred maintenance Existing but unfulfilled requirements for repairs and rehabilitation.

depreciation Loss of value in real property brought about by age, physical deterioration, or functional or external obsolescence; a loss in value from any cause.

dormer A projection built out from the slope of a roof.

double hung windows Windows with an upper and lower sash, each supported by cords and weights.

dry rot A fungus-caused decay in wood.

easement A right or interest in the land of another which entitles the holder thereof to some use, privilege, or benefit (such as to place utility poles, pipe lines, roads thereon, or travel over, etc.) out of, under, or over said land.

eaves The extension of a roof beyond house walls; overhang.

effective age The age of a structure based on the actual wear and tear and maintenance, or lack of maintenance, that the structure has received.

encroachment When a building, a wall, a fence, or other fixture encroaches upon (overlaps) the land of an adjoining owner, there is said to be an "encroachment," provided such adjoining owner has not consented thereto.

escrow Written instructions given by a seller and buyer to an impartial party (escrow holder) authorizing the delivery of a deed or other instrument upon the payment of the purchase money, or other money or things, and upon compliance with the other provisions of the escrow instructions.

estate tax A tax levied upon the transfer of property by reason of the death of a person, the amount of the tax being determined by the value of the entire net estate.

fee simple An estate of inheritance in land without qualifications or restrictions as to the persons who may inherit it as heirs. Also called an "Absolute Fee" or "Fee Title." Denotes absolute ownership.

fenestration The arrangement of windows in the walls of a building.

floor furnace The furnace is suspended below the floor and hot air rises from the furnace through a flush grille in the floor. There usually are no ducts.

formica A trade name for a hard laminated plastic surfacing such as countertops and bath wainscoting.

function of the appraisal The reason for which the appraisal is written or is intended to be used.

graduated payment loan Allows smaller than usual loan payments to initially be made, with small increases in later years. After approximately five years, a payment level is reached which remains fixed for the loan term.

grant deed The written instrument by which the title to real property is transferred.

gravity furnace A warm air heating system usually located in a basement. Warm air rises through ducts to the upper levels.

heat pump Self-contained, reverse cycle, heating and cooling unit. On the heating cycle, heat is collected on the outside coil and pumped inside. During the cooling cycle, heat is collected from the inside and pumped to an outside coil where it is dissipated.

indirect costs Costs in erecting a new building not involved with either building construction or site preparation.

jalousies Windows with movable, horizontal glass slats angled to admit ventilation and keep out rain. This term is also used for outside shutters of wood constructed in this manner.

lanai Balcony, veranda, porch, or covered patio.

landlocked parcel A parcel of land without access to any type of road, street, or highway.

land residual technique A method of capitalization using the net income remaining to the land after return on and recapture of the building value have been deducted.

leasehold The interest of a lessee under a lease.

lessee The person to whom a lease is given.

lessor The person who grants a lease.

louver An opening with horizontal slats to permit passage of air, but excluding rain, sunlight, and view.

modernization Minor or major changes to the structure which bring the property into conformity with current standards.

molding A strip of decorative material having a plane or curved narrow surface prepared for ornamental application. These strips are often used to hide gaps at wall junctures.

mudsill The lowest sill of a structure usually placed in or on the ground.

observed condition depreciation A method of computing depreciation in which the appraiser estimates the loss in value for curable and incurable elements of depreciation.

orientation Positioning of a structure on its lot with regard to exposure to the sun, prevailing winds, views, privacy, and protection from adverse influences.

outbuilding A detached building subordinate to a main building.

overimprovement An improvement that is not the highest and best use for the site on which it is placed by reason of excess size or cost.

panel heating Uses copper coils embedded in concrete floor slabs and low-temperature heated water. The floor radiates gentle heat throughout the room and is never cold to walk on. It is readily tied in with solar heat because it does not require hot water.

pilaster A projection or the foundation wall used to support a floor girder or stiffen the wall or an architectural feature in the form of a rectangular pillar or column projecting from and constituting part of a wall.

plottage value The subsequent increase in value when adjacent properties are combined into one property.

points A fee charged by a lender for making a loan. For instance, two points represents a fee of 2 percent of the loan amount.

prefabricated house A house manufactured, and sometimes partially assembled, before delivery to the building site.

principal The employer of an agent.

purpose of the appraisal The reason for the appraisal assignment, for example, to estimate a defined value of real property interests or to conduct an evaluation study pertaining to real property decisions.

radiant heat Coils of electricity, hot water, or steam pipes embedded in floors, ceilings, or walls to heat rooms.

real property Land and anything permanently affixed to it, incidental or appurtenant to it, or immovable by law.

rehabilitation The restoration of a property to its former capacity without changing the plan, form, or style of the structure.

remaining economic life The period of time over which the structure may reasonably be expected to perform the function for which it was intended.

remodeling Changing the plan, form, or style of the structure.

replacement cost The cost of constructing a building which has the same or similar utility using current prices; in accordance to today's standards of design and materials.

reproduction cost The cost of constructing an exact replica of the structure using current prices and the same or similar building materials.

restrictions Public restrictions imposed on the use of the land usually as a part of a comprehensive plan for the development or protection of the area. Private restrictions may be established by owners, subdividers, or others to create uniformity in a tract or to restrict the use of the land for private reasons.

rollover loan Permits a lender to renegotiate the rate of interest with the borrower, usually, every three to five years.

scuttle A small opening either to the attic, to the crawl space, or to the plumbing pipes.

septic tank A sewage settling tank in which part of the sewage is converted into gas and sludge before the remaining waste is discharged by gravity into a leaching bed underground.

setback ordinance A zoning ordinance which designates the distance a building must be set back from the property lines.

sheathing The first covering of boards or other material on the outside wall or roof prior to installing the finished siding or roof covering.

shingles Pieces of wood, asbestos, or other material used as an overlapping outer covering on walls or roofs.

shiplap Boards with rabbeted edges overlapping.

sill A horizontal stone or timber on which a structure rests; the horizontal piece at the bottom of a window, door, or similar opening.

site When land is improved by the addition of utilities, street improvements, and other improvements it becomes a site.

special assessments Tax levied upon property to pay costs of public improvements of special benefit to property assessed, such as street paving, sidewalks, and sewers.

subfloor Usually, plywood sheets that are nailed directly to the floor joists and that receive the finish flooring.

sublease A lease by a tenant to another person of all or a part of the premises held by him or her; an underlease.

tongue-and-groove Carpentry joint in which the jutting edge of one board fits into the grooved end of a similar board.

undue influence Taking any fraudulent or unfair advantage of another's weakness of mind, distress, or necessity.

variable interest rate loan or VIR A loan in which the interest rate is not fixed and can increase or decrease according to a standard index.

venetian window A window with one large fixed central pane and smaller panes at each side.

wainscoting Wood lining of an interior wall; lower section of a wall which is finished differently from the upper part.

zero lot line Sometimes referred to as "offset lot line"; the structure is built on the property line providing a greater setback on the opposite side of the structure.

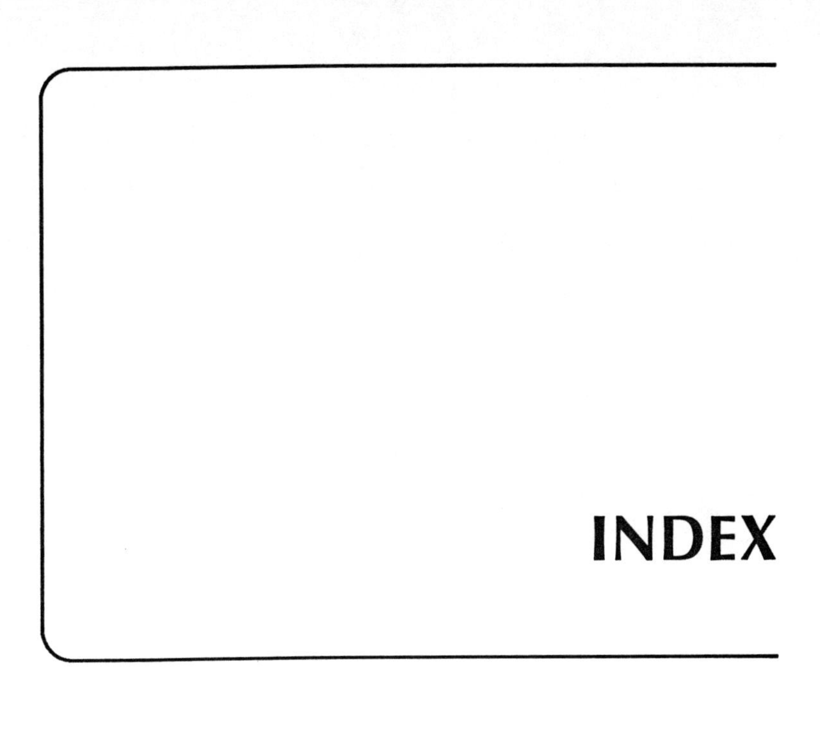

INDEX

A

Abbreviations
listing of, 450–453
in written report, 149
Actual age, of structure, 216, 314–315
Addenda, to written report, 150–153
Additions, 242–247
code violations, 244–245
garage conversions, 243
kitchen, 243–244
nonpermitted additions, 247
permits, 244, 246–247
recognizing additions, 124–125
Adjustments, in comparable sales method, 9,297–294
Adverse external influences, in neighborhood analysis, 186, 187
Age of structure
actual age, 216, 314–315
effective age, 217, 218–219, 314–315
Air traffic, 210–211
Alleys, as site improvements, 203
Amenities
civil amenities, 43–44
definition of, 40–41
market adjustments for, 83
Appraisal data
address register, 27
assessor's description vs. appraiser's descriptions, 28–29
description of property, 18–20, 24
disclosure statements, 16
fee quotes, 20–21
microfiche data, 27–28
parcel list, 27–28
plat map, 26–27
sales contracts, 16
Appraisal plan, 91–93
sequence of events in, 92–93
Appraisal report
census tract numbers, 160
Appraisal report (*cont'd*)
compliance with FNMA Form 1004, 148–150
date of sale/sales price, 160
example of, 426–442
financing data, 161–162
FLHMC Form 442, 14
legal descriptions in, 158–159
names of parties, 159, 163
neighborhood analysis ratings, 177–189, 190–191
neighborhood description, 168–174
property rights, 164–168
rating stability of value, 189–190
sales history, 160–161
single-housing price/age ranges, 174–177
special assessments, 163
tax information, 162–163
Appraisal reviews
procedure in, 404–410
review summary, 412–413
Uniform Standards of Professional Appraisal Practice, 410–411
Appraisals
appraisal plan, 91–93
"as is" conditions, 250, 251
client pressure and, 21–22
construction quality appraisal, 105–111
dealing with clients questions, 143–144
design and appeal appraisal, 101–105
disclosure of final estimate, 146
equipment for, 88–91
error reduction in, 131–134
expiration date, 32
limitation in scope type of, 22–23
neighborhood appraisal, 93–98
photographs, use in, 90–91
physical inspection, 120–131
postponement of, 25–26

Appraisals (*cont'd*)
  preliminary access arrangements, 24–25
  problems related to, 1–6
  property description, 112–120
  rejecting assignments, 21
  scheduling appointment for, 88
  site appraisal, 98–101
  timeliness, importance of, 30–32
  See also individual topics.
Appraiser's signature, 350
Architect's Scale, 90
"As is" conditions, 250, 251
"As is" site improvements, 277–282
"As is" value, 344–345
Assessments, special assessments, 163, 210
Attic, inspection of, 127
Attics, 230

B

Basement, inspection of, 126–127, 221–222
Bathrooms, types of, 226
Bedrooms, number of, dollar amount of adjustments, 82–83
Boundaries, neighborhood, 41–42
Bracketing comparable sales, 39–40
Budget analysis, condominiums, 375–377
Builder sales, use of, 45–47
Building calculations, 264–271
Building costs
  discrepancies in, 65
  learning about, 64–65
Building diagram, 155
Building size, calculation of, 263–264

C

Camera, 89
Cash equivalency adjustments, 296–301
Census tract numbers, 160
Cesspool, 201
Civil amenities, 43–44
Code violations, changes to property, 244- 245
Comparable sales
  adjustments to value, 139–141
  analysis/reconciliation, 336–342
  arms-length transactions in, 285–286
  avoiding mistakes, 47–48
  bracketing comparable sales, 39–40
  builder sales, use of, 45–47
  cash equivalency adjustments, 296–301
  cost approach to valuation, 48–50, 53
  data from alternate cities, 44–45
  date of sale and, 55–57
  financing in, 294–296
  inconsistent comparable sales, elimination of, 51–52
  information sources, 35–37, 52–53
  insufficient market data problem, 52–54
  listings, use in, 286–287
  listings/sales in escrow, use of, 54
  market adjustments, 287–294
  multiple-listing books, use of, 57–58
  neighborhood in, 40–44
  order of importance of data, 38
  presentation of market analysis, 303–333
  price per square foot estimation, 50
  sales terms/concessions, use of, 55
  subjective adjustments, 38–39
  tax stamps, to determine sale price, 37
  three closed sales in, 283–284
  upper limits of value in, 54–55
  visual inspection, 139–141
Condominiums
  addenda to report, 385–388
  appraisal of, 68–73, 360–365
  budget analysis, 375–377
  cost approach, 377–378

Condominiums (*cont'd*)
inclusionary zoning restrictions, 373-374
income approach, 383
individual unit descriptions, 374-375
market data analysis, 378-383
project improvements, 365-372
rating of project, 372-373
compared to town house, 358-360
Construction quality appraisal, 105-111
exterior characteristics, 106-107
interior characteristics, 108-109
learning about, 110-111
roofing, 107-108
shape of house, 106
of very-good-quality homes, 110
windows/doors, 107
Convenience factors, neighborhood analysis ratings, 179-181
Cooling system, 230, 328
Cooperatives
addenda to report, 391-392
project analysis, 392-401
proprietary lease, 388
unique features of appraisal, 383-391
Cost approach, 48-50, 53
advantages of, 260-261
"as is" site improvements, 277-282
building calculations, 264-271
condominiums, 377-378
cost estimates, sources of, 262-263
depreciation, estimation of, 272-277
error reduction and, 262
land values, 280-281
total estimated cost new, 271-272
Cost handbooks, 274-275
Crawl space, 116
Curable depreciation, 272-273
Curable obsolescence, 275
Curbs/gutters, as site improvements, 202
Custom-built homes, appraisal of, 63-65

D

Date of sale
incomparable sales method, 55-57
sales price, 160
Deferred maintenance, 117-118, 120, 122
Depreciation
based on economic life, 273
curable depreciation, 272-273
estimation of, 272-277
improvements and, 247-249
physical depreciation, 272
Design and appeal appraisal, 101-105
additions, 103
architectural style, 102, 104-105
color, 102
consistency aspects, 102, 103
Disclosure statements, 16
Doors, interior, 228
Doors/windows, ill-fitting, 123
Downzoning, 172
Drainage
checking lot drainage, 121-122
in site appraisal, 205-206
Drip edge, roof, 108
Driveway, in site appraisal, 206-207
Dry rot, inspection for, 124

E

Earthquakes, 209
Easements, 207
Effective age, of structure, 217, 218-219, 314-315
Effective tax rate, 162-163
Electrical service, 129-130
Encroachments, 207
Energy addendum, 223
Energy-efficient items, 131, 269, 331
high rating items, 223-224
Equipment for appraisal, 88-91
Architect's Scale, 90
camera, 89
measuring aid, 89
measuring tape, 89

Errors, reducing in appraisal, 131–134
Escrow, listings/sales in, 54
Estimation of dimensions, measurement of property, 134–135
Expiration date, appraisals, 32
Exterior characteristics, construction quality appraisal, 106–107
Exterior improvements, 219–221
  gutters/downspouts, 220
  roof, 220
  walls, 219–220
  windows, 220–221
Exterior walls, inspection of, 123–124
External obsolescence, 276–277

F

Fannie Mae, 56, 68
Fee quotes, 20–21
FHLMC Form 70A, 269
FHLMC Form 442, 14, 153
FHLMC Form 465, 357, 387
FHLMC Form 465 Addendum A, 365, 387, 391, 392
FHLMC Form 465 Addendum B, 391, 400
Financing
  cash equivalency adjustments, 296–301
  reasons for, 297–299
  statements related to, 252
Financing data, 161–162
  lenders, 163
  sales concessions, 162
  types of, 161
Fireplaces, 229, 332
Fixtures, tests of personal property, 118- 119
Flood hazard, 208–209, 210
  maps for, 208
Flood insurance, 208
Floor coverings, 226–227
  types of, 114
FNMA Form 216, 150, 343, 385
FNMA Form 439, 349
FNMA Form 1004, 74, 85, 146–156, 224
  exhibits/addenda to, 150–153
  guest houses, 147–148
  recertification of value, 153–154
  single-family residential property, 146- 147
  two-family property, 147
  written report, 148–150
FNMA Form 1004B, 349
FNMA Form 1007, 150, 343, 385
Foundation
  inspection of, 123–124, 221
  types of, 116
Functional obsolescence, 255–257
  curable obsolescence, 275
  external obsolescence, 276–277
  incurable obsolescence, 276
Functional utility rating, 324–328

G

Garage, 231, 269, 329
  garage conversions, 243
  inspection of, 126
  nonconforming uses, 126
Geological hazards, 209
Grandfather clause, zoning, 196
Gross living area, 322–323
  basement, 323
Gross rent multiplier, 343
Growth rates, neighborhood, 168–169
Guest houses, FNMA Form 1004, 147–148
Gutters/downspouts, 220

H

Heating system, 229, 328
Higher-priced homes, appraisal of, 65–66
Highest/best use analysis, 197–200
Hillside property, 264
House style, types of, 113

I

Improvements, 70
additions, 103
age/life cycle of neighborhood and, 77–78
appraisal of, 74–82
buyers options and, 76
compatibility factors and, 80
consistency aspects, 102, 103
documentation of, 78
economic factors and, 79
modernization in older homes, 78–79
neighborhood factors and, 80–81
objectivity in appraisal of, 77
overimprovements, 75–77, 79, 81, 103
price/value aspects, 76–77
range of sales approach to, 79
recognition of, 125
types of higher priced neighborhoods, 81
underimprovements, 79, 82
See also Exterior improvements; Site improvements.
Improvements appraisal
additions, 242–247
age of structure and, 216–217
cosmetic improvements, 218
depreciation factors, 247–249
descriptions in, 239–241
design/style of, 215
detrimental conditions, 233–234
estimated physical life, 238
exterior improvements, 219–221
insignificant improvements, 241–242
neighborhood influences, 233
proposed improvements, 215–216
quality aspects, 234
remaining economic life, 238
Income approach
condominiums, 383
market value estimate, 342–348
Incompatible uses, 99
Incurable obsolescence, 276
Insulation, 114–115
harmful type, 114–115
hazardous types, 222
R-values, 114, 115, 222
Interior characteristics, construction quality appraisal, 108–109
Interior inspection
attics, 230
closets/storage, 236
condition, 129–130
conformity, 129
cooling system, 230
doors, 228
electrical system, 129–130, 237
fireplaces, 229
floor coverings, 226–227
of garage, 231
heating system, 229
kitchen, 230, 237
plumbing, 130, 236
ratings for, 228–229
rooms, listing of, 225–226
room/size layout, 128–129, 234–236
trim, 227–228
wall finishes, 227
water damage, 130–131

K

Kitchen, 230, 237, 332–333
extra-kitchen, 243–244

L

Landscaping, in site appraisal, 206
Land values, 280–281
Laundry rooms, 226
Leasehold land, 43, 164–165
Legal but nonconforming uses, zoning, 197
Limiting conditions, certification and statement of, 349–350
Listings/sales in escrow, use of, 54
Lot appraisal *See* Site appraisal

Lot size, calculation of, 70
Lot utility, rating of, 100

M

Maintenance, deferred maintenance, 117–118, 120, 122
Maintenance level
  neighborhood, 43–44
  neighborhood appraisal, 97
Manufactured houses
  appraisal of, 83–85
  classification of, 84
Market analysis, presentation of, 303–333
Market data
  analysis of, 59–62
  builder sales, 45–47
  data from alternate cities, 44–45
  information sources, 35–37, 52–53
  insufficient data problem, 52–54
  listings/sales in escrow, 54
  multiple-listing books, 57–58
  neighborhood information, 40–44
  order of importance, 38
  for unusual property, 67
Marketing time
  neighborhood, 169
  rate of, 86
Market trends, 11–14
  information sources, 12–13
  signs of declining market, 170–171
Market value
  basis of approach, 7–8
  cost/price versus value, 10
  definition of, 8–9
  market trends, influences of, 11–14
  recertification of, 14–15
  sales representing market value, 10–11
Market value estimate
  comparable sales, analysis/reconciliation, 336–342
  final estimate, 348–352
  income approach, 342–348
Measurement of property, 133–138
  estimation of dimensions, 134–135
  guidelines for, 135–138
  measuring aid, 89
  measuring tape, 89
  second story, 136–137
  setbacks in, 137–138
  square-off structures, 138
Misplaced improvement, 66
Mixed uses
  classification of, 195
  in neighborhood analysis, 186–187
Mobile homes, appraisal of, 85
Model homes, appraisal of, 71
Multiple-listing books, use of, 57–58
Multiresidential zoning, 200

N

Narrative appraisal report
  example of, 424–425
  letters of acceptance, 422–424
  requirements for, 416–422
Neighborhood, 40–44
  boundaries of, 41–42
  civil amenities, 43–44
  defining amenities, 40–41
  effective age of structure and, 218–219
  growth rates, 168–169
  locational/external/environmental factors, 42
  maintenance level, 43–44
  marketing time, 169
  market trends, declining, 170–171
  percentage of present land use, 171–172
  percentages of built-up areas, 168
  predominant occupancy, 172–173
  property rights, 43
  vacancy ratio, 173–174
  visual inspection for comparable sales, 139–141
Neighborhood analysis ratings, 177–189, 190–191

Neighborhood analysis (*cont'd*)
- adverse external influences, 186, 187
- average, 177
- conflicting statements, avoiding, 178–179
- convenience factors, 179–181
- employment stability, 179
- fair, 178
- general appearance of properties, 183
- good, 177
- mixed uses, 186–187
- poor, 178
- property compatibility rating, 182
- protection from detrimental conditions, 183
- public transportation, 181
- rating stability of value, 189–190
- recreational facilities, 181
- socioeconomic characteristics, 185
- utilities, 181–182
- writing neighborhood comments, guidelines for, 184–189, 190–191

Neighborhood appraisal, 93–98
- buffers to negative influences, 95–96
- maintenance level, 97
- physical inspection, 95–96
- proximity to facilities, 97
- reasons for, 94–95
- static/changing neighborhood, 97–98
- traffic patterns, 96–97

New housing, older homes located in area, 73–74
New subdivisions. *See* Residential housing tracts
Nonconforming uses, 196–197
"No value assigned," 121

O

Older homes, appraisal of, 73–74
Omissions in appraisals, 4–5
Outside entries, 231–232
- illegal, 117

Overimprovements, 75–77, 79, 81, 103, 278
- handling of, 177

P

Parking, 231
- types of facilities, 117

Percentage of present land use, 171–172
Percentages of built-up areas, 168
Permits, changes to property, 244, 246–247
Personal property
- classification of, 241
- determination of, 118–119

Photographs
- in appraisal report, 89, 90–91, 140, 151- 152
- uncompleted structure, 216
- use in appraisal, 90–91

Physical inspection, 120–131
- additions, 124–125
- attic, 127
- basement, 126–127, 221–222
- drainage/slippage, 121–122
- for dry rot, 124
- foundation, 123, 221
- garage, 126
- interior inspection, 128–131
- physical depreciation, 120
- professional's involvement in, 121
- roof, 122–123
- for termite damage, 124

Planned unit developments (PUDs)
- appraisal of, 68–73
- characteristics of, 166
- homeowner's association dues, 167
- property rights, 165–167
- *See also* Condominiums.

Plat map, 26–27, 151, 209
Plumbing, 130
Poor utility, 254–255

Predominant occupancy, neighborhood, 172–173
Predominant price, 175–176
Price per square foot estimation, 50
Principles of progression and regression, 44
Private deed restrictions, 207
Property address, listing of, 158
Property compatibility rating, 182
Property description, 112–120
  confirmation of year built, 112–113
  deferred maintenance, 117–118, 120, 122
  flooring, 114
  foundations, 116
  house style, 113
  insulation, 114–115
  outside entrances, 117
  parking facilities, 117
  physical depreciation, 120
  wall finishes, 116
  window styles, 113–114
Property rights
  leasehold land, 164–165
  planned unit developments, 165–167
Proprietary lease, 388
Public restrictions, 207–208
Public transportation, 181
Public utilities, 201

R

Railroad traffic, 211
Real estate agents, use of, 29
Recertification of value, 153–154
Recreational facilities, 181
Regulation, of appraisals, 2
Rental absorption rates, 344
Repairs, deferred maintenance, 117–118
Reproduction costs, 259
Residential housing tracts
  appraisal checklist, 72–73
  appraisal of, 68–73
  lot size, calculation of, 70
Residential housing tracts (*cont'd*)
  sample appraisal, 72
  takeoff list, 69–70
  tract appraisal information, 70–71
  upgrades, handling of, 70
Restrictions, 207
Roofing, 220
  appraisal of, 107–108
  checking for wear, 122–123
  drip edge, 108
  materials used, 108
Rooms
  listing of, 225–226
  room count, above-grade, 318–322
  room layout, 128–129, 234–236
R-value, 114, 115, 222

S

Safety/health factors, 250–251
Sales contracts, 16
Sales history, 160–161
Satisfactory completion certificate, 153
Scheduling appraisal, 88
Scuttle, 230
Second story, measurement of, 136–137
Setbacks, in measurement of property, 137- 138
Shape of house, appraisal of, 106
Shingle-shakes, 116–117
Sidewalks, as site improvements, 203
Single-family house pricing, 174–177
  age range, 174–175
  detached/attached, 214–215
  FNMA Form 1004, 146–147
  overimprovements, handling of, 177
  predominant price, 175–176
  values exceeding predominant price, 176
Site appraisal, 98–101
  air traffic, 210–211
  drainage, 205–206
  driveway, 206–207

Site appraisal (*cont'd*)
easements, 207
encroachments, 207
favorable site factors, identification of, 101
flood hazard, 208–209, 210
geological hazards, 209
highest/best use analysis, 197–200
incompatible uses and, 99
landscaping, 206
lot utility, rating of, 100
measurements of property, method for, 133- 138
mixed uses, 195
nonconforming uses, 196–197
railroad traffic, 211
restrictions, 207
setbacks in, 205
shape of lot, 204–205
site improvements, types of, 201–207
size, 98–99, 194, 204
special assessment, 210
topography of lot, 204
traffic patterns, 99, 100
utilities, 201
view, 206
zoning classification, 194–195, 200
Site improvements
alleys, 203
curbs/gutters, 202
sidewalks, 203
street lights, 203
streets, 202
Site value, estimation of, 279–280
Slippage, 209
checking for, 121–122
Socioeconomic characteristics, in neighborhood analysis, 185
Special assessments, 163, 210
Square-off structures, measurement of property, 138
Street lights, as site improvements, 203
Streets, as site improvements, 202
Structural damage, 123
Subdivisions, appraisal of, 69–73
Subjective adjustments, 38–39
Sump pumps, in basement, 127
Swimming pool, 331
adjustments for, 112

T

Taxes
effective tax rate, 162–163
special assessments, 163
Tax stamps, to determine sale price, 37
Termite damage, inspection for, 124
Time factors, timeliness and appraisals, 30- 32
Total estimated cost new, 271–272
Town house, compared to condominiums, 358- 360
Traffic patterns
neighborhood appraisal, 96–97
site appraisal, 99, 100
Trim, interior, 227–228
Two-family property, FNMA Form 1004, 147

U

Underimprovements, 79, 82
Undue influence, 3–4
Uniform Residential Appraisal Report, 354- 355
Uniform Standards of Professional Appraisal Practice, 410–411
Unusual property
appraisal of, 66–68
building cost estimation, 267–268
market data for, 67
Utilities, 181–182, 201
public utilities, 201

V

Vacancy ratio, neighborhood, 173–174

Variances, zoning, 196–197
View, 310–311
  in site appraisal, 206
Visual inspection, of comparable sales, 139- 141

W

Walls
  exterior, 219–220
  wall finishes, 227
Water
  checking lot drainage, 121–122
  water damage, interior, 130–131
Windows, 220–221
  appraisal of, 107
  types of, 113–114
Written report
  abbreviations in, 149
  addenda, 148–150
  building diagram, 155
Written report (*cont'd*)
  documentation from public records, 150
  FNMA Form 1004, 148–150
  terms used in, 149

Y

Yard, types of improvements, 121

Z

Zoning
  classifications for, 194–195
  development of site and, 200
  grandfather clause, 196
  inclusionary zoning restrictions, 373–374
  legal but nonconforming uses, 197
  multiresidential zoning, 200
  variances, 196–197